Toward social welfare

An analysis of programs and proposals
attacking poverty, insecurity, and
inequality of opportunity

Toward
social welfare

An analysis of programs and proposals attacking poverty, insecurity, and inequality of opportunity

CLAIR WILCOX

Professor Emeritus of Political Economy
Swarthmore College

1969
Richard D. Irwin, Inc. Homewood, Illinois
Irwin-Dorsey Limited, Nobleton, Ontario

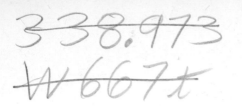

First Printing, February, 1969

Library of Congress Catalog Card No. 69–17158
Printed in the United States of America

To the memory of Florence
*   who shared my first concern*
and to Marcia
*   who helped me bring it to fruition*

Acknowledgments

A number of people have helped me in the writing of this book. Eveline M. Burns, Emeritus Professor at the School of Social Work of Columbia University, and Joseph A. Pechman, Director of Economic Studies at the Brookings Institution, permitted me to pick their brains, as did Frank C. Pierson, Professor of Political Economy, and Charles E. Gilbert, Professor of Political Science at Swarthmore College. The entire manuscript was read by Everett E. Hagen, Professor of Economics and Political Science at the Massachusetts Institute of Technology. The material on income maintenance was read and criticized by Dr. Burns; the material on labor markets, manpower development, job creation, and minimum wages by Dr. Pierson; the chapter on income supplements by Dr. Pechman; and the chapter on public assistance by Dr. Gilbert. These friends caught a number of errors and made an even larger number of helpful suggestions. Responsibility for the final text, however, is mine alone. Howard H. Williams, head of the Reference Department at the Swarthmore College Library, ran down fugitive materials with his accustomed efficiency. My wife, Marcia Lincoln Wilcox, acquiesced in a schedule that left us little time for recreation and, as usual, helped with the index and the proof.

C. W.

Table of contents

ployment. The Negro's occupations. The Negro's wages. Discriminatory practices. Discrimination in housing. The Negro rebellion.

Part II.   Attacks on insecurity

Government support for segregation. State and local fair housing laws. The federal fair housing law. Prospects for open housing. Toward racial equality: *Prejudice and discrimination. Integration and black power.*

Part IV.   Attacks on poverty

Minimum wage laws: *State minimum wage laws. Federal minimum wage laws.* Minimum wage administration: *Issues in wage determination. Enforcement of minimum wages.* Effects of minimum wages: *Economic analysis of effects. Empirical studies of effects. The incidence of harmful effects.* Minimum wage policy.

The federal-state assistance program: *The pattern of public assistance. The scope and level of assistance. The growing burden of assistance.* Administration of public assistance: *Determination of eligibility. Determination of payments. Disqualification for assistance. The problem of disincentives. The welfare workers.* Relief or rehabilitation? *Cash and services. The social work approach. The 1962 amendments.* The politics of public assistance: *The assistance constituency. The revolt against assistance. The 1967 amendments.* Proposals for reform.

Proposals for income guarantees: *The minimum income. The offsetting tax. Suprapoverty income guarantees. Intrapoverty income guarantees. Relation to other welfare programs. The cost of income guarantees.* Income guarantees pro and con: *The case for income guarantees. Inconsistency of objectives. Administrative difficulties.* Children's allowances: *Allowances in other countries. Allowance proposals in the United States. The case for children's allowances. The case against children's allowances.* How support incomes?

Private enterprise in housing: *The housing market. The housebuilding industry. The decay of the cities.* Governernment housing policy: *Regulation of private housing. Promotion of private housing. Public housing. Urban renewal.* Problems of urban renewal: *Planning for renewal. Relocating residents and businesses. Results of urban renewal.* Problems of public housing: *The cost of public housing. Occupancy of public housing. Life in a housing project. The failure of public housing.* New approaches to housing: *Demonstration cities. New towns. Interest subsidies. Rent supplements.*

Part V.   The prospects

The strategy of welfare: *How attack insecurity? How attack inequality of opportunity? How attack poverty? Benefit-cost analysis. Cost-effectiveness analysis. Priorities in the attack on poverty.* The feasibility of welfare: *The cost of welfare. Can we afford social welfare? Prospects for social security. Prospects for equality of opportunity. Prospects for the abolition of poverty.*

Bibliography

Index

Introduction

In the richest country on earth at the peak of prosperity, one family in seven—if not more—lives in poverty. In a country that has the capacity to assure every one of its citizens a continuing income, the future for millions is insecure. In a nation that professes its devotion to democracy, an eighth of the people, members of racial minorities, are denied equality of opportunity. This is America in the last third of the 20th century. These are its social problems: poverty, insecurity, and inequality of opportunity.

Measures designed to solve these problems are frequently denounced as instruments of a welfare state. Concern for social welfare, it is said, makes men dependent on government and thus is alien to the American tradition of self-reliance, industry, and thrift. But it is difficult to accept the view that welfare is unworthy as a goal of policy—that its alternative, illfare, is to be preferred. And it certainly is not true that concern for social welfare is un-American. From the initiation of free public education, the abolition of slavery, the enactment of protective labor legislation, and the provision of public charity to the needy, all in the 19th century, to the inauguration of the social security system in the 20th, action to ease the lot of the less fortunate has sprung from the American soil. Measures proposed today may differ in detail from those adopted a century or more ago. But the purpose that inspires them is the same.

Advances in welfare provisions come by fits and starts as social crises impress the need for action on the public consciousness. It was a crisis of major proportions that produced the social reforms of the Roosevelt New Deal. The nation's economy had broken down. The national product had dropped from $80 billion in 1929 to $40 billion in 1932. Fifteen million workers were unemployed. Wage payments had declined by three fifths. Nine million savings accounts had been wiped out. Between 1932 and 1938, the average number of families living on public charity was more than six million, nearly a fifth of the nation's households. During the period as a whole, 20 million families were dependent for a time on public aid. It was against this background that Congress moved to enact a program of social reform. In these circumstances, its emphasis was on social security.

During the forties, attention shifted to the war and to the problems of international reconstruction. In the fifties, the existence of social problems was generally ignored or denied. It was not until the sixties that social reform again moved to the center of the stage. Now the situation was different than in the thirties. The economy as a whole was functioning successfully. Business depressions had been brought under control. Unemployment was of minor proportions. Poverty was far less extensive than before. The problems of social welfare were now problems of particular groups. But these problems were persistent. Despite continued prosperity, there remained, year after year, a hard core of the unemployed. Despite pervasive affluence, there remained a hard core of the poor. And among the groups presenting these problems, there were disproportionate numbers from racial minorities.

In this situation, under the Johnson administration in 1965 and 1966, there came the greatest rush of social legislation in the nation's history. There were measures to extend and strengthen existing programs (social security, urban renewal), new programs affording opportunities for employment (area redevelopment, vocational retraining), programs embodying new policies (federal scholarships for higher education, rental subsidies for the poor), and programs that had long been bitterly opposed (health insurance for the aged, federal aid to local schools). There was the declaration of a "war on poverty" with federal support for varied programs developed by local bodies, their membership including representatives of the poor. And finally, there were measures designed to put an end to racial discrimination in education, in employment, and in the field of civil rights.

How was this rush of reform to be explained? The country was prosperous. Jobs were plentiful. Levels of living were high. Most people felt reasonably secure. The troubles that led to the reforms of the Roosevelt New Deal were virtually unknown. But there was one new driving force that demanded change. A century after his emancipation from slavery, the Negro was asserting his right to equality. A host of other problems were allied with the problem of race: the deterioration of the cities, the failure of urban education, growing child dependency, youthful unemployment, increasing delinquency, violence in the city streets. All of this stirred the conscience of the white community and aroused its fears. Something had to be done. In addition, there was the fact that President Johnson, elected in 1964 with large majorities in both houses of the Congress, now exerted his leadership to move the country toward the eradication of poverty and the assurance to every American of an equal chance.

This brave beginning came to an untimely end with the escalation of the war in Vietnam. Attention was diverted from America to Asia. Guns were given priority over butter. The programs inaugurated in the earlier years were continued, but not expanded. The zeal that had inspired them was gone. But the problems they sought to solve remained. These problems are still with us. They will have to be faced again someday, some way, somehow.

A great variety of measures have been adopted or proposed for the purpose of ameliorating poverty, assuring security, and providing equality of opportunity. Some of them, however well intentioned, may operate to do more harm than good. Some of them may serve only as palliatives, lightening the burdens of those who are less fortunate, but not preventing their misfortune. By attacking the causes of misfortune, some of the measures may prevent its recurrence.

There are certain questions that must be asked of every program for social reform, adopted or proposed. What will be its economic effects? Will it be politically acceptable? Can it be efficiently administered? How is it to be brought about? These are the questions that will be asked in this volume concerning programs that attack the social problems of poverty, insecurity, and inequality of opportunity.

PART I

The problems

Inequality in income
and wealth

In no country at no time have income and wealth been distributed equally. Everywhere and always there have been some people who were relatively rich, others who were relatively poor. The extent of inequality has varied from place to place and from time to time. In some cases, the disparity has been extreme: the rich living at the height of luxury, the poor enduring the deepest misery. In others, the disparity has been moderate, with no one enjoying great luxury, no one condemned to misery. But even here some people have been better off than others: income and wealth have been distributed unequally.

In this chapter, we shall examine the extent of inequality in the distribution of income and wealth in the United States, comparing it with that found in other countries and observing its changing pattern over time. Then we shall go on to consider the consequences of inequality—its disadvantages and its advantages.

The extent of inequality

There is substantial inequality in the distribution of income in the United States, but greater inequality in the ownership of wealth. The degree of inequality, however, is about the same in this country as in other advanced countries of the West and much lower than in the less developed countries of the world. And inequality is far less marked in

7

the United States today than it was a few decades ago. These are the highlights; we turn to the details.

The distribution of income

The earliest estimates of income distribution were pieced together by adding data on larger incomes taken from tax reports, data on wage incomes obtained by multiplying the numbers of workers in various occupations by their average wages, and data on the incomes of farmers and other self-employed persons obtained by making sample surveys. Later estimates were based on studies of larger samples made for a variety of purposes by several agencies of the federal government. Each of these estimates had its imperfections. In 1940, questions on personal income were included in the decennial census, but the information requested was fragmentary. In 1950, the Bureau of the Census addressed a longer list of questions to every fifth respondent on its rolls. And in 1960, it enlarged its sample to cover every fourth household. A sample of this size, running to millions of cases, affords a virtual count of incomes in each tenth year. In every year between the census years, moreover, the Bureau makes another estimate. In connection with its monthly survey of employment covering a carefully designed nationwide sample of 35,000 households, each March it asks three fourths of these households to report all of the cash income received during the previous year. On the basis of this information, it presents a current estimate of income distribution, along with estimates for earlier years, in an annual report on *Consumer Income* as one of its *Current Population Reports*.[1]

The Bureau's estimate for 1966 shows family income to be distributed as follows:

Income Class	Percent of Families
Under $3,000	14.3
Between $3,000 and $5,000	13.9
Between $5,000 and $7,000	17.8
Between $7,000 and $10,000	24.4
Between $10,000 and $15,000	20.4
Over $15,000	9.2

[1] On the validity of the various estimates of income distribution, see T. Paul Schultz, *Statistics on the Size Distribution of Personal Income in the United States* (88th Cong., 2d sess., Joint Economic Committee [Washington, D.C.: U.S. Government Printing Office, 1965]), chap. iii; and Herman P. Miller, *Rich Man, Poor Man* (New York: Thomas Y. Crowell Co., 1964), Appendix.

In that year, 28 percent of the families were below and 72 percent above $5,000; 50 percent below and 50 percent above $7,400; and 70 percent below and 30 percent above $10,000.[2] When families are divided into fifths, income is shown to be distributed among them in this way:

Income Class	Percent of Income
Lowest quintile	5.4
Second quintile	12.4
Third quintile	17.7
Fourth quintile	23.8
Highest quintile	40.7

The third and fourth quintiles, 40 percent of the families, received 41.5 percent of family income, just about their equal share. The two lowest quintiles, another 40 percent of the families, received 17.8 percent of the income, less than half their share. The bottom quintile received a fourth of its share; the top quintile received twice its share. The top 5 percent of the families received 14.8 percent of the income, three times its share.[3]

The degree of inequality in any distribution of income may be shown graphically by a Lorenz curve, a device originated by Max Lorenz. Along the horizontal axis of such a graph are plotted cumulative percentages of income recipients; along the vertical axis, cumulative percentages of income. If income were distributed equally, the distribution would be represented by a diagonal line, with 10 percent of the recipients having 10 percent of the income, 20 percent having 20 percent, 30 percent having 30 percent, and so on. A curve plotted to show an actual distribution invariably sags below this line. Where inequality is moderate, the sag is small. Where it is extreme, the sag is great. The distribution of family income in 1966 is shown by the Lorenz curve in Figure 1.

Estimates of distribution, such as that shown in the table and in the curve for 1966, have their defects. In some respects, they tend to overstate inequality. First, the estimates are based on figures for a single year. A family may have a low income in some years and a

[2] U.S. Bureau of the Census, *Consumer Income,* Series P-60, No. 53, December 28, 1967, p. 2.
[3] *Ibid.,* p. 7.

Figure 1. Lorenz curve for the distribution of family income in 1966

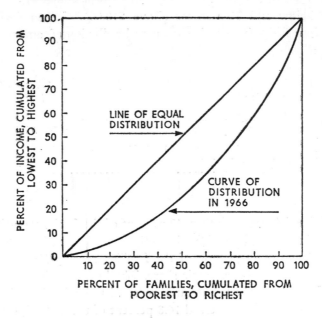

higher income in others. If they could be made, estimates based on incomes received over longer periods would doubtless reveal less inequality. Second, the estimates are based, not on disposable incomes but on incomes before payment of income taxes: incomes are less equal before taxes, more equal after taxes. Third, a family's welfare depends not only on its income but also on the cost of living where it resides and on the ages of those who depend upon it for support. The lower incomes are received in large part by people on farms and in small towns where the cost of living is low; the higher incomes, by people in cities where the cost of living is high. The lower incomes are received, moreover, by younger and older persons who do not have dependents; the higher incomes, by middle-aged persons who do. In these respects, the estimates overstate inequality.

In other respects, however, estimates tend to understate inequality. First, many forms of income enjoyed by the rich are not included in income subject to taxation; larger incomes are more likely to be under-reported than smaller ones; the sampling process covers the former less adequately than the latter. Second, the higher incomes are more largely based on property ownership; they continue when their recipients are disabled or unemployed; they thus afford security. The lower incomes are more largely derived from wages; they stop when their recipients are disabled or unemployed; they afford no security. Third, a family's welfare depends upon the number of those who depend upon it for support. Family size in general varies inversely with income. Money available for the care of children is distributed less equally than income as a whole. The estimates of inequality of income thus understate the inequality of opportunity.

The distribution of wealth

There is no census of the distribution of wealth. Only two estimates of such distribution have been made in recent years. The first, for the year 1953, was prepared by Robert J. Lampman on the basis of information regarding estates subject to the federal estate tax. Assuming that property was distributed among the living in the same way as among those who had died, Lampman employed the pattern of distribution found in the taxed estates as a means of computing the distribution of wealth among property owners as a whole.[4] The second estimate, for the year 1962, was made by the Federal Reserve Board on the basis of a sample survey of consumer finances.

In 1953, according to Lampman, title to wealth in the United States was distributed as follows:[5]

Percent of Adults	Percent of Wealth
Lowest 50	8.3
Next 18.4	10.2
Next 21.2	29.3
Next 8.8	24.6
Top 1.6	27.6

In 1962, according to the Federal Reserve Board, the concentration of ownership was even greater:[6]

[4] For a detailed explanation of his method of estimation, see Robert J. Lampman, *The Share of Top Wealth Holders in National Wealth* (Princeton, N.J.: Princeton University Press, 1962), chap. ii.

[5] *Ibid.*, p. 213.

[6] See Edward C. Budd, *Inequality and Poverty* (New York: W. W. Norton Co., Inc., 1967), pp. xxi–xxiii.

	Percent of Consumers	Percent of Wealth
Bottom quintile		Less than 0.5
Three middle quintiles		23
Top quintile		77
Top 5%		53
Top 1%		33

As is evident, there is far greater inequality in the distribution of wealth than in the distribution of income, with the top fifth holding 77 percent of wealth and getting 40 percent of income, the top 5 percent holding 53 percent of wealth and getting 15 percent of income, and the top 1 percent holding 33 percent of wealth and getting 8 percent of income. This contrast, based on the Census distribution of income and the Lampman distribution of wealth, in 1953, is depicted in the Lorenz curves in Figure 2.

Figure 2. Lorenz curves for the distribution of income among families and the distribution of wealth among adults in 1953

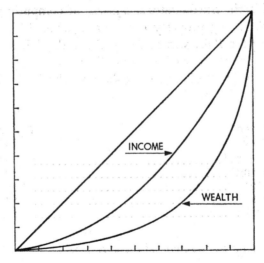

Distribution in other countries

The distribution of income found in different countries may be compared by plotting Lorenz curves, but the curves fall so close together that they are difficult to distinguish. These distributions may also be compared numerically by means of the Gini index of concentration.

This index, originated by Corrado Gini, measures the portion of the lower triangular area on a Lorenz curve which falls between the diagonal line of equal distribution and the curve of actual distribution. It will stand somewhere between 0, representing complete equality, and 1, representing the greatest possible inequality.[7]

The Gini index for some year during the 1950's stood at 23 for Denmark; 28 for the Netherlands; 31 for Japan; 35 for Australia; 39 for Great Britain, Norway, Sweden, and the United States; and 41 for Italy. The share of income going to the top 5 percent of recipients during the same decade stood at 18.2 for Norway, 18.9 for Australia, 20.1 for Denmark and Sweden, 20.4 for the United States, 20.9 for Great Britain, 23.6 for Western Germany, and 24.1 for Italy.[8] These figures are not precisely comparable. Different definitions of income and of recipients are used in different countries. Some distributions are computed before and others after taxes. And the estimates are made for different years.[9] After allowing for these differences, it appears that inequality during the 1950's was greater in the United States than in the Scandinavian countries, the Netherlands, and Australia; about the same as in Canada, Great Britain, and Japan; and smaller than in West Germany and Italy.

Information on the distribution of income in the Soviet Union is not available. There is little property income since industry is not privately owned. In incomes from wages, however, inequality is greater than in other industrial countries. In the iron and steel industry, for instance, the range of wages from the highest to the lowest paid employee in a typical plant is 20 to 1, a spread that is twice as great as that found in the United States.[10]

Inequality is less pronounced in the advanced countries than in the less developed ones. In the advanced countries during the 1950's, the Gini indexes averaged 0.37; in the less-developed countries they averaged 0.44. In the advanced countries, the top 5 percent of recipients got around 20 percent of the income; in India they got 33 percent; in

[7] The Gini index is ambiguous in that it does not distinguish the income level at which inequality exists. In practice, however, the skewness of the Lorenz curves varies so little that this is not a serious defect.

[8] Irving B. Kravis, *The Structure of Income* (Philadelphia: University of Pennsylvania Press, 1962), pp. 238, 252.

[9] See James N. Morgan *et al.*, *Income and Welfare in the United States* (New York: McGraw-Hill Book Co., Inc., 1962), chap. xx.

[10] M. Gardner Clark, "Comparative Wage Structures in the Steel Industry of the Soviet Union and Western Countries," Industrial Relations Research Association, *Proceedings of the Thirteenth Annual Meeting*.

Mexico, 37 percent; in Kenya, 50 percent; and in Southern Rhodesia, 65 percent.[11]

In other countries, as in the United States, there is less information on the distribution of wealth than on the distribution of income. England and Wales are the only places in which a comparable study has been made. In the United States in 1953, as we have seen, the top 1.6 percent of adults owned 27.6 percent of the wealth. In England and Wales in 1946–47, the top 1.5 percent owned 53 percent.[12]

Changes in distribution

The pattern of income distribution in the United States has changed markedly over time. Earlier studies show inequality narrowing between 1890 and 1920 and increasing during the decade of prosperity that followed World War I. From the extremes of 1929, inequality declined sharply during the depression of the 1930's and the years of World War II. The change in the distribution of family income is shown in the following table and in the curves of Figure 3:

	Percent of Income	
Income Class	1929	1944
Lowest quintile	3.5	4.9
Second quintile	9.0	10.9
Third quintile	13.8	16.2
Fourth quintile	19.3	22.2
Top quintile	54.4	45.8

The Gini index fell from 0.49 in 1929 to 0.39 in 1944. The share of income going to the top 5 percent of recipients dropped from 30 percent to 20 percent.[13]

This decline in inequality is to be attributed in part to a decline in inequality of wealth and thus of income from property. It is to be attributed more largely to the fact that a smaller share of income came to be derived from property, a larger share from work. Business recovery and wartime demand produced a high level of employment.

[11] Simon Kuznets, "Quantitative Aspects of Economic Growth of Nations," *Economic Development and Cultural Change*, Vol. 9 (1963), pp. 13, 18, 60, 61.
[12] Lampman, *op. cit.*, pp. 210–15.
[13] The estimate of distribution is that made by the Office of Business Economics of the Department of Commerce. See Herman P. Miller, *Income Distribution in the United States* (Washington, D.C.: U.S. Government Printing Office, 1966), p. 21. The Gini index is taken from Budd, *op. cit.*, p. xiii.

Figure 3. Distribution of income among families in 1929 and 1944

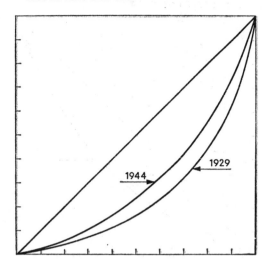

More members of a family joined the labor force. A larger share of this force was employed in high-wage occupations. Wage differentials between skilled and unskilled occupations were reduced. Labor organization was strengthened and wage rates were increased through collective bargaining. The workweek was lengthened, and the amount of overtime pay was increased. All of these factors operated to enlarge the total of wages. At the same time, strong markets for agricultural output, together with a government program of price supports, made for larger incomes on the farms.

Impressed by these striking changes, some economists came to speak of a revolution in distribution which was producing an egalitarian society. But with the war's end, the movement toward equality slowed down. The distribution of income among families in 1966 did not differ sharply from the pattern obtaining in 1947, as is shown below and by the curves in Figure 4:

	Percent of Income	
Income Class	1947	1966
Lowest quintile	5.0	5.4
Second quintile	11.8	12.4
Third quintile	17.0	17.7
Fourth quintile	23.1	23.8
Top quintile	43.0	40.7

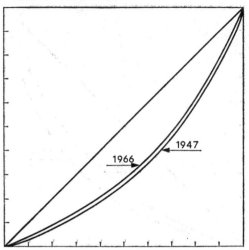

The Gini index stood at 0.38 in 1947 and at 0.34 in 1966. The share of income going to the top 5 percent of recipients dropped from 17.2 percent to 14.8 percent, but the share going to the top fifth remained around 41 percent and the share going to the two bottom fifths remained around 17 percent.[14]

In relative terms, the poorer groups experienced little gain after 1947. In absolute terms, however, their gain was substantial. The whole distribution was pitched at a higher level. Disposable income per capita in constant (1958) prices rose from $1,513 in 1947 to $2,294 in 1966, a gain of nearly 50 percent.[15]

Less information on changes in distribution is available for wealth than for income. According to Lampman, the share of personal wealth held by the top 1 percent of adults fell from 36.3 percent in 1929 to 20.8 percent in 1949 and then rose to 28 percent in 1961. The degree of inequality in ownership was thus higher in 1961 than in 1949, but lower than it had been in 1929.[16]

---

[14] U.S. Bureau of the Census, *op. cit.*, p. 7. The Bureau's estimates are not strictly comparable with those formerly made by the Office of Business Economics, cited above.

[15] *Economic Report of the President*, 1967, p. 232.

[16] Lampman, *op. cit.*, p. 220.

Inequality—pro and con

Inequality is usually found in association with poverty. Those with the smaller incomes in a typical distribution are poor not only relatively but absolutely. It is the poverty that is found at the lower end of the income scale that most often leads reformers to denounce inequality. But poverty and inequality should not be confused. It would be possible to have a society in which everybody was in real poverty with no inequality. It would also be possible to have a society in which there was great inequality but nobody was really poor. We shall postpone until the next chapter the problems that are peculiar to poverty. We turn now to those that are peculiar to inequality.

Earned incomes

In a market economy, production is guided by dollar votes that are cast by consumers. The many consumers with smaller incomes each have fewer votes; the few consumers with larger incomes each have many votes. Production is thus diverted from meeting the needs of the many to satisfying the desires of the few. The resulting allocation of productive resources is to be justified only if it can be shown that the distribution of income is fair. Inequality, moreover, may be resented by those whose incomes are low. It may well give rise to social unrest and political disorder. It is less likely to do so if the higher incomes can be shown to have been earned; more likely to do so if they cannot.

Incomes can be regarded as earned if they have been received in payment for the performance of a socially useful service and if they have been determined in a competitive market. There are many large incomes that can be justified in this way. But there are others that cannot.

Incomes from work, even though very large, may be earned. Most conspicuous among such incomes are those received by entertainers and corporate executives. The services provided by these groups are obviously in demand. The salaries paid the entertainers are also determined in the market. They are high because talented performers are scarce. These salaries are earned. The pay of some corporate executives is determined by arm's length bargaining. The pay of many others is not. Managements, in control of the proxy machinery, fix their own

been earned. Though originally indefensible as earned, these incomes have been legitimatized by transfers of ownership.

Great fortunes can no longer be made in the ways in which most of the older fortunes had their origins. The resources of nature have long since been appropriated. Land values are not advancing at their earlier pace. Special privileges are still conferred, but with a somewhat less liberal hand than in the past. Monopoly has been brought under control by regulatory commissions and by the antitrust laws. Financial manipulation has been outlawed by the securities acts, and financial operations brought under surveillance by the SEC. It may still be possible to become a multimillionaire, but it is not as easy as it used to be.

Inheritance

Great fortunes, whatever their origin, may be perpetuated through the rights of bequest and inheritance. Under the right of bequest, a wealthy man may leave his property to whomever he may please. Under the right of inheritance, if he dies without a will his property may be claimed by his widow, his children, his grandchildren, his brothers, sisters, nephews, nieces, cousins, and other relatives to the remotest degree of relationship. The heir, obviously, is not responsible for the source of his wealth. The son does not create the father; the causation is the other way around. There are few who would attempt to argue that inherited capital has been earned. Nor can the return obtained on such capital in the form of interest or dividends be regarded as earned. But many have attempted to justify inheritance on other grounds.

It is said, first, that a man's widow and his orphans should be assured a livelihood. This argument, of course, carries no weight where other heirs are concerned. As for the rich man's widow, the fact is that she has usually been well provided for before he died. And the average age at which his orphans come into their inheritance is 42. It is said, second, that ability to leave his money to whom he pleases affords a man an incentive to work and save. This argument applies to the right of bequest but not to the right of inheritance. It is scarcely to be assumed that a man will be driven to greater effort by the confidence that his wealth will someday be shared by relatives who are detested, remote, or even unknown. And even though his incentive may have been strengthened, his heir's incentive will have been impaired. For the heir has known that society can be required to support him and his children if he never does a day's work as long as he lives. It is said, finally, that the problem of the idle heir will solve itself since his inheritance will soon be lost. The family, according to the adage, will move from shirtsleeves to shirtsleeves in three generations. But this need not be the case. It is possible, for a reasonable fee, to hire a trustee who will see to it that a fool and his money are not soon parted.

There are arguments, too, against the institution of inheritance. If the heir chooses to live in idleness, it burdens the community with his support and deprives it of his services. If he chooses to exert himself, it affords him opportunities that are denied to others. It perpetuates class differences. It is not consistent with the principles of democracy.

Estates passing at death are subject to progressive taxation. But the provisions of the law are such that substantial sums may be inherited even though the full tax rates are paid. And there are means of legal avoidance that can be—and are—utilized to keep a major part of the greater fortunes out of the tax collector's hands. Taxation, in short, has not gone far toward the abolition of inheritance.

The defense of private riches

Is great inequality socially desirable or undesirable? A number of arguments have been advanced in justification of private riches: (1) It is said that rich people perform a useful function when they spend their money, since their expenditures (*a*) provide other people with employment; (*b*) make other people envious, thus giving them an incentive to work and save; and (*c*) promote culture, establishing and maintaining higher values for the rest of the community to imitate. (2) It is said that the rich perform a useful function when they save their money, thus providing the economy with capital. (3) It is said that they perform a useful function when they give their money away, financing great foundations, universities, and other worthy undertakings.

These attempted justifications of great riches are partly fallacious, partly exaggerated, partly true. (1) As for the function of spending: (*a*) it is fallacious to argue that the rich must engage in sacrificial self-indulgence in order to provide the rest of us with jobs. Money spent by the poor on bread and milk provides employment as surely as does money spent by the rich on caviar and champagne. (*b*) It is true that inequality affords an incentive to work and saving. But for this purpose a moderate degree of inequality would probably suffice. Extreme inequality would not seem to be required. (*c*) Whether inequality contributes, on balance, to culture is open to question. Culture is not a private entertainment for a fastidious minority. It is not promoted by buying up old masters and first editions and putting them under lock and key. A living culture requires an open door to talent and a large and appreciative audience. And these are to be promoted not by extreme inequality but by greater equality. (2) It is true that the rich save a larger portion of their incomes than do the poor. But society can obtain capital through the reinvestment of corporate profits, from savings made by persons of moderate means which are assembled and invested by large financial institutions, and through public investment financed by taxation. Extreme inequality is not required. (3) As for charity, it is true that the rich do good by giving their money away. The foundations that bear the names of Ford, Rockefeller, and Carnegie are cases in point. But many of the rich make no such benefactions. The great bulk of charitable giving, moreover, is channeled through churches, community chest drives, and the like, and comes from persons whose incomes are not large.

Extreme inequality is unnecessary. It is also socially undesirable. It perverts social values—establishes materialistic standards to guide behavior. It denies to those with lower incomes an equal opportunity to participate in the life of the community, robbing them of their self-respect. It makes for bitterness and antagonism among the poor, and for callousness and arrogance among the rich. It obstructs the development of social morality. It divides the nation into contending groups. It checks the free flow of sympathy and hinders action for the common good. We should be better off without it.[17]

The uses of inequality

Such are the objections to extremes of inequality. Does it follow that society would be better served by precise equality? There are considerations that compel a negative reply.

Inequality has its uses. It affords the major incentive for productive effort. Unequal wages persuade men to work harder. Unequal profits

[17] See R. H. Tawney, *Equality* (New York: Harcourt, Brace & Co., 1931).

promote managerial efficiency. The lure of larger incomes stimulates invention, innovation, and technical progress. Other incentives could be used: differences in leisure, titles, decorations, and other symbols of prestige. But these would be as open to criticism as are differences in income. And they would be more difficult to administer. Pecuniary motivation is both effective and convenient.

Inequality promotes the proper allocation of scarce resources among competing uses. Some goods are wanted more than others. To obtain them, consumers will pay a higher price. Those who produce them will command labor by paying a higher wage. Industries which satisfy growing demands will expand. Those whose products are less wanted will decline. Men will move into the one and out of the other. The necessary transition will be effected without compulsion. It will be brought about by differences in prices and in incomes.

A society which abandoned inequality as an allocator would be compelled to adopt one of two alternatives. It might coerce consumers. It might apply compulsion to labor. Neither of these measures is to be desired. Coercion of consumers would obviate the necessity of transferring workers from one occupation to another, but it would do so by forcing people to go without things they wanted and to take things for which they had less use. It would lessen satisfaction in consumption. Compulsion might be employed, alternatively, to place workers where they were needed. But this measure, too, is unattractive. If equality is to be purchased at the cost of liberty, it may well be concluded that the price is too high. Of the possible methods of accomplishing the allocation of resources among competing uses, variation in income appears to be the most desirable.

If it tried hard enough, a government might succeed in making incomes equal. But it would have to employ stern measures to do so. Since private enterprise would result in differences in profit, the government would have to forbid it. Since private saving would yield different amounts of interest, the government would have to prohibit accumulation of capital by anyone but the state. Since private employment would involve differences in wages, the government would have to make every workman an employee of the state. The implication of such measures must be plain. Exact equality is not to be obtained in a market economy. It would require the public ownership and operation of all industry and the concentration of economic authority in the hands of the state.

In conclusion

Extreme inequality has one set of disadvantages. Exact equality would have another. It is possible to avoid them both. Society can escape the unhappy consequences of the one extreme without plunging into the obvious difficulties of the other. It can eliminate the abuses of inequality without abandoning its uses. It need only eradicate the extremes and with them the evils which they entail. The moderate inequality which will remain can be productive of little harm and much good.

So much for the issues that are peculiar to inequality of income and of wealth. Their thorough exploration would require a book as long as this. Our task, however, is a different one. We shall confine ourselves in the chapters that follow to the questions that are peculiar to poverty and to its related problems of insecurity and inequality of opportunity.

Poverty

We turn now to poverty—to the problems that are usually encountered at the lower end of the income scale. We first consider the meaning of poverty, its definition and measurement, mark its character and its extent, and note its changing incidence. We then go on to analyze the causes of poverty, both personal and social. And we examine, finally, the deprivation that is inherent in poverty and assess its consequences.

The extent of poverty

How extensive is poverty in the United States? The answer will depend upon the standard that is used for its measurement. Poverty may be defined either in relative or in absolute terms. It has been proposed, for instance, that families in the bottom quintile of the income scale or families getting less than half of the median family income be defined as poor. Poverty, it is said, is a matter of social status. If one man gets less than another, he feels that he is poor; and if he feels poor, he *is* poor.

The phenomenon that would be measured by such a definition would be inequality, not poverty. But it is to the problems that are peculiar to poverty that the attention of society should be turned.

These are the problems that are created by serious deprivation and by the misery that it entails. With a relative standard, there would be no measure of those who were really in need. In a prosperous country, a family might be counted as poor even though it was well housed, well clothed, well fed, and otherwise well cared for. Nor would there be a measure of the progress that might be made in lifting people out of poverty. The same percentage of the population would always be defined as poor, no matter how much their condition might have been improved.

The standards by which poverty is usually judged are stated as absolutes. Such standards are established by preparing family budgets that cover the costs of goods and services that are found to be needed to satisfy basic requirements. The cost of food is estimated by determining the calories and nutrients needed for an adequate diet for persons of different sexes and ages, translating them into the types and quantities of foods customarily consumed, and pricing these foods at the markets where the families in question customarily buy. Rents are based on standards of structural safety, sanitation, ventilation, and cubic feet of space per person. Clothing rations for each member of the family are designed to assure cleanliness, dryness, warmth, and presentability. On similar bases, allowances are made for household equipment, toilet articles, medical and dental care, school supplies, streetcar fares, and so on. All these goods and services are priced, and the cost of the total budget is thus obtained. Such budgets are set at different levels, depending upon the character and the quantity of the goods and services that they include. Most of them allow for something more than bare subsistence; some of them for much more than others. Even though stated as absolutes, these standards are not rigid; they are adjusted from time to time, not automatically but through the exercise of judgment as conditions change.

Measures of poverty

The most widely publicized estimate of the extent of poverty in the United States was that made by the Council of Economic Advisers in 1964.[1] The Council's estimate was based upon a study by the Social Security Administration of the income needed to support a nonfarm

[1] *Economic Report of the President, 1964,* chap. ii.

family of four. The SSA had established two standards for such a family, both based on estimates of dietary costs prepared by the Department of Agriculture. One provided for a "low-cost" budget, permitting the minimum diet consistent with the food preferences of the lowest third of the population and adequate to avoid basic nutritional deficiencies. This budget allowed 28 cents per person per meal, or $3.36 per family per day. On the basis of an Agriculture study made in 1955 showing that 35 percent of the expenditures of low-income families went for food, the size of the total budget was calculated by multiplying the food allowance by three. The resulting budget stood at $3,955. This called for a far higher level of expenditure than welfare agencies were allowing for families receiving public assistance. To meet the administrative need of these bodies, the SSA prepared a second budget. This was an "economy budget" based on a deficiency diet designed for temporary or emergency use. It allowed 23 cents per person per meal for food or $2.74 per family per day. Multiplied by three, this allowance set the total budget for a nonfarm family of four in 1962 at $3,165.[2] On the basis of this figure, the CEA adopted $3,000 as its family poverty line. In the same way, it arrived at $1,500 as the line for a single individual. It thus found more than 9,000,000 families and 5,000,000 unrelated individuals, altogether some 35,000,000 people, a fifth of the nation, to be in poverty in 1962.

The Council's estimate was criticized on many grounds. By taking as its basis a budget for a family of four not living on a farm, it set its figure for income needed by smaller families and by families living on farms too high. By confining its figure for income received to money income, it disregarded such real income as the rental value of owners' homes and the value of food produced by families in their own gardens. By confining this figure to income received during a single year, it disregarded the ability of many families to draw upon savings from earlier years or to borrow and repay in later years. In all of these ways, it tended to overstate the extent of poverty.

In response to these criticisms, the Social Security Administration reworked its budget estimate to make allowance for differences in the size and composition of families and in their location. As a result, it counted fewer aged people and fewer residents of farms among the poor, but more families with many children and more families living in

[2] Mollie Orshansky, "Counting the Poor: Another Look at the Poverty Profile," *Social Security Bulletin*, Vol. 27 (1965), pp. 3–29.

urban areas. Though the composition of the group in poverty differed, its size remained the same: about one fifth of the population.[3] The SSA did not attempt to correct the Council's estimate to allow for income in kind, for past savings, or for possible borrowing. In this respect, the tendency toward overstatement of the amount of poverty remained.

There are other respects, however, in which the estimates of the SSA and the CEA tended to understate rather than overstate the numbers of the poor. The budget used was built on the foundation of a diet that was deemed appropriate only for temporary use in an emergency. It assumed that foods would be bought more economically, handled less wastefully, and prepared more skilfully than would in fact be the case. It was to be doubted that families could be adequately fed for as little as 23 cents per person per meal. If the budget had been built on the foundation of the low cost rather than the emergency allowance for food, it would have stood closer to $4,000 than to $3,000. To get the total budget, moreover, the food allowance was multiplied by three, a ratio held to be appropriate in 1955. But according to a study made in 1961, the fraction of total expenditures then going for food was not a third but a quarter. Accordingly, unless allowances for items other than food were to be held below their customary share, the multiplier should have been not three but four. On this basis, the total economy budget would have stood at more than $5,000 a year. When these considerations are weighed against the Council's failure to allow for income in kind, for savings, and for ability to borrow, it does not appear that its estimate of the extent of poverty can have been too high.

Family budget studies

It was the purpose of the Council's estimate to establish a rough index by which to mark the overall dimensions of the problem of poverty. Budget studies made for more than 60 years have had a number of other purposes. They have been used in fixing the amount of money paid to persons on relief, in measuring changes in the cost of living, and in setting wage rates in union contracts. Most of these

---

[3] Mollie Orshansky, "Recounting the Poor: A Five-Year Review," *Social Security Bulletin*, Vol. 29 (1966), pp. 20–37.

studies not only specify the family's need for food but spell out its requirements for other goods and services. Here, the budget maker must decide what items are to be included and what quantities and qualities are to be allowed. He will begin by prescribing the way in which the family's income ought to be spent, basing his prescriptions on standards of adequacy established by experts in the various fields. He will then seek to determine how these standards are to be met by resorting to sample studies to discover how expenditures are actually made. There is thus a large element of subjective judgment in the figure at which he finally arrives.

Budgetary requirements may be set at lower or higher levels, depending upon the budget maker's purposes. The fraction of families whose incomes will not permit them to satisfy these requirements will vary accordingly. In 1960, the Social Security Administration found 22 percent of the people living in households that fell below its economy budget described above. It prepared another budget costing a third more, basing it on a more adequate dietary provision; and it found another 8 percent of the people whom it characterized as "near poor," altogether 30 percent of the population, falling below this line.[4] Oscar Ornati prepared budgets at three levels for a family of four in New York City in 1960. The first was a "minimum subsistence" budget, appropriate for a family living on relief; its cost was $2,660, and the incomes of one tenth of the city's families fell below this level. The second was a "minimum adequacy" budget, appropriate for families receiving other welfare services; its cost was $4,348, and the incomes of one fourth of the families fell below this level. The third was a "minimum comfort" budget, appropriate for civil service employees; its cost was $5,600, and the incomes of two fifths of the families fell below this level.[5]

The best known of the budgets is the "modest but adequate" City Worker's Family Budget prepared by the Department of Labor. This budget is designed for a standard family consisting of a man aged 35, his wife, a son aged 13, and a daughter aged 8. It can be adjusted, however, for differences in the size and composition of different families. The budget, originally based on living standards prevailing around the time of World War II, was priced in each of the major

[4] *Ibid.*, p. 25.
[5] Oscar Ornati, *Poverty Amid Affluence* (New York: Twentieth Century Fund, 1966), chap. ii.

cities of the United States in 1946–47.[6] It was revised to conform to
standards prevailing in the 1950's and priced in 1959[7] and again revised
to embody the standards of the 1960's and priced in 1966.[8] The
average cost of the budget stood at $3,118 in 1947, at $6,148 in 1959,
and at $9,191 in 1966.

The costs of all such budgets have risen sharply over the years, and
so, in consequence, have the figures taken as representing the poverty
line. In part, this increase is to be attributed to a rise in the level of
prices. In part, it reflects an increase in the standard of living. Robert
Hunter[9] set the cost of supporting a family of five in New York City
in 1904 at $460, a figure that would run to $1,500 at the prices prevailing in 1964, or only half of that used as a poverty line by the CEA.
Ruth Mack records a poverty line based on current welfare budgets as
rising by 40 percent, at constant prices, between 1935 and 1960.[10] The
Department of Labor attributes a minor part of the 50 percent increase
in its budget from 1959 to 1966 to a rise in prices; a major part to the
fact that it provided for the purchase rather than the rental of housing,
for more general ownership of automobiles, for better dental care, and
for other improvements in the standard of living.

The City Worker's Family Budget was not intended, nor has it been
used, to serve as a basis for a poverty line. The incomes of more than
half of the country's families fell below the level at which it stood in
1959; the incomes of nearly two thirds fell below its level in 1966. Yet,
according to the Department, it provides nothing more than the goods
and services needed for a healthful, self-respecting mode of living, for
the nurture of children, and for normal participation in the life of the
community. Detailed examination of the items it contains reveals none
that appears to be luxurious or extravagant.[11] If a $9,000 budget is
indeed "modest," the $3,000 poverty line adopted by the CEA was
even more so.

[6] Lester S. Kellogg and Dorothy S. Brady, "The City Worker's Family
Budget," *Monthly Labor Review*, Vol. 66 (1948), pp. 135–70.
[7] Helen H. Lamale and Margaret S. Strotz, "The Interim City Worker's
Family Budget," *Monthly Labor Review*, Vol. 83 (1960), pp. 785–808.
[8] Phyllis Groom, "A New City Worker's Family Budget," *Monthly Labor
Review*, Vol. 90 (1967), pp. 1–8.
[9] Robert Hunter, *Poverty* (New York: Macmillan Co., 1907), p. 52.
[10] Margaret S. Gordon (ed.), *Poverty in America* (San Francisco: Chandler
Publishing Co., 1965), p. 98.
[11] "The City Worker's Family Budget," *Bureau of Labor Statistics Bulletin*,
No. 1570–1, 1967.

The American poor

How many Americans are poor? The answer, as we have seen, depends on where the poverty line is drawn. In the early sixties, a number of writers put the fraction at a fourth or more.[12] Others set it around one fifth.[13] The fraction whose incomes fall below the level required for bare subsistence is estimated at a tenth.[14]

Each of these estimates has to do with the fraction of people in poverty in a single year. The fraction in poverty at some time during the life cycle would be larger. Until he is 15, a child may be one of many in a family that is too large and therefore poor. Between the ages of 15 and 20, his contribution to the family's income, together with those of his parents, brothers, and sisters, may raise it above the poverty line. When he first marries, particularly if he and his wife are both at work, he will not be poor. But with the birth of children if his family is too large, his expenses will rise, his wife will stop working, and the family income will fall, and he will again find himself in poverty. After he is 40, his children may contribute to the family's income, and when they leave home, he will have only his wife to support. During these years, he will not be poor except in periods when he is ill or unemployed. But when he retires, his income will decline, and he will end his years in poverty. If less than a fifth of the American people are in poverty at any one time, it is probably safe to say that more than a fifth will know poverty at some time during their lives.

Poverty has declined sharply since the Great Depression of the 1930's and since World War II. By taking as his poverty line a figure

[12] Michael Harrington, *The Other America* (Baltimore, Md.: Penguin Books, Inc., 1962), Appendix; Gabriel Kolko, *Wealth and Power in America* (New York: Frederick A. Praeger, Inc., 1962), p. 129; James N. Morgan *et al.*, *Income and Welfare in the United States* (New York: McGraw-Hill Book Co., Inc., 1962), pp. 188–91; Ornati, *op. cit.*, chap. ii; and Eugene Smolensky, "The Past and Present Poor," Task Force on Economic Growth and Opportunity, *The Concept of Poverty* (Washington, D.C.: Chamber of Commerce of the United States, 1965), p. 59.

[13] Leon H. Keyserling, *Progress or Poverty* (Washington, D.C.: Conference on Economic Progress, 1964), p. 17; Robert J. Lampman, *The Low Income Population and Economic Growth* (Washington, D.C.: Joint Economic Committee, 1960), p. 13; Herman P. Miller in Task Force on Economic Growth and Opportunity, *op. cit.*, p. 48; Ruth Mack in Gordon, *op. cit.*, p. 98, and Orshansky, "Recounting the Poor," *Social Security Bulletin*, Vol. 29 (1966), pp. 20–37 at p. 24.

[14] Ruth Mack in Gordon, *op. cit.*, p. 98; and Ornati, *op. cit.*, chap. ii.

of $1,956 for 1935 and $3,000 for 1959 (both at 1959 prices) and thus allowing the standard of living to rise by half, Smolensky found that the part of the population in poverty dropped from 37 percent in 1935 to 23 percent in 1959.[15] Using current subsistence budgets at constant prices, Mack found that the portion of people in poverty dropped from 28 percent in 1935–36 to 10 percent in 1960. Using a 1960 budget, she found that it dropped from 47 percent to 10 percent.[16]

As of 1966, the government has adjusted its poverty index to allow for the change in the level of prices. The resulting figure for the standard urban family of four is $3,335. Using this measure, it is found that the number of persons below the poverty line fell from 22.1 percent in 1959 to 15.4 percent in 1966 and the number of families below the line from 18.0 percent to 12.4 percent.[17] In the words of Herman P. Miller:

In 1929, at the height of the prosperous twenties, 31 per cent of the families and individuals had incomes under $2,000. Using the same dollar standard adjusted for price changes, we find that 32 years later only 12 per cent of the families and individuals has incomes this low. This decrease clearly means that there has been a sharp drop in the proportion of persons living at near subsistence levels, and that for millions of people absolute want has been eliminated.[18]

The reduction in poverty has not been accompanied by a reduction in inequality. As we saw in Chapter 1, inequality has not changed markedly over the past two decades. Poverty has been reduced rather by continued prosperity which has raised the level of income in every income group.

In the United States today, poverty differs strikingly from the poverty that was known to earlier generations and from the poverty that is still encountered abroad. The American poor enjoy many things that would have been regarded as luxuries by their forebears and that would mark them as belonging to the middle class in Europe or to the upper class in much of Latin America, in Asia, or in Africa. Among the fifth of the people who fell below the CEA poverty line in 1962, 14

[15] Smolensky, *op. cit.*, p. 59.
[16] Gordon, *op. cit.*, pp. 98–99.
[17] *Economic Report of the President, 1968*, chap. iv; and Mollie Orshansky, "The Shape of Poverty in 1966," *Social Security Bulletin*, March, 1968, pp. 3–32. According to a preliminary announcement for 1967, only 10.6 percent of American families were in poverty in that year (*New York Times*, August 9, 1968).
[18] Herman P. Miller, *Income Distribution in the United States* (Washington, D.C.: U.S. Government Printing Office, 1966), p. 12.

percent had bought an automobile within the previous year, 19 percent had a home freezer, 73 percent had a washing machine, and 79 percent owned a television set. In the poorest county in the poorest state in the union, where four fifths of the families had incomes under $3,000, 37 percent owned washing machines, 46 percent owned automobiles, and 52 percent had television sets.[19] These things had doubtless been purchased at the expense of proper housing, a nutritious diet, adequate medical care, and provision for the upbringing of children. The food, clothing, and shelter of the American poor today is little better than that enjoyed by earlier generations or by those who are in poverty abroad.

Causes of poverty

Economists distinguish three types of poverty: First, there is general poverty which results from a deficiency of aggregate demand—from business depression and mass unemployment. This type of poverty they feel is no longer a problem. It is being eliminated by economic stabilization and by continued economic growth. Second, there is insular or community poverty. This occurs when a region loses its economic base and when its resources have been exhausted and demand for its products has declined. Here, nearly everybody is poor. The remedy for this type of poverty is to be found in outward migration or in programs of regional economic development. Third, there is personal or case poverty. This type of poverty is found not only in depression but also in prosperity—not only in depressed regions but also in prosperous ones. It is caused in part by the characteristics and the fortunes of the individual and in part by social factors that are beyond his control.

Personal factors

There are among the poor a number whose poverty is caused by personal defects. Among them are those who are lazy, irresponsible, dishonest, and depraved: tramps and beggars, men who have deserted their families, habitual criminals and perverts, alcoholics and drug addicts, the derelicts along Skid Row. These are outcasts known to

[19] Ben B. Seligman (ed.), *Poverty as a Public Issue* (New York: The Free Press, 1965), pp. 23–27.

sociologists as the "disreputable poor."[20] Their defects may be a consequence of poverty as well as a cause. But their demoralization has carried them beyond redemption. They present a serious social problem. Their number among the poor is small.

Poverty may also result from forms of personal inadequacy that carry no disrepute. A man may be poor because he is incapable of earning a living wage. He may be physically or mentally handicapped. He may be emotionally disturbed, alienated, and withdrawn. His productivity may be small. The only employment for which he can qualify may be casual or seasonal or in occupations where wages are low. He may lack the skill or training that is required to enable him to earn a living wage. His inadequacy may be due to inherent incapacity. It may be due to lack of opportunity.

Poverty may be caused by personal shortcomings. It may also be caused by misfortune. A family may be deprived of its income by accident, sickness, and resulting disability, by the death or desertion of the breadwinner, or by dependent old age. In 1962, of the families that were found to fall below the poverty line set by the Council of Economic Advisers, one fourth had no male breadwinner, one third were headed by persons over 65, and two fifths had no member in the labor force.[21] The poverty of these families was clearly to be charged in some part to hard luck.

Social factors

Poverty is caused in large part by factors which are social rather than personal. A family is poor because the breadwinner is unemployed. The breadwinner may be unemployed because the economy as a whole has gone into a slump, because the region where he lives is depressed, because the demand for his product has declined, because the methods of production and distribution have changed, because progress in technology has left him behind. He may fail to find new employment because the labor market does not provide the necessary information, because the educational system does not equip him with the needed skills. Like personal misfortune, these are matters for which the individual is not responsible and over which he has no control.

[20] David Matza, "Poverty and Disrepute" in Robert K. Merton and Robert A. Nisbet, *Contemporary Social Problems* (2d ed.; New York: Harcourt, Brace & World, Inc., 1966), pp. 619–68.
[21] *Economic Report of the President, 1964*, pp. 56–57, 61–73.

The breadwinner may be refused employment altogether or denied employment in well-paid occupations because he belongs to a racial minority. Only one seventh of the nation's white families but nearly half of its colored families fell below the poverty line in 1962. Only a tenth of all families but a fifth of those in poverty were nonwhite. Color to be sure is a personal characteristic. But discrimination on account of color is a social phenomenon.

Poverty may be caused, finally, by inflation. As prices rise, real income falls. And this, too, is a development that the individual cannot control.

Consequences of poverty

The low incomes of the poor are reflected in a low level of living, in substandard housing, deficient diets, and inadequate medical care. The children of the poor attend inferior schools—get an inferior education. This deprivation has its economic cost, impairing the capacities of men as agents of production. It has its social costs, adding to the burdens of dependency and delinquency.

The low level of living

The United States Census of Housing in 1960 found a fifth of all housing units in the country to be substandard, but more than a third of these units were occupied by families with incomes under $3,000 and half were occupied by families with incomes under $2,000. Part of this housing was in rural areas; much of it in city slums. Here, there are apartments that lack plumbing, adequate light and ventilation, facilities for washing and for storing food. There are buildings that are obsolete, deteriorated, and neglected, infested with vermin and with rats. There are hallways and stairways that are dark and dilapidated; common toilets that are not kept clean. Living quarters are overcrowded, allowing too little space for quiet and privacy, for homework, and for rest. And these habitations are located in neighborhoods devoid of play space, where the streets are littered with waste and the pavements and sidewalks go unrepaired—neighborhoods where health, education, and welfare services are inadequate to meet community needs.[22]

[22] Ornati, *op cit.*, chap. ix.

Along with substandard housing go deficient diets. One family in seven and one child in five fall below a poverty line built on a diet deemed adequate only for temporary use in an emergency. A high degree of correlation exists between the incomes and the diets of nonfarm families. The Department of Agriculture reported in 1968 that the diets of 9 percent of the families with incomes over $10,000 and 36 percent of those with incomes under $3,000 were nutritionally inadequate. In quantity, the poor get fewer calories; in quality, they get fewer nutrients.[23] Within the first month after his enrolment, the average youth serving in the government's Job Corps in 1967 gained 15 pounds.[24] For the first time in his life, he had had enough to eat.

Poverty is also a barrier to the use of preventive medical services. A National Health Survey made in 1960–61 revealed that children under 14 years of age saw a physician only two thirds as often and a dentist only one third as often where the family's income was below $4,000 as where it was above. Immunization and pediatric service, in particular, vary inversely with income.[25] Half of the youths, aged 16 to 21, given medical examinations in the Job Corps had never before seen a physician.

Inferior schooling

The schools that are attended by the children of the poor are generally inferior in quality. Some of them are in backward rural areas; some of them in urban slums. All of them are poorly supported. Expenditure per pupil is only two thirds as high in the southern states as in the rest of the country; only half as high in the slums as in the suburbs. These schools, typically, are housed in buildings that are old and dilapidated. They are ill-equipped and overcrowded. They are staffed with teachers who are underpaid and poorly qualified. Staff morale is low; the rate of turnover is high.[26]

As a learner, the slum child is seriously handicapped. Lack of medical care may leave him with uncorrected defects in eyesight or in

---

[23] Lenore Epstein, "Some Effects of Low Income on Children and Their Families," *Social Security Bulletin*, Vol. 24 (1961), pp. 12–17; *New York Times*, February 25, 1968.

[24] *New York Times*, August 13, 1967.

[25] Epstein, *op. cit.*; and Ornati, *op. cit.*, chap. x.

[26] See James B. Conant, *Slums and Suburbs* (New York: McGraw-Hill Book Co., Inc., 1961); and Patricia C. Sexton, *Education and Income* (New York: Viking Press, 1961).

hearing. Lack of needed rest and nourishment saps his energy. Living in the midst of constant clamor, he grows inattentive and fails to develop the ability to distinguish differences in sound. He finds no mental stimulation in his home. He has no objects to manipulate—no toys, books, paper, or pencils. Nobody reads to him, talks to him, or answers his questions. The child lacks motivation. He expects no reward for achievement, receives no encouragement from his parents, has no hope for the future, sees no purpose in learning. He is apathetic, discontented, restless—antagonistic to the teacher and the school.[27]

The school responds to this child by subjecting him to a stereotyped curriculum that is not suited to his needs. It emphasizes verbal comprehension and fluency where his preparation has been poor. It uses teaching materials that are built on problems of middle-class life—problems that are meaningless to him. The child's teacher, usually a woman, comes from a middle-class background and is unfamiliar with the environment that makes him what he is. If he is indifferent or hostile, she may grow impatient, may show her irritation, and may make it clear that she holds him in contempt. Frequently, the child's reaction is disorderly behavior. It then becomes the function of the teacher to maintain discipline rather than to teach and the function of the school merely to keep the children off the streets.

In such a situation, schooling ends in failure. Children fall two or three years behind their grade level in reading and are similarly retarded in arithmetic. More than half of them drop out before they finish high school. They leave as functional illiterates, ill prepared for employment or for successful participation in the life of the community.

The costs of poverty

Poverty has serious economic costs. It makes for ill health. The darkness and dampness of slum dwellings—the lack of fresh air and sunlight—contribute to respiratory diseases. Inadequate provision for sanitation and for the storage of food cause digestive ailments. Overcrowding and lack of immunization promote the spread of epidemics. Malnutrition causes skeletal and organic damage, checks growth in

[27] See Frank Riessman, *The Culturally Deprived Child* (New York: Harper & Row, 1962); and Benjamin S. Bloom *et al., Compensatory Education for Cultural Deprivation* (New York: Holt, Rinehart & Winston, 1965).

height and weight, and lowers resistance to disease. The poor are sick more often and are afflicted more commonly with acute and chronic diseases than are members of the upper income groups. Ill health, in turn, results in impairment of strength and vitality.

The damage done by poverty is mental as well as physical. There is increasing evidence that protein deprivation in the first two years of life can cause permanent damage to the brain.[28] Studies of foster children and studies of identical twins placed in different homes have shown that favorable environments raise measurable intelligence while unfavorable environments depress it. Poverty also contributes to emotional disturbance. A study in New York City showed psychiatric illness to be three times as common among the lower fifth of income recipients as it was at the top.[29]

Poverty thus impairs the poor as instruments of production. It leads to absenteeism and high labor turnover; to fatigue and danger of accident; to bad morale, soldiering, and poor discipline; and to reduced efficiency and poor performance on the job. In all these ways, it retards industrial output and impedes the improvement of levels of living.

Poverty also has its social costs. Where opportunity has been afforded to the children of the slums, they have sometimes gone on to careers of distinction in public affairs, in scholarship, and in the arts. Where opportunity has been denied, as is more usually the case, hidden talents have not been developed and the community has been deprived of the contributions that their possessors might have made.

Poverty leads to delinquency, vice, and crime. The slum child is brutalized at home and on the streets. The slum dwelling affords opportunities for molestation of children, for sexual assaults, for premature sexual experience ending in illegitimacy and in prostitution. The life that awaits the school dropout on the streets is that of the organized gang engaged in continuous warfare, going on from minor to major infractions of the law, from probation to the reform school to the penitentiary.

All this imposes on the community heavy costs for the maintenance of law and order and for correctional and charitable activities. Cities must spend more on police and fire protection, on courts and jails, on

[28] Citizens' Board of Inquiry into Hunger and Malnutrition in the United States, *Hunger: U.S.A.* (Washington, D.C.: New Community Press, 1968), chap. ii.
[29] *Business Week,* February 1, 1964, p. 40.

public health and medical services, on welfare programs and institutional care. And money thus spent cannot be used in meeting vital needs of the community as a whole.

The transmission of poverty

Poverty breeds poverty. The poor man's son grows up in a poor environment. He is poorly fed, clothed, and housed, and suffers from malnutrition and ill health. He goes to a poor school, drops out at an early age, does not acquire the skills that would qualify him for a good job. He is lacking in aspiration and in hope. He marries early and has more children than he can give a proper start in life. They, too, will be physically and culturally deprived. They will live as he has lived—in poverty. So poverty perpetuates itself from one generation to the next.

Insecurity

A family is insecure if its income may be cut abruptly, reducing its ability to pay for shelter, food, and other needed goods. It is even more insecure if its expenses may rise at the same time. For the rich, insecurity is not a problem. If income from work is cut off and if expenses rise, bills can be paid out of income from property or by drawing on savings. For the poor, on the other hand, the problem of insecurity is serious in the extreme. They have little or no property income or savings on which to draw. Curtailment of income from work drives them deeper into poverty. But insecurity is not a problem for the poor alone. Loss of income and added expense may drive the near-poor—the 12,000,000 families with incomes between $3,000 and $6,000—below the poverty line. For the middle income group, too, loss of income may force a drastic reduction in levels of living, destroy long-standing expectations, exhaust savings, and drive families deeply into debt. Even here, where 16,000,000 families have incomes between $6,000 and $10,000, the problem of insecurity is all too real.

Loss of income

The income that has supported a family may be cut off by old age. It may be cut off by desertion or by the premature death of the breadwinner. Where a man is self-employed, his income may be cut

off by business failure. Where he works for another, it may be cut off
by unemployment. In any of these cases, loss of income is a hardship,
creating problems that must somehow be solved.

Old age

The death rate in the United States has been declining. The span of
life has been lengthening. More people are living beyond the age of 65.
As a result, the portion of the aged in our population has grown. At
the turn of the century, only 4 percent of our people were over 65.
Today the figure stands at 10 percent. Some 20,000,000 Americans are
in their later years.

Generations ago when a larger portion of the labor force was self-
employed, the onset of old age did not put an end to productive
activity. The old man continued to do chores around the farm or to
putter around the shop as long as he kept his strength. But as self-
employment was superseded by wage labor, the situation changed. At
the onset of old age, the worker is now laid off. Only a fifth of those
past 65 are at work. The aged contribute little to the national product.
Their incomes are low: the median for all American families in 1966
was $7,436; the median for families headed by a person over 65 was
$3,645.[1]

Retirement—with cessation of earnings—may be an economic ca-
tastrophe. Generations ago, aged parents lived in the homes of their
children, in the village, or on the farm. This situation, too, has
changed. There is less room for the old folks in a city apartment and
less that they can do to be of help. Today only 1 in 10 of the aged live
with relatives; more than half of them live alone.[2]

The old people must pay for shelter, for food, clothing, and medical
care. Their expenses may be small. They no longer have dependents to
support. They are not buying a home. Their demands for food and
clothing are modest. But their medical bills are likely to be high. Inflation steadily adds to other living costs. Expenses continue though
income has stopped. Savings, where they exist, are steadily depleted.
Some are not readily convertible; liquid savings are small.

The consequence all too often is poverty or near-poverty. The

[1] U.S. Bureau of the Census, "Income in 1966 of Families and Persons in the
United States," *Current Population Reports*, Series P-60, No. 53 (1967), p. 24.
[2] Mollie Orshansky, "Recounting the Poor: A Five-Year Review," *Social
Security Bulletin*, Vol. 29 (1966), pp. 20–37 at pp. 31–34.

Bureau of Labor Statistics' modest but adequate budget for a retired couple was priced at $3,000 in larger cities and at $2,500 in smaller cities in 1959. The incomes of nearly two million aged couples fell below this level.[3] A fifth of the aged couples in the United States was in poverty in 1964; another sixth was near poverty.[4]

Even in the middle income groups it is difficult to make provision for retirement. Some families lack the imagination or the responsibility required to plan ahead. Others who possess these qualities still may not save enough to meet their needs. To provide for retirement, they must look 40 or 50 years into the future, estimating their probable needs and resources, the probable degree of inflation, and the probable yield of investments of various types. They may lack the knowledge or the judgment required for making such projections. Their projections, however careful, may turn out to be wrong. For the middle income groups as for those of lesser means, the threat of dependency in old age is a major source of insecurity.

Loss of the breadwinner

A family may be deprived of its source of income through loss of the breadwinner. In 1962, a tenth of American families were without a male head.[5] The breadwinner may be removed by divorce, by desertion, or by premature death. The divorce rate climbed from 0.7 per 1,000 population in 1900 to 2.2 in 1944 but has remained fairly steady since that time. The rate of desertions not leading to divorce is unknown. The chances of premature death have steadily declined, the death rate dropping from nine per 1,000 population in 1900 to four in 1960. On balance, the problem of deprivation through loss of the breadwinner is less serious today than it was a half century ago.

When a couple with minor children is divorced, the court requires provision for their support. In the case of desertion, too, an order for support may be obtained. But a man can put himself beyond the jurisdiction of the court. Or his whereabouts may be unknown. In the case of death, of course, the possibility of compelling support is gone.

The consequences of removal of the breadwinner vary. A woman who has been divorced or widowed may remarry. But this solution of

[3] Louis A. Ferman *et al.* (eds.), *Poverty in America* (Ann Arbor, Mich.: University of Michigan Press, 1965), p. 120.

[4] Orshansky, *op. cit.*

[5] *Economic Report of the President, 1964*, p. 61.

her problem cannot be regarded as a certainty. She may find employment. Her ability to do so depends upon her circumstances. If a couple was childless or if their children have finished school, the wife will be free to support herself by going to work. If there are older children who are still in school, she must support them also and may find employment that will enable her to do so. If there are younger children, the mother cannot take employment unless someone else can be made responsible for their care. This may not be possible, and even where it is, the children might be better off if the mother stayed at home.

It is in the last of these cases that the loss of the breadwinner is most serious. Without a source of current income, the mother's burden may be a heavier one than she can bear. Of the families that lacked a male head in 1962, nearly half had incomes that fell below the poverty line.[6]

Unemployment

The family's income may be cut off by unemployment. Here, however, the loss may be temporary. Some of those who are counted as unemployed are in the process of moving from job to job. Others have jobs that are seasonal or casual. Three fourths of those who are unemployed at any one time have been idle less than four months.[7]

Unemployment of longer duration may be caused by a business depression. During the 1930's the rate of unemployment ranged from a tenth to a quarter of the labor force, averaging nearly a fifth. Nearly 13,000,000 workers were unemployed in 1933. Nothing of this sort has been experienced for nearly three decades. Recessions have occurred, but they have been less protracted and less severe. By adopting monetary and fiscal policies designed to maintain aggregate demand, the government has succeeded in preventing a major depression. The risk of massive cyclical unemployment has virtually disappeared.

But unemployment has persisted. Despite continued prosperity, the number of unemployed averaged more than 3,000,000 during the 20 years between 1948 and 1968, and the rate of unemployment in 10 of those years stood above 5 percent.[8] Much of this idleness has been

[6] *Ibid.*, p. 71.
[7] William Haber and Merrill G. Murray, *Unemployment Insurance in the American Economy* (Homewood, Ill.: Richard D. Irwin, Inc., 1966), p. 10.
[8] *Economic Report of the President, 1968*, pp. 237–38.

caused by structural changes in the economy: by innovations in technology that have displaced workers with special skills, by declines in demand for particular goods and services, and by depressions concentrated in particular regions. Jobs closed in this way are not reopened. The resulting unemployment persists until workers are able to move into different occupations, different industries, or different regions.

Protracted unemployment carries heavy costs. The worker loses his skills, his job rights, his morale. His family exhausts its savings, goes into debt, and finally goes on relief. It loses status and suffers impairment of self-respect. The specter of unemployment remains a major source of insecurity.

More expenses with less income

The breadwinner's income may be cut off by accident or illness. With accident, the loss is sudden; with illness, it may be gradual. The resulting disability may be temporary; in time, the worker's earning power may be restored. It may be permanent. The disability may be partial, with capacity to earn a smaller income retained. It may be total.

In all these cases, the normal expenses of the family must be met. The father, the mother, and their dependent children must be sheltered, clothed, and fed. Provision must be made for the children's health and education and for their other needs. And in addition there will be the cost of medical care for the disabled man—the hospital bills, the doctor's bills, the surgeon's bills, the nurses' pay, the charges made for therapy, the prices of drugs and prosthetic devices, and so on and on. Without earned income and with expenses multiplied, the family suffers a heavy blow.

Accidents

Injuries account for a minor part of the total burden of accident and illness, but they still involve substantial costs. Injuries in 1966 resulted in wage losses of $5.9 billion and in medical expenses of $2 billion, a total of $7.9 billion.[9]

[9] Estimate by National Safety Council, *World Almanac, 1968*, p. 895.

More than 2,000,000 disabling accidents occur in industry in the course of a year, leaving some 15,000 workers dead and 85,000 permanently crippled.[10] But industrial accident is not the major source of injury. More people are killed and injured in accidents on the highways and in their homes than in factories. The wage loss and medical expense resulting from automobile accidents in 1966 was $3.2 bill.on; from industrial accidents, $2.2 billion; from accidents in the home, $1.5 billion.[11]

The amount of disability resulting from industrial accident has steadily declined. Safeguards have been imposed by law in hazardous employments. Safety measures have been voluntarily adopted by employers. In 1945, there were 33 fatal accidents for every 100,000 employees; in 1966, there were 20.[12] Provision has also been made to meet some part of the cost of industrial accidents through workmen's compensation laws.

No such progress has been made in the prevention of accidents on the highways or in the homes, or in meeting the costs that they entail. In all of these cases, the impact of disabling injury on the family is the same. But government has gone much farther toward meeting the problems created by industrial than by nonindustrial accidents.

Illness

On an average day in 1963, disabling illness kept more than five million people from going to work, attending school, or doing the housework.[13] In 1964–65, according to the National Health Survey, sickness restricted the activity of the average person for 16.4 days, kept him in bed 6.2 days, kept the average child home from school for 5 days and the average worker off his job for 7 days.[14]

Workers lost $51 billion in income in 1964 through illnesses not caused by their employment. Consumers paid out $25 billion for medical care. The private cost of nonoccupational disability in that year thus reached $76 billion. Its cost to the economy as a whole,

[10] John G. Turnbull *et al., Economic and Social Security* (3d ed.; New York: Ronald Press Co., 1967), pp. 310–17.
[11] National Safety Council, *op. cit.*
[12] Estimate by National Safety Council, *New York Times,* February 1, 1968.
[13] Margaret Gordon (ed.), *Poverty in America* (San Francisco: Chandler Publishing Co., 1965), p. 240.
[14] Turnbull *et al., op. cit.,* p. 353.

including losses of efficiency and public expenditures for medical care, was even higher.[15]

Illness is distributed unequally. Its incidence is lower among those who are young, white, married, and employed; and it is higher among those who are old, colored, single, and idle. The trend is away from communicable diseases and the ailments of childhood and toward the degenerative diseases of old age. The cost of medical care is therefore shifting toward the aged. The burden of sickness is heavier on those in the lower income groups than on the well-to-do; their ailments are more frequent, more serious, and more prolonged.[16]

The heaviest blow that can fall upon a family is the breadwinner's permanent and total disability, resulting either from accident or from illness. His income has stopped as certainly as if he had died. His wife cannot obtain support by remarriage. If he requires attendance, she must stay at home to care for him. Or she must find employment at wages that are high enough not only to meet the family's normal expenses and the husband's medical bills but also to cover the cost of alternative personal care. The burden is one that few women are prepared to carry.

The incidence of medical costs

Expenditures per family for health services and supplies in 1964 were about $400, or 6 percent of median family income. This figure does not appear to be unduly high. But the burden was not distributed evenly. A quarter of the families paid less than $100 and a twentieth paid more than $1,000. The lower the family income, the higher the share that went for medical costs. For an income over $7,500, the share was under 4 percent; for an income under $2,000, it was 13 percent.[17] Various studies made between 1918 and 1951 showed 10 to 15 percent of the families covered paying 40 percent of the medical bills. In 1957–58, half of the families met 88 percent of medical costs; the other half met only 12 percent.[18]

Medical costs are unpredictable. No family can foresee when they will occur or how large they will be. The costs of an unexpected illness

[15] *Ibid.,* p. 357.
[16] *Ibid.,* p. 354.
[17] *Social Security Bulletin,* Vol. 29 (1966), p. 15.
[18] Herman M. Somers and Anne R. Somers, *Doctors, Patients, and Health Insurance* (Washington, D.C.: Brookings Institution, 1961), p. 215.

may be staggering. An illness like cancer, for instance, may cost as much as $5,000 or $10,000 or even $15,000. Such a charge cannot be met by foresight or by careful budgeting. It cannot be paid from income or from savings by persons of modest means. The need is one that should be met through the insurance principle of pooling extraordinary risks.

If people are unable to meet the costs of proper medical care, they may allow their illnesses to go unattended, attempt self-medication, or resort to faith healers. At best, the result will be a prolongation of their disabilities; at worst, deaths that could have been prevented.

Insecurity or security?

Consideration of the consequences of insecurity and of the advantages and disadvantages of public action to assure security raises three questions: First, how would action to lessen insecurity affect human character? Second, how would it affect industrial output and economic progress? Third, how would it affect social and political stability? It is to these questions that we now turn.

Security and character

Public action to lessen insecurity has often been opposed on the ground that it would impair strength of character. It is said that insecurity makes people ambitious, industrious, and self-reliant and that the assurance of security makes them lazy, indolent, and irresponsible. It is said, too, that measures assuring security lead to immorality, that people feign illness and avoid employment in order to collect insurance benefits, and that they conceal their financial resources in order to collect relief.

These allegations are unproven. There is no evidence that people have worked less or saved less during the 30 years since the Social Security Act was passed than they did before. Nor have sample studies of the Social Security Administration disclosed a significant amount of fraud. A stricter standard seems to be applied in judging measures that benefit the poor than in judging benefits enjoyed by other groups. There is little concern, apparently, that the price supports given to farmers, the tariff protection given to manufacturers, the subsidies given to ship builders and operators, or the depletion allowances given to oil producers will undermine their character. Among those who fear that security programs will be abused, moreover, there is little complaint concerning the evasion that is common in the upper brackets of the income tax. In a small minority of security cases, it is possible that incentives may be impaired and that payments may be made to persons who are not deserving. But this does not justify denial of protection to all those who are insecure.

The fear that security payments will be damaging to character is relevant in the case of able-bodied people of working age. But four fifths or more of those for whom such payments are made are physically disabled, too old to work, or still in childhood. Whatever the validity of preachments concerning self-reliance, they have a hollow ring when addressed by an able-bodied and prosperous man in the prime of life to a cripple, an aged couple, or an impoverished child.

There is one way, it must be admitted, in which provision for social security may threaten public morality. Where the beneficiaries of security programs are politically powerful, candidates for office may vie with one another in promising larger benefits. Political advantage may thus be purchased at the expense of other citizens. But this differs in no way from competition among politicians for the votes of subsidized farmers or businessmen. It is one of the problems of democracy.

Security, output, and progress

The influence of insecurity on output can be none other than adverse. As a source of anxiety, it saps the worker's physical vitality, threatens his emotional stability, and thus impairs his productivity. Assurance of security, on the contrary, makes for contentment, contributes to health, and ministers to morale. And this is reflected in output. Men who have confidence are better productive instruments than men who are afraid.

Economic progress causes insecurity. Changes in demand, in the technology of production, in market organization, and in production costs all threaten to deprive men of their accustomed livelihoods. Sensing the danger, they organize for mutual defense. Characteristically, they seek legislation to obstruct the changes that they fear—laws that will prevent or delay innovation and enable them to stay in the old occupations, producing the old things in the old way. They demand that barriers be erected to the progress that the rest of the community desires. Social security affords a different remedy. If the burden of change need not be borne entirely by the individual who loses but can be shared by the community that gains, the need to stand in the path of progress will disappear. Security will no longer be purchased at the cost of stagnation.

Security and stability

Insecurity creates attitudes that are congenial to radical social change, invites resort to violence, and opens the way to revolution, with consequences that no one can foresee. Security affords an atmosphere that is conducive to gradual adjustment, where workable solutions to social problems can be devised, debated, and adopted, where the bad in society can be corrected without endangering the good. Insecurity makes for disorder; security makes for social and political stability.

4

Inequality of opportunity

Poverty, as we have seen, may be caused by personal delinquency, incapacity, and misfortune; by imperfect functioning of the economy; and by economic change—factors that may affect the welfare of all men. It may also be the consequence of deliberate discrimination. The welfare of some men may be impaired because they are refused equality of opportunity. Even though they are capable and industrious, though their potential contribution would meet the needs of a smoothly functioning economy, they may be denied an equal chance.

Discrimination intensifies the problems raised by poverty. The incidence of poverty is much higher among the members of minority groups than in the rest of the community. Poverty is thus a matter not only of class but also of race. Indeed, it is the growing protest against racial discrimination that has made the amelioration of poverty a major issue in the United States.

Discrimination not only intensifies the problems of poverty but it also raises problems of its own. It is social rather than economic in origin. It is based on the psychology of prejudice. Its impact is concentrated on racial minorities. Its manifestations and its consequences go beyond those that are presented by poverty alone. It is with these matters, peculiar to discrimination, that the present chapter is to deal.

Minorities in the United States

Before World War I, the groups regarded as minorities in the United States were the European immigrants in eastern cities (the Irish, Italians, Slavs, and Jews) and the Orientals on the Pacific Coast. These groups were feared, attacked, and made the objects of discrimination. They have now been successfully absorbed. At present, the minorities toward whom attention is turned are quite different: the Negroes in the South and in the cities of the North, the Mexican-Americans in the states of the Southwest, the Puerto Ricans in the cities along the Eastern Seaboard, and the Indians on their reservations in the West. In the Census of 1960, these peoples numbered about 24,000,000, or 13 percent of the nation's population. Among them, the Negroes numbered nearly 19,000,000, or 10½ percent; the Mexican-Americans 3,500,000, less than 2 percent; the Puerto Ricans around 850,000, less than half of 1 percent; and the Indians around 500,000, less than a third of 1 percent. These numbers have grown since 1960, the Negroes reaching 21,500,000, or 11 percent of the population, by 1966; the other minorities rising to some 5,500,000, still only 3 percent. Individuals in each of these groups have prospered, but their average level of living is pitifully low.

The American Indian

The red native of North America, conquered by the white invader, was dispossessed of his lands, segregated on reservations, and virtually abandoned. Legally, he became a ward of the government under the guardianship of a federal Bureau of Indian Affairs. For more than a century the Bureau's performance was marked by indifference, incompetence, and recurrent corruption. The Indian was pauperized instead of being equipped for self-support. His treatment was a black mark on the history of the time. Since the 1930's, this treatment has improved. Health services have been provided to the reservations. Educational programs have been upgraded and expanded. A start has been made toward the provision of better housing and the establishment of small industries. The Indian has come increasingly to manage his own affairs. He has been recognized as a citizen and given the right to vote.

But of all American minorities, the Indian is still the worst off. He suffers most from malnutrition and disease; his death rate is 70 percent above that of the general population; his life-span is only 42 years. He has the poorest housing: nine tenths of it is below the minimum standards of safety, health, and decency. He is the least educated: his literacy rate is only 50 percent. He has the least secure employment: his unemployment rate is seven times the national average. He is in the deepest poverty: his average family income in 1962 was $1,500, only half of the figure then taken as the poverty line.[1]

On the reservation, the Indian is typically a farmer. His land is infertile, arid, and difficult of access; his knowledge and equipment are meager; his labor therefore yields a small return. The reservation, moreover, is so far from markets and its resources are so scant as to prevent development through the growth of large-scale industry. Off the reservation, the Indian may be absorbed into the white community. Frequently, this has happened. But usually he is handicapped, lacking the experience and the training that he would need if he were to compete. If the Indian is to be lifted out of poverty, it will require a more determined effort than has yet been made.

The Mexican-American

The Spanish-surname population of the five southwestern states forms the second largest minority in the country. Ethnically, these people are mestizos, being of mixed Spanish and Indian blood. Eighty-five percent of them were born in the United States, half of them to parents who were born here, some of them descendants of persons who were already here when the territory was annexed. Only 15 percent are immigrants from Mexico. Four fifths of them live in California and in Texas. In California, they are the largest minority, outnumbering the Negroes two to one.

The Mexican-Americans live in cultural isolation. Their family groups are closely knit. They resist learning English. Their children are among the most underprivileged in the United States. In California they fall three years behind the whites in schooling; in Texas, four and a half years. Their drop-out rate and their delinquency rate are high.

The Mexican-Americans are better off than the Indians—no worse

---

[1] House of Representatives, Committee on Education and Labor, *Poverty in the United States* (Washington, D.C.: U.S. Government Printing Office, 1964), chap. v.

off than the Negroes. But a third of those in the cities and half of those in rural areas are in poverty. In California their median income is four fifths that of the whites; in Texas, three fifths; in the other states, two thirds.

These people find employment as common laborers and as farm hands. But their employment is irregular, their unemployment rate is high, and the conditions under which they work have been bad. They have long lacked organization and leadership. They are only now beginning to give expression to their demands for a better life.[2]

The Puerto Ricans

The Puerto Ricans, unlike the Indians, the Mexican-Americans, and the Negroes, are recent immigrants, coming from their overcrowded island in search of a better living on the mainland. Nearly all of them have settled in urban areas in the Northeast, and three fourths of them in New York City. Here, their language sets them apart. But they are nonetheless regarded by the whites much as if they were Negroes. The two groups are crowded into the same ghettoes, subjected to the same sorts of treatment.

On balance, the Puerto Rican is worse off than the Negro. His housing, if anything, is poorer. He gets less schooling. He is handicapped in competing for jobs. His income is lower. Politically, the Puerto Rican is weaker than the Negro. His fate, for better or worse, appears to be linked to that of the Negro.

The Negro[3]

The Negro minority is to be distinguished from other minorities in the United States. It is the largest, accounting for three fourths of the

[2] U.S. Department of Agriculture, Economic Research Service, *Low Income Families in the Spanish-Surname Population of the Southwest*, Report No. 112, 1967.

[3] Some Negroes now repudiate the word "Negro" as a white man's term of opprobrium and demand that it be replaced by "black" or "Afro-American." But, according to W. E. B. Du Bois, writing in *Crisis* magazine for March, 1928, " 'Negro' is a fine word. Etymologically and phonetically it is much better and more logical than 'African' or 'colored' or any of the various hyphenated circumlocutions." John A. Morsell, assistant executive director of the N.A.A.C.P., adds: "Only 'Negro' possesses, by reason of years of wide and continued usage, a clear, specific, and exclusive detonation: a person of black African origin or descent." (Editorial page, *New York Times*, July 20, 1968.) Accordingly, the word "Negro" is used in this text.

numbers in minority groups. It is the most widespread, not being confined as are the others to particular regions. It is the most conspicuous. Three fourths of all Negroes now live in cities, a third of them in the 12 largest: Washington is nearly two-thirds black, Newark more than half black, Baltimore and St. Louis more than a third black, Chicago and Philadelphia nearly a third black. More than any other minority, the Negro is identified with the more serious of our domestic problems: with urban deterioration, with social disorganization, with mounting welfare costs. Of the minorities, the Negro alone has a history of servitude that imposes a special burden on the conscience of the white community. More than the others, the Negro is fighting for recognition, for equality of opportunity, and for civil rights. For all of these reasons, we shall be concerned in the rest of this chapter with the Negro. But much of what is said with regard to the treatment of the Negro will apply to other minorities as well.

The changing Negro problem

Once a slave on the plantations of the rural South, the Negro has moved in recent times from South to North, from country to city, from agriculture to industry. He has advanced in legal status; the statutes and the court decisions that condemned him to inferiority have been removed. Some of his numbers have risen in the social scale, filling positions that carry prestige and being absorbed into the larger community. Psychologically, the Negro has moved from subservience to self-assertion and from shame to self-respect. He has come a long way from slavery. But he is still an object of discrimination—in education, in employment, in housing, and in other social areas. His long march toward equality is but begun.

Slavery and caste in the South

The Negro in the American colonies worked not only as a farm hand but also as a builder, a mechanic, a warehouseman, and in other occupations requiring special skills. His status was the same as that of an indentured servant who was white. He was not accorded different treatment on the ground that he was black. But early in the 19th century, his status was radically altered following the invention of the cotton gin. This invention made possible the plantation system of cotton culture. The plantation system in turn called for a supply of cheap labor. The planters saw that large profits were to be obtained if they could make the Negro's bondage permanent. And laws were enacted under which this was done.

The status of the Negro under slavery was that of a chattel, comparable to livestock. He could be bought and sold without his consent. He could be separated from his wife and children. He had no legal rights. He could not own property or enter into contracts. He had to do whatever work his master required of him. He could claim no wages. His food, clothing, and housing might be good or poor; he might be given medical care or not, educated or not, treated with consideration or brutality as his master chose. He could not protest; he had no standing in the courts. This inhumanity of man to man came to be defended by the white majority on the theory that the Negro was biologically inferior. Racism emerged as a *post hoc* rationalization of slavery.

Legally, emancipation freed the slaves. Socially, slavery was replaced by a caste system whose rules were strictly enforced. Negroes were denied employment in industry and confined to agriculture. Where they worked as laborers, their wages were low. Where they became tenants and sharecroppers, their holdings were small, their skills limited, and their capital scant. They were exploited by landlords and tradesmen and kept in debt by money lenders. Their status was that of virtual peonage. Negroes were segregated in the schools, at work, in housing, and in public accommodations. They were made to travel in separate sections, use separate lavatories, eat in separate areas, enter buildings by separate doors. In personal contacts, they were compelled to assume an attitude of subservience that manifested their inferiority. And in sexual relations, most significantly, where the Negro female was made subject to the demands of the white male, contact with the white female was forbidden to the Negro male. The Negro was kept from voting and from exercising his legal rights. The rules that bound him were enforced by segments of the white community through extra-legal sanctions, and ultimately by lynching.

Migration and urbanization

In 1910, nine tenths of the nation's 9,000,000 Negroes lived in the South. By 1966, nearly half of its 21,000,000 Negroes lived in the

North. Between 1940 and 1967, more than 3,500,000 moved north-ward. And the migration countinues at the rate of 200,000 a year.

The Negro was pulled off the southern plantation during the two world wars by a manpower shortage that created a demand for added labor in industry. He was afforded continuing opportunity for employment in the cities by the industrialization of the South. He was attracted to the North by the prospect of a better living than he could make in southern agriculture or industry. He was attracted, too, by the fact that the North—even the northern ghetto—offered him better welfare services than did the South, better amenities, and a friendlier environment in which to live.

The Negro was pushed off the southern plantation after 1933 by the government's agricultural program and by a revolution in agricultural technology. The price of cotton was raised; its markets abroad surrendered to foreign competitors. The acreage that could be planted to cotton was sharply curtailed. At the same time, the introduction of chemical fertilizers and herbicides reduced the need for hand labor. The mechanical cotton picker displaced the field hand; in 1966, more than nine tenths of the crop was harvested by these machines. Less labor was needed per bale of cotton. Its displacement, moreover, was accelerated by a minimum wage law that increased its cost. Cotton culture became a large-scale, highly mechanized, capital-intensive industry. The Negro farmer abandoned the competition and left the land.

In 1910, three fourths of the nation's Negroes lived on farms. In 1966, three fourths lived in cities. From 1960 to 1967, the Negro population of the major cities rose by more than 2,000,000. Through high birth rates and continued migration, this population is still growing at the rate of 500,000 per year. Within two decades it will number more than 20,000,000. No longer confined to the rural South, the Negro problem has also become a problem of the urban North.

The Negro's welfare today

When the Negro's position today is compared with that of a generation ago, it will be seen that striking progress has been made. More Negroes now finish high school; more go on to college. Negroes have entered occupations that were formerly closed to them; more of them are now employed in skilled and semiskilled trades. The Negro's median real income has risen. More than a quarter of Negro families have climbed into the middle brackets: those making $7,000 or more (in dollars of constant value) stood at 6 percent of such families in 1947 and at 28 percent in 1966. The percent of Negroes owning their own homes has risen; the percent living in substandard housing has declined.

But these gains have not been equally distributed. A minority of Negroes has succeeded in climbing into the middle class. The majority is little better off than it was before. The Negro's recent gains, moreover, have been made during a period of prolonged prosperity. Impressive in themselves, they are less than proportionate to the gains made by the whites. When the two races are compared, it is clear that the Negroes are still at a disadvantage.

The income of the average Negro family is still only 60 percent of that of the average white family. The Negro's chance of poverty is more than three times that of the whites. In 1966, only 10 percent of white families but 35 percent of Negro families fell below the poverty line. Of the nation's children, only 16 percent of the whites but 60 percent of the Negroes were living in poverty.[4]

The Negro has won notable victories in the legislatures and in the courts. He is now free to vote not only in the North but also in the border states and increasingly in the South. Public accommodations have been almost completely desegregated, and a start has been made toward desegregating the schools. A beginning has also been made toward the elimination of barriers to employment. But these reforms still encounter opposition. And discrimination in housing is even more resistant to change. Prejudice endures and with it the inequality of opportunity that prejudice demands.

Discrimination in education

Usually in the South and in the urban areas of the North, the races are separated in the public schools, with most of the Negro children going to one group of schools and most of the white children to

---

[4] U.S. Department of Health, Education, and Welfare, *White-Nonwhite Differentials in Health, Education, and Welfare,* 1965; U.S. Department of Labor, Office of Policy Planning and Research, *The Negro Family,* 1965; U.S. Department of Labor, Bureau of Labor Statistics, *The Negroes in the United States,* Bulletin No. 1511, 1966; U.S. Department of Labor, Report No. 332, *Social and Economic Conditions of Negroes in the United States,* 1967.

another. In 75 cities in 1966, three fourths of the Negroes attended elementary schools where the enrollment was 90 percent black; more than four fifths of the whites attended schools where it was 90 percent white. Not only is Negro schooling separate but it is inferior in quality. The Negro pupil, retarded by special handicaps, needs more attention than does the white; he gets less. As a result, his educational attainment is inferior, and he is less well equipped than is the white pupil for successful participation in the life of the community.

Segregation in the schools

In the South, in conformity with the regime of caste that followed slavery, a dual system of public schools was eventually established, with separate facilities and staffs; and separation of the races was required by law. In the North, there has been a single system and racial segregation has not been required. But segregation has nonetheless occurred. As Negroes have moved into the northern cities and sent their children to the public schools, white families have moved to the suburbs or sent their children to parochial and other private schools. Discrimination in housing has barred the Negroes from white neighborhoods, and the schools in these neighborhoods have remained predominantly white. Discrimination has confined the Negroes to other neighborhoods, and the schools in these neighborhoods have become predominantly black. In some cases, local governments have promoted segregation by the way in which they have drawn the boundaries of school districts, located new school buildings, and handled requests for transfers, refusing them to Negro pupils and granting them to whites. As a result, segregation has become almost as common in the cities of the North as it is in the South. In 200 northern communities in 1962, the enrollment in 738 schools was more than nine-tenths black. In New York City in 1967, the enrollment in public schools was more than half Negro and Puerto Rican. In Philadelphia, Baltimore, Detroit, St. Louis, and Chicago, it was more than half Negro; in Washington, more than nine-tenths Negro. The white pupils, most of them, went to public schools in the suburbs or attended private schools.[5]

Even if the education provided to both races were of equal quality,

---

[5] Commission on School Integration, *Public School Segregation and Integration in the North* (Washington, D.C.: National Association of Intergroup Relations Officials, 1963); and U.S. Commission on Civil Rights, *Racial Isolation in the Public Schools* (Washington, D.C.: U.S. Government Printing Office, 1967).

segregation in the schools would still have undesirable effects. It imposes a social stigma on the colored child, instils in him a feeling of inferiority, destroys his self-confidence, discourages his efforts, and worsens his performance. There is evidence to suggest that the Negro's educational attainment is better when he is taught in schools where he associates with whites: his self-esteem is enhanced by equal treatment, his aspirations raised, and his efforts stimulated by interracial contacts. His attainment is poorer when these advantages are denied. This evidence will be examined in Chapter 10.

The quality of Negro schooling

The Negro pupil in the public school is subject to the same disabilities as are all children who come from poor homes. In addition, he suffers from handicaps of his own. In a fourth of the Negro families, the mother has not been married or has been widowed, divorced, or deserted. The absence of a father deprives the son of a model and robs him of self-respect. The Negro parent has experienced discrimination in employment; he gives his child no goal to strive for, no hope for the future. The child learns that effort is futile; his motivation is impaired. Between the teacher and the Negro child, coming from different worlds and speaking different languages, there is a failure of communication more complete than with other children of the poor. If the child perceives that the teacher holds him to be inferior, he may accept her evaluation as his own.

To overcome these handicaps, an effort greater than that expended on other children would be required. In fact, however, the schools attended by Negroes are poorer than those attended by whites. The expenditure per pupil is lower. The facilities provided are less adequate. The teachers are less well trained and less well paid. The ratio of pupils to teachers is higher. There are fewer programs designed to evoke interest and stimulate achievement. There is little effort to discover and satisfy the Negro pupil's special needs.

As a consequence in part of the handicaps that burden him and the poor quality of the schooling that is provided him, the Negro child's educational achievement is inferior to that of the whites. Typically, he has difficulty in learning to read. The average third-grade Negro is a year behind the average third-grade white in reading. Year by year, he drops farther behind. By the time he reaches the 12th grade he lags by three years. In general, the Negro is more likely than the white to fall below the grade level normal for his age. In 1960, among children 14 and 15 years old, 12 percent of the whites and 30 percent of the Negroes were in such lower grades. The Negro is more likely to drop out of school; in 1960, among males between the ages of 16 and 24, drop-outs were 26 percent of the whites and 44 percent of the Negroes.[6]

Opportunity for higher education

A youth's opportunity for higher education depends in large measure on his family's income. Even where no tuition is charged, education is not free. The student must be freed for some years from the need to earn a living. He must be fed, clothed, housed, supplied with books and other educational materials, and enabled to participate in undergraduate life. All this costs money. The family's income not only influences the youth's ability to go to college but it may determine where he goes, how long he remains there, and the character of the course he takes. Financial assistance is increasingly available for able students who are in need. But enrollment in the best of the private institutions is a privilege that is enjoyed in the main by the children of the well-to-do.

In a study of 440,000 youths made at the University of Pittsburgh in 1964, it was found that nearly all of the males whose scholastic aptitude scores put them in the top 2 percent of the group taking aptitude tests went to college regardless of the size of their family income. But below this level, income was often crucial. Where income was over $12,000, half of those whose scores were so low as to put them in the bottom 50 percent of the group went on to college, as did four fifths of those who were above this level but in the bottom 75 percent. But where income was below $3,000, a fourth of those whose scores were so high as to put them between the upper 25 percent and the upper 10 percent of the group and an eighth of those whose scores put them between the upper 10 percent and the top 2 percent did not receive a college education.[7]

---

[6] U.S. Department of Health, Education, and Welfare, *op. cit.*, p. v; and U.S. Department of Health, Education and Welfare, *Equality of Educational Opportunity* (Washington, D.C.: U.S. Government Printing Office, 1966), *passim*.

[7] House of Representatives, Committee on Education and Labor, Subcommittee on the War on Poverty, *Hearings on the Employment Opportunity Act of 1964*, March 19, 1964, pp. 205–7.

Whatever his color, a youth's opportunity for higher education, is influenced not only by his parents' income but also by their aspirations for his future, and these depend on their own education, on the father's occupation, and on their social class. Among Negroes, the level of aspiration as well as the level of income is lower than among whites. As a result, though Negroes comprised 12 percent of the population of college age in the early sixties, they accounted for only 6 percent of those who were enrolled in colleges and professional schools.

Not only is the Negro's chance of going to college less than the white's; when he does go, he often attends institutions that are inferior in quality. Three fifths of Negro students are enrolled in predominantly Negro schools. There are 111 such institutions in the United States, 76 of them accredited by academic authorities. With some exceptions, the quality of their performance is said to have been low.[8] Two fifths of Negro students attend institutions that are predominantly white. Until recently, desegregation was resisted by the universities in the deep South, but now it is accepted. Elsewhere, desegregation started earlier and spread more rapidly in institutions of higher learning than in the public schools. Today, efforts are being made to seek out able Negro students and assist them to obtain an education.

In a number of northern states, beginning with New York in 1948, laws were enacted prohibiting discrimination against applicants for admission on the basis of race, color, or creed and forbidding the inclusion of questions concerning these matters on application blanks. State commissions were authorized to receive complaints of discrimination, to persuade or order institutions to accept qualified applicants, and to bring suit, if necessary, to have such orders enforced by the courts. In practice, the commissions received few complaints; they never brought an enforcement suit. The laws have now become dead letters, not because institutions are refusing Negro applicants but because they are actively seeking them. In this situation, the rule against including racial questions on application blanks is a handicap. Institutions wishing to discriminate in favor of Negro applicants now argue that the laws should be repealed.

For the Negro with superior capacities and adequate preparation, the opportunity for higher education is assured. For the Negro of

[8] David Riesman and Christopher Jencks, "The American Negro College," *Harvard Education Review,* Vol. 37 (1967), pp. 3–60; and Nathan Hare, "The Legacy of Paternalism," *Saturday Review,* July 20, 1968, pp. 44 ff.

ordinary attainments, it is not. In colleges and universities, as else-where, complete equality of opportunity is yet to be attained.

Discrimination in employment

The Negro is at a disadvantage not only in getting an education but also in getting a job. He is twice as likely as the white man to be unemployed. And where employed, he is three times as likely to be in an unskilled or menial occupation. He is handicapped in seeking white-collar work by lack of training. And even where qualified, he may be barred from such employment by deliberate discrimination. Whatever his job, his wages are lower than those paid to whites.

Rates of unemployment

Negroes comprised 11 percent of the civilian labor force in 1966; they accounted for over 21 percent of the unemployed. In 1961 when the rate of unemployment was high, 6 percent of the white workers and 12.5 percent of the Negroes were reported as jobless. In 1968 when the rate of unemployment was low, 3.1 percent of the whites and 6.7 percent of the Negroes were so reported. And these figures under-state the extent of Negro joblessness because Negroes who have become discouraged and stopped looking for work are not counted as belonging to the labor force. When these potential workers are taken into account, the rate of Negro unemployment rises by half. In 1968, for instance, instead of being under 8 percent, it would have been as much as 12 percent.

Negroes are unemployed more frequently than whites. When busi-ness improves, they find work. When business worsens, they are the first to be laid off. For them, moreover, unemployment lasts longer than for whites. In 1966 when Negroes comprised 21 percent of the unemployed, they accounted for 25 percent of those who had been out of work for more than six months.

The rate of unemployment is higher in the ghettoes of the great cities than in other areas. In 1966 when the rate for the nation as a whole stood at 3.6 percent, the average rate in the ghettoes of 10 cities was 10 percent; in some of these cities it was as high as 13 percent. The rate of unemployment is higher among teen-agers than among adults and higher among Negro teen-agers than among whites. In 1967, it stood at 11.2 percent for white males between the ages of 16 and 20 and at 25.3 percent for Negroes. An even higher percent of Negro youths was unemployed at some time during the year.

It is in this group that Negro unemployment presents its most serious social problem. While jobless, young people get no work experience and they do not obtain the skills that jobs require. And the longer unemployment persists, the less is the likelihood that jobs will ever be found. Without work and without hope, the youth in the Negro ghetto provokes public disorder, resorts to violence, and drifts into delinquency and crime.[9]

The Negro's occupations

Less than a tenth of Negro workers are left in agriculture and more than nine tenths have moved into urban jobs. In southern industry, however, the caste system survives. Negroes and whites do not work side by side. Negroes are not hired to supervise white or mixed crews. Seniority lines are separate; a white newcomer may outrank a Negro who has been on the job a longer time. In the rest of the country, such discrimination is less likely to be found, but everywhere the occupational pattern of the Negro differs markedly from that of the whites.

Among Negroes who are gainfully employed, only a fraction of 1 percent are entrepreneurs. Most of these people operate small service establishments in Negro communities: barber shops, restaurants, and the like. There are few large Negro businesses. The obstacles to the creation and growth of such undertakings are formidable. The Negro lacks entrepreneurial experience. He is without financial resources. He finds it difficult to raise capital, to get credit, to obtain insurance. He is overcharged by lenders, insurers, and suppliers. Finding the risks of enterprise too great, the ambitious Negro seeks to enter the professions or to find salaried employment.

More than half a million Negroes are engaged in professional and technical work, many in teaching and the ministry, with smaller numbers in medicine and in the practice of law. Although 12 percent of the labor force, they are only 6 percent of those working in these fields. Around 200,000, or 3 percent of their numbers, have managerial or official positions. Around 800,000, or 9 percent, are in clerical or sales

[9] U.S. Department of Labor, Bureau of Labor Statistics, Bulletin 1511, *op. cit.*, chap. ii.

work. Altogether, a sixth of the Negroes as compared with half of the whites are in white-collar jobs.

Negroes have their share of government employment: more than a million work for local, state, and federal governments, serving as policemen, postal workers, and the like. They have their share, too, of semiskilled jobs: more than 1,500,000 of them work as factory hands, truck drivers, and the like. They have less than their share of employment as craftsmen and foremen: 14 percent of white workers but only 6 percent of Negroes are so employed. Negroes gain access to new occupations when labor is scarce, but it takes an acute shortage to enable them to break into fields such as these.

In general, Negroes get the poorer jobs. Half of Negro men are common laborers and service workers, performing heavy manual tasks and serving as janitors, waiters, and the like. A third of the female workers are domestic servants. Altogether, Negroes supply a quarter of all laborers and two fifths of all service employees.[10]

The Negro's wages

Negroes are paid lower wages than are whites. In 1960, the median earnings of Negro men in professional and technical work were 32 percent less than those of whites; in managerial work, 37 percent less; in clerical work, 16 percent less; in sales work, 44 percent less; among craftsmen and foremen, 36 percent less; in semiskilled work, 32 percent less; among service workers, 30 percent less; and among common laborers, 27 percent less. The wage differential was narrowed during the forties and the early fifties: in 1939, the median wage income of Negro families was 63 percent below that of whites; from 1954 to 1956, it was 44 percent below. Thereafter, this movement was arrested; in 1963, the Negro's lag had increased to 47 percent. In part, these differences may be due to differences in productivity. But even though he has the same qualifications and does the same work, the Negro is paid less than the white.[11]

---

[10] *Ibid.;* Ray Marshall, *The Negro Worker* (New York: Random House, Inc., 1967), chap. vi; and Arthur M. Ross and Herbert Hill (eds.), *Employment, Race and Poverty* (New York: Harcourt, Brace & World, Inc., 1967), chap. ii.

[11] *U.S. Census of Population, 1960, Detailed Characteristics,* Summary Tables 205 and 208; and U.S. House of Representatives, Committee on Education and Labor (88th Cong. 2d sess.), *Poverty in the United States,* 1964, p. 268, Table 18.

Discriminatory practices

The Negro's record of unemployment, poor jobs, and low pay is to be attributed to a number of factors. In the mind of the employer, he is stereotyped as being suited only to inferior occupations. He lacks needed skills and is wanting in experience. His employment is irregular, and this deprives him of seniority. His housing is confined to segregated neighborhoods, and this limits his choice of jobs. He has crowded into a contracting urban labor market more rapidly than he could be absorbed. But another factor outweighs all the rest: the Negro worker is the object of deliberate discrimination.

The labor union may discriminate against the Negro. It may exclude him from union membership. And where its contract with the employer requires a union shop, this bars him from employment. The union may refuse the Negro admission to apprenticeship training. Its contract may require the employer to maintain separate seniority lines. It may compel him to lay Negroes off first and call them back last, and to prefer whites to Negroes in making promotions. Such discrimination has not been practiced by industrial unions; it has been common among craft unions, such as the railway brotherhoods and the building trades.

The employment agency may discriminate. It may refuse to register Negro applicants. It may fail to recommend them to employers. Or its references may differ according to race. Such practices have been usual among private agencies.

The employer may discriminate. Flat refusal to hire Negroes is rare. But the employer may recruit new workers from white schools and white unions and from among the relatives and friends of his white employees. He may instruct employment agencies to refer none but whites. He may deny Negroes admission to training programs. He may place them in inferior jobs, pay them at lower scales, and delay their promotion. Such practices have been common for many years in most industries in most parts of the country.[12]

[12] Paul H. Norgren and Samuel E. Hill, *Toward Fair Employment* (New York: Columbia University Press, 1964), chaps. ii and iii; and Michael I. Sovern, *Legal Restraints on Racial Discrimination in Employment* (New York: Twentieth Century Fund, 1966), chap. i.

Discrimination in housing

Discrimination in housing contributes to discrimination in other fields. If the Negro must live in a segregated housing area, his choice of employment will be limited and his children will have to go to a segregated school. Discrimination in housing, moreover, is more deep-rooted than in other fields—more stubbornly resistant to reform.

The Negro finds it almost impossible to own a home in the suburbs. He can rarely buy a house in a new development; commercial developers build almost exclusively for whites. Nor can he often buy land in the suburbs and build a house of his own. The landowner will refuse to sell to him. The mortgage lender will not finance his building costs. Most homeowners buy their houses secondhand. But the Negro can rarely buy a used house in a suburban community. The realtor will not show him a house. The mortgage lender will not finance his purchase. Almost the only houses that Negroes can buy are secondhand dwellings in segregated urban areas or in decaying areas nearby. It is only here that the realtor will be willing to offer places for sale and the mortgage lender willing to extend credit.

Instead of buying, the Negro usually rents the quarters where he lives. And since new housing is not built for this purpose, he must rent a dwelling that is old and may be in a poor state of repair. But where? Not in a white suburb. Here, again, the realtor will profess to have nothing to show him. Almost the only rental housing available will be in colored neighborhoods.

When the Negro does succeed in breaking into a restricted area, he may be subjected to harassment by his neighbors, to indignities, and even to physical violence. Such behavior like the discrimination practiced by realtors and mortgage lenders is a product of the fear that the entry of Negroes will lead to an exodus of whites, that the schools and other institutions will deteriorate, that the character of the community will be worsened, and that property values will decline. Such fears may be unjustified, but they operate nonetheless to obstruct desegregation.

The result is that the Negro is confined in large measure to the ghettoes of the cities: more than half of urban Negroes live in areas where the population is nine-tenths black. Here, much of the housing is antiquated, dilapidated, and poorly maintained. But the demand—

even for such housing—exceeds the supply. Buildings are over-crowded, and rents are high. Property owners profit while Negroes spend more for housing than they can afford.

Segregation, though pervasive, is not complete. Even in housing, there is growing tolerance. There are mixed neighborhoods here and there into which Negroes have been permitted to move. But the principal avenue of escape from the ghetto has been into other urban areas or into decaying suburbs where the whites move out as the Negroes move in. The boundaries of the ghetto may be extended, and the average quality of the housing it affords may rise. But the segregation of the races survives.

The Negro rebellion

Riots broke out in the ghettoes of scores of American cities during the summer months from 1963 to 1967. Starting usually with some minor incident involving police action, they rapidly exploded into general disorder, with window smashing, looting, and burning, ending in open warfare between mobs of Negro youths and the police, re-enforced by the National Guard. In Newark in 1967, warfare lasted five days and killed 23 people. In Detroit, five days' warfare left 43 dead.

The proximate causes of these disorders were the Negro's familiar grievances: discrimination in education, in employment, and in housing; gouging by white storekeepers; the poor quality of municipal services; the inadequacy of welfare programs; and most of all the alleged brutality of the police. The ultimate causes were to be found in the Negro's bitter experience and its effect on his psychology. Under slavery and under the caste system in the South, for centuries the Negro had suffered degradation and humiliation to which he was forced to submit with docility. Now, he had hoped his victories in the legislatures and the courts would assure him equality and his migration to the North would bring him prosperity. His expectations were not fulfilled. In the North as in the South it appeared that the white man was his enemy. He found his race rejected; his color still regarded as a mark of inferiority. He had no pride in his identity, and no bond with the community in which he lived. His rage, pent up for years, was now released. It was released in mass hysteria, in contagious violence, in blind destruction. In all of this, the Negro took pride. Through rebellion, he succeeded in forcing the whites to recognize him. He found dignity through self-assertion. He experienced the taste of power.

The white community's reaction to the riots was mixed. Some men saw in them the need for reforms that would attack the fundamental causes of the Negro's rebellion. Others demanded measures that would suppress the rebellion through the exercise of overwhelming force. President Johnson appointed a commission to study the causes of the riots and propose remedies. This body, consisting of 11 members—8 of them responsible officials in federal, state, and local governments and 3 of them eminent private citizens, with 2 of them Negroes and 9 of them white—made its report on March 1, 1968. It laid responsibility for the riots flatly at the door of "white racism," "the racial attitude and behavior of white Americans toward black Americans," and it came to this conclusion:

Our nation is moving toward two societies, one black, one white— separate and unequal. Reaction to last summer's disorders has quickened the movement and deepened the division. Discrimination and segregation have long permeated much of American life; they now threaten the future of every American . . . . To pursue our present course will involve the continuing polarization of the American community and, ultimately, the destruction of basic democratic values. The alternative is not blind repression or capitulation to lawlessness. It is the realization of common opportunities for all within a single society.[13]

[13] *Report of the National Advisory Commission on Civil Disorders* (New York: Bantam Books, 1968), p. 1.

PART II

Attacks on insecurity

5

Private provision
for security

The risks that threaten security, discussed in Chapter 3, are met in part through private efforts. A family may save a portion of its income, putting money aside to provide for a rainy day. It may be aided in an emergency by relatives or friends or by organized private charity. It may provide for its own protection through the purchase of private insurance policies. Insurance companies sell policies that provide for the payment of annuities during old age, though this part of their business is comparatively small. They undertake on a much larger scale to pay benefits in case of sickness or in the event of death. Protection is also afforded by retirement systems and by survivorship, sickness, and unemployment benefit plans set up by employers or by unions or established through collective bargaining. Taken together, these arrangements go part of the way, but far from all the way, toward giving assurance of security.

Private charity

Private saving cannot suffice to offset the risks that expenses will be increased through misfortune and that income will be reduced. These risks are unpredictable. No one can tell with any certainty when he is going to suffer an accident or fall ill, how long he will be incapacitated, how much his care will cost, or how much income he will lose. No one can foresee whether he is going to be thrown out of work or how long his idleness will last. No one knows whether his death will be so timed that it deprives his dependents of an income. No one knows whether with the onset of old age he will be capable of self-support. There are few people who can save enough to meet all these contingencies. For those below the poverty line, saving is virtually impossible. For the middle income group, the saving that is possible cannot be large enough to bear the burden of any misfortune that may come.

Their own savings exhausted, people turn first for help in an emergency to relatives and friends. If this fails them, they may turn to organized private charities.

Relatives and friends

In simple societies, the family has usually been the principal source of security. In earlier days in societies that are now industrial and urban, this was also the case. The son who met with failure in town came back to his father's farm. The aged parent found room in his son's home. The widowed sister and her children found food at her brother's table. The brother who could no longer pay the rent moved in with the one who could.

In advanced societies, all this has changed. Industrialization and urbanization have supplanted the family farm. People still contribute to the support of relatives outside the home. But the provision of food and lodging in the home has all but disappeared.

Family responsibility is a slender reed on which to lean. Some of those who encounter misfortune may have no relatives to whom to turn. Where there are relatives, their resources may be small. If the relatives are well-to-do, they may refuse to help. If they refuse to help, they cannot be forced to do so. And even where they are willing, the help they give may be inadequate.

The victims of misfortune are also assisted by neighbors and by friends. When a house burns, its former residents are sheltered for a time by neighbors. When persons are stricken by injury or illness, neighbors appear with offers of aid. Such support is helpful. But it is temporary. It cannot be claimed as a matter of right. It cannot be relied upon.

Organized charity

As urbanization has proceeded and as people have become more mobile, personal relations have become less intimate. Private charity, as a consequence, has come to be extended through channels that are formally organized. There are neighborhood agencies such as settlement houses in city slums, community agencies such as welfare councils and community chests, and nationwide organizations such as the Red Cross and the Y.M.C.A. There are churches, the largest of charitable organizations, handling more than half of private philanthropic funds. There are fraternal and service organizations (the Masons, the Elks, the Rotarians, the Kiwanians) each with a welfare program of its own. These agencies give aid in many different ways in amounts that run into billions every year. But the needy cannot depend upon them. Access to their aid is uncertain. It cannot be demanded as a right.

In the great depression of the thirties, the government first took the position that the needs of the unemployed should be met through private charity. But the magnitude of the task proved to be so great and the resources of the private agencies by comparison so small that they could not begin to do the job. The government therefore shouldered the burden of relief. It has carried the burden since that time, making payments in cash to those in need. Most of the private agencies have moved into other fields, rendering services to special groups, providing counseling and therapy to clients from the lower middle class, seeking to bring about social rehabilitation through the methods of case work. These services, sometimes rendered for a fee, do not reach the masses of the poor.[1]

Life insurance

There are more than 1,700 life insurance companies in the United States. A tenth of the benefits distributed by these companies take the form of periodic payments under annuity contracts. Around three

[1] Alfred De Grazia and Ted Gurr, *American Welfare* (New York: New York University Press, 1961), chaps. i–xi; and James N. Morgan, Martin H. David, Wilbur J. Cohen, and Harvey E. Brazer, *Income and Welfare in the United States* (New York: McGraw-Hill Book Co., Inc., 1962), chap. xviii.

tenths are payments for health insurance. More than six tenths are life insurance benefits. Life insurance, of course, does not guarantee a man continued life. What it does is to make sure that funds will be available for the support of his dependents in the event of his untimely death. This is the principal function of the life insurance business.

Survivorship protection under private contracts is general among American families. It is estimated that four fifths of all households and nine tenths of those containing children had some form of this protection in 1965. Policy holding varied with income: where income was over $3,000, nine tenths or more of the families were insured; where it was under $3,000, only seven tenths were insured. The average protection provided by the policies held by an insured family was nearly $20,000. In nearly half of the families with minor children, however, the protection amounted to less than $10,000.

Types of insurers

Insurance policies are written by different types of carriers. More than half of the life insurance in force has been written by mutual companies. These concerns are owned by their policyholders. The premiums they charge are reduced by the amount of the dividends they pay. Around two fifths of the insurance has been issued by stock companies. These concerns sell participating and nonparticipating policies. Under the former, around an eighth of the total, they share some of their profits with policyholders. They distribute some part of the rest as dividends to their stockholders. A smaller amount of insurance (about one sixteenth) is issued by other types of carriers: by the Veterans Administration to former servicemen, by fraternal organizations to their members, and by savings banks in New York, Connecticut, and Massachusetts to residents of those states.

These companies carry on their operations in different ways. The savings banks employ no outside salesmen but sell their policies over the counter. Most of the other companies employ salesmen. They collect their premiums annually by mail. Four companies issue "industrial insurance," sending agents around not only to sell their policies but also to collect weekly premiums. Of the three methods of operation, the one used by the savings banks is the least costly and the one used by the industrial companies is the most costly.

Insurance contracts provide protection both to individuals and to members of groups. Three fifths of the protection provided in 1966 was under individual contracts and two fifths under group contracts. There were 250,000 group contracts covering 64,000,000 persons in that year. The great majority of such contracts are entered into by employers on behalf of their employees, and a small minority by labor unions or jointly by unions and employers. Premiums may be paid by the employer, by the worker, or by both. The member of a group receives a certificate showing his participation. The average protection afforded under individual policies in 1966 was $4,930; that afforded under group certificates was $5,350. Group insurance has marked advantages for the insured. Its cost is lower because protection can be sold more cheaply at wholesale than at retail. The applicant for an individual policy must pass a physical examination; the member of a group need not.

Types of protection

Insurance companies sell policies of different types. Under term insurance, the benefits promised are stable but premiums rise from year to year as risk of death increases. Under decreasing term insurance, premiums remain the same and benefits decline. These policies are written for a fixed term. Some of them may be renewed without a physical examination; others may not. Term insurance is pure insurance; no savings are accumulated under such a policy. A tenth of individual policies and nearly all group policies are of this type.

Under level-premium policies, the premium and the promised benefit remain the same from year to year. For younger people, with a longer life expectancy, the premium exceeds the cost of insurance, the surplus being deposited in a savings account. For older people, the premium falls short of the cost of insurance; the deficiency is made up from the savings account. Under straight-life policies, 38 percent of individual insurance in 1962, premiums are paid until death. Under limited-payment policies (13 percent of the total), premiums, necessarily higher, are paid for a fixed term after which the insurance remains in force. Under endowment policies (7 percent of the total), premiums that are still higher are paid for a fixed term; the policyholder then receives the money that is in his savings account, and his insurance protection is terminated.

Under level-premium policies, the linkage of the insurance business and the savings business in a common contract gives the companies enormous reserves, totaling $167 billion in 1966, which they must invest. Their return on this investment determines the dividends they pay and thus in the case of policies of mutual companies and participating policies of stock companies affects the net cost of the protection that they sell.

The cost of insurance

There is a wide range in the premiums that must be paid for the same amount of insurance issued by different companies under different types of policies. These premiums are all based on the same table of life expectancy. Other factors explain the differences in cost. One company's method of selling policies or collecting premiums may be costlier than another's. Some protection is sold at retail; some at wholesale. Some policies provide for nothing but insurance; others combine insurance with a savings account. The number of premiums required differs from policy to policy as does the date when benefits must be paid. Some policies participate in earnings, and others do not; some companies earn more than others.

Industrial insurance, so-called, is by all odds the costliest form of protection since it involves the employment of agents to sell small policies to poor families and to collect weekly premiums. Two thirds of these policies provide for limited-payment or endowment types of insurance that the poor cannot afford. Policies are written not only on the breadwinner but also on his wife and on each of his children. The average policy pays around $450, about enough to cover the cost of a funeral. This type of protection has come, therefore, to be known as "burial insurance." It provides little or nothing for the support of dependents if the breadwinner dies. Industrial insurance exploits the poor by charging the highest premium for the least protection. Fortunately it has declined in importance, from 17 percent of the insurance written two decades ago to 4 percent in 1966.

The young husband with dependent children should buy the policy that will give his survivors the largest possible benefits for the lowest possible costs. He should obtain protection, if possible, as a member of a group. If he is a citizen of New York, Connecticut, or Massachusetts, he should buy individual insurance from a savings bank. Elsewhere, he should buy from a mutual insurance company or buy a participating policy from a stock company. He should buy renewable term rather than level-premium insurance. The agent who seeks to sell him a policy will doubtless expound the virtues of straight-life, limited-payment, and endowment contracts, whose sale will bring him a higher commission. Such contracts will force the purchaser to save. They will spare him the necessity of managing his investments. They will provide him with protection at a lower cost after he has passed middle age. But the young man needs insurance more than he needs savings. In his later years, his income will probably be larger and the needs of his dependents smaller. In his earlier years, the premiums paid on term insurance will provide larger benefits than the same amount spent on level-payment policies. And this is when his wife and children will need all of the protection that he can afford.[2]

Employee benefit plans

An increasing share of compensation to employees of large firms has come to take the form of fringe benefits. These include paid vacations, retirement systems, survivorship insurance, medical care, and unemployment benefits. The number and scope of such plans has grown rapidly since World War II. Workmen now regard their benefits as part of their regular pay.

Many of these plans have been initiated by employers as an element of personnel policy. More than half of them have been products of collective bargaining, in some cases between a union and a group of employers and in most cases between a union and a single firm. Half of the plans are financed jointly by an employer and his employees. A growing number of them are financed by the employer alone. In 9 cases out of 10, the plan is administered by the employer. Some plans, relatively few in number, are administered by unions or jointly by unions and managements. The welfare plan of the United Mine Workers, one of the largest, is financed by a levy on every ton of coal that is mined; and it is administered, as required by law, by three trustees representing the union, the coal operators, and the public.

Retirement and survivorship

By the end of 1965, some 28 million workers, nearly half of those employed in private industry, were covered by retirement plans.

[2] For a full exposition of life insurance operations, see Dan M. McGill, *Life Insurance* (rev. ed.; Homewood, Ill.: Richard D. Irwin, Inc., 1966). For current data, see *Life Insurance Fact Book* (New York: Institute of Life Insurance, 1967).

Under these plans all workers who have served for a certain period, attained a certain age, or earned more than a certain wage are eligible for benefits. Benefits usually start at age 65 and are either a flat amount or a function of the worker's past service or earnings or both. The retired worker's widow may also be assured a fraction of these benefits as long as she survives. Benefits paid by the government under the social security system are subtracted in determining the amount to be paid under a private plan. The resulting total, however, will be higher than the public benefits alone.

Nearly two thirds of all civilian wage and salary earners are covered by plans assuring benefits to their survivors. Eligibility for such coverage is determined by length of service. Benefits may be set at a flat figure or made proportionate to earnings. They are paid in addition to those provided by the government under the social security law. The adequacy of survivorship provision is increased accordingly.

The employer who promises these benefits may bear the risk himself, depositing the funds that will be needed with a trustee. Three fourths of private pensioners are covered by plans that are financed in this way. Alternatively, the employer may shift the risk to an insurance company by purchasing a group insurance policy. Nine tenths of all the welfare plans are so insured.

The plans have certain weaknesses. Their coverage is not complete, being confined in the main to large firms and to industries where labor is strong. Coverage may be limited, moreover, to those workers who are better paid. Few of the plans are fully funded; it is not certain that the benefits promised can be paid. If a plant shuts down, is absorbed in a merger, or is sold, the worker's protection may be lost. The plans operate, moreover, to impede labor mobility. Where all the employers in an industry participate in a common system, this is not the case. But where an employer has a separate plan, the worker who transfers to another firm will lose his accumulated rights to benefits.[3]

Unemployment

Protection against unemployment is also provided under employee benefit plans, though on a much smaller scale than protection against retirement or survivorship. Five million workers were covered in 1965

[3] John G. Turnbull, C. Arthur Williams, Jr., and Earl F. Cheit, *Economic and Social Security* (3d ed.; New York: Ronald Press Co., 1967), pp. 175–96.

by union contracts which guaranteed them dismissal compensation or severance pay in addition to wages due if they should be permanently separated from employment for reasons beyond their control. A half million workers were covered by plans for a guaranteed annual wage that assured certain classes of employees a fixed number of weeks of work or a stated income each year. Two million workers were covered by plans for supplementary unemployment benefits. Under such a plan, a worker who has qualified for benefits under a state unemployment insurance law commonly gets around 60 percent of his previous earnings, plus allowances for dependents for as long as a year. The employer pays the difference between the benefits paid by the state and those provided by the plan. These plans reach only a small percentage of those who are covered by the unemployment insurance laws, leaving the rest with less protection. If the benefits paid by the states were made more nearly adequate, there would be less need for supplementary benefit plans.[4]

Meeting the cost of medical care

People with low incomes have long been assisted in one way or another in meeting the cost of medical care. Philanthropy has provided the funds to build most private hospitals. The prices charged for hospital services have been designed to cover not the cost of capital but only the cost of current operation and even here a tenth of the cost is met by charity. The difference between the prices charged for private rooms and for beds in wards has been greater than could be justified by differences in cost. Doctors associated with hospitals have been expected to care for needy patients in clinics and wards without charge. Doctors have also adjusted their fees to the incomes of other patients, making them higher for the rich and lower where they have served the poor. As a result of these policies, it has been argued that the private practice of medicine has not barred people with low incomes from access to medical care.

All this has been changing. With the spread of health insurance, an increasing number of people have become able to pay their hospital bills and their doctors' bills. Free service in clinics and wards is less needed; it will eventually disappear. The sliding scale of fees, likewise,

[4] *Ibid.*, pp. 272–98.

is less needed; save in the case of surgery, it, too, is likely to disappear.

Taking the place of these arrangements is a great variety of private plans for meeting the cost of medical care: insurance against various risks by commercial carriers with individuals and groups; insurance against the cost of hospitalization and surgery, respectively, by the Blue Cross and the Blue Shield; medical service provided under employee benefit plans; and protection of various sorts provided by group practice clinics, consumers' cooperatives, and other community groups. In 1966, nearly 150 million people were insured in one or more ways against health risks, 97.4 million of them by commercial companies, 63.4 million by Blue Cross, 54.5 million by Blue Shield, 4.6 million under employee benefit plans, nearly 2 million under consumer and community plans, and less than 250,000 under group clinic plans. Four fifths of the civilian population had some sort of protection against the cost of hospital care, three fourths against the cost of surgery, and two fifths against the cost of doctors' office and home calls.[5]

Commercial health insurance

More than 900 insurance companies sell protection against health risks, nearly 40 million of their beneficiaries being covered by individual contracts and 70 million (with overlapping) as members of groups. Among the individual contracts the most frequent is one which covers basic medical expenses such as the costs of hospitalization, surgery, and other physician's services. Another type of contract, less frequently sold, covers major medical expenses, obligating the insurer to meet a share of the costs that exceed a stated figure, up to a maximum amount. A third type is comprehensive in its coverage, combining the sorts of protection provided by the other two. Other policies compensate in part for income lost in the event of continued disability. Still others cover both medical expenses and income loss.

The individual contracts have a number of disadvantages. Their benefits have sometimes been misrepresented. At best, their terms are so diverse and so complicated as to make it difficult for the consumer to make a rational choice. The companies refuse protection under certain circumstances, such as the preexistence of illness. They may cancel their policies or refuse to renew them. The cost of the protection they provide is high. In 1966, it took 43.2 percent of their

[5] Louis S. Reed, "Private Health Insurance: Coverage and Financial Experience," *Social Security Bulletin,* November, 1967, pp. 3–22.

premium income to cover operating expenses; only 54.4 percent was used to settle claims.

The group contracts sold by the commercial companies offer the same protection as the individual contracts: insurance against basic medical expenses, major medical expenses, and comprehensive insurance combining the two; also insurance against loss of income and against both medical expenses and income loss. These contracts, however, have marked advantages. The purchaser is well equipped to evaluate their terms. They cover all the members of a group. The protection afforded a member cannot be cancelled; its renewal cannot be refused. Group contracts are less expensive than individual policies. In 1966, the companies spent 12.8 percent of their income from such contracts on operating expenses and used 93.1 percent to settle claims, incurring a loss on this part of their business of 5.9 percent.[6]

Blue Cross and Blue Shield

The first Blue Cross associations were established by hospitals in the depression of the thirties to meet the problem of financing hospital costs. There are now 80 such associations serving nearly 7,000 participating hospitals in the United States. A Blue Cross association is a local nonprofit body set up under state law and governed by a board that represents the hospital administrations, the medical profession, and the public. It sells hospital services to the public, usually under group contracts, and buys them from the hospitals at a price that covers their costs. It does not provide physician's services or any services rendered outside a hospital. It pays its beneficiaries no cash. What it does is to pay the hospitals for specified services rendered on their behalf. A Blue Cross check typically covers 85 percent of the hospital bill. The cost of Blue Cross protection is the lowest in the health insurance field. Only 4.9 percent of its income was required in 1966 to cover operating expenses; 93.4 percent was paid out in benefits.

Blue Cross has had its problems. In order to assure broad coverage, it set flat rates based upon the average risk in a community, not differentiating according to an individual's sex, age, occupation, or past experience. The commercial insurers, on the other hand, differentiated their rates, basing them on individual risks. Charging lower rates on

[6] *Ibid.,* p. 17; Turnbull, Williams, and Cheit, *op. cit.,* pp. 415–29; and Herman M. Somers and Anne R. Somers, *Doctors, Patients, and Health Insurance* (Washington, D.C.: Brookings Institution, 1961), chap. xiv.

better risks, these concerns got their business, leaving the poorer risks to the Blue Cross. In self-defense, the Blue Cross, adopted the commercial pattern of pricing. As a result, the poorer risks were discouraged from participating in the plan.

Hospital costs have been rising. Blue Cross cannot raise its own charges without permission from the state. Such increases are opposed by the consumers of hospital services, and the permission requested is frequently denied. Blue Cross is thus caught in a financial squeeze. Attention turns, then, to the possibility of reducing hospital costs. To this end, more economical means of hospital operation might be devised. But the hospitals contend that this is not the business of Blue Cross. The number of hospital admissions might be limited, the duration of hospital stays curtailed, and the services rendered reduced. But these are matters that physicians have held to be exclusively within their competence. The intrusion of insurers into such fields is resisted by the hospitals and the doctors alike. This is a conflict that arises under public as well as private health insurance plans. We shall refer to it again in Chapter 9.

Blue Shield follows the pattern set by Blue Cross, except that the majority of an association's board must be physicians. It usually employs the same administrative staff as does Blue Cross. There are 75 such associations in the United States, with nine tenths of the country's doctors participating in the plan. Blue Shield contracts cover nothing but surgeon's fees and charges for other doctor's care in the hospital. Each association negotiates with the local medical society to fix its scale of fees. Where a patient's income falls below a certain level, the doctor agrees to charge no more than the benefit that is stipulated in the plan. Where incomes are higher, however, he may charge as much as he pleases, the patient paying the difference between the benefit and his fee. Blue Shield is more costly to administer than is Blue Cross, nearly 10 percent of its income being required to cover operating expenses in 1966 and only 90 percent being distributed as benefits.[7]

Other health plans

There is a large number of other health plans serving fewer patients than do the commercial insurers, Blue Cross, or Blue Shield. Some of

---

[7] Reed, *op. cit.;* Somers and Somers, *op. cit.,* chaps. xv, xvi; and Turnbull, Williams, and Cheit, *op. cit.,* pp. 429-37.

them are sponsored by employers, by unions, or jointly as part of an employee benefit plan. Some are sponsored by physicians, others by consumers' cooperatives, still others by community organizations. The provisions of these plans differ in considerable detail.

An outstanding union plan is that of the United Mine Workers welfare fund. It operates regional hospitals and clinics in a score of states under contract with doctors' groups, providing a complete medical service to members of the union and their dependents, including hospitalization, surgery, inpatient physicians' care and drugs, and outpatient diagnostic and therapeutic services. These benefits, like the others administered by the fund, are financed by the tax on coal. The fund also sells its medical services to other residents of the mining areas. Another union plan, sponsored by the International Ladies Garment Workers, operates a chain of outpatient clinics and mobile facilities in New York City, employing doctors on a salaried or per session basis to render outpatient services. It also provides hospital, surgical, and maternity benefits under an insurance plan. Its operations are financed under a collective bargaining agreement by the employers in the industry. A similar plan is maintained by the Amalgamated Clothing Workers.

Some of the plans operated by physicians have been set up by local medical societies on the Blue Shield pattern but are not affiliated with that group. Others have been established by group clinics controlled by participating doctors. The earliest of these was the Ross-Loos clinic in Los Angeles. This organization operates a large central office and a number of branch offices in that city, providing diagnostic and therapeutic service on a prepayment basis. Its patients get their hospital protection from Blue Cross.

Well known among the consumer cooperative plans are the group health associations of Washington and New York. The Washington association provides comprehensive medical services, including dental, optical, and psychiatric care, through group-practice units attached to four medical centers and operating in the main on a prepayment basis. The association has 68,000 members, 70 percent of them employees of the federal government and 14 percent employees of the city's transit system, covered by agreements with the Civil Service Commission and the transit company. It is governed by a board of nine unpaid trustees elected by its members. Group Health Insurance of New York provides cash benefits to cover surgical and medical charges. For protection against hospital costs, both associations depend upon Blue Cross. A third such association, the Group Health Cooperative of Puget Sound in Seattle, has built and operates a hospital of its own.

The community health plans include the Kaiser Foundation plan on the Pacific Coast and the Health Insurance Plan of Greater New York. The Kaiser Foundation operates a dozen hospitals and scores of out-patient centers under contract with hundreds of doctors combined in group practice units. It provides comprehensive hospital and medical services. The HIP in New York, with more than a half million subscribers served by a thousand doctors, contracts with group practice units, each owning and operating its own facilities, to render hospital, home, and office service to its subscribers, including home nursing and a yearly physical examination, for a fixed amount per subscriber per year. Like several of the other plans, it relies on Blue Cross to meet the costs of hospitalization.[8]

How adequate is private health insurance?

The overall coverage of private health insurance is incomplete. It affords no protection to the unemployed, the disabled, the aged, or to people on relief. There is no protection for a fifth of the civilian population against hospital costs, for a fourth against the cost of surgery, for three fifths against the cost of doctors' home and office calls. There are regional differences in coverage: the fraction of the population having protection is higher in the North, much lower in the South. There is also inequality in the coverage of different income groups. In 1962–63, hospital insurance covered nearly all of those with incomes above $7,000, but it failed to cover a fifth of those between $4,000 and $7,000, half of those between $2,000 and $4,000, and two thirds of those below $2,000.[9]

Private health insurance does not cover all health risks. Protection against loss of income during illness is provided under the disability laws of four states (California, New Jersey, New York, and Rhode Island) and in the case of railway employees, under federal law. Other workers are covered by formal or informal sick leave plans adopted voluntarily by employers. Under a typical plan, salaries are continued

---

[8] Somers and Somers, *op. cit.*, chap. xvii.

[9] Eugene Feingold, *Medicare: Policy and Politics* (San Francisco: Chandler Publishing Co., 1966), p. 14.

in full for one or two weeks, whereupon the payments cease. Some employers carry this risk themselves; others meet it by buying group insurance. Only a half of the labor force is protected against income loss; only a sixth in states where such protection is not required by law. And where protection is provided, less than 30 percent of the loss is recovered in the payments that are made.[10]

Private insurance covers some medical risks inadequately; others not at all. It pays only part of the doctor's bill, making little provision for diagnosis and preventive care. It barely begins to meet the cost of drugs. It offers little or no protection against the costs of dentistry, mental illness, and chronic illnesses.

Even where benefits are provided, they meet only a fraction of the costs incurred. In 1966, private insurance benefits covered less than a third of the total costs of medical care.[11]

[10] Alfred M. Skolnik, "Income-Loss Protection against Illness," *Social Security Bulletin*, January, 1968, pp. 3–14.

[11] For evaluations of private health insurance, see Somers and Somers, *op. cit.*, chaps. xviii–xx; and Turnbull, Williams, and Cheit, *op. cit.*, pp. 440–55.

6

Social security

Social provision for security, unlike private provision, involves action by government. It is based upon a recognition that self-reliance and private charity are not adequate to meet all human risks; that the community, in common decency, cannot permit people to die of starvation or exposure; that society, in its own interest, cannot deny its members the minimum support they need in order to subsist. It is based, too, upon a recognition that the misfortunes that may befall an individual or a family are the result in large measure of conditions for which society as a whole is responsible. If employment is curtailed by business depression or by technological displacement, if reemployment is obstructed by faulty operation of the labor market, if jobs are denied by racial discrimination, or if real incomes are reduced by inflation, the individual should not be expected to shoulder all the costs. A part, at least, of the burden should be borne by the community as a matter of public policy.

Approaches to social security

The public means of meeting social risks fall into two categories: public charity and social insurance. Public charity is provided specifically to the poor; it is designed to alleviate their poverty. It goes under the names of "relief," "assistance," and "welfare." It may take the form of institutional care, of goods and services, or of payments in cash. It is financed by appropriations from the general revenues of governments. If the taxes that supply these revenues are progressive, it brings about a transfer of income from the upper to the lower income groups. The extent of such transfers cannot be without bounds. A limit is therefore established by denying public charity to persons who have resources of their own, confining it to persons who can show they are in need. This is done by requiring a "means test" of applicants for aid. Eligibility for aid and the amount of aid provided depend not on past employment or earnings but on present need. Determination of need is a matter of administrative discretion. The needy person cannot claim public charity as a right. He cannot count upon it as a certainty.

Social insurance differs both from private insurance and from public charity. Like private insurance, it pools definable risks in a large statistical population. It is financed by contributions made by or for prospective beneficiaries. Eligibility for its benefits and the amount of such benefits are not determined by need.

But the differences between private and social insurance are great. Participation in private insurance is voluntary; in social insurance, compulsory. The contributions and the benefits that are stipulated in a private insurance contract cannot legally be changed; the contributions required and the benefits provided by social insurance can be altered by legislative action. Private insurance is financed exclusively by premiums paid by the prospective beneficiary; social insurance may be financed in various combinations by taxes paid by the beneficiary or by his employer on his behalf and by contributions from general revenues. Under private insurance, the individual's own payments purchase his own benefits. Under social insurance, the contributions made for workers who are currently employed finance the payments made to those who are currently receiving benefits. With private insurance, the beneficiary can claim his benefits as a matter of legal right. With social insurance, having paid taxes to provide benefits to an earlier generation, he has the right to expect that a later generation will pay taxes to provide benefits to him. This is a moral rather than a legal right, but one that government most certainly will recognize. Private insurance does not redistribute income; social insurance has this effect.

Social insurance differs from public charity in many ways. It aims to prevent, not merely to alleviate, poverty. It is financed by contributions made on behalf of those who are insured. The contributions are earmarked to pay the benefits; both are handled through a separate insurance fund. Eligibility for benefits depends on past employment, not on lack of means; the applicant is not required to prove he is in need. Contributions and benefits are both related to past earnings and thus to one another. The beneficiary feels, however mistakenly, that he has bought and paid for the benefits he gets. Their amount and their duration are not a matter of administrative discretion. He can expect their payment as a matter of right. They are predictable, guaranteed, and thus dependable.

Such is the difference in principle between social insurance and public charity. In practice, as we shall see, the line is not so clearly drawn.

The background of social security

Social security had its origins abroad; it was late in coming to the United States. Public charity in this country was patterned after the English poor laws enacted during the reign of Elizabeth I. Under these measures, relatives were held to be primarily responsible for the support of the poor. But where this was unavailing, the local parish assumed responsibility, taxes were imposed to finance relief, and overseers appointed for its administration. Relief was given to paupers who were aged or handicapped and denied to paupers who were able-bodied unless they entered a public workhouse. These principles—primary family responsibility, residual government responsibility, local financing and administration, and different treatment for the unemployable and the employable—were carried over into the poor laws of the American colonies and, later, the American states.

Social insurance made its appearance much later, coming first in Germany under Chancellor Bismarck. Here, compulsory health insurance was inaugurated in 1883, old-age and disability insurance in 1889, and survivors' insurance in 1911. Health, disability, and unemployment insurance were also introduced in Great Britain in 1911. The movement had spread to 40 other countries before the first social insurance laws were enacted in the United States.

The evolution of public charity

Until the 20th century, people incapable of self-support were cared for by local governments in institutions known as poorhouses or poor farms or, later, as county homes or county farms. Within their walls,

the aged, the disabled, the unemployed, and the orphaned or abandoned child were housed and fed together with the imbecile, the
insane, the derelict, and the depraved. The atmosphere typically was
one of squalor and degregation. The food provided might be no more
than was required for bare subsistence, the keeper pocketing what he
could withhold from the funds allowed. There was little medical care
for the handicapped, the aged, or the disabled, and inadequate training
for children. To be relegated to the poorhouse was to be disgraced.

Early in the 20th century, private charity and state and local governments came increasingly to establish specialized institutions for the
care of particular groups—the aged, the orphaned or abandoned child,
the physically handicapped, the feeble-minded, and the insane. Here,
inmates were spared the degrading influence of the poorhouse and
were supposedly given care adapted to their needs. But these institutions were starved for funds; the quality and quantity of their services
were low.

It soon came to be realized that institutionalization was often unnecessary, even harmful, and always costly. The aged would be hap-
pier if given a modest income that would enable them to remain in
their own homes or to live with relatives or friends. The orphaned or
abandoned child would stand a better chance of development if he
could be brought up by a relative or in a foster home. It would be
cheaper to support an aged person or a child in the community than in
an old folks' home or in an orphanage. State legislatures, therefore,
began providing for cash relief. Beginning in 1911 with Illinois and
Missouri, 45 states had enacted widows' pension laws by 1935, authorizing county governments to assist mothers left with dependent
children to support them in their own homes. And beginning in 1923
with Montana, 28 states had authorized their counties to pay pensions
to the aged. This authority was not fully utilized. But where it was, a
declining portion of the needy—those who were seriously handicapped
or advanced in senility—was kept in institutions and an increasing
portion was helped to live in the community.

The present pattern of public charity dates from the great depression of the thirties. The need for help was then so great that it exceeded the capacities of state and local governments. The federal
government came to their aid, providing emergency employment and
making grants to finance the distribution of relief. Its continuing
commitment to share in the provision of assistance to certain categories
of the needy—the aged, the handicapped, and dependent children—

was written into the Social Security Act of 1935. Then regarded as dealing with a passing emergency, the public assistance provisions of that law became a permanent feature of the structure of public charity.

The evolution of social insurance

Until the thirties, social insurance in the United States was limited to compensation for workers injured in industrial accidents. The first of the workmen's compensation laws was enacted in New York State in 1910. Such laws had been passed by 44 of the states by 1935. But that was all. Introduction into this country of the types of protection afforded by the insurance systems of other industrial states was delayed by America's traditional belief in the sufficiency of individual initiative and self-reliance. It took the great depression to shake the country loose from this philosophy. The first new measure then to be adopted was an unemployment insurance law enacted by Wisconsin in 1932. This was the extent of social insurance in the United States until the Social Security Act was passed by Congress in 1935.

The Social Security Act contained a provision (explained in Chapter 7) whereby the federal government induced the remaining states to follow Wisconsin in providing insurance against unemployment. It also set up a federal system of insurance against dependent old age. Establishment of this system marked the beginning of comprehensive social insurance in the United States. The law was attacked in the national campaign of 1936 by Alfred M. Landon, the Republican candidate for the presidency, who thereupon carried the states of Maine and Vermont. Since that time, the program has had bipartisan support. Its scope has been enlarged, extending its coverage and affording protection against more risks—against survivorship in 1939 and permanent total disability in 1954—and providing medical care for the aged in 1965. The level of its benefits has repeatedly been raised. Social insurance is now a permanent institution, generally accepted, and enjoying widespread popular support.

The American pattern of social security

The social security system of the United States is a complex combination of different measures enacted at different times by different legislative bodies and altered from time to time by amendment. The system includes both social insurance and public charity. Some risks are covered by both; others by neither. The benefits provided by some of the programs are available to all; those offered by others are limited to particular groups. Some parts of the system are financed and administered exclusively by the federal government, others by state and local governments, and still others involve the different levels of government in a variety of relationships. Administration of the programs, both in the nation and in the states, is entrusted to a number of different agencies. Nowhere is there provision for consistency of policy or central responsibility for the system as a whole.

This complicated pattern may be better understood if its elements are presented in outline form:

SOCIAL INSURANCE | PUBLIC CHARITY

Federal Programs

Social Insurance	Public Charity
Old age	Institutional care and
Survivorship	welfare services in
Permanent disability	federal jurisdictions
Hospital costs for	
the aged	Veterans' benefits
Supplementary medical	
costs for the aged	
Railroad employees	
Federal employees	

Federal–State Programs

Social Insurance	Public Charity
Unemployment	Welfare services
	Categorical assistance:
	Old age
	Blindness
	Permanent total
	disability
	Dependent childhood
	Medical care for the
	medically indigent
	Food programs
	Housing programs

State and Local Programs

Social Insurance	Public Charity
Occupational injury	Institutional care
and illness	Welfare services
Temporary disability	General assistance
State and local employees	

The relative significance of the several elements in this pattern may be shown in a rough order of magnitudes by figures covering the number of persons receiving benefits and the amount of money being spent on benefits in 1967. Around 60 million out of 200 million Americans received benefits in some form. Of these, some 18 million received institutional care, free goods, or welfare services, and around 42 million received cash. Among the latter, about 27 million collected insurance benefits and 15 million had charitable grants. Cash payments were made to some 2 million persons through state and local programs, to 9 million through federal-state programs, and to 31 million through federal programs. (In every case allowance should be made for overlapping; its extent, however, is unknown.) Expenditures on the security programs ran around $48 billion. Of this, some $6 billion went for aid in kind and $42 billion for benefits in cash. Of the cash, about $32 billion took the form of insurance benefits, more than $5 billion was in public charity, and nearly $5 billion was in aid to veterans.

There is a certain logic in the relationship between social insurance and public charity. Social insurance is taken to be the first line of defense against misfortune. But it cannot be the sole defense. Its coverage cannot be complete. Where the collection of contributions is not feasible, people cannot be insured. And where those covered by the law have not worked long enough or had sufficient earnings to establish eligibility, no benefits are paid. In the federal insurance program, moreover, the size of one's benefits depends upon the amount of his earnings while covered; the benefits paid in the early years of the program were therefore small. In all such cases, the needs not met by insurance benefits are to be met, if at all, by public charity.

As its coverage has been extended, more people have come to be protected by social insurance. With the passage of time, moreover, those covered by the federal program have earned the right to larger benefits. Insurance thus has come to shoulder more of the burden of security, leaving less of it to charity. It has sometimes been said that this process will continue until the need for charity has disappeared. This would not seem to be the case. There will always be needs that the insurance method cannot handle and needs so great that the benefits earned under this method will not suffice. Here, there will be a place for public charity. But the share of insurance in providing security should continue to rise and that of charity to decline.

Insurance programs

The several insurance programs contained in the social security system are marked by their diversity. The programs differ in coverage, in benefits, in financing, and in administration. The problems presented by state programs of insurance against occupational accident and illness and those presented by the federal-state program of insurance against unemployment are to be considered in Chapter 7. The issues raised by the federal program of insurance against old age, survivorship, and permanent disability will be discussed in Chapter 8; those raised by federal insurance against the costs of hospital and medical care for the aged in Chapter 9. The general character of these programs is noted briefly below. The remaining insurance programs—state insurance covering temporary disability and affording protection to state employees and federal insurance for railroad workers and for federal employees—are also noted but are not to be discussed at greater length.

State insurance programs

Protection against occupational injury is provided by the laws of all the states; protection against occupational illness by all but one or two. The coverage afforded and the benefits paid vary from state to state. Payments are made to meet the cost of medical care and to compensate for loss of income and earning power. Benefits are also paid to survivors when occupational injury or illness results in death. The programs are financed by employers who insure themselves with state or private carriers. The rates charged for insurance vary with the risks involved. The programs are administered by state authorities.

Four states (California, New Jersey, New York, and Rhode Island) have programs that provide cash benefits to employees who have been temporarily disabled by injuries or illnesses that are not related to their employment. The coverage of these programs is similar to that provided for unemployment. Eligibility for benefits depends on previous employment and the size of benefits on previous earnings. Payments may be continued for as long as 26 weeks. The programs are financed in the main by contributions made by employees. They are administered by state industrial accident or unemployment compensation agencies.

All states have insurance programs for government employees. All of them provide protection against old age; most of them against permanent disability; some of them against survivorship. The programs differ in the amount and duration of promised benefits. They are financed by contributions from governments and from their employees.

All of the states have programs of insurance against unemployment. But here the federal government also plays a part. It imposes a tax on payrolls, but waives a major part of it where states have set up acceptable insurance programs financed by a similar tax. It pays the costs of state administration. It serves as a trustee for unemployment insurance funds. The state programs differ in coverage, in eligibility for benefits, and in their amount and duration. Benefits are related to past earnings, within lower and upper limits set by law. A typical beneficiary will receive less than half of his previous weekly earnings for less than 13 weeks. The programs are financed by the tax on payrolls, the employer's tax rate depending on his unemployment rate.

Federal insurance programs

The federal government operates the most comprehensive of the social insurance programs, providing the largest number of people with protection against the greatest variety of risks. The program covers more than nine tenths of the labor force. It pays benefits to workers who have retired or have been permanently disabled and to the survivors of workers who have died. And for people over 65, it also provides protection against the costs of hospitalization and supplementary medical care. Eligibility for benefits depends on previous employment. The amount and duration of old age, disability, and survivors' benefits are related to the beneficiary's previous earnings and the number of his dependents. The benefits paid the aged for hospitalization and for other medical care are specified in detail. With one exception, insurance against the risks that are covered is compulsory and is financed by equal taxes on workers' wages and on employers' payrolls. Insurance of the aged against supplementary medical costs is voluntary but is virtually complete. These benefits are financed by equal contributions from the insured and from the government. The program as a whole is administered by the Social Security Administration in the Department of Health, Education, and Welfare.

A separate insurance program covers all railroad employees. Benefits for old age, total disability, and survivorship are financed by contributions by employers and employees. By law, these benefits must be at least 10 percent higher than those provided for other workers under the Social Security Act. Benefits for loss of income through unemployment, injury, or illness are financed by the employers alone. These benefits cannot be less than 60 percent of wages; they thus are higher than those paid other workers under the unemployment insurance programs of the states. The protection against the costs of hospitalization and other medical care provided under the Social Security Act is also extended to railroad employees. The railroad insurance program is administered by the Railroad Retirement Board.

A number of insurance programs apply to employees of governmental agencies. Of these, the Civil Service Retirement System is most important, covering more than nine tenths of federal employees. This program affords protection against old age, disability, and survivorship and is financed by contributions made by the government and the employee. There is also protection against occupational injury and illness, financed by the government, and a voluntary program of medical benefits. The system is administered by the Civil Service Commission.

Charitable programs

There is even greater diversity in public charity than in social insurance. Some charitable care is given in institutions; some out of doors. Some is given in the form of goods and services; some in cash. Some is confined to limited categories of the needy; some is offered to all. Some types of need are met more fully than others. Some charitable programs are financed and administered exclusively by state and local governments, and some by the federal government; some are financed, in part, by federal grants to the states, conditioned on conformity with federal rules. The welfare programs of the several states differ in coverage and in the adequacy of the aid that they provide. In the states, administration is in the hands of state departments of public welfare. In the federal government it is entrusted to a Welfare Administration in the Department of Health, Education, and Welfare. Particular programs, however, are handled by other agencies: a food program by the Department of Agriculture; aid to veterans by the Veterans Administration. The principal charitable programs are briefly described below. The problems of welfare administration are to be considered at greater length in Chapter 14.

Welfare services

Institutional care is still provided by state and local governments for the handicapped, the aged, the orphaned or abandoned child, and others who are in need. In addition, governments perform a great variety of welfare services. They concern themselves in many ways with the welfare of children. Instruction in prenatal and postnatal care is given to prospective mothers. Day care is supplied to children whose mothers are at work. Crippled children are given prosthetic devices and trained to use them; those who are mentally defective are given care. Children who are abandoned, neglected, or abused are given protection. Children are placed in foster homes; arrangements are made for their adoption. Governments also perform services for youths in the form of employment counseling, job training, and probational care. They offer health services to adults, giving rehabilitative training to persons who are handicapped, instruction on family planning to women of child-bearing age, and advice on diagnosis and treatment to persons with other health problems. And they provide counseling services where there are other difficulties, such as alcoholism, drug addiction, emotional illness, and marital discord. Some of these services are provided only to persons who can pass a means test; others are offered freely to all. Some are financed entirely by state and local governments; others are financed, in part, through federal aid.

Categorical assistance programs

State and local programs making payments to certain categories of needy persons—the aged, the blind, the totally and permanently disabled, and families with dependent children—are financed in part by federal grants. Under the public assistance provisions of the Social Security Act, the federal government pays half of the administrative cost of such programs and a share of the welfare payments that varies from state to state under formulas that are designed to favor the poorer states. In 1964, for instance, the federal grant supplied 48 percent of the money distributed to the aged in California and 81 percent of that distributed in Mississippi. A state must satisfy certain requirements if it is to receive these funds. It may pay benefits only to the needy. Its program must be in operation in all its counties. The state itself must contribute to its cost. The program must be administered or supervised by a single state agency. There must be a merit system for the welfare staff.

Apart from these requirements, administrative provisions are left to the states. They make the rules that govern eligibility for aid, usually holding applicants to be eligible if their resources fall below the amount required to meet a subsistence budget and if they have no relatives who can be charged with their support. The states also determine the amount of aid to be provided, usually basing it on the amount by which the applicant's income falls short of the budgetary standard they have set. In practice, the payments made by the several states fall below the sums their standards would require. There is inequality, moreover, among the states, the lowest average payment for the aged being only two fifths as large as the highest and the lowest average payment for a dependent child being only a sixth of the highest.

The categorical assistance program is one of major magnitude. Eight million people were receiving payments at the end of 1967, among them two million of the aged, five million in families with dependent children. Expenditures were running to five billion dollars a year.

Medical aid to the indigent

Since 1965, the federal government has aided the states in financing medical care for persons not covered by social insurance who are unable to meet its costs. A state may give such help not only to persons receiving public assistance but also to people held to be medically indigent whose incomes are higher than the figure that would qualify them for other forms of aid. It may finance a wide range of medical services, extending eventually to comprehensive care. The federal government puts up half of the state's administrative costs and a major part of its medical costs, in accordance with a formula that favors the poorer states. This program, still in its formative years, will be discussed in Chapter 9.

Food programs

The federal government supports the prices of certain agricultural commodities by making loans and purchases at levels higher than would be justified by the forces of demand and supply. In the process, it accumulates substantial surpluses. Some of these surpluses are sold abroad at world market prices, the government taking a loss. Some of them are distributed—also at a loss—to needy people in the United States.

Under one program, foodstuffs that happen to be in surplus, such as flour, corn meal, rice grits, and dry beans, are given to the states and passed on by them to local welfare authorities for distribution to the poor. Some of this food is given to charitable institutions; some of it to people on relief. Packed in cartons weighing 95 pounds and designed for families of four, it is given once monthly to those who can come to collect it at designated distribution points. There were more than three million persons in households receiving such commodities in 1967. The food is made available only where the states request it. In certain states, particularly in the South, it reaches no more than a minor fraction of the poor.

Under another program, local welfare authorities supply the needy with stamps, issued by the federal government, entitling them to purchase food. People who are destitute are given the stamps without charge. Others may purchase them at prices that depend upon their income and the size of their families. The average charge for a stamp that will buy a dollar's worth of food is 64 cents. The plan thus provides an average subsidy of 36 percent. Those holding stamps may spend them at retail stores for any domestic foods they want. The plan requires no duplication of distribution facilities—no physical handling of foodstuffs by agencies of government. The retailers redeem the stamps at their banks. The banks in turn are compensated by the federal government. State and local authorities have merely to handle the distribution of the stamps. The federal government finances the subsidy. Two and a half million people were benefitting from this program in 1968.

Governments subsidize the lunches that are provided to children in the elementary and secondary schools, selling them to the needy at reduced prices or giving without charge and selling them to others at prices that do not cover their costs. Around 20 million of the 50 million public school children in the United States participated in this program in 1968. A fourth of the cost is met by the federal government; three fourths is locally financed. State and local governments contribute little, however, from tax revenues, meeting their share of the cost from the charges made for meals. The benefits of the program are distributed unevenly. Fewer than two million children get food at a reduced price or without charge. Many schools in poorer areas do not participate, lacking cafeterias and unable to raise the funds with which to build them. Elsewhere, lunches are provided to the children of the well-to-do, subsidizing the nonpoor rather than the poor. Two other programs are set up on an experimental basis and designed to finance the feeding of needy children: One, authorized in 1966, provides school breakfasts. The other, authorized in 1968, provides lunches through settlement houses, day-care centers, and the like to preschool children in poverty areas.

Housing programs

Charitable aid is extended by the federal government in the form of housing subsidies. The government in effect provides the capital required for the construction of public housing projects. The rents collected by municipal housing authorities need cover only the costs of current operation. They fall far short of meeting total costs. Occupancy is limited to families who can pass a means test. The number of families aided in this way—about 700,000 in the country as a whole—is relatively small.

An alternate method of subsidization, introduced in 1966, takes the form of a cash rent supplement. Apartments in nonprofit private housing projects are rented to needy tenants at figures that cover all their costs. The tenants pay a quarter of their incomes in rents. The federal government pays the difference. As his income rises, the tenant pays more, the government less. When a quarter of the tenant's income equals the rent, the subsidy ceases. The funds appropriated to finance this program have been minuscule. The number of tenants aided is therefore insignificant.

The housing problem is to be discussed at greater length in Chapter 16.

General assistance

Payments are made by state and local governments to needy persons who are not eligible for aid under the categorical assistance programs. These may be people who are temporarily disabled or deprived of income by unemployment or by the death or desertion of the bread-winner. They are not aided unless they can pass a means test. And the aid that is given them is lower than that provided under the categorical programs, meeting but a fraction of their needs. General assistance is financed and administered exclusively by state and local governments; the federal government takes no part.

Veterans' benefits

Veterans of the country's wars are given public assistance on a scale more generous than that accorded any other group. A number of measures have been designed to facilitate their readjustment to civilian life. Under the G.I. Bill of Rights, the government has financed the veterans' continued education, paying their tuition and expenses, and providing them with living allowances. It has assisted veterans in ob-taining reemployment and accorded them preference in appointments to the civil service. To those who were unemployed or partially em-ployed, it has given readjustment allowances in cash. Under a system of loan guarantees, the government has also aided veterans in starting businesses, buying farms, and building or buying homes.

In addition to readjustment assistance, there are two programs of continued financial aid. Veterans with incomes below a specified level who have been totally disabled as a result of military service are given a lifetime pension. For those who are under 65, disability must be proven. For those who are over 65, it is generally assumed. Under this program, benefits are also paid to the veterans' widows and their children. No means test is imposed.

The other program covers veterans who have no disability con-nected with their service but have incomes below a certain level and can show themselves to be in need. These veterans are pensioned on a sliding scale: larger payments being made where incomes are lower, smaller payments where they are higher. Pensions are also paid to their widows and children if their incomes are low and they can establish proof of need. Most veterans over the age of 65 are also eligible for old-age benefits under the Social Security Act. The widows and children of veterans, likewise, are eligible for survivors' benefits. The combina-tion of the two programs affords the veterans and their dependents assurance of ample support.

The veterans' benefits are financed out of general revenues by the federal government. Three million veterans and two million survivors were receiving payments at the end of 1967 at an annual cost of $4.5 billion. Aid has also been given to veterans in a variety of forms by many of the states. The veterans, nearly 27 million in number, together with their families comprise almost half of the population and constitute a potent voting bloc. Their interests are effectively represented by the American Legion and the Veterans of Foreign Wars. Their favored position among the recipients of public charity would seem to be secure.

The adequacy of social security

Taken together, the federal and state insurance programs afford a measure of protection against all the forms of insecurity except the cost of medical care for persons under 65. The coverage of federal insurance against old age, survivorship, and total disability is all but complete. But state insurance against occupational injury and illness covers only four fifths of the civilian labor force, insurance against unemployment only three fourths, and insurance against temporary disability only one sixth. The benefits paid under the federal program have been repeatedly increased, but they still lag behind the growth in living standards and costs. The average payments made to the aged, to survivors, and to the disabled are well below the poverty line. In some cases, by supplementing other income, they suffice to lift their recipients out of poverty; in others, they do not. The benefits paid under state insurance programs to the victims of occupational injury and illness and to the unemployed, averaging a third of their wages, are seriously inadequate.

The coverage of the public assistance programs is restricted by arbitrary eligibility requirements and by the obstructive procedures employed in their administration. Aid is denied to new residents of a state and to persons who are held to be employable even though opportunities for employment do not exist. Applicants for aid are required to prove beyond a doubt that they are without resources and in desperate need. Categorical assistance does not cover persons under 65 who are temporarily disabled or unemployed. In some localities, no supplementary assistance is provided; in others, it is not continuously available. Public charity, therefore, does not begin to cover all who are in need. In general, only a quarter of the poor and less than a third of the children living in poverty are being helped. Where aid is given, it falls far short of meeting proven need. Each state sets its own budgetary standard for determining need, but many states meet only a fraction of the budgetary deficit. The payments made under the categorical assistance program run at half or less of the figure taken as representing the poverty line. Those made on behalf of dependent children lag behind those made to the aged and the blind. Payments under the general assistance programs are the lowest of all. In 1965, among households receiving public assistance in any form, five out of six remained in poverty after they got it. The nation's support of its poor is grudging and niggardly.

Occupational injury
and unemployment

Two programs of social insurance are administered by the states. Insurance against industrial accident and occupational disease, known as "workmen's compensation" and first introduced in 1911, is a program in which the federal government takes no part. Insurance against unemployment, dating from 1935, involves both state and federal governments. But the federal role, originally stimulative, is now supportive and supplementary. Detailed administration is handled by the states.

Occupational disability

A half century or more ago, the only recourse of a man who was injured at his work was to sue his employer for damages. To win such a suit, he had to prove that his employer had been negligent, a fact to which other workers were understandably reluctant to testify. The law, moreover, gave the employer three defenses: He could plead that the worker's injury had been due to the negligence of a fellow servant; that the worker himself had been guilty of contributory negligence; or that the worker had knowingly assumed the risk of injury when he took the job and accepted the wage it paid. In the face of these defenses, 9 plaintiffs out of 10 lost their suits. The first improvement in this situation came around the turn of the century with the enactment of employers' liability laws by most of the states. Under these laws, the employer's defenses were weakened and the worker's chances of winning a suit improved. But litigation was still costly—its outcome uncertain. It was not until the workmen's compensation laws were enacted that protection against industrial accidents was assured.

Workmen's compensation

The compensation laws require employers to make specified payments to workers who have been disabled as a result of their employment, not because the employers are held to be responsible for the disabilities but on the ground that occupational disability is a social cost and therefore a cost that is properly to be met through social action. The laws were originally limited to industrial accidents, but nearly all of them have now been extended to cover occupational disease. Typically, they exempt farm laborers, domestic servants, casual workers, and employees of religious and charitable organizations. Half of them exempt firms with very few employees. Their coverage, altogether, protects some 50 million workers—around four fifths of the civilian labor force.

Half of the laws require employers to insure against the risk of disability, making it certain that they will be able to meet the payments required. Under the other half, insurance is voluntary, but all legal defenses are denied to employers who do not insure. Strictly speaking, the latter programs do not provide for social insurance. In practice, however, the great majority of employers do insure. In 18 states, insurance is sold by a state fund. In six of these states, the fund has a monopoly. Here, all risks are covered in a common pool and the cost of insurance is low. In 12 states, the state fund competes with private insurance companies. Here, the private carriers attract the employers whose risks are low, leaving to the state the employers whose risks are high. In the remaining states, insurance is left entirely to the private concerns. Here, the competition for business makes for high costs. With the state funds, 12 to 15 percent of premium income goes to cover the costs of operation and 85 to 88 percent is distributed as benefits. With the private carriers, 23 to 38 percent of income goes for costs and 62 to 77 percent for benefits.[1]

[1] Alfred M. Skolnik, "Twenty-five Years of Workmen's Compensation Statistics," *Social Security Bulletin*, October, 1966, pp. 3–26, at p. 26.

Workmen's compensation has been supported not only as a method of aiding victims of occupational injury and illness but also as a means of reducing the occurrence of disability. Insurance rates are set high where disability is frequent, set low where it is rare, thus giving the employer an incentive to take preventive action. It is true that the rate of industrial accidents has declined in the half century since the compensation laws were first enacted. And this may be in part because possible insurance savings have directed the attention of employers to safety measures and because insurance companies have conducted safety campaigns and provided safety services. But it may also be because safety measures have been required by law and because employers have adopted them voluntarily without regard to savings in insurance rates. Such savings, at most, are small. The average cost of insurance to employers is only 1 percent of payrolls. The inducement to safety offered by variations in this figure cannot be very great.[2]

The benefits promised

The benefits promised under the compensation laws take two principal forms: payments in cash to maintain a portion of the incomes of disabled workers and their survivors, accounting for two thirds of the outlay; and medical and rehabilitative services, accounting for the other third. In most cases, disability is total but temporary, the worker recovering completely in a matter of weeks and returning to his job. Here, after a waiting period of around seven days, the worker receives a weekly payment, usually set at two thirds of his previous wage, within a maximum figure fixed by law. In some states, these payments continue as long as his disability lasts. In others, they are limited in duration to a period running from 300 to 500 weeks. Where disability is total and permanent, as with the loss of eyesight, an arm, or a leg, similar payments are made, but for a longer time. In some states, they are continued for life. In others, they are subject to maxima set in weeks or in dollars. Where disability is permanent but partial, payments are not only made on the same basis as in other cases of disability —to compensate for the loss of wages—but they are also made to compensate for the impairment of future earning power. In most states, the latter payments conform to a schedule fixed by law. The

[2] *Ibid.,* p. 20; John G. Turnbull, C. Arthur Williams, Jr., and Earl F. Cheit, *Economic and Social Security* (3d ed.; New York: Ronald Press Co., 1967), pp. 337–38.

amount and duration of the indemnities provided in such schedules are purely arbitrary and vary sharply from state to state. The loss of an eye brings a maximum payment of $18,000 in Hawaii and $3,100 in Alabama; loss of a foot brings $22,000 in Arizona and $3,800 across the line in New Mexico. The benefits paid to a worker's widow are set by different states at half or two thirds of his own benefit, or if she has dependent children, at the full amount; and they are continued until she remarries or dies, or in most states up to a maximum of 300 to 500 weeks. Benefits at a fraction of the worker's rate are paid to children until they finish school or come of age.[3]

Medical benefits were not originally provided under the compensation laws. Added later, they now apply to the costs of hospitalization, surgery, doctors' services, and other care. In some states, these benefits pay for full treatment; in others, they are subject to maximum limits. In general, they are more nearly adequate in cases of industrial accident than in those of occupational disease. Rehabilitative services are even more recent, being provided by only half of the states. In a few states, such services are supplied by the workmen's compensation authorities. In most cases, these authorities do no more than pay for the maintenance of disabled workers while they are being retrained by other public agencies.

The benefits provided

In administering the compensation laws, someone must determine whether a claimant is eligible for benefits and how large the benefits are to be. In a few states, this is left to the courts. But in all the others, it is delegated to an administrative agency such as the department of labor or a special commission. If claims are not disputed, their payment may be ordered on notice of disability. This method of settlement is economical. Where the administrative agency has an adequate staff, it is also speedy. More often, claims are settled by agreement among the worker, the employer, and the insurance carrier, requiring no action by the administrative agency. There is danger in such a situation that the worker will be persuaded to accept a lump sum rather than a periodic income or to settle for a smaller amount than is his due. About

[3] Turnbull *et al., op. cit.,* pp. 325–31; and Robert J. Myers, *Social Insurance and Allied Government Programs* (Homewood, Ill.: Richard D. Irwin, Inc., 1965), pp. 201–4.

a tenth of all cases are appealed to the courts by employers or by insurance companies. Here, the worker must bear the costs and the delays of litigation that the compensation laws were supposed to prevent.[4]

Cash benefits paid under the workmen's compensation laws are far from adequate. Disabled workers are promised two thirds of their previous wages. But the maximum limits fixed by law, typically running between $35 and $50 per week, prevent them from getting this amount. In only five states are the maxima high enough to permit the worker to get the two thirds which is his due. In the country as a whole, the average benefit runs around one half. Benefits paid the permanently disabled are even less adequate than those paid for temporary disability. In 42 states in 1963, these beneficiaries recovered less than 50 percent of the wages they lost; in 29 of these states, less than 35 percent; in 19, less than 15 percent. The payments made fall well below minimum budgetary standards. The cost of disability must thus be borne in large part by the worker and his family and by private and public charity.[5]

There are shortcomings, too, with the benefits provided in the form of services. The compensation agencies exercise little or no control over the quality of medical care. The disabled worker selects his own doctor; his choice may not be well informed. The fees allowed may be too low to attract physicians of proven competence. The insurance companies may put pressure on the physicians to limit their treatments and keep their charges down. Rehabilitation services, potentially of great importance, are sadly neglected. In half of the states, they are not provided. And where provided, they are seldom fully staffed or adequately supervised.

Unemployment insurance

When the provisions of the Social Security Act were being devised in the thirties, it was generally agreed that insurance against old age should be a wholly federal program. But the form of the unemployment insurance program was in dispute. There were those who contended that it, too, should be wholly federal. The risks of unemployment varied from state to state; a federal program would bring them

[4] Turnbull *et. al., op. cit.,* pp. 343–44.
[5] Skolnik, *op. cit.,* pp. 12–18.

into a common pool. Eligibility for benefits under state programs would discourage the movement of workers across state lines; a federal program would permit such mobility. State programs would establish different levels of protection in different states; a federal program would provide a uniform level for the country as a whole. But there were those who argued, on the contrary, that unemployment insurance was still in an experimental stage; that some states preferred one type of program and some another; that each of the states should be free to adopt the one that it might choose. It was argued, too, that a federal program once set up and under way would be abolished as unconstitutional. These arguments prevailing, unemployment insurance was left to the states.

But how were the states to be persuaded to enact insurance laws? Such enactments were obstructed by the contention of employers that a tax imposed to finance insurance would increase their costs and handicap them in competing with employers in other states, thus reducing their state's industrial activity. Congress undercut this argument by adopting an ingenious device. It imposed a federal tax on employers' payrolls and provided for the remission of nine tenths of this tax in states imposing an equivalent tax to finance acceptable programs of unemployment insurance. As a result, enactment of an insurance law would no longer put a state's employers at a competitive disadvantage. On the contrary, it would render funds available for local unemployment benefits which would otherwise have gone to the federal government. The Social Security Act thus provided a powerful inducement for the enactment of unemployment insurance laws. By July, 1937, within two years of its passage, all of the states had such laws.

Coverage and eligibility

In general, the coverage of the State laws is the same as that of the federal tax. Agricultural workers, domestic servants, and casual laborers are excluded, as are employees of nonprofit organizations and of state and local governments. Firms with fewer than four employees are exempt under federal law, but smaller firms are covered by more than half of the states. Altogether, the laws cover less than three fourths of wage and salary earners, providing no protection to some 15 million employees.

To be eligible for unemployment benefits, a worker must recently have been employed for a certain number of weeks or have earned a certain amount of wages or both. He must also be able to work and be available for work, demonstrating his continued attachment to the labor force by registering at a public employment office and actively seeking reemployment. Newcomers to the labor force and persons with little employment experience are found to be ineligible as are those who are disabled or not looking for work. As a result of limitations on coverage and eligibility and exhaustion of rights, less than half of those who are unemployed at any time will be entitled to benefits.

Disqualification for benefits

Unemployment insurance is designed to maintain income in cases where unemployment is involuntary. Workers are therefore disqualified for benefits where they are at fault. There are three principal causes for such disqualification. Two of them, considered when the worker first applies for benefits, relate to the manner in which he was separated from his job. First, the worker may voluntarily have quit without good cause. For instance, if the work assigned him was not suited to his training and experience, he may be held to have had good cause to quit. But if the work was suitable, he may be held to have lacked good cause, and benefits will be denied. Second, the worker may have been fired for misconduct. If he was discharged for mere incompetence, he will be eligible for benefits. But if he has repeatedly been absent, has been drunk on the job, has refused to do the work assigned him, or has otherwise been insubordinate, he may be disqualified.

The third major cause of disqualification may come at any time while the worker is drawing unemployment benefits. This is the case where he refuses an offer of suitable work. Jobs that would endanger the worker's health, his safety, or his morals are always found to be unsuitable. So is employment at hours or wages or under conditions substantially less favorable than those prevailing for similar work in the locality. During the early months of unemployment, moreover, a worker may be permitted to draw benefits while he looks for work at his accustomed occupation, at his former wage, and in his own vicinity, refusing jobs in other fields, at lower wages, or far away. In time, however, the worker may reasonably be expected to adjust to changes in the labor market. Employment in a different occupation at a lower wage or at a distance may then be held to be suitable, and a worker who refuses it may be disqualified for benefits. The questions to be answered here are how much time should pass before the stricter rule is applied and how different an occupation, how much lower a wage, or how distant a location will then be regarded as suitable.

Another cause of disqualification is participation in a labor dispute. If a worker goes out on strike, he may not have done so voluntarily. But if unemployment benefits were paid to strikers, the insurance funds would be diverted to financing strikes. So strikers are disqualified. But, on the other hand, employment as a strikebreaker is held to be unsuitable and the worker who refuses such employment continues to draw benefits. The law is thus neutral in labor disputes.

There are still other cases in which continued benefits may be denied. A woman who quits work to have a baby, to care for a sick child, or to move away with her husband may be disqualified. So, too, may a student who quits to return to school. Workers receiving payments under other insurance plans, public or private, may have their unemployment benefits suspended or reduced. Those who misrepresent their status are disqualified.

The duration of disqualification may vary with the seriousness of the case. In less serious cases, it may be temporary, typically running around six weeks. In more serious cases, it may last throughout the period of unemployment or even for some weeks after a worker has been reemployed.

In some of these matters, rules are prescribed by law. In others, they are within the discretion of an administrative agency. In all of them, policy varies from state to state. In general, over the years, the causes for which workers are disqualified have increased in number and in severity.[6]

The level and duration of benefits

Unemployment benefits may take the form of a flat amount or be related to previous earnings or to family needs. Under the laws of the several states, they are made proportionate to earnings, within a maximum limit, in accordance with formulas that are relatively more generous in compensating the worker with lower wages than the one who is better paid. The general goal is half of the previous wage. An additional allowance for dependents is made by a fifth of the states.

[6] William Haber and Merrill G. Murray, *Unemployment Insurance in the American Economy* (Homewood, Ill.: Richard D. Irwin, Inc., 1966), chap. xv.

Here, as with insurance against occupational disability, the maximum limits prevent the beneficiaries from receiving the share of previous earnings that the law allows. In some states, the maxima are set at a fraction—usually half—of previous wages, but more often they are fixed as absolute amounts. The maxima obtaining in 1967 ranged from $30 a week in Mississippi to $66 in Hawaii, falling in most cases between $40 and $50. In two thirds of the states they stood at less than half of the average weekly wage. The benefits paid since the forties have run around a third of this wage. The average payment at the end of 1967 was $41 a week, falling far below the government's poverty line.

Unemployment benefits are paid after a waiting period, typically a week in length. The worker can usually manage to meet his costs for this short a time. The delay, moreover, reduces the burden of administration and prevents the dissipation of insurance funds in payments to persons who are merely shifting from job to job. The average duration of subsequent benefits during the sixties has run between 12 and 15 weeks. The maximum permitted by law in most of the states stands at 26 weeks. Payments were extended beyond this limit during business recessions in 1958 and 1961 through special action by the federal government. Opinions differ as to whether unemployment insurance should be confined to compensating for short-term unemployment or extended to cover long-term unemployment as well. In the former case, the duration of 26 weeks might well suffice. In the latter, benefits might well be paid for as long as 52 weeks where it appeared that a worker's reemployment at his previous occupation, after such a period, was reasonably assured or where he was willing to enter training for a different kind of work.[7]

Administrative problems

Administration of the unemployment insurance system is shared by state and federal governments. The states collect taxes on employers' payrolls and pay benefits to workers who are unemployed. They deposit their tax receipts in separate state accounts in a federal Unemployment Trust Fund and draw on these accounts to finance their

[7] Haber and Murray, *op. cit.*, chaps. xi–xiii; and Milton J. Nadworny, "Unemployment Insurance and Income Maintenance" in Sar A. Levitan *et al.* (eds.), *Towards Freedom from Want* (Madison, Wis.: Industrial Relations Research Assn., 1968), pp. 88–104.

benefits. The federal government also collects payroll taxes, though on a smaller scale. It establishes standards to govern the state insurance systems, supervises their administration, and draws on its payroll tax revenues to meet all of their administrative costs.

State administration is usually in the hands of an agency that manages both the unemployment insurance program and the state's system of public employment offices. Workers file their claims for benefits at the employment offices. The staffs of these offices determine whether a claimant has had enough earnings or service to be eligible, whether he quit work without good cause, and whether he was discharged for misconduct. They compute the amount of benefits that is due. Thereafter, they determine whether a beneficiary is able to work and is actively seeking work, and if he refuses a job that is offered him, whether the job was suitable. The volume of this work is heavy. It diverts employment office staffs from their major function, that of matching all available manpower and all available jobs. It gives employers and workers the impression that the public employment offices are really unemployment offices, thus making it less likely that they will be called upon to fulfill their purpose. An effort has therefore been made in recent years to separate the two functions, providing a special staff to handle insurance cases and freeing employment office personnel for their larger responsibility.

The arrangement under which the federal government meets the entire costs of state administration is unique in federal-state relations. It was designed by Congress to make certain that this administration would be competent and well financed. It now involves the distribution of more than $500 million per year. To get the federal money, a state must have a merit system to protect administrative personnel and must meet administrative standards which the federal government prescribes. The arrangement presents its problems. It offers state authorities no incentive to economize. It has given rise to controversies concerning the principles which govern the distribution of federal funds among the states. But however defective it may be in principle, the arrangement seems to work.

Merit rating

An outstanding feature of the unemployment insurance system, known as "merit rating," is the variation of state payroll taxes in accordance with differences in rates of unemployment. If an employer over the years has laid off substantial portions of his work force, his tax rate will be high. If he has kept his work force steadily employed, his rate will be low.[8] This variation is patterned after the differentiation of insurance premiums in accordance with safety records under the workmen's compensation laws. In that case, the variation was designed to give the employer an incentive to prevent accidents. In this case, it is supposed to give him an incentive to prevent unemployment.

The analogy with insurance against accidents is dubious. There are steps that the employer can take to prevent accidents. He may also attempt in various ways to reduce seasonal fluctuations in employment. But before the other causes of unemployment he is powerless. He cannot compel fickle consumers to continue to use his product. He cannot forbid competitors, domestic and foreign, to invade his market. He cannot prohibit technological innovation. He cannot exorcize business recessions. The variation of payroll tax rates can have little effect on the volume of employment.

The result of merit rating is a rate structure which imposes low rates on employers who produce goods for a stable market and high rates on employers who produce for a market subject to fluctuations. The rates paid by producers of necessary consumers' goods and services are low. The rates paid by producers of durable goods, capital goods, and luxury goods are high. The reward of rate reduction goes to employers who have done nothing to earn it. The penalty of high rates is imposed upon employers who are not so much inefficient as unlucky. Thus merit ratings bear little or no relation to merit. Their determination depends less on good management than on good fortune.

Variation of tax rates in accordance with employment experience can be defended, however, on other grounds. It can be argued that unemployment in an industry is a cost that should be covered in the prices paid by the industry's consumers, and that taxes and prices should be high in an industry where employment is irregular, low in an industry where it is stable. Such a position is tenable. But it can also be argued with equal force that unemployment is a social cost to be met by imposing taxes on the basis of ability to pay, and that customers of stable industries are able to contribute to benefits for workers who are

---

[8] To make this possible, the federal law is so written that the employer can deduct from his federal payroll tax the full amount of the offset allowed where states have insurance laws, even though the tax he has paid the state is less.

laid off by irregular industries. The choice between these views is a matter of public policy.

Rate variation under merit rating has had two undesirable effects. For one thing, it has lowered the level of taxes paid and the size of insurance reserves. Taxes in stable industries have been drastically reduced, those in the stablest industries being cut to zero. Instead of standing at the 2.7 percent of payrolls contemplated when the Social Security Act was passed, the average tax rate has stood at less than 1.5 percent. Some states raise rates when the shortage of revenues threatens the adequacy of their reserves. But others do not. Merit rating not only produces automatic reductions in tax rates but it also gives employers a strong incentive to demand tighter disqualifications and to oppose the liberalization of benefits. It operates to keep reserves low and benefits down.

The other unfortunate effect of merit rating is its impairment of the potential usefulness of unemployment insurance as a built-in stabilizer of economic activity. During prosperity, supposedly, money will be taken out of circulation as employers pay taxes into the insurance fund. During recessions, money will be put back into circulation as the insurance fund pays benefits to the unemployed. With merit rating, however, the system is not allowed to operate this way. In prosperity, with little unemployment, less money is taken out of circulation by taxes. Insurance reserves are not as large as they otherwise would be. In recessions, therefore, less money can be put back into circulation as benefits. Even worse, taxes not only decline in good times but in bad times they rise with more unemployment. Money in circulation is increased when it should be reduced, and reduced when it should be increased. Instead of functioning as a stabilizer, the system has the opposite effect.

Problems of multiplicity

Problems are presented by the fact that insurance against unemployment is provided not by a single federal system but by separate systems in more than 50 jurisdictions. One such problem is that of interstate migration. If a worker were to lose his eligibility for unemployment benefits by taking a job in another state, he might hesitate to move. If a worker drawing benefits were to lose them by going to another state to look for work, he might prefer to remain unemployed. In either case, the state insurance system would obstruct mobility. This outcome is prevented through interstate cooperation. Each state acts as an agent for the others in handling out-of-state claims. The agent state receives the claim and transmits it to the state that is liable. The liable state determines whether the claimant is eligible for benefits and if so computes their size and informs the agent state. The agent state pays the benefits and obtains reimbursement from the liable state. The procedure is clumsier than would be the case in a federal system. But it does permit mobility.

A second problem is created by the unequal strength of separate state reserve funds. If its solvency is to be assured, such a fund should be one and a half to two times as big as the largest amount of benefits paid during any previous 12 months. The reserves of most states fulfill this requirement. But the incidence of unemployment differs among the states. It is low in states that produce a variety of goods and high in states that specialize in producing a few, and low in states that produce necessary consumers' goods and high in states that produce luxury and capital goods. Accordingly, the reserve funds of some states may be too low to meet the demands that may be made upon them. In such a situation, benefits due in one state would not be paid even though surplus funds stood idle in the reserves of other states. At the end of 1964, the reserves of 20 states were less than one and one half times as great as their largest previous 12-month benefits.

A state could increase its reserves, of course, by raising tax rates, but such action is certain to be opposed by employers. Another solution is offered by the federal government. Under a law enacted in 1954 and amended in 1960, a state can get an interest-free loan from the federal government if its reserve fund and its estimated tax receipts fall so low that it would otherwise be unable to make the benefit payments that are due in the coming month. Since these loans are interest-free, the states would have no incentive to repay them were it not for the fact that the tax credits given its employers will be canceled in the second following January if payment has not been made. This solution is not a happy one. The federal loans are doled out month by month. A state cannot get one unless it faces bankruptcy. And a loan does nothing to remove the causes of its trouble.

Other solutions have been suggested. If the state insurance systems were to be replaced by a single federal system, the diverse risks of all the states would be covered in a single pool. Failing this, the federal government might establish minimum standards to govern the solvency of state insurance funds, reducing or canceling employers' tax credits if the standards were not met. Alternatively, the government might provide reinsurance against extraordinary increases in insurance costs or make grants to finance the excessive costs of particular states.[9] These, again, are clumsy solutions to a problem that could be solved more simply if the system were to be federalized.

Possible reforms

The state unemployment insurance systems fall far short of giving workers the protection that the country could afford. Coverage could be extended to millions who are now excluded. Rules governing eligibility and disqualification for benefits could be relaxed. The level of benefits could be raised, assuring the average worker half of his previous wage plus an additional allowance for dependents, within a maximum set not as an absolute amount but at two thirds of the previous wage. Benefits for short-term unemployment could run for 26 weeks. Benefits for long-term unemployment could be provided under stricter conditions for an additional 26 weeks.

All this would cost more money. The needed funds could be provided in various ways. First, merit rating could be abolished. Second, if this proved to be impossible, a figure—say 1 percent—could be established below which rate reductions in the payroll tax would not be permitted to go. Third, the base on which the tax is levied could be enlarged. When the Social Security Act was passed in 1935, the base of the tax imposed to finance federal old-age benefits was set at the first $3,000 of the worker's annual earnings, and the base of the tax for state unemployment benefits was set at the same amount. Now the tax that supports the federal insurance program applies to the first $7,800 of earnings. The tax for state unemployment insurance still stands at the first $3,000. This figure could be substantially increased. With a broader base, larger revenues could be more readily obtained when needed by moderately raising rates. Fourth, taxes could be imposed not only on employers but also on employees. This is done in nearly all the countries that have unemployment insurance laws. It is done in only three American states. Employee participation in financing insur-

---

[9] Haber and Murray, *op. cit.*, chap. xix.

ance benefits might have its advantages. It should contribute to the worker's understanding of the system and give him a sense of responsibility for its proper use.

There are two radical reforms that might be made in the present program: merit rating might be abolished, and the several state insurance systems might be replaced by a single federal system. Abolition of merit rating would increase tax revenues and give greater assurance of solvency. It would weaken employer opposition to the liberalization of benefits. Creation of a single federal system would obviate the need for federal financing of state administration. It would simplify the handling of interstate migration. It would make the payment of claims more certain and the use of reserve funds more efficient by combining all risks in a single pool.

As a matter of practical politics, these changes are unlikely to be made. The way to reform must therefore lie through the establishment of federal standards to govern state performance and their enforcement through possible denial of credits against the federal payroll tax. Such standards could put a floor under merit rates and require the maintenance of reserves at a level that would assure solvency. They could encourage expansion of coverage. They could ease the rules controlling eligibility and disqualification. They could require more generous benefits. The weaker state systems could also be strengthened through a program of federal grants. Even these reforms will encounter employer opposition. But they are likely to come in time.

8

Old age, survivorship,
and disability

Unlike unemployment insurance, the system of old-age, survivorship, and disability insurance (OASDI) set up under the Social Security Act is wholly federal. It is more comprehensive in its coverage
than unemployment insurance; the benefits it provides are more nearly
adequate. In sheer size, OASDI is outstanding among the nation's welfare programs. It has been well administered, effective, and successful.
It is generally accepted; its survival is assured. But it has shortcomings;
there is room for reforms.

Federal social insurance in 1935

The Social Security Act of 1935 was a product of the great depression of the thirties. Its provisions were based upon the recommendations made by a committee of public officials and private citizens set up
by President Roosevelt to study and report on the problem of achieving economic security. This committee was faced with a number of
fundamental issues of policy. What risks should be insured? What
groups should be covered? What sort of system should be set up?
How should benefits be determined? What taxes should be imposed?
Should the system be put on a pay-as-you-go basis or should it be

financed in part by accumulating and investing a reserve fund? The significance of these issues and the nature of their original resolution are examined in the section that follows.

Risks to be insured and groups to be covered

All social risks might be insured under a single federal system or insurance might be limited to certain risks. The committee and the Congress took the latter course. Occupational disability was excluded from the federal system because it was insured by the states. Unemployment, for reasons explained in the preceding chapter, was also left to the states. The risks resulting from sickness, though serious and clearly susceptible to reduction through insurance, were omitted because their inclusion was opposed by the medical profession. The hardships suffered by the unemployed were in the forefront of attention. It was thought that the number of workers competing for jobs could be reduced by encouraging the aged to retire and that distress could be alleviated by paying old-age benefits. Little or no attention was given to the need of survivors for care following the death of the breadwinner or to the need of the family for care following his disability. The federal insurance system was confined to the risk of dependency in old age.

At the outset, an effort might have been made to make the system of old-age insurance universal. But administrative difficulties were anticipated and initial coverage was limited. Railroad workers and civil servants were excluded because they had insurance systems of their own. Agricultural laborers, domestic workers, and the self-employed were omitted because it was thought to be too difficult to collect contributions from them. Employees of nonprofit institutions (churches, hospitals, schools, and the like) were left out because they were customarily exempt from taxes. Doctors were left out because their coverage was opposed by the medical profession.

The character of old-age insurance

In determining the essential character of provision for old-age security, there were two possibilities. One would have called for a simple system of transfers, with benefits to all of those who had attained a certain age, financed by taxes levied on incomes. The other called for benefits related to past employment, financed by taxes on wages and payrolls. There was no chance at the time that a simple system of transfers would be enacted by Congress. Most other countries paying benefits to the aged had rejected or abandoned this approach. Under their systems, benefits were usually based on previous earnings and were financed in major part by taxes imposed on employers and employees. This precedent was followed in the United States.

A consequence of this approach was to emphasize the system's seeming similarity to private insurance. The taxes levied on employers and employees were called "contributions," denoting their likeness to private insurance premiums. The yields of these taxes were earmarked and deposited in a reserve fund which was invested in interest-bearing obligations of the government, the taxes and the interest providing the money required to pay the promised benefits. This, too, resembled private life insurance, with its accumulation of reserves to assure the payment of indemnities. In short, the system appeared to be one in which an individual by his contributions had bought and paid for his benefits—one in which, accordingly, he could claim his benefits as a matter of right.

This analogy with private insurance undoubtedly made it easier to pass a law that promised old-age benefits. The operating methods of private insurance companies were known to be sound; the operations of the old-age insurance system, resembling them, were also accepted as sound. But the analogy was never true. Congress having promised the benefits would doubtless appropriate the money to pay them. But the aged worker, though he had made his contributions, could not compel it to do so. The reserve fund, moreover, added nothing to the soundness of the plan. A private insurance company needed a reserve to guarantee its payment of indemnities since it had no way of knowing what its income from premiums would be when the indemnities fell due. The government, on the other hand, had no need for a reserve fund since it would always be able to meet whatever payments might be due by imposing taxes. Payments into the reserve in the form of tax receipts and interest on government bonds depended on the ability to tax. Essentially, whatever its business-like appearance, the system was one under which the government paid benefits to the aged and financed them by taxation. But its characteristics were determined by the insurance approach.

Eligibility and the determination of benefits

Eligibility for benefits could be based on age alone, upon need, or upon past earnings or contributions. If based on age alone, say 65, the numbers claiming benefits would be so large that individual benefits would be too small to be helpful or the cost of the program would be prohibitively high. If based on need, the number of recipients could be held down and the total cost of the program kept within bounds, but it would be necessary to employ a means test to determine need, administration would be costly, and the program would take on the nature of public charity. If eligibility were made to depend upon past earnings (or on contributions related to earnings), the number of beneficiaries could be controlled and the right to collect benefits without submitting to a means test could be preserved. This is the usual method of determining eligibility for insurance benefits; it is the method adopted for the old-age program in 1935.

The amount of benefits payable might be determined in a number of different ways. A flat sum could be paid to every beneficiary, as was done in Great Britain. The size of benefits could be based on need. Or benefits could be related to past earnings. A flat payment would be easy to administer, but it would be too low for the high-paid worker or too high for the low-paid worker, and too low for the worker with dependents or too high for the worker with none. A benefit calculated on the basis of need, again, would require a means test, with all its disadvantages. A benefit related to previous earnings could be objectively determined; its payment could be claimed as a right.

Under the Social Security Act, benefits were related to past earnings. But this was not without unfortunate consequences. It meant that benefits were low for persons entering the system in their later years and for persons with low wages. It meant, too, that benefits were less adequate for persons with dependents than for those without. Allowances could be made for these factors, computing benefits on a more generous basis for the older and less well-paid workers than for the younger and better-paid ones, and making extra payments for dependents. But this would mean that benefits would no longer be proportional to earnings. It would require departure from the insurance character of the plan.[1]

Taxes for social insurance

Old-age benefits might be financed by a variety of taxes, most important among them being the personal income tax and the wage and payroll taxes. The incidence of the income tax is on the person on whom it is levied; in general, it cannot be shifted backward in lower prices or forward in higher prices. The rates of the tax are progressive, rising as income rises. If this were the only source of revenue employed, the system would bring about a large-scale transfer of income from the upper to the lower income groups. It would look less like insurance and more like charity. The income tax payers might demand the imposition of a means test to hold benefits—and taxes—down. If the insurance character of the system were to be preserved, it appeared that benefits would have to be financed by taxes paid for the prospective beneficiaries. Such taxes might be imposed at a flat rate per head, as in Great Britain, or at a rate proportionate to earnings. A flat rate would be simple and easy to administer, but it could not be made to yield a sum sufficient to provide substantial benefits. A tax proportionate to earnings is equally enforceable, and it affords a larger yield. This was the choice.

It was decided that benefits would be financed by two taxes imposed at equal rates—one on the workers' wages and one on the employer's payroll. The distinction between the two taxes has little real significance. The incidence of a payroll tax as well as a wage tax is usually on the worker, its burden being shifted back to him when the employer reduces—or, more often, fails to raise—his wages. These taxes were imposed at a proportionate rate on the first $3,000 earned each year. Their burden was regressive. For incomes above $3,000 it declined as a share of total income, the larger such income became. But the use of wage and payroll taxes, by relating contributions as well as benefits to earnings, and thus to one another, did emphasize the insurance aspect of the plan.[2]

[1] See Eveline M. Burns, *Social Security and Public Policy* (New York: McGraw-Hill Book Co., Inc., 1956), chaps. i–iii.
[2] *Ibid.*, chap. ix.

Current or reserve financing?

One policy issue remains. Should the insurance system be put on a pay-as-you-go basis or should it be financed in part by accumulating and investing a reserve fund? Pay-as-you-go financing is clearly workable for sickness and accident insurance. In the case of unemployment, more taxes are collected during prosperity and more benefits paid during depression; income is thus shifted over time, but the period involved is relatively short. In the case of old age, however, it appears that taxes are paid during youth and middle age for benefits collected after retirement and that income must therefore be shifted over periods as long as four decades. This would seem to argue for the use of a reserve. But the argument has no validity. The young worker's taxes are not in fact put away to be returned to him years later as benefits. They are used to finance the benefits paid to people who have already retired. When the worker himself grows older and retires, his benefits will be financed in turn by another generation of workers, many of whom are not yet on the scene. No reserve is needed. Income can balance outgo, year by year.

Nonetheless, the framers of the Social Security Act created a reserve. Tax collections were begun in 1936. Benefit payments were not to start until 1942. Taxes were to exceed benefits until 1980 when the reserve, invested in government bonds, would amount to $47 billion. Thereafter, benefits would exceed taxes, the difference being financed by interest on the bonds. On the surface, this resembled the reserve financing of private insurance. But underneath something quite different was happening. From 1935 to 1980 that part of the taxes collected from the lower income groups that exceeded the benefits paid them was to be used by the government to buy up bonds to reduce the national debt. After 1980, benefits were to be financed in part by taxing wages and payrolls and in part by taxing incomes to raise the money needed to pay the interest on the bonds. The reserve arrangement served merely to obscure the fact that old-age benefits were to be financed not only by requiring contributions for prospective beneficiaries but also by imposing taxes unrelated to such benefits on the community as a whole.[3]

[3] *Ibid.,* chap. x.

Evolution of federal social insurance

In the three decades since the Social Security Act was made a law, it has been amended many times. The Act has been extended to meet more risks and to protect more people. The rules governing eligibility have been relaxed. The level of benefits and taxes has repeatedly been raised. The structure of benefits has been altered. The system has been put on a basis of pay-as-you-go.

Risks insured and groups covered

Under the Social Security Act as originally written, workers for whom wage taxes were paid but who failed to recover the full amount of these payments in benefits were entitled to collect the balance, plus interest, in a lump sum. Those who retired without becoming eligible for benefits got their money back. Payments due those who died were made to their estates. This provision reflected the insurance orientation of the law. But the payments it provided bore no relation to family needs. The provision was superseded in 1939 by one requiring the payment of benefits to the survivors of workers who might die before retirement. The system came to be known as OASI. The need for benefits where workers were permanently and totally disabled was recognized in 1950. With provision for these benefits, the system became OASDI. Insurance of medical care for the aged (to be discussed in the following chapter) was added in 1965. The system is now OASDHI.

Coverage has gradually been extended to groups originally excluded. When it appeared to be administratively feasible, protection was given to certain agricultural workers, to domestic servants, and to the self-employed. Employees of nonprofit organizations and of state and local governments were given the option of electing to participate. And the law, finally, was applied to the professions, including lawyers and doctors.

Benefits and taxes

The formula governing eligibility for benefits has been changed from time to time, always with the effect of increasing the numbers eligible. The level of benefits has steadily been raised. For example, a single worker who had retired after earning $300 a month would have drawn $40 a month in 1940, $80 in 1951, $98.50 in 1955, $105 in 1959, $112 in 1966, and $127 in 1968. In most cases, the money benefits payable to an aged person in 1968 stood at three or four times the level that had obtained in 1940.

The taxes required to finance old-age benefits have been raised at the same time. The base of the wage and payroll taxes was increased in successive stages from $3,000 of the worker's earnings, where it stood in 1935, until it reached $7,800 in 1967. The combined rate of the two taxes was raised in similar stages from 2 percent to 6.65 percent. (With taxes for disability and health insurance added, it stood at 8.8 percent.) In levying taxes to pay for benefits, Congress has assumed that wages (the tax base) would remain the same. But wages, in fact, have risen and the yield of wage and payroll taxes has grown. Surpluses have accumulated, and their existence has encouraged Congress to raise benefits, a move that is always popular.

The structure as well as the level of benefits has been changed. Originally, benefits were made proportionate to the beneficiary's total earnings while covered by the law. On this basis, the benefits paid those who were covered for only a short time before retirement and those whose wages were small would have been very low. To prevent this, the formula governing the computation of benefits was changed in a number of ways, by successive amendments. Benefits were related to average annual earnings rather than total earnings, and the base period used in the calculation was shortened. These changes operated to increase the benefits payable to older workers. At the same time, a higher percentage was used in calculating benefits where average earnings were low and a lower percentage where they were high. This operated to the advantage of workers who were less well paid. It also came to be recognized that beneficiaries with dependents had greater needs than those without. The worker's own benefits were therefore supplemented with dependents' allowances. As a result, benefits came to be higher for married than for single beneficiaries, and for those with children than for those with none. The effect of these changes was to attenuate the tie between contributions and benefits, relating benefits increasingly to need.

Pay-as-you-go financing

The reserve fund provision of the law has been substantially modified. As it stood, the provision had two unfortunate effects. While the reserve was being built up, benefits would be delayed and when paid would be unnecessarily low. Until 1942, moreover, the system was to take money out of the economy in taxes and return nothing to it in benefits. Until 1980, the taxes taken out would exceed the benefits returned. This would have a depressing influence on the economy. Indeed, the initiation of tax collections contributed to a recession in 1937. As a consequence, the plan to build up a big reserve fund was abandoned in effect in 1939. The beginning of benefit payments was moved up from 1942 to 1940. And the first benefits, as we have seen, were determined under a formula that made them larger than originally planned. The reserve did grow as taxes exceeded benefits, but at a slower rate than had been intended, reaching a peak of $22.5 billion in 1956. Income roughly balanced outgo over the next decade. Reserves that are roughly equivalent to a year's benefits are still held in old-age and disability trust funds in the Treasury. They give assurance that benefits will be paid when due, whether Congress acts in time to appropriate the needed funds or not. But their importance is not great. The system in effect is on a basis of pay-as-you-go.

Federal social insurance in 1968

The coverage of OASDI is virtually complete, extending to 84,000,-000 people in 1966 and to nearly all of those in the labor force, both employees and self-employed, who were not protected by railroad or civil service plans. Monthly payments were being made to 24,000,000 people early in 1968, among them 16,000,000 who had retired, more than 2,000,000 who were disabled, and nearly 6,000,000 survivors of workers who had died. Altogether, these payments amounted to $2,000,000,000 a month. The system, clearly, is gigantic. We now summarize its characteristics as it stands today.

Eligibility for benefits

As a general rule, to be eligible for old-age benefits a person must have earned $50 or more in one fourth of the calendar quarters since 1950, or after age 21, the coverage required ranging from 18 months for older workers to 10 years for younger workers. Since 1966, however, persons over 72 not meeting this requirement have been entitled to draw benefits on the basis of age alone. To be eligible for disability benefits, a worker must have earned $50 or more in 6 of the last 12 quarters before he was disabled or in half of the quarters since he was 21. For his widows and orphans to be eligible for survivors' benefits, a deceased worker must have earned $50 in 6 of the 13 quarters preceding his death. These qualifications are by no means stringent.

Under certain circumstances, the right to benefits may be lost. Payments to a widow under 62 are terminated if she remarries or when her youngest child reaches the age of 18, or 22 if still in school. Payments to a beneficiary between the ages of 62 and 72 may be curtailed or eliminated if he earns more than a stipulated sum. Where earnings in any year are between $1,680 and $2,880, benefits are cut by half of the excess over $1,680. Where earnings are over $2,880, benefits are cut by all of the excess. This provision is designed to prevent the dissipation of insurance funds in making payments to persons who do not need them. It applies, however, only where income is earned by employment, not where it is derived from ownership of property. And it does not apply to persons past the age of 72.

Determination of benefits

The benefit that is paid to a worker without dependents who retires at 65 or is disabled is known as the primary insurance amount. All other allowances are related to it. The primary amount is never less than $55 a month. Above this figure, it is graduated with respect to earnings up to $7,800 a year. Thereafter, earnings are ignored. Determination of the benefit involves two steps: First, one calculates the average monthly wage earned during a specified period, the period being shorter for workers who were older when first covered and longer for those who were younger. Second, one computes the monthly benefit by taking the following percentages of the average monthly wage:

71.16% of the first $110.
25.88% of the next $290.
24.18% of the next $150.
29.43% of the next $100.

In accordance with this formula, workers whose average monthly wage was $200 receive about half of that amount as a benefit; those whose wage was $650 receive about a third. Workers are permitted to retire at 62 instead of waiting until 65, but the benefits of those who take this option are reduced.

The allowances added for dependents are percentages of the primary amount. The sum allowed for a wife over 65 is 50 percent of that amount up to a maximum of $105. For a widow over 62, the figure is 82½ percent; for a surviving parent, 82½ percent; for a widow with a dependent child, 75 percent; for a child of a worker who is disabled or deceased, 75 percent. Maximum benefits are set for families, ranging from 100 percent of average earnings for workers whose pay is lowest to 67 percent for those whose wages are the highest taxable. Examples of benefits that will be paid in accordance with these rules are shown in the accompanying table.

Examples of monthly cash benefits

Average monthly earnings during base period	$150.00	$250.00	$400.00	$550.00
Retired worker over 65 ..	88.40	115.00	153.60	189.90
Retired couple over 65 ..	132.60	172.50	230.40	284.90
Widow over 62	73.00	94.90	126.80	156.70
Disabled worker, wife, and child	132.60	202.40	307.20	379.90
Widow and child	132.60	172.60	230.40	285.00
Maximum family benefit ..	132.60	202.40	230.40	395.60

The combined rate of the wage and payroll taxes imposed to finance OASDI stood at 7.6 percent of the first $7,800 of earnings in 1968. It was scheduled to rise every second year until reaching a maximum of 10 percent in 1973. The tax paid by the self-employed is set at three fourths of this rate.

The character of the system

Critics of the old-age insurance program claim that workers entering the system at an early age will be shortchanged. If instead of having wage and payroll taxes paid for them they were given the money and permitted to invest it at interest, using the proceeds to purchase an annuity from a private insurance company, their monthly benefits would be larger than those now scheduled under OASDI.

Indeed, the taxes paid for them over the years will exceed the benefits they are now entitled to collect. The arithmetic on which this complaint is based may be accurate. But the conclusion to which it leads is not. The critics assume that the economy will be static, that average earnings will remain the same, and that average benefits, therefore, will not increase in size. They assume, moreover, that the legal level of benefits will not be changed. But growth in the economy, with earnings and benefits rising, is more probable. And the legal level of benefits in the future as in the past is likely to be raised. The workers for whom taxes are paid are likely to get more than this in benefits. They may even do better than they would have done by investing privately.[4]

The federal insurance system, however, is a hybrid. It does not conform to the purchased-benefit principle of private insurance. Benefits are not strictly proportionate to contributions. They are computed on a more generous basis for those who have been covered for a short time before retirement than for those who will be covered for many years. The old folks have had a bargain. The share of benefits actuarially purchased by those retiring in the early decades of operation has ranged from less than 1 percent to around 10 percent.[5] Benefits are figured more generously, too, for those whose wages have been low than for those whose wages have been high. The minimum benefit affords a higher return on taxes than do benefits above the minimum. The self-employed get the same benefits as do employees, though their taxes are a quarter less. Benefits are denied to persons over 65 if they earn more than $1,680 a year, even though their taxes have been fully paid. Benefits are given to some persons over 72, even though they have never been taxed. The system, clearly, is not one in which the beneficiary takes out just what he puts in.

The system, on the other hand, does not conform to the principles of public charity. Benefits are paid to persons in the middle and the upper income groups. In 1965 two fifths of the households receiving OASDHI benefits had incomes apart from such payments that were above the poverty line.[6] Beneficiaries are not required to prove they are in need. Their benefits in all but a small minority of cases are thought

[4] Joint Economic Committee, *Old Age Income Assurance* (Washington, D.C.: U.S. Government Printing Office, 1967), Part III, pp. 72–84 and 109–32.
[5] Robert J. Myers, *Social Insurance and Allied Government Programs* (Homewood, Ill.: Richard D. Irwin, Inc., 1965), pp. 140–41.
[6] Joint Economic Committee, *op. cit.,* Part II, pp. 222–26 and 313–16.

to be earned by taxed employment. They claim them as a right. In these respects, the system resembles insurance more than charity.

The system redistributes income. Taxes paid for bachelors help finance the benefits of married men. Taxes paid for workers who do not have children help finance the benefits of those who do. Taxes paid for younger workers help finance the benefits of older ones. Taxes paid for workers whose wages are high help finance the benefits of those whose wages are low. In these respects, the system has the appearance of charity. But its redistributive function is limited. The wage and payroll taxes stop at $7,800. As income rises above this figure, the share that is taken by these taxes steadily declines. The system shifts income from the middle class to the poor. It does not shift income from the rich to the poor in proportion to their ability. This is because taxes are related to benefits, following the insurance pattern. The system in short is a compromise between the principles of insurance and those of charity.

Proposals for reform

A number of reforms are needed for the improvement of OASDI. The level of benefits should be raised and the structure of benefits modified. In financing the system, less reliance should be placed on the taxation of wages and payrolls and more on the taxation of income. Ultimately, there should be a dual system of income maintenance, with a guaranteed income based on need serving as a floor and insurance benefits related to past earnings affording protection at levels above this floor.

The level and structure of benefits

The benefits paid early in 1968 averaged about $100 a month for a retired worker, $150 for a retired couple, less than $200 for a disabled worker with a wife and child, and less than $150 for a widowed mother and her child. The benefit paid a worker who had been employed full time at the legal minimum wage was less than half of that amount. The minimum benefits, paid to about 9 percent of the beneficiaries, were only half of the amount required for subsistence: the retired worker, needing $132 a month, collected $55; the aged couple, needing $165, collected $82.50. The payments made to those retiring before the age of 65, around 7 percent of the beneficiaries, were even lower. In 1965, old-age benefits reduced the number of households in poverty from 14.8 million to 11.2 million, lifting 3.6 million above the poverty line. But half of those who were poor before receiving benefits remained poor afterward. A million beneficiaries have been able to make ends meet only by proving their need for supplementary assistance.[7]

In their recent study of the federal insurance system, Joseph A. Pechman, Henry Aaron, and Michael K. Taussig propose that minimum benefits be raised immediately to $75 for a retired worker and $105 for an aged couple and ultimately to $120 and $150, respectively—these amounts being required along with other resources to lift them out of poverty. Above the minimum, they propose that benefits be fixed according to a formula that will reflect previous standards of living, leaving families in the same relative position among beneficiaries that they had occupied among the employed. Treating the earnings of husband and wife as a unit, they would set the basic family benefit at $90 a month plus 30 percent of average monthly earnings (never figured at less than $100) up to the median level of family income, adding $30 a month for each dependent. Where earnings had been as high as $7,800 a year, this formula would pay $315 a month to an aged couple, or 48 percent of such earnings.[8]

There are shortcomings not only in the level but also in the structure of benefits. Pechman, Aaron, and Taussig propose that it be modified in several ways. A single beneficiary is treated less generously than a couple; they would give a single person relatively more, a couple relatively less. The dependent's allowance of 75 percent of the primary benefit is larger than is needed; they would cut it to $30 a month. A widow needs as large a benefit as did her husband; they would raise her payment from 75 and 82½ percent to 100 percent of the primary benefit amount. The ceiling on family benefits discriminates against children in larger families; they would remove it.[9]

The purchasing power of benefit payments declines with inflation. Congress has repeatedly raised the benefit level to compensate for this

---

[7] *Ibid.*, pp. 222–26; and Mollie Orshansky, "The Shape of Poverty in 1966," *Social Security Bulletin*, March, 1968, pp. 3–32 at p. 29.

[8] Joseph A. Pechman, Henry Aaron, and Michael K. Taussig, *Social Security: Perspective for Reform* (Washington, D.C.: Brookings Institution, 1968), pp. 217–20.

[9] *Ibid.*, chap. v.

decline. But its action has been belated and inadequate. The level of benefits should be adjusted automatically in accordance with changes in the cost-of-living index.

Financing benefits

The wage and payroll taxes bulk large in public finances. They yielded more than $31 billion in 1967. They are the third largest and the fastest growing source of federal revenue, accounting for a fourth of federal tax receipts. The rates of these taxes have steadily been raised. The combined OASDHI rate will reach 11.8 percent by 1987. These taxes take more money than does the income tax from three fifths of those who pay both.

The taxes have three advantages. Their yield is large. The cost of collecting them is low. They make it appear that insurance benefits have been purchased and can therefore be claimed as a matter of right. But there are also disadvantages. The taxes fall heavily on the poor, taking $1.5 billion each year from people below the poverty line. Their incidence in general is on the worker. Their burden is regressive, the rate rising as income falls. They make no allowance for the different circumstances of different families, providing no exemptions for dependents and no deductions for unusual medical costs.

Steps should be taken to reduce the burden imposed by these taxes on the lower income groups. Pechman, Aaron, and Taussig suggest two ways in which this might be done. For one, exemptions and deductions might be incorporated in the wage tax, eliminating payments for those below this level and reducing them for those above. For another, the wage tax might be credited, dollar for dollar, against the income tax, with refunds made to those whose wage tax payments exceeded their income tax liabilities. Either plan would involve a loss of revenue which would have to be made up from other sources.[10]

The harm done by the wage and payroll taxes is serious enough when their rates are low; it is even greater when their rates are high. These rates have now approached—if they have not already reached—the limits of political tolerance. If money is needed to finance increased insurance benefits, the government will have to draw, again, on other sources of revenue, presumably on the personal income tax.

There are those who fear that such a move would endanger the

[10] *Ibid.*, pp. 189–94.

insurance system. They feel the payment of benefits has been assured by linking them to wage and payroll taxes. It might be resisted if it were charged in substantial part against the income tax. In the early years of the system this would doubtless have been true. But it is not likely today. The support that has been promised to the aged, to survivors, and to the disabled will be provided, whatever its financing. The government is too deeply committed to withdraw. In other countries, the insurance systems have been supported not only by employer and employee contributions but also by appropriations from general revenues. Their systems have survived; so will the system of the United States.

A dual system of income maintenance

Social insurance benefits fulfill two quite different functions. First, they help to ameliorate poverty, putting a floor, ideally at the subsistence level, under the incomes of those who are unable to work. Second, they protect people who are not in poverty against contingencies, many of them unforeseeable, that would necessitate a sudden and radical reduction in their standards of living, thus giving them a measure of security. The first of these purposes is also served by various forms of public charity such as the public assistance program discussed in Chapter 14. It would be served by the several proposals for guaranteed incomes discussed in Chapter 15. The second purpose is served by social insurance. It is the combination of these two functions in a single program that has caused the ambiguity that characterizes the insurance plans. The situation could be clarified by adopting a dual system of income maintenance. Under such a system, the basic benefits would be provided by public charity or by an income guarantee, conditioned on a test of means or income and financed from general revenues. Protection above this level would be afforded by a system of insurance, with benefits related to earnings and paid without a test of means or income, financed by taxes on wages and payrolls. This is the direction in which the income maintenance programs of other countries have been moving. It is a road that might well be followed by the United States.[11]

[11] *Ibid.*, pp. 197–201, 215–17; and Margaret S. Gordon, "The Case for Earnings-Related Social Security Benefits Restated," Joint Economic Committee, *Old Age Assurance*, Part II (Washington, D.C.: U.S. Government Printing Office, 1967), pp. 312–39.

Medical care

There are six questions to be asked concerning the provision of medical care. Four of them relate to its adequacy. (1) Are there enough facilities and enough personnel to satisfy all needs? (2) Are these resources so distributed among places and among people as to meet their several needs? (3) Are the resources so organized as to economize their use? (4) What is the quality of medical care? Two other questions have to do with the cost of care. (5) Are costs excessive and increasing? (6) How are the costs to be met? The present chapter will offer answers to these questions as they apply to medical care in the United States.

The health services industry

The health services industry is partly public, partly private. More than a fourth of the money that is spent on medical care comes through governments. Governments carry on public health work, assuring the safety of the water supply, inspecting dairies, restaurants, and swimming pools, imposing quarantines, providing immunization, and otherwise preventing the spread of communicable disease. They do a large part of the work of medical research and education. They supply a fourth of the hospital beds and nearly all of the beds in mental hospitals. They provide full care for veterans and for members of the armed services.

Nearly three fourths of the expenditure on medical care is private. Of this, 38 percent goes for the services of doctors, dentists, nurses, and other personnel; 28 percent for hospital services; around 20 percent for drugs; and the rest for eyeglasses, medical appliances, insurance, and a variety of other costs.[1]

Neither the overall provision nor the distribution of medical facilities are centrally planned. The number and the location of hospitals are a consequence in the main of the charitable impulses of community groups and individual philanthropists. The supply and distribution of personnel are the result of private initiative, acting in response to market opportunities. The doctors, most of them solo practitioners, function as small-scale entrepreneurs. Their services, once almost completely lacking in orientation, have come to be organized in the main around the hospitals. The drug companies are large-scale enterprises seeking profits without professional status or obligation. The American Medical Association has long been the trade association of the market-oriented health services industry.

The supply of resources

There are some 7,000 hospitals in the United States, providing around 1,700,000 hospital beds. In the forties, hospital facilities were far from adequate. But during the next two decades, under a program of federal loans to the states, their supply was substantially increased. Most of the new construction, however, was in small towns and rural areas; there was little improvement in urban facilities. As a result, the total number of beds is fairly adequate. But a third of them are in obsolete buildings with obsolete equipment. The need, here, is for extensive modernization.[2]

There are 260,000 practicing physicians in the country, 136 per 100,000 population compared to 157 at the turn of the century, 172 in Israel today and 238 in the Soviet Union. There is a doctor shortage which is worsening year by year. Each year the hospitals have openings for more than 12,000 interns. But the medical schools produce

[1] Dorothy P. Rice and Barbara S. Cooper, "National Health Expenditures," *Social Security Bulletin*, April, 1968, pp. 3–22.
[2] President Johnson's Message to Congress, *New York Times*, March 6, 1966.

only 7,000 graduates. More than a fourth of the openings are filled by foreigners, graduates of schools in the Philippines, Iran, India, and Pakistan. A fifth of them stand vacant. In the decade from 1965 to 1975, the demand for physicians will rise by a fourth. It is unlikely that the supply of medical graduates will keep pace.[3]

The prestige of the medical profession is high. Its average income is higher than that of any other professional group. But applications for admission to medical schools have declined. Why? For one thing, the schools attract students almost entirely from the upper income groups; they offer little scholarship aid to students who are poor. For another, the doctor's training, during his years of internship, is onerous and poorly paid. The workweek of interns and first-year residents runs from 85 to 100 hours; their average salary stands at $4,000.[4] The big money is a long way off. It is not surprising that many of the abler students are attracted by fellowships for scientific research. And finally, it must be noted, the profession deliberately restricts its numbers to keep its incomes high. The medical schools reject qualified applicants. State licensing authorities cooperate to keep the numbers down.[5]

The shortage of doctors has been offset in part by increases in productivity. Doctors work longer hours than they formerly did—up to 60 hours a week for 50 weeks a year. They make fewer home calls, saving time once spent in travel, and have more office calls. They see more patients a day and spend less time with each. In 1935, the average doctor saw 50 patients a week; in 1965 he saw 124; the general practitioner saw 169; some doctors as many as 250 or 300.[6] The physician is equipped, of course, with knowledge that he did not have before. And he gets more help from laboratory workers and other paramedical personnel. But whether this speed-up has been effected without impairment of the quality of service, it is impossible to say.

If the increased demand for doctors is to be met in the coming

[3] Rashi Fein, *The Doctor Shortage* (Washington, D.C.: Brookings Institution, 1967), chaps. ii, iii.
[4] Herman M. Somers and Anne R. Somers, *Medicare and the Hospitals* (Washington, D.C.: Brookings Institution, 1967), p. 110.
[5] Seymour E. Harris, *The Economics of American Medicine* (New York: Macmillan Co., 1964), pp. 472–82; and Herbert E. Klarman, *The Economics of Health* (New York: Columbia University Press, 1965), pp. 89, 94.
[6] Somers and Somers, *op. cit.*, p. 106; Harris, *op. cit.*, pp. 131–41; and Klarman, *op. cit.*, pp. 150–55.

years, it will be necessary to step up the output of the medical schools, to accept more foreigners, and still further to lengthen the doctor's hours, increase his patient load, and shorten his calls.[7]

The distribution of resources

As a result of new construction over the past two decades, the geographic distribution of hospitals is fairly equal, with more facilities in small towns and rural areas than was formerly the case. But the facilities available for the treatment of the lower income groups are still less adequate than those available for the well-to-do. And hospitals for the treatment of chronic illnesses and mental disorders are less adequate than those for other ills.

There is serious inequality in the geographic distribution of medical personnel. Rural areas have 30 percent of the country's population but only 12 percent of its doctors. The number of doctors per 100,000 population is 195 in metropolitan centers and 53 in isolated rural regions. It stands at 180 in Massachusetts and 70 in South Dakota, and at 184 in New York and 58 in Mississippi. There were 1,442 towns in the United States in 1962 that had no physicians in residence.[8] Doctors pick their own locations, and in doing so, they are more likely to settle in places where incomes are high and a better living can be made. As Rashi Fein has remarked, "Creating physicians because Appalachia or Harlem are without sufficient services is not likely to bring those physicians and their services to Appalachia or to Harlem."[9]

There is also inequality in the distribution of doctors as between general practice and specialization. The number of general practitioners fell from 89 per 100,000 population in 1940 to 50 in 1965. Only a third of the office doctors are now in general practice. Only an eighth of the interns are planning to enter such practice. This trend is readily explained. There is more to learn in medicine than was previously the case. There is satisfaction in obtaining fuller command of a narrower field. There is also more prestige in specialization—and more money. A pediatrician may make $27,000 a year, but a psychiatrist can

[7] Fein, *op. cit.*, chap. v.
[8] President's National Advisory Commission on Rural Poverty, Report, 1967, pp. 63–67.
[9] Fein, *op. cit.*, p. 143.

make $65,000 and a senior surgeon as much as $250,000.[10] The result of overspecialization, unfortunately, is neglect of the fundamental process of diagnosis and possible failure to meet the patient's needs through inability to see him whole.

Solo practice versus group practice

Of the 260,000 doctors in the United States, more than 70,000 are salaried employees and around 190,000 are in private practice, 160,000 of them as solo practitioners. The solo practitioner is both a professional worker and a businessman. He runs a private enterprise similar in scale to a delicatessen, say, or a shoe repair shop. He provides his own quarters, equipment, and supplies, keeps his own books or hires someone to keep them, collects his fees, pays his bills, and keeps whatever profit there may be.

This way of doing business is not only wasteful but threatens the quality of the service it provides. Investment in facilities is needlessly duplicated. The doctor is always on call; his hours are long and irregular. Part of his time is wasted. His opportunity for consultation is limited. He is unable to keep abreast of new developments. If he takes time off for study, he does so at his own expense. The quality of his performance is not supervised.

Group practice offers an alternative. Here, a number of physicians are associated in a common enterprise, sharing facilities, costs, and earnings, and cooperating in their work. This arrangement has many advantages. Money can be invested in a greater variety of equipment; the waste of duplication can be avoided. Manpower, too, can be economized. Business operations can be delegated to a common staff. Doctors can take turns on duty; hours can be shorter and more regular. General practitioners and specialists can cooperate in diagnosis and treatment. Opportunity for consultation is always at hand. A member of a group experiences continuous education. He can be given leaves for study to bring him up to date. His performance is subject to constant observation by his peers.

Group practice is not only more economical than solo practice but it can also provide superior service. It must be noted, however, that

[10] A. M. Butler, "Innovations in U.S. Medical Care," *The Center Diary*, May–June, 1967, pp. 4 ff., at pp. 9–10.

less than a tenth of American doctors are conducting their practice in this way.

The role of the hospital

Among the 7,000 hospitals in the United States, 5,700 are voluntary general hospitals handling short-term cases. These institutions have 70 percent of the country's hospital beds and care for 90 percent of its patients. At one time, the function of such institutions was primarily custodial. Today, they offer a great variety of services, including obstetrics, surgery, and emergency care, laboratory aids to diagnosis, radiology, and physical therapy. They conduct outpatient clinics, carry on social work, and supervise the services of nursing homes. They engage in research and participate in medical education. The voluntary hospital is thus evolving into a community health center, serving as a focus for all health services.

The hospital is a nonprofit institution. Legal responsibility for its administration lies, as in a university, with lay boards of trustees. Its business operations are in the hands of a professional manager. In some but not all cases, its medical operations are subject to oversight by a salaried director. In every case, the hospital has a full-time salaried staff. Private practitioners, also, are admitted to membership in the staff.

Development of the modern hospital has radically changed the character of private practice. Upon approval by the staff, the solo practitioner is accorded staff privileges. He can bring his patients to the hospital for diagnosis and treatment. He can use the hospital's facilities and can consult with the specialists on its staff. But he remains in charge of his cases, controlling their admission, diagnosis, prescription, treatment, and discharge. The private practitioner is not controlled by the hospital. He has no responsibility for its financing or its administration. But the hospital has institutionalized his practice. It has integrated the provision of medical care.[11]

The drug industry

A fifth of the consumer's health dollar goes for drugs. A third of this is spent on patent medicines and two thirds on prescription drugs.

[11] Somers and Somers, *op. cit.*, chap. iii.

There have been great advances in recent years in the use of "wonder drugs"—sulfas, antibiotics, steroids, and the like. But there are doctors who contend that Americans are taking drugs where they are not needed, where they are not beneficial, where they may even be doing harm; and that patients are overmedicated, overinoculated, and over-stuffed with tranquilizers and barbiturates. The use of drugs, per capita, is two and a half times as great in the United States as it is, for instance, in Great Britain.

New drugs are developed in the laboratories of the pharmaceutical manufacturing companies. They cannot be marketed until the government's Food and Drug Administration has found them to be safe. Such a finding depends on tests the manufacturers have made on animals, followed by tests that a number of doctors have made on their patients. This procedure is less than rigorously scientific and on occasion has been subject to abuse. But under the Drug Amendments of 1962, if a drug once cleared for use is later found to be unsafe, the F.D.A. can order it withdrawn from the market and forbid its further use. Advertisements of drugs may withhold or minimize information on the possibility of harmful side effects or may overstate their possible advantages. Under the law, however, full disclosure of side effects is now required and drugs must be shown to be beneficial as well as safe.

The drug manufacturers spend four times as much money on sales as they spend on research. They bombard physicians with direct mail advertising and deluge them with samples of new drugs. They employ some 15,000 "detail men," salesmen who have no medical training, to call on doctors and urge that their products be prescribed. Before this onslaught, the average practitioner is helpless. He lacks the time and the facilities to evaluate the hundreds of new drugs that are put on the market each year. His patients urge him to prescribe well-publicized cures. Checking, perhaps, with equally helpless colleagues, he often takes a chance. As a result, he may prescribe drugs that are worthless, if not harmful, and greatly overpriced.

In the United States, in contrast to other countries, drug manufacturers can patent their wares. Where a product is unique, the patent authorizes its producer to sue a possible competitor for infringement, thus giving him a monopoly and enabling him to charge a monopoly price. Where an identical product is sold by many manufacturers, it is differentiated by giving it a brand name and doctors are urged to prescribe it under this name rather than its generic name, thus removing it from competition and enabling each of its producers to charge a higher price. As a result, the prices of drugs are high. The range of prices for identical products sold under different names is as much as 20 or 30 to 1. In one case, a committee of Congress found a pill that had cost $1.57 per bottle to produce was sold at $106.20, a markup of 1,118 percent. The high prices bring high profits. The committee found that drug manufacturers as a whole averaged a return after income taxes of 18.9 percent on their investment—a figure twice that realized by manufacturers in general—and that three of the major companies had made profits after taxes of 33 to 38 percent.[12]

To the price that is charged by the manufacturer, the retail druggist adds an average markup of 66⅔ percent. The consumer is helpless. He must buy the drug the doctor prescribes, usually under the manufacturer's brand, and he must pay a noncompetitive price. The companies that manufacture and distribute drugs are money-making enterprises without professional responsibility. It is here that the performance of the health services industry is most open to criticism.

The American Medical Association

Four fifths of the doctors in the United States belong to 2,000 county medical societies. These bodies elect representatives to state medical societies, and these societies in turn elect representatives to the House of Delegates of the American Medical Association. This body chooses the trustees of the AMA. The trustees supposedly control the Association's staff. But the staff constitutes a permanent bureaucracy that strongly influences Association policies. Control by practicing physicians is tenuous in the extreme. The Association is supported by members' dues, by the publication of magazines, and by the sale of advertising space in these magazines, much of it to manufacturers of prescription drugs.

The AMA maintains one of the best financed and one of the most powerful lobbies in Washington. Over the years, it has been determined in its opposition to any change that might threaten the independence and the prosperity of the solo practitioner. It has opposed expansion of the health activities of governments: compulsory vaccina-

[12] *Administered Prices: Drugs* (87th Cong., 1st sess.), Senate Report 448, 1961; Richard Burak, *The Handbook for Prescription Drugs* (New York: Pantheon Books, 1967); Reed Harris, *The Real Voice* (New York: Macmillan Co., 1964); and Morton Mintz, *The Therapeutic Nightmare* (Boston, Mass.: Houghton Mifflin Co., 1965).

tion against smallpox, clinics for the treatment of venereal disease, maternal and child health services, federal grants for the construction of medical schools, public health insurance, and so on. It has been equally vigorous in its opposition to private initiative in the field, to the Red Cross blood bank, to group practice, and to Blue Cross. Almost every forward step in health care in the United States has marked a victory in a battle won against the opposition of the AMA.[13]

The quality of medical care

Great strides have been made in health care. Epidemics have been brought under control. Diseases that once were serious—tuberculosis, smallpox, polio—have virtually disappeared. The life-span has lengthened. It is a mark of the advance of medicine that the ills now regarded as most serious are those of old age. But the record still leaves much to be desired. Infant mortality is higher in the United States than in 14 other countries. Life expectancy is shorter than in Great Britain, France, and Czechoslovakia; three to four years shorter than in the Scandinavian countries and the Netherlands.

The quality of hospital care is safeguarded in a number of ways. Hospitals are accredited by a joint commission representing medical and hospital authorities and are examined, thereafter, every third year. Their internship and residency programs are approved by the AMA; and their medical school affiliations by an association of medical colleges. But there is some doubt concerning the efficacy of these controls. The National Advisory Commission on Health Manpower, reporting in 1967, cited studies of the quality of hospital care. In two major teaching hospitals, the care received was found to be poor or only fair in 46 percent of the medical cases, 39 percent of the surgical cases, and 50 percent of the obstetrical and gynecological cases. In two community hospitals, the respective figures were 74, 60, and 74 percent. Among 438 patients admitted to 98 hospitals in New York City, only 57 percent of the whole group and 31 percent of the general medical cases received optimal care.[14]

The physician's initial competence is attested by his graduation from medical school, his approval by state licensing authorities, and his

[13] Oliver Garceau, *The Political Life of the American Medical Association* (Cambridge, Mass.: Harvard University Press, 1941); and Reed Harris, "Annals of Legislation: Medicare," *The New Yorker,* July 1, 1966, pp. 29–62.
[14] *Report of the National Advisory Commission on Health Manpower* (Washington, D.C.: U.S. Government Printing Office, 1967), pp. 39–40.

acceptance to practice in a hospital. His continued competence is not so well controlled. Upon complaint, the county medical society will review the pattern of his practice and in case of serious malpractice may drop him from membership. A committee of the hospital medical staff may review his hospital practice, and where there is serious abuse, it may withdraw his hospital privileges. But these controls offer little protection against a physician's failure to keep abreast of new developments in medicine. For this purpose, doctors might be reexamined periodically and the licenses of those who failed to pass might be suspended or revoked. There are cases, finally, where a doctor is competent but where he is inaccessible and where his service when obtained is perfunctory. Here, a shift to a competitor where possible is the consumer's only defense.

The cost of medical care

Americans spend between $45 billion and $50 billion a year for health services. This runs around 6 percent of the gross national product and is less than 10 percent of personal consumption expenditures. It is only three fifths as much as is spent on national defense and is only two and a half times as much as is spent on liquor and tobacco. The average health outlay per family at $400 is only 6 percent of the median family income. Overall, the cost of medical care does not appear to be excessive. But it has been increasing at a rapid pace. And its incidence among individuals and families is unequal and unpredictable.

The increasing cost of care

Health costs during the fifties and the sixties have risen twice as rapidly as other items in the index of consumer prices. Hospital charges have risen five times as rapidly, gaining 8 to 9 percent per year from 1950 to 1965 and 16.5 percent in 1966. Doctors' bills rose 3 percent per year from 1960 to 1965 and 7.8 percent in 1966. The cost of an average prescription for drugs jumped from 93 cents in 1940 to $3.10 in 1964. If this trend continues, health costs in general will rise by 140 percent between 1965 and 1975, hospital rates by 250 percent, doctors' bills by 160 percent, and drug prices by 65 percent.[15]

[15] Somers and Somers, *op. cit.*, p. 226; and President's Message to Congress, *New York Times*, March 5, 1968.

In large part, the rise in prices is to be attributed to increases in demand. The population has grown. A larger portion of the population is aged and thus in poorer health. The automobile adds to the number of accidents. New drugs and new methods of treatment carry higher costs. The spread of education and the rise in standards of living lead people to demand more health service than they did in earlier years. The growth of insurance for hospital and surgical care increases the demand for hospitalization and surgery, since treatment need not be foregone by the insured for want of means.

In the case of hospitals in particular, there have been striking increases in costs. Hospitalization is more usual than was formerly the case, patients being admitted not only for emergencies and for surgery but also for childbirth and diagnostic tests. More kinds of therapy are provided, and more types of service performed. The hours of hospital workers have been shortened; their wages raised. High hospital costs are also to be attributed in some part to the backwardness of hospital managements. The average length of hospital stays has been shortened. But apart from this, there has been little if any improvement in hospital productivity. Hospital administrators have done little in the way of cost analysis. Hospital pricing is traditional, bearing no relation to differences in cost. Charges for obstetrics and gynecology, for instance, are too low; charges for laboratory and X-ray services too high. If the runaway in hospital charges is to be brought under control, there must be stricter supervision of hospital admissions, the duration of hospital stays, and the prescription of hospital services. Cost accounting must be introduced, and charges for services related to costs.

Meeting the cost of care

The incidence of the cost of medical care is uneven, as we saw in Chapter 3, falling lightly on some and heavily on others. It is also unpredictable; it is not to be met through careful budgeting. Hospitals have sought to ease the impact of unmanageable costs by varying their prices, charging more for beds in private rooms and less for beds in wards. Physicians have attempted to meet the situation by varying their fees.

Around three fourths of the private practice of medicine is on a fee-for-service basis. This creates a curious disincentive. You do not pay the doctor when you are well but only when you are ill. It is therefore to his advantage not to cure you but to keep you sick. Fortunately, physicians do not customarily respond to pecuniary motivation. But fee-for-service payment does have another unfortunate effect. It discourages people from going to the doctor for a check-up when they are well, but not from seeking his care when they are ill. It thus puts its emphasis on curative rather than preventive medicine.

Physicians contend that they have compensated for the inequality and unpredictability of medical costs by adopting a sliding scale of fees—fixing high prices for the rich and low prices for the poor. But this device has serious shortcomings. It operates in effect as a private system of taxation. But it operates with less precision than the income tax. It is based on hunches rather than facts. Its rates are not progressive or even proportionate. In some cases, moreover, a doctor has only rich patients or only poor ones and he cannot tax the rich to subsidize the poor. And even if he has both, he can impose his higher charges only on the rich who happen to fall ill. The rich whose health is good contribute nothing.

There is another method by which the poor get medical service without going deeply into bankruptcy. They simply fail to pay their bills. Somewhere between a tenth and a fifth of doctors' bills go uncollected. But this is a matter about which less is said.

Sickness affords the perfect example of the sort of risk that should be met through insurance. A small, predictable burden can thus be substituted for a large and unpredictable one. The patient need no longer be deterred from seeking service by its unmanageable cost. The emphasis in medical practice can be placed on prevention rather than cure. The doctor can be paid for all the service he renders instead of giving some of it at a cut rate and some of it free.

Health insurance may be private or public, voluntary or compulsory. Private provision of health insurance in the United States, as we saw in Chapter 5, fails to cover a substantial fraction of the population, is uneven in its coverage of geographic areas and income groups, does not cover certain risks at all, and altogether meets less than a third of the costs of care. We now examine the ways in which these costs are met through governments.

Government intervention in medical care

In every advanced country save the United States, beginning with Germany in 1883, governments have long intervened in financing medical care. Medical services were supported through public action in more than 60 countries in 1964. Their programs fall into three major types: (1) Salaried personnel employed by government render services directly to patients through facilities owned and operated by government. (2) Services are rendered by independent personnel who are paid under contract by government. (3) Independent personnel are paid by patients who then get refunds from government. All of the programs cover workers; some of them also cover their dependents. The forms of service provided differ from country to country. They usually include general practitioner care, some hospitalization, and essential drugs. Many of them also include specialist care, some dentistry, and the cost of such appliances as eyeglasses, hearing aids, and artificial limbs. The programs are generally financed by taxes on wages and by contributions from general revenues.[16]

There has been a long struggle over the financing of health care in the United States. The first bill providing for compulsory health insurance was introduced in Congress in 1939. It was not until 1965 that such a bill was enacted into law, and then its coverage was limited to persons over 65. The federal government also aids the states in providing charitable assistance to aged persons who are medically indigent. Younger persons are covered, if at all, by the voluntary private plans described in Chapter 5.

Socialized medicine

Under a system of socialized medicine, the government owns and operates all clinics, hospitals, and dispensaries. It employs all doctors, dentists, nurses, and other medical personnel. It provides medical services without charge to all who may need them. The system is financed by taxation. It is operated much as the public school system is operated in the United States.

The best-known example of socialized medicine is that of the Soviet Union. Here, except for drugs for home use, medical care is provided without charge. Every child is assigned to a pediatric clinic, and every adult to a doctor at a polyclinic. If he wishes to change to another doctor, he must make a written request and may then be permitted to do so. The polyclinic is the center for basic treatment. It is staffed with general practitioners and specialists. It has no hospital beds; such care is

[16] Social Security Administration, *Social Security Programs Throughout the World,* 1964 (Washington, D.C.: U.S. Government Printing Office, 1964).

given separately. By American standards, the salaries of ordinary practitioners, many of them women, are low. To American observers, also, the quality of care that is given appears to be lower than that provided in the United States. But it is superior to that provided to poorer people in many countries of the West.[17]

This is the pattern of medical care in 9 communist countries and in 28 others, a total of 37. Care is also provided in this way in certain regions or for certain patients in seven other countries.

Health insurance abroad

There are two types of compulsory health insurance. Under the first, services are rendered to patients by private practitioners who are paid under contract by the government. This is the pattern in 13 countries, including Great Britain, the Netherlands, Denmark, West Germany, Switzerland, Austria, and Japan. In the seven other countries where part of the population is served directly by the government, the other part is served in this way.

In Great Britain since 1948 the National Health Service has provided complete medical care to the whole population without regard to prior contributions. The Service provides doctors, surgeons, hospitals, and nurses, provides dentistry for children, and supplies glasses, hearing aids, and the like at moderate prices. Five percent of the system's cost is met by fees for service designed to discourage excessive use, 19 percent by insurance contributions, and 76 percent from general revenues, mostly from taxes on alcohol and tobacco. No doctor is required to join the Service; in practice, 95 percent of them have chosen to do so. These doctors may have private patients as well as patients under the NHS; in general, they get a tenth of their income from the former group and nine tenths from the latter. The patient is free to select his own doctor and to shift from one doctor to another. The doctor is paid on a per capita basis according to the number of persons on his panel. This may be as many as 4,000; the average is 2,200. The amount of the per capita payment is determined through negotiations between the NHS and the medical associations. The incomes of physicians under the Service are lower than those enjoyed in the United States but higher than they were before the Service was

[17] Harrison E. Salisbury (ed.), *The Soviet Union: the Fifty Years* (New York: Harcourt, Brace & World, Inc., 1967), pp. 323–41.

inaugurated and higher than those in other professions in Britain. The system has enlarged the quantity of medical facilities and personnel and improved their distribution. It has raised the quality of care provided to the lower income groups and has improved the health of the people as a whole.[18]

Under the second type of compulsory insurance, the patient pays the doctor's fee and the hospital's charges and buys his own drugs, subsequently obtaining a refund from the government. In France, the patient bears 20 percent of the cost of care and the government meets the other 80 percent. All of the country's doctors participate in the plan. The size of their fees is determined through negotiations between the medical associations and the insurance authorities. The system is financed by taxes imposed on wages and payrolls. Similar systems exist in six other countries, including Belgium, Norway, and Sweden.

The attack on health insurance

Compulsory health insurance has come under heavy attack in the United States. According to a statement by the AMA, it "would regiment patients and doctors alike under a vast bureaucracy." It "would not only jeopardize the health of our people but would also endanger our freedom. It is one of the final, irrevocable steps toward state socialism."[19] Such critics usually equate health insurance with socialized medicine. But there is a world of difference between the two. Health insurance does not change the organization of medical care. It does not turn the physician into a government employee. Under the British system, it substitutes per-capita per-annum payment for fee-for-service payment. Under the French system, it does not even do that. All it does is to make certain that the doctor's bill will be paid.

According to another familiar argument, health insurance destroys the traditional relationship between doctor and patient. It prevents the intimate knowledge and the confidence that are essential to accurate diagnosis and successful therapy. The truth is that the sympathetic relationship between doctor and patient, pictured as normal under private practice, has never existed for much of mankind. And today, with urbanization, increased mobility of population, and the growth of

---

18 Harris, *op. cit.*, chaps. xvi, xvii.
19 *New York Times*, April 25, 1949.

medical specialization, the family doctor has virtually disappeared. Complaints are heard, moreover, concerning the impersonal and perfunctory character of the service rendered by solo practitioners operating on a fee-for-service basis. And here the government is not involved.

A third criticism is that under health insurance, the doctor will no longer have an incentive to do his best and will allow the quality of his service to decline. This, indeed, is said to have happened under the National Health Service in Great Britain. Such an argument is a libel on the integrity of the profession. Physicians are nowhere motivated solely by a desire for monetary gain. And in Great Britain, there is scant evidence to support the charge that the quality of medical service has declined. Interviews with patients have found 90 percent of them to be satisfied and only 3 percent positively dissatisfied with the treatment they have received.[20] It is unlikely that a stronger vote of confidence could be obtained for the fee-for-service system in the United States.

Problems of health insurance

The popular arguments against compulsory health insurance carry little weight. But there are other scores on which physicians may have reason for concern. For one thing, as we have seen, medical personnel is not distributed according to need. There are too few doctors in the South, too few in rural areas, and too few in urban areas where incomes are low. There are too few doctors in general practice. Physician's services are now distributed in response to economic opportunity. If it held the purse strings, the government might require that they be distributed in accordance with need.

The profession and the government might differ, too, concerning the method and the amount of the doctor's compensation. The profession is accustomed to fee-for-service payment. The government may favor annual salaries or payments per capita. Physicians are accustomed to incomes higher than those obtained in other professions. Seeking to balance expenses with revenues, the government may attempt to hold the doctors' charges down. The doctors may have to unionize and bargain collectively if they are to increase their pay, ultimately en-

[20] See Paul F. Gemmill, *Britain's Search for Health* (Philadelphia, Pa.: University of Pennsylvania Press, 1960).

forcing their demands by threatening to strike. This has been happen-ing to school teachers. Physicians do not want it to happen to them.

A third problem is created for the profession by the fact that under an insurance system some doctors will prescribe for patients a larger quantity and a higher quality of service than they require, hospitalizing patients who do not need hospital care, keeping patients in hospitals longer than they need to stay, prescribing remedies that are unduly expensive and forms of therapy that are unnecessary. Without in-surance, excessive service would be prevented by its cost. With in-surance, this barrier is removed. The resulting overprescription may threaten the solvency of the insurance funds. This is a threat that must be brought under control. A usual procedure is to have the doctor's pattern of prescriptions reviewed not by the insurance authorities but by a committee of his peers. On this basis, a physician who persistently overprescribes may be reprimanded or fined. This procedure does interpose a third party between the doctor and his patient. It calls his professional judgment into account. It is therefore disliked by doctors and reenforces their opposition to health insurance plans. This prob-lem, it should be noted, arises not only where insurance is public and compulsory but also where it is private and voluntary.

Health insurance in the United States

National health insurance was a plank in the platform of Theodore Roosevelt's Progressive Party in 1912. It was kept out of the Social Security Act of 1935 by the opposition of the AMA. Bills to set up an insurance system were introduced in every Congress from 1939 to 1945. Health insurance was advocated by Harry S Truman in his presidential campaign in 1948, and a bill to require it was introduced in Congress in 1949 but failed to pass. During this whole period, health insurance came to be provided to growing numbers of people through the private programs described in Chapter 5. The proponents of public insurance therefore turned their attention to care for the aged, where needs were more acute and private insurance less adequate.

The strategy now adopted by the foes of health insurance was that of meeting the health needs of the aged through federal grants to support assistance payments made by the states on the basis of a means test. Under the Kerr-Mills Act, which was passed in 1960, the federal government paid 50 to 80 percent of the cost of the assistance given not only to aged persons who were on relief but also to others who might be found by the states to be medically indigent. By the end of 1964, such programs were in operation in 39 states, were getting under way in five others, and had been rejected by six.

Bills to provide compulsory medical insurance for the aged were introduced in Congress with the support of John F. Kennedy in each of the years of his presidency, but they failed to pass. Such insurance was made an issue in the national campaign of 1964, with Lyndon B. Johnson for it and Barry Goldwater against. In 1965, after Johnson's landslide victory, it was enacted into law.

Medical care for the aged

In their need for medical aid, the aged present a special case. Their health is poorer and their need for care is greater than that of younger folks. Their former incomes have declined or ceased. Many of them are in poverty. For them, the burden of medical costs is great. They may have lost private insurance protection on retirement. Some of them cannot obtain new policies. For those who can do so, the benefits are restricted and the premiums high. If the aged were to be protected against the costs of medical care, some sort of public action was required.

Two bills were introduced in Congress, one by the administration, the other by the Republicans. The administration bill made health insurance compulsory, financing benefits for aged persons who were under the federal insurance system by increasing the tax rates on wages and payrolls, and financing benefits for those not so covered by drawing on general revenues. The Republican bill made coverage voluntary, with the government matching contributions made by those who chose to be insured. The final act, popularly known as Medicare, was a compromise, embodying both approaches. It applied the administration plan to hospital insurance and the Republican plan to other medical benefits. This bifurcation is administratively awkward, but it facilitated the enactment of the law. The law also provided for further grants to the states to support their programs of medical assistance to the indigent.

The insurance programs

The compulsory hospital insurance program embodied in Medicare covers all persons, some 17,000,000 in number, who are over 65 and are covered by OASDI or the Railroad Retirement System, and it is extended to another 2,000,000 persons who are over 65 and not so covered. The program pays for the following care: (1) all services rendered during 60 days in a hospital except for the first $40, and all but $10 per day for another 30 days; (2) all services subsequently rendered during 20 days in a nursing home and all but $5 per day for another 80 days; (3) up to 100 health visits by nurses in the year following release from a hospital or nursing home; and (4) four fifths of the cost of outpatient diagnostic tests. In the case of persons covered by OASDI, these benefits are financed by an increase in wage and payroll taxes that started at 0.35 percent each in 1966 and will rise to 0.8 percent each by 1987. In the case of other aged persons, they are financed by contributions from general revenues.

Medicare's accompanying program of voluntary medical insurance pays 80 percent of the charges for the following services after the first $50 in each year: (1) physicians' and surgeons' services; (2) up to 100 home health visits by nurses in a year not following hospitalization; (3) half of the costs of mental illness up to $250 per year; and (4) a number of other items such as ambulance service, diagnostic tests, and the cost of a variety of medical appliances. These benefits are purchased by a payment of $3 per month which is matched by a contribution from the general revenues of the government. More than nine tenths of those who were eligible for this program enrolled during the first year. Taken together, the benefits of the two programs are expected to meet two fifths of an aged person's medical costs.

Insurance administration

In its management of Medicare, the Social Security Administration does not deal directly with hospitals or physicians but operates through intermediaries, chosen by them. For this purpose, the hospitals in a region usually choose Blue Cross and the doctors choose Blue Shield. These agencies pay the hospitals and the doctors and are reimbursed by the government.

To be included in the program, hospitals must abandon racial segregation of patients and staff and must satisfy quality standards adopted by the SSA. For this purpose, the administration has accepted standards that were developed by an accrediting commission created by the hospitals themselves. In no section of the country have less than nine tenths of the hospital beds been approved.

The SSA must pay each hospital the "reasonable" cost of the service it renders plus 2 percent. It is thus faced with the problem of determining what costs are "reasonable." So far, it has had to accept the statements made by hospitals much as they stand. But this basis for compensation should force the hospitals eventually to introduce systems of cost accounting and to overhaul the structure of their rates. Cost-plus payment, moreover, has the disadvantage of offering no inducement to economy. If a hospital engages in wasteful practices or makes extravagant outlays, the costs must be covered in its rates. Compensation on the basis of the average costs of groups of hospitals, with less than 2 percent being added for those whose costs are high and more than 2 percent for those whose costs are low, would make for greater efficiency. This is a problem that may well lead in time to government regulation of hospital rates.

The fees that are paid to doctors under the program must also be "reasonable." These payments are not based on costs but on the charges that are customary or typical in each region. They permit city doctors to charge more than country doctors, specialists more than general practitioners, and all of them more to some patients than to others. The reasonableness of fees is determined by intermediaries, usually the Blue Shield. As doctors proceed with inflation to raise their charges, this will create another problem for the government.

The program permits two methods of collecting the doctor's bill. Under the first, the doctor collects 20 percent of his bill from the patient and 80 percent from the intermediary, the total not exceeding his reasonable fee. Under the second, he collects his entire bill from the patient who must then recover his 80 percent from the intermediary. But here the doctor can charge whatever he pleases. If his charge exceeds his reasonable fee, the excess is borne by the patient. This method of collection, not surprisingly, is favored by the AMA.

Provision is made, finally, to prevent overutilization of hospital facilities and services. To this end, utilization committees are established, composed of professional personnel, to review justifications for admission, the length of stays, and the character of services prescribed.[21]

---

[21] On the administration of Medicare, see Somers and Somers, *op. cit.*, particularly chaps. ii, v, viii, x.

The medical assistance program

Along with insurance for the aged under Medicare, Congress expanded federal aid for programs of medical assistance in the states. Those eligible for such assistance include not only the aged but also the blind, the disabled, and dependent children; not only persons on relief but also persons with somewhat higher incomes who are unable to meet the costs of catastrophic illnesses. Assistance is limited to those who pass a means test. The benefits provided under state assistance plans may be more generous than those obtaining under Medicare. Instead of being listed item by item, they can be comprehensive, covering a broad range of services. Recipients of assistance, moreover, are not usually required to pay the first part of their hospital or doctors' bills or to pay a fraction of the rest. The programs are administered by the states, with the federal government putting up half of the administrative costs and 50 to 83 percent of the medical costs of programs meeting federal standards. This is to supersede the Kerr-Mills Act.

Forty-three jurisdictions had such programs by mid-1968. The character of the assistance provided differs from state to state. In some states, assistance is limited to persons who are on relief. In general, for families of four, it is limited to those with incomes of less than $3,500. Some states have been more generous. In New York, for instance, assistance was initially extended to families with incomes up to $6,000. The costs of this program proved to be much larger than had been expected. In 1968, New York reduced its ceiling on eligibility to $5,300 and required beneficiaries who were not on relief to pay 20 percent of their medical bills. The federal government, too, took steps to limit its outlays, declining to provide matching funds for assistance where incomes exceeded 150 percent of the state's welfare budget and reducing this figure by 1970 to 133 ⅓ percent.

The future of health insurance

The future direction of public provision for medical care in the United States is difficult to predict. It is possible that Medicare will be extended to all who receive benefits under OASDI—to survivors and the disabled as well as to the aged; that benefits not now provided will be added (physical examinations, dentistry, drugs, glasses, hearing aids, the service of private-duty nurses); that the requirement of initial and fractional payments will be modified. Such changes would reenforce the insurance approach, maintaining health care as a right. It is possible, on the other hand, that the assistance program will be liberalized, the means test eased, and comprehensive care provided to larger numbers who are in need. It is even possible that the country will move eventually to a system like that in Britain where health care is provided freely to all. At present, the first approach appears to be more likely.

PART III

Attacks on inequality
of opportunity

Educational opportunity

Equality of opportunity has long been part of the American credo. Social stratification, characteristic of older countries, was officially rejected by the United States. Here, every mother could hope that her son would become President, moving, according to tradition, from log cabin to White House. And the rise of the poor but honest lad from bootblack to banker was celebrated by Horatio Alger, Jr., in a score of popular books for boys.

Basic to equal opportunity is free public education, but this was slow to gain acceptance, making its way against the opposition of church and private schools. It was not until the middle of the 19th century that the struggle was won—justified, finally, as giving every child an equal chance.

But practice continued to lag behind profession. Slavery persisted in a land where the Declaration of Independence had held that all men were created equal. And after slavery came the caste system that persists to the present day. This has been reflected in segregated education, with inferior schooling provided for children who are black. At the same time, schools in poorer areas have been less well supported than schools in richer ones, and poor whites as well as blacks have been denied an equal chance.

The issue of educational opportunity was brought to the forefront of public attention in the fifties and the sixties, a century after free public education was widely established. It was brought there by judicial decisions and by governmental action attacking racial segregation and by measures providing massive federal aid for the first time to local schools attended by the children of the poor. These were accompanied by aid extended on a major scale to students seeking higher education. When the record of recent years is compared with that of the preceding century, it must be acknowledged that striking progress has been made. But opportunity for education is still unequal. There is much remaining to be done.

Desegregation of schools

In the South, racial segregation in the public schools was required by state law. In the North, it was not. In 1954, the Supreme Court found such a requirement to be unconstitutional, and since that time, the federal government has sought to force desegregation in the South. But this effort has been accompanied by the Negro's migration and his concentration near the centers of the cities in the North. This concentration has been a product in large part of discrimination in housing. In some neighborhoods, the residents are white and the pupils in the schools that serve them are white. In others, the residents are black and the pupils in the schools are black. White parents have put their children in private schools or have moved to the suburbs to get them into better public schools. Negro children have filled the city's public schools. While *de jure* segregation has given ground, if slowly, in the South, *de facto* segregation has gained ground rapidly in the North. During the years when the federal government has really undertaken to do away with racial segregation in the schools, the number of Negro children attending segregated schools has actually increased. It is with the fight against *de jure* segregation and the problems presented by *de facto* segregation that the present section is concerned.

De jure segregation before the courts

In the case of *Plessy* v. *Ferguson* in 1896[1], the Supreme Court upheld a Louisiana statute that required railroads to provide separate

[1] 163 U.S. 537.

facilities for white and Negro passengers, finding it not to be in violation of the Constitution as long as the facilities provided were "separate but equal." This ruling was never applied explicitly to education. But for half a century it was taken as justifying segregated schooling even though the schools provided for Negroes, while separate, were by no means equal. Then, in cases decided from 1936 to 1950, the Court held that segregation of the instruction offered by the states of Maryland, Missouri, Texas, and Oklahoma to Negroes in their law schools and graduate schools was a denial of equal protection of the laws by these states, a denial that was forbidden by the Fourteenth Amendment. These precedents were followed in 1954 when the Court handed down its unanimous decision in the case of *Brown* v. *Board of Education.*[2] It is upon the foundation laid by this decision that the fight for desegregation has been based.

The Court's decision covered cases involving public schools in Kansas, Delaware, Virginia, and South Carolina, and in the District of Columbia. Segregation by the states, said the Court, was a denial of equal protection of the laws and thus forbidden by the Fourteenth Amendment. Segregation by the District of Columbia was a denial by the federal government of the due process of law that was guaranteed by the Fifth Amendment. In short, segregated schooling for Negroes was held to be unconstitutional. Said Justice Warren, "To separate them from others of similar age and qualifications solely because of their race generates a feeling of inferiority as to their status in the community that may affect their hearts and minds in a way unlikely ever to be undone. Separate educational facilities are inherently unequal." It should be noted that the Court did not require the mixing of races in the schools. It did not forbid separation on the basis of residence or ability. What it did was to outlaw separation solely because of race.

The Court recognized that governments would encounter difficulties in complying with its decision, granting them time to plan for the adjustments that would be required. Then, in 1955 in a second unanimous decision in the same case,[3] it instructed the federal district courts to order a "prompt and reasonable" start toward desegregation with a view to "good faith compliance at the earliest practicable date." It set

[2] 347 U.S. 483.
[3] 349 U.S. 204.

no deadline for completion of the process but said that it should be carried out "with all deliberate speed."

Desegregation in the South

In some of the border states, compliance with the law's requirements was fairly prompt: cities such as St. Louis, Louisville, Baltimore, and Washington proceeded to desegregate their schools. In the deep South, desegregation was resisted. Obstructive legislation was enacted. Laws requiring school attendance were repealed. Public schools were closed. Grants were made to support private schools. In Prince Edward County, Virginia, in 1959 the white children were moved into a private academy and the Negro children were given no schooling for the next four years. Elsewhere, segregation was continued under pupil placement plans, separation of the races being attributed to differences in residence and in ability. Desegregation was resisted, too, by individual action. Negroes who sought to send their children to white schools were subjected to economic pressure, being fired from their jobs, evicted from their homes, or dropped from the welfare rolls. They were threatened with violence and physically attacked. The Office of Education could do little more than coax and beg school districts to obey the law. And in this they had little success. In the school year 1964–65, a decade after the Brown decision, only 2.5 percent of the Negro children in 11 southern states were attending integrated schools.

This situation was changed by the Civil Rights Act of 1964. Title VI of this law forbade discrimination because of race or color under any program receiving federal aid and directed the agencies extending loans and grants to issue regulations carrying out its purpose. The law required these agencies first to seek voluntary compliance. But where this was not forthcoming, it authorized them to cut off federal funds. This provision gained added importance in the following year when Congress passed the Elementary and Secondary Education Act of 1965, making federal funds available on a massive scale for aid to local schools. Equipped with this authority, the Office of Education issued guidelines to govern the process of desegregation. These rules required visible signs of compliance, starting in good faith in the school year 1965–66. They asked for immediate desegregation of four grades: the first grade, the first grade in junior high schools, and the first and last grades in senior high schools; and they set the year 1967–68 as the target date for desegregation of the remaining grades. They directed schools that were partially integrated to double their rates of integration by that time. The guidelines were contested in suits by local governments but were upheld consistently by the federal courts. The Office of Education began cutting off funds from recalcitrant school districts. It had taken such action in 247 cases by the fall of 1968. For this, the Office was attacked by southern Congressmen. Its appropriation was cut, its staff curtailed, and its enforcement effort handicapped by requiring time-consuming procedures. Despite this, it made substantial progress. The share of Negro children in mixed classes in 11 southern states rose from 2.5 percent in 1964 to 12 percent in 1966. But the figure differed among the states, standing at 30 percent in Texas, at 15 percent in Virginia, and at 12 to 14 percent in Arkansas, North Carolina, and Florida, but at only 6 percent in Georgia, 4 to 5 percent in South Carolina, and 2.5 percent in Alabama, Mississippi, and Louisiana. By 1967, the rate of integration in the 11 states stood around 17 percent. The Office of Education had set the school year 1969-70 as a deadline when the process of desegregation should be complete.

Under a form of compliance adopted by nine tenths of the southern school systems, a child's parents are free to choose the school he is to attend. Formally, Negroes are thus permitted to enroll their children in white schools. Actually, they may hesitate to do so. And where they make the attempt, they are likely to encounter administrative obstacles that make enrollment difficult if not impossible. In a unanimous opinion handed down in the Spring of 1968 in a case brought by Negro parents from Virginia, Tennessee, and Arkansas, the Supreme Court held the freedom-of-choice plans to be inadequate and directed the school boards to dismantle "the state-imposed dual system" and to create "a unitary non-racial school system."[4] Thereupon, the Department of Justice announced a major drive to compel 159 school districts in nine southern states to replace their freedom-of-choice plans with more effective methods of desegregation by the following fall.

Desegregation in the North

The Court's decision in the Brown case was not without significance in the North. Its condemnation of *de jure* segregation would apply, for instance, where officials so drew the boundaries of school districts or so

[4] *Green v. County School Board*, 36 Law Week 4476.

assigned pupils to schools as to keep the races separate. But the decision did not outlaw *de facto* segregation where it resulted from the residential character of different neighborhoods. Where segregation was innocent, said the Courts of Appeal in a number of cases, governments were not required to desegregate.

In 1967, a different ruling was made by Judge J. Skelly Wright in the case of *Hobson* v. *Hansen* involving the public schools of the District of Columbia. Judge Wright found that the District school authorities had assigned children to neighborhood schools; that they had created optional attendance zones, permitting white children to choose white schools; that they had employed a "tracking system," so assigning pupils according to ability that members of different races were assigned to different curricula and different classes; that they had segregated teachers as well as pupils; and that all of these practices had operated to perpetuate segregation. He found, too, that school expenditures were $100 lower per pupil in Negro than in white neighborhoods and that the schooling provided Negroes was inferior to that provided whites. The judge did not hold *de facto* segregation as such to be unconstitutional, but he did hold that the school authorities were under obligation to take affirmative action to desegregate. "Racially and socially homogenous schools," he said, "damage the minds and spirit of all children who attend them—the Negro, the white, the poor, the affluent—and block the attainment of the broader goals of democratic education, whether the segregation occurs in law or in fact." He ordered the District authorities to transport Negro children where possible from overcrowded black schools to under-utilized white schools, to discontinue optional attendance zoning, to abolish curricular tracking, and to integrate teachers as well as pupils.[5]

Early in 1968, the Office of Education issued guidelines to govern desegregation in the North. It did not order school districts to put an end to segregation caused by residential patterns. It did not require, for instance, that children be transported from one district to another to achieve racial balance in the schools. But it did order the districts to eliminate segregation caused by factors other than housing, forbidding them to redraw boundaries or to assign pupils in ways designed to keep the races separate. More than this, it directed the districts to provide Negro children with educational opportunities as favorable as those enjoyed by whites, requiring them to equalize expenditures per pupil,

[5] *Saturday Review,* July 15, 1967, pp. 51–52, 65.

to do away with overcrowded classes, to raise the qualifications of teachers, and to improve inferior facilities, equipment, and instructional materials. Shortly thereafter, the Office filed its first compliance suit against a northern school system, charging that a district in Cook County, Illinois, had so discriminated against Negro children as to deny them equal protection of the laws.

The feasibility of desegregation

Under some circumstances, desegregation may be readily attained. Where the percentage of Negro pupils in a school system is low, they can be scattered among the schools by so redrawing district boundaries that they differ from those of racial neighborhoods. Where white schools are not overcrowded and black pupils are few, black schools can be closed and their pupils redistributed. Where white and Negro districts are contiguous, schools can be paired, with all pupils in certain grades attending the schools that had been white and those in other grades attending the schools that had been black. New schools can be located, not in centers of ethnic concentration but between such areas, so as to be equally accessible to children of both races. Such steps have been taken without great difficulty in smaller cities in the North and West.

Where the percentage of Negro pupils is high, desegregation is more difficult. Under a system of open enrollment, pupils in many cities are permitted to apply for admission to schools in districts other than those where they live. But Negroes are reluctant to apply to white schools, and where they do, their applications may be denied on the ground that the schools are full. White pupils, on the other hand, are unlikely to enter schools that are black. The racial homogeniety of the white schools may be modified; that of the black schools will not. District lines can be redrawn and a measure of integration thus attained, but segregated schools will remain within the altered boundaries. New schools can be sited between racial neighborhoods, but a shift in population may surround them with the members of a single race. The principle of neighborhood attendance can be abandoned in the case of secondary schools, and children of both races drawn from larger areas. But this will not affect the racial composition of the elementary schools where integration is as important as in the pupil's later years.

In large cities where Negroes are in a minority in the school system as a whole, school authorities may attempt to force desegregation by two-way compulsory bussing, transporting black children to white schools and white children to black schools. Even if this procedure were effective, it would be open to question. It would separate children from extra-hour school activities, would cut community contacts, and would obstruct communication between parents and teachers. But the procedure is unlikely to succeed. As soon as the fraction of Negroes in an integrated school passes a certain point, perhaps a third to two fifths, white parents, whether justifiably or not, will put their children in private schools or move to the suburbs. Instead of retreating, segregation will advance. Where the schools within a city's boundaries are predominantly black, moreover, as they are in Washington where 93 percent of the pupils are Negroes and 7 percent are whites, racial balance cannot be achieved by intracity bussing, since there are not enough whites to go around. It might be achieved if the suburbs would cooperate, creating school districts with boundaries that comprehended whole metropolitan areas. But such consolidation will not be accepted by suburban voters and cannot be ordered by the courts.

There are other proposals for desegregation. One of them calls for the establishment of magnet schools, offering special programs of superior quality and thus attracting white as well as Negro pupils from wide areas. But such an undertaking would not affect the character of the remaining schools. A more ambitious proposal envisages the creation of vast school parks, housing great complexes of secondary, feeder, and specialized schools, all of the latest design, with the most advanced programs, serving as many as 5,000 pupils from the largest possible attendance zones. Such complexes, it is hoped, would draw both Negroes and whites from their ethnic neighborhoods and submerge the problem of race in overwhelming numbers, superior instruction, and diverse activities. This proposal, like others, would not change the racial pattern in the elementary schools. It deals only with the problem of desegregation, leaving unanswered innumerable questions of educational purpose and method. Its realization would take many years and necessitate heavy expenditures. The conclusion is inescapable: desegregation of the schools of northern cities faces an uphill fight, with the prospect of victory remote.[6]

[6] See U.S. Commission on Civil Rights, *Racial Isolation in the Public Schools* (Washington, D.C.: U.S. Government Printing Office, 1967), pp. 140–83.

Desegregation pro and con

A study of the comparative effects of segregated and mixed instruction on the educational achievements of Negroes in 4,000 public schools made by James Coleman and others was published by the Office of Education in 1966. The study found that as measured by standard tests, the performance of these pupils was little influenced by differences in school facilities, curricula, or even teaching staffs, but it was positively correlated with the race and social background of the Negroes' classmates. Black pupils did better in schools where most pupils were white. Advantaged Negroes did better in classes with advantaged whites than in classes with other advantaged Negroes. Disadvantaged Negroes did better in classes with disadvantaged whites than in classes with other disadvantaged Negroes. The study concluded that a pupil's performance depends primarily upon his aspiration and that his aspiration depends in turn upon the character of his classmates. A black pupil in a black school is wanting in self-esteem, in self-confidence, in ambition and enthusiasm. Accordingly, his achievement is low. A black pupil in a mixed school, on the other hand, shares the ambitions of the whites, develops self-confidence, and grows in self-esteem. Accordingly, his achievement is improved.[7]

Samuel Bowles and Henry M. Levin have subjected the Coleman study to critical analysis. They find that the sample of cases used was not representative. The criteria employed in measuring school resources and pupil achievement were faulty. The correlations obtained were not statistically significant. Negroes in schools that were mixed made higher scores in reading and mathematics than those in schools that were not, but the difference was miniscule. Their superior performance might have been explained by the fact that Negroes entering the mixed schools were drawn from a higher socioeconomic class. In short, the evidence was inconclusive.[8] The Coleman thesis finds some support, however, in the results of a study published in 1967 of the educational performance of Negro pupils in White Plains, N.Y., three years after integration of the schools. Here, the third graders, who had

[7] James Coleman *et. al., Equality of Educational Opportunity* (Washington, D.C.: U.S. Government Printing Office, 1966).

[8] Samuel Bowles and Henry M. Levin, "The Determinants of Scholastic Achievement," *Journal of Human Resources,* Vol. III (1968), pp. 3–24.

never been in segregated classes, did better than the sixth graders who had been in segregated classes for three years and in mixed classes for three, and both groups did better than the sixth graders who had been in segregated classes all six years.[9]

Racial integration does not invariably assure equality. If pupils are classed according to ability, Negroes with less ability may find themselves in the same buildings with whites but in different rooms with different teachers. They will still be segregated, with psychological effects the same as those experienced in segregated schools. If both races are taught in the same room with whites moving ahead of their age level and Negroes lagging behind it, more damage may be done the Negroes' self-confidence and self-esteem than if they were segregated. Even where the educational performance of the races is equal, Negroes may suffer discrimination on social grounds. The effects of poverty and prejudice cannot be overcome simply by putting blacks in school with whites. The colored pupil, moreover, may be less well served in integrated than in segregated schools. He needs special programs, special materials and methods of instruction, and teachers with special training. He needs counseling and guidance. The integrated school may not be equipped to meet these needs. Integration also cuts the ties between the pupil and his neighbors, between parent and teacher, between the school and the community. Desegregation may do harm as well as good.

Improvement of schools

When it appeared that desegregation of city schools might not always be feasible or even desirable, educators turned their attention to the possibility of improving the quality of schooling in the city slums. They held that such improvement should not duplicate the education given to middle-class suburbanites but should be designed to overcome the handicaps imposed by poverty. The schools should provide the basic skills, the receptivity to learning, and the mental stimulation that were not provided in the home. More instruction should be given, more materials supplied, more money spent per pupil in slum schools than in other schools. Unequal education was required to assure equality of opportunity. Proposals were therefore advanced and programs undertaken in the name of compensatory education for the disadvantaged child. At the same time, there were those who urged a

[9] *New York Times,* October 16, 1967.

larger role for the school in the life of the slum community. And there were demands from slum dwellers that they be given control of neighborhood schools.

Compensatory education

Educators agree that compensatory education should start much earlier than the usual beginning age of six. Listening habits should be developed and speaking ability improved. Skills prerequisite to reading should be acquired. Learning should be stimulated through manipulation of blocks and toys and through creative play. Educational experiments with children in the slums now begin before the age of three; one experiment in Washington, D.C., began as early as 15 months.[10] In time, there may be children's centers in every neighborhood, with programs beginning in the second year.

The quantity of schooling offered to older children should be increased. Instead of being locked in the evening, over the weekend, and during vacations, school buildings should be kept open 14 hours a day and six days a week, all year round, the added hours being filled with educational activities. In summers, children should be sent to camps outside the urban areas.

Stereotyped curricula in the schools should be replaced with programs related to the child's problems, employing materials that reflect his experience. Methods of instruction should be changed. The lockstep of grades should be abandoned, permitting each child to advance at his own speed. The school should provide more individual attention, reducing the size of classes, giving remedial instruction, counseling on personal problems, and offering guidance in the selection of courses and the choice of careers.

These changes would require an increase in the ratio of teachers to pupils and an improvement in teaching skills. Teachers should be informed concerning the handicaps of their pupils and should come to understand their attitudes and learn how to communicate with them. More men should be engaged in teaching. The ablest teachers should be attracted to the slums by offering higher salaries and quicker promotion than are obtainable elsewhere.[11]

[10] *New York Times,* October 15, 1967.
[11] Benjamin S. Bloom, Allison Davis, and Robert Hess, *Compensatory Education for Cultural Deprivation* (New York: Holt, Rinehart & Winston, Inc., 1965); and A. Harry Passow (ed.), *Education in Depressed Areas* (New York: Teachers College, Columbia University, 1963).

Such are the proposals for compensatory education. Experiments embodying one or more of them have been undertaken in scores of cities, particularly in the North and West. Expenditures per pupil have been doubled, larger staffs employed, more services provided. The results have been disappointing. There has been no significant impact on academic achievement. Where initially promising, improvements have not been sustained. Some educators argue that the school, however great its efforts, cannot hope to compensate for handicaps imposed by the environment. Others attribute the failures of compensatory education to the fact that the experiments were not properly carried out. The teachers who participated in them are said to be ill prepared; their approach was conventional; and their techniques were not adapted to the pupils' needs.[12] It follows, not that the idea of compensating for the slum child's handicaps is mistaken, but that more research and experimentation are needed. One thing, at least, is clear: if ultimately adopted, compensatory education will require larger expenditures per pupil, larger school budgets, higher local taxes, and more federal aid.

School and community

Many reformers envisage a larger role for the slum school. Some of them would make it into a neighborhood center, offering facilities for community meetings, programs of adult education, and cultural and recreational activities. Others would go farther, making the school an agency for social casework, with visiting teachers offering advice on the rearing of children and on other problems of family life. Both groups seek to promote the child's education by drawing his parents into a closer relationship with the school. The neighborhood center proposal has much to commend it. The social agency approach would probably be unacceptable to those it was designed to help.

Urban school systems are generally governed by citywide boards. Such a body may be racially integrated, nonpolitical, hardworking, and competent. But slum parents may regard its members as outsiders, denouncing their control of education in the ghetto as a form of colonialism. The parents, not unreasonably, want a say in how the schools attended by their children are to be run. They demand, ac-

---

[12] Edmund W. Gordon and Doxey A. Wilkerson, *Compensatory Education for the Disadvantaged* (New York: College Entrance Examination Board, 1966), chap. vii.

cordingly, that control be decentralized, asking that they be given power to determine educational programs and to hire and fire educational personnel. Such a change might have the advantage of developing a sense of responsibility. But it would also have its dangers. The neighborhood school boards might be turned into forums for racial conflict. Even worse, they might be captured by black racists who would proceed to discharge white teachers without regard to competence, replacing them with blacks. If this occurred, the whites who were not discharged would leave and no other whites could be recruited. The fight for desegregation would be lost. Unless Negro teachers of equal competence could be obtained in sufficient numbers, the schooling given Negro children would suffer. The alternative of compensatory education would be out of reach. It is undoubtedly desirable to delegate a measure of self-determination to neighborhood boards. But it is also important that enough authority be retained by the city to protect the tenure of teachers and preserve the quality of the educational enterprise.

Federal aid to local schools

The level of financial support for public schools varies from place to place in the United States. Less is spent per pupil in the South than in the North, in rural than in urban areas, in the slums than in the suburbs, with resulting inequality in educational opportunity. The lower support in the poorer states does not result from a failure to tax. Indeed, the burden of taxes is heavier here than in the richer states. The basic difficulty is that children of school age are distributed according to one pattern and taxable capacity according to another.

Until 1965, three fifths of the money spent on the schools came from local governments and two fifths from the states. The local governments obtain their revenues in the main by taxing real estate. The yield of this tax depends upon the value of realty and the height of the tax rate. In most areas, the value of realty has not kept pace with the cost of education, and realty interests consistently oppose increases in the rate. State taxing capacity in general is weak. Increases in taxes affecting business are opposed because of fear of competition from other states. State funds are granted to local school districts, but not on bases that favor the poorer communities. One solution to the problem of school financing lies with the federal government. The system of federal revenues based on the taxation of corporate and personal income is highly productive. Further support for education is now provided by federal grants, distributed on the basis of need.

Before 1965, aid was extended to local schools on a 50-50 matching basis for special purposes: in 1917, aid was given to stimulate the development of vocational training; and under the National Defense Education Act of 1958, aid was given to finance the purchase of equipment for instruction in mathematics, science, and foreign languages. But proposals to give aid for general purposes aroused the opposition of two powerful blocs; the southerners and the Catholics. The southerners feared that the leverage afforded by federal grants would be used to force desegregation. The Catholics, who provide the schools attended by 6,000,000 children, insisted that aid should not be given to public schools unless it was given to parochial schools as well. Non-Catholics, on the other hand, held that aid to church schools would violate the constitutional principle of separation of church and state. The two sides to this debate were deadlocked until 1965. In that year, the Johnson administration succeeded in effecting a compromise. Federal aid would be given for buildings, equipment, and salaries to public schools and not to parochial schools. But it would be given on an equal basis for materials and services supplied to pupils in both. On this basis, federal aid for general purposes was enacted into law.

The Elementary and Secondary Education Act of 1965

Under the Act of 1965, federal funds are directed to public schools attended by children who are in poverty. For a school district to be eligible for a grant, 3 percent of its pupils, at least 100 in number, must come from families whose incomes are under $2,000 or who are subsisting on relief. The basic grant to a school is determined by multiplying half of its average expenditure per pupil by the number of those who come from poor families. As an incentive, an additional grant is made to districts whose expenditures per pupil are increased.

These funds can be used by public schools for construction, for the purchase of equipment, and for enlargement of their teaching staffs. They can be used by both public and parochial schools for programs that involve the sharing of educational facilities and services, such as mobile equipment, radio, and television. Other grants are made to finance the improvement of libraries and laboratories, the acquisition of teaching machines, and the provision of textbooks for the use of children in both public and parochial schools. And grants are made, finally, for supplementary educational centers and services. These may provide health care, physical education and recreation, special classes for the physically handicapped or the mentally retarded, remedial instruction, counseling and guidance, courses in music and art, advanced work in science and in foreign languages, and a variety of other programs, all of them open on an equal basis to pupils in public and parochial schools.

The Act of 1965 is a landmark in the progress of elementary and secondary education in the United States. It marks the first extension of federal aid for general purposes to local schools. It directs the flow of federal money to those children who are most in need. It has prompted the provision of aid on a massive scale, reaching 9,000,000 children in 17,500 school districts in 1967.

Not all has been smooth sailing. In 1967, state school administrators supported by a number of Congressmen undertook to shift control of the program from the federal government to the states. Instead of making grants for specific purposes, the Office of Education would have been required to make them in blocks, with state officials determining how the money was to be spent. There was danger, if this were done, that states would use the funds to finance their accustomed programs, with help no longer going to children who were most in need. There was danger, too, that states would cut the aid provided for pupils in parochial schools, thus putting an end to the entire program by destroying the compromise on which it was based. Fortunately, Congress rejected this proposal as it applied to aid in general. And it proceeded to appropriate $9.3 billion to carry out the purposes of the Act in the fiscal years 1969 and 1970, the largest sum provided for aid to education in the country's history.

The Teachers Corps

Positions as teachers in schools attended by the children of the poor are unattractive. Energy is exhausted in maintaining discipline. Hope for creative experience is small. As a result, the tenure of teachers in these schools is short. Those who remain are poorly qualified. If the schools are to be improved, ways must be found to recruit teachers who are competent and committed. One possibility would be to rotate teachers on assignment among the schools of richer and poorer areas. A second would be to attract teachers to schools in poorer areas by offering lighter work loads and higher pay. Both solutions are opposed by teachers in the better schools. A third possibility is to recruit highly motivated young people and give them training to serve as specialists in the education of disadvantaged children. This is the approach that was adopted by Congress when it created the Teachers Corps in 1965. Under this program, 6,000 young people who were trained for the work by their universities were to be assigned at the request of local school boards to work in teams, under skilled supervision, in the schools of poverty areas. The program shortly evoked congressional opposition. The Corps was seen as an army of federal teachers taking over control of local schools. Its members were depicted as outside agitators, fighting for desegregation. An effort to kill the Corps in 1967 did not succeed. But the Corps was denationalized. Recruitment and selection of its members was taken away from the Office of Education and given to local school districts, under supervision of the states. The Corps has been starved for funds. Its appropriation for fiscal 1966 stood at only $17 million of the $100 million authorized. Its authorization for fiscal 1970 stands at $56 million for 5,000 to 6,000 Corpsmen. The Corps numbered some 300 team leaders and 1,500 interns in the spring of 1968, a fraction of the number that could have been recruited and usefully employed.

Aid for higher education

Expenditures on higher education in the United States are growing. College and university enrollments are expanding. More facilities are being provided. Academic salaries are being raised. Costs per student are mounting. The total outlay on higher education, now around 2 percent of the gross national product, will stand at 3 percent by 1975.

How are the larger expenditures to be financed? Private institutions will get more income from endowments and from current giving. Public institutions will get more from state and local taxes. But these sources of income are unlikely to keep pace with the growth of expenditures. An expanding share of the cost of higher education will have to be met by further increases in tuition and student fees. Charges per student are likely to rise by another 50 percent in the next decade. This raises the question of how these bills are to be paid, particularly by students from the lower income groups.

With higher education as with elementary and secondary education, attention turns to the federal government. Aid may be given by the government to colleges and universities, enabling them to acquire added facilities and personnel. Such aid, however, may carry with it a measure of control over research and teaching, distorting the purpose and endangering the integrity of the academic enterprise. Aid may be given to students, enabling them to pay their college bills. Here, the government exercises no control over educational policy. It is neutral among institutions, permitting students to attend whatever ones they choose.

Forms of student aid

Aid to students may take a variety of forms: (1) City and community colleges and state colleges and universities charge no tuition. This practice is supposed to assure equality of opportunity. It does not do so. It does not give the poor boy money to meet his other expenses. It gives the boy whose parents are in an upper income bracket a subsidy he does not need. (2) It is frequently proposed that parents be allowed to deduct their children's college bills from income subject to taxation. This device would be of no help to those whose incomes are too small to be taxed. It would give to those who pay taxes a subsidy that would increase as incomes rose. (3) Educational institutions give scholarships in amounts that vary with the students' needs. In effect, they have a sliding scale of fees. This arrangement does not subsidize the rich. It does help students from the middle income groups. It rarely provides enough to help the really poor, for the costs that they must meet include not only college bills but also maintenance and freedom for a number of years from the need to go to work. (4) Since World War II, under the G.I. Bill of Rights the government has financed the education of veterans, not only meeting their college bills but also giving them living allowances and paying the institutions they have attended for the costs involved. In this case, aid has been given on the basis of status, not ability or need. But it has made higher education possible for many to whom it would otherwise have been denied. Its general adoption as a method of financing is prevented by its cost.

The cost of higher education is not properly to be regarded as a current expense to be met out of current income. It is rather a form of capital investment that should be financed from the larger earnings that result. Money should be borrowed during college years and paid back throughout one's working life. But the cost of such financing under commercial terms is too burdensome, particularly for the poor. Economists have proposed that this obstacle be overcome by making loans for long periods and delaying repayment for some years. The burden would then be light for persons whose incomes were large, but it would still be heavy for those whose incomes were small. This has led to the further suggestion that payment be made proportionate to income. If such an arrangement were voluntary, people who expected to have large incomes would borrow elsewhere. Only those who expected to have small incomes would take advantage of the plan, thus increasing its cost. Parents would borrow to educate their daughters but not their sons. Those who chose to loaf would be excused from paying for their educations; those who worked would be compelled to pay. If the arrangement were compulsory, it would be an added tax on income, imposing a heavier burden on those who had been to college than on those who had not. It would impose a double burden on families where husband and wife were both college-bred. A workable and equitable solution to the problem of spreading the cost of higher education through later years is yet to be found.

The federal role

Under the Morrill Act of 1862, federal land was granted to the states for the support of colleges to provide instruction in "agriculture and the mechanic arts." Since that time, the land-grant colleges have grown into state universities, and support of higher education has become a major function of the states. It is only in recent years that the federal government has come to provide aid to institutions of higher learning, financing their facilities and supporting their students.

The G.I. Bill of Rights, enacted in 1944, marked the beginning of large-scale federal aid. This legislation was designed to compensate veterans of World War II whose education had been delayed or interrupted by service in the armed forces. Under its terms, as has been noted, the government paid their bills at institutions of their own choice and provided them with living allowances for periods up to four years. This support was given to 10,000,000 former servicemen, a third of whom used it for higher education. The academic achievement of these men on the average was high. Similar provision was made on a smaller scale for veterans of the wars in Korea and Vietnam.

Congress came to the aid of students again when it passed the National Defense Education Act of 1958. Under this law, loans up to $1,000 per year ($5,000 altogether) were made with interest at 3 percent, with repayment to begin a year after graduation and to be completed within the next 10 years. Nine tenths of the money involved was put up by the government, and the other tenth by the student's college or university. These institutions administered the loans.

Under the Higher Education Act of 1965, the government moved a third time to give support to students on a major scale. (1) Under a work-study program, an institution may pay a student up to $450 for work done during the academic year and up to $500 for work done in the summer, with the government putting up nine tenths of the money. (2) Under a program of guaranteed loans to families with incomes under $15,000, sums running to $1,000 per year ($5,000 total) for undergraduates and to $1,500 ($7,500 total) for graduate students may be borrowed from private lenders, with the government paying all of the interest while a youth is still in college and part of it during the 5 to 10 years after his graduation while the loan is being repaid. (3) Under a program of educational opportunity grants, scholarships of $200 to $800 (plus $200 for students in the upper half of their classes) are given to students who would not otherwise be able to go to school. Nearly 1,500,000 students were being aided under federal programs in the spring of 1968, more than 300,000 of them receiving work-study payments, nearly a million receiving NDEA and HEA loans, and more than 200,000 receiving educational opportunity grants.

There are now many programs that help the ambitious student of limited means to obtain a higher education: the scholarships granted by private institutions; the system of National Merit Scholarships financed by the Ford Foundation; the tuition-free education offered by city and community colleges and by state colleges and universities; and the employment afforded, the loans made, and the grants given by the federal government. In one way or another, the student who is able and industrious will be given educational opportunity.

Higher education for Negroes

Steps are being taken to improve the quality of education offered in predominantly Negro institutions. The federal government finances cooperative arrangements among these institutions involving the joint use of facilities and personnel and partnerships between these and stronger institutions involving exchanges of faculty and students and the introduction of new curricula. It offers teaching fellowships, encouraging junior professors and graduate students to serve on the faculties of these schools. A commission set up by the Southern Regional Education Board has called upon its member states to provide "catch-up" funds to enable the Negro colleges to overcome their handicaps.

An effort is also being made to improve the preparation of Negro high school students for college work. Through its program known as Upward Bound, the Office of Economic Opportunity stages summer coaching sessions and offers assistance during the school year. There were 26,000 pupils enrolled in this program in 1968. Four fifths of the Upward Bound students have gone on to college; two fifths have stayed for a second year.

Half of all Negro students come from families with incomes of less than $4,000 a year. Scholarship money is now being provided them in increasing volume. The sources of aid that were listed above are open to blacks and whites alike. In addition, there are two national scholarship funds that are open only to Negroes. One of them, bringing graduates of southern high schools to northern colleges and universities, is supported by the Rockefeller Foundation. The other, providing achievement scholarships in proportion to the colored population in each of four regions, is supported by the Ford Foundation. No Negro of outstanding ability need now be denied a higher education for want of means. It should be noted, however, that no such effort has been made on behalf of other minority groups.

Employment opportunity

As we saw in Chapter 4, the Negro is at a serious disadvantage in the labor market. His rate of unemployment is higher than that of the white man. He is unemployed more frequently and for longer periods. When he does find work, he gets a poorer job, one that pays lower wages and offers less hope of advancement. The Negro's disadvantage is attributable in part to lack of training and experience. But it is also a result of deliberate discrimination. Discrimination is practiced by labor unions, by employers, and by employment agencies. It affects every aspect of the Negro's work: his chances of being hired, well placed, and promoted; and his tenure and wage. It denies him equality of opportunity.

At the end of World War II, this denial became a matter of public concern. In the years that followed, laws and ordinances forbidding discrimination in employment were enacted by state legislatures and city councils, and measures to control discrimination were adopted by the federal administration and enacted by Congress. All of these measures put more reliance on persuasion than on coercion to carry out their purposes. But progress has been made. While far from equal, the Negro's opportunities today are better than they were a score of years ago. The nondiscrimination measures, moreover, can be strengthened. The Negro's opportunities can be further improved.

State and local control of discrimination

The first of the measures forbidding discrimination, known as the fair employment practice laws, was enacted by the legislature of New York State in 1945. This came to be a model for the laws of other states and for municipal ordinances. Twenty years later, there were statutes in 34 states and ordinances in more than 50 cities, covering almost all employment outside the South. In the present section of this chapter, we examine the substantive provisions of these measures, the organization and procedures provided for their enforcement, and the manner in which their purposes have been carried out.

Fair employment practice laws

The FEP statutes make it unlawful to discriminate in employment because of race, creed, color, or national origin. In general, they cover employment in all fields except domestic service, nonprofit organizations, government agencies, and firms with fewer than four employees. The laws forbid employers to discriminate in hiring and firing workers, determining their wages and working conditions, transferring and promoting them, and fixing other terms of employment. They forbid unions to discriminate in admitting workers to membership, and they forbid employment offices to discriminate in accepting applicants and referring them to employers. To administer these prohibitions, the laws create commissions consisting of 3 to 10 members appointed by governors or mayors for staggered terms, all but the members of the New York State commission serving part-time. These bodies are empowered to receive complaints, conduct investigations, hold hearings, and issue orders, appealing for their enforcement, if necessary, to the courts.

Following the usual procedure, a person who has suffered from discrimination by an employer complains to his state or city commission. In only a few jurisdictions can a complaint be made by others on his behalf. A member of the commission's staff makes an investigation, visiting the employer's establishment, interviewing his personnel manager, and checking on his employment practices. He then reports to the commission. If a complaint appears to be unfounded, the case is dropped. If it appears to have substance, the commission invites the employer to confer in private with one or more of its members. At such a conference, it seeks to persuade the employer to abandon his discriminatory practices. If it succeeds, his agreement is put in writing, committing him to take such action as employing, transferring, promoting, or reinstating the complainant and paying him such back wages as may be due. If conciliation is not successful, the commission may hold a public hearing which the employer must attend, producing his books and papers and giving testimony under oath. Following such a hearing, the commission may dismiss the case or may issue a formal order directing the employer to cease and desist from his illegal practices in general and to take affirmative action to redress the damage done by his illegal conduct in the complainant's case. If the employer does not obey this order, the commission may bring suit before a court to have it enforced. If he still does not obey, he can be punished for contempt of court. Willful violation of the law is made a misdemeanor, punishable by fine or imprisonment, or both.

Enforcement of fair employment practices

The commissions operate under serious handicaps in their enforcement of the laws. With only one or two exceptions, their budgets have been too limited and their staffs too small to enable them to mount a vigorous enforcement drive. Half of the commissions can act only when they receive complaints. The other half are empowered to initiate action but usually lack the resources to do so. Employers who are guilty of persistent violation may not be called to account because nobody files a complaint. Employees who suffer from discrimination may fail to complain because they are ignorant of the law, because they fear reprisals, or because they are cynical about their chances of obtaining redress. Where complaints are received, relief may be limited to particular cases instead of dealing with discrimination in general.

Nearly all of the commissions are required by law to exhaust the possibilities of conciliation before proceeding to order compliance. The process of conciliation may be protracted. The terms of the agreement that the commission finally accepts may be unduly lenient. The fact that the commissions have in reserve the power to issue orders should strengthen their hands in these negotiations. But they rarely require that a complainant be immediately reemployed or that he be given back pay. The complainant gains little; the employer suffers no penalty. Businessmen get the idea that the law is not to be taken seriously. They are unlikely to cooperate voluntarily in carrying out its purposes.

In 99 percent of the cases brought to the commissions, their action does not go beyond this point. Few cases go on to an order to cease and desist. Even fewer are carried to the courts. Only one or two commissions follow up their agreements and orders to determine whether their terms are being observed. Enforcement against employers, thus, is lax. Enforcement against unions and employment agencies is even more so. Here, the obstacles to obtaining compliance are greater. Few of the commissions make the attempt. Aside from handling individual cases, some of the commissions have carried on educational campaigns, working with employers, unions, and civic groups, explaining the importance of integration in employment and dispelling fears regarding its effects.[1]

Federal control of discrimination

It was not until 1964 that Congress enacted a law forbidding discrimination in employment. In Title VII of the Civil Rights Act of that year, it laid down prohibitions that paralleled those contained in the state FEP laws and set up an agency—the Equal Employment Opportunity Commission—comparable to the state FEP commissions to enforce them. Where a complaint originates in a state that has an FEP law, the federal commission cannot receive it unless the state commission has failed to act for 60 days. But when a complaint comes from a state without such a law, the federal commission can accept it at once. As a result, the coverage of the laws forbidding discrimination is now complete. In the North and West, cases are handled by the state commissions. In the South, they can be taken directly to the EEOC.

This law does not mark the first or the only attempt by the federal government to deal with discrimination in employment. Under a series of executive orders issued since 1941, the government has undertaken

---

[1] Michael I. Sovern, *Legal Restraints on Racial Discrimination in Employment* (New York: Twentieth Century Fund, 1966), chap. iii; Paul H. Norgren and Samuel E. Hill, *Toward Fair Employment* (New York: Columbia University Press, 1964), chaps. v and vi; and Paul Bullock, *Equal Opportunity in Employment* (Los Angeles: Institute of Industrial Relations, University of California, 1966), chap. iv.

to prohibit discrimination by firms receiving government contracts. Under an order issued in 1948, it has abolished segregation in the armed forces. Under an Equal Employment Program dating from the Kennedy administration, it has increased the Negro's share of jobs in the civil service. And discrimination by labor unions has almost inadvertently been brought under control by the National Labor Relations Board under the provisions of the National Labor Relations Act.

Discrimination in government employment

Until 1948, Negroes in the armed forces were assigned to separate units and required to use separate facilities; Negro officers did not command white men. In that year, President Truman, in his capacity as Commander-in-Chief, issued an order abolishing segregation. Now all units in all the services are integrated and all facilities desegregated. The percentage of Negroes among officers is lower than among privates. But there are Negro officers at all ranks, with integrated commands. Desegregation started earlier and has gone farther in the armed forces than in the civil service.

Until recent years, discrimination was common in federal employment. Negroes were confined in the main to menial and clerical tasks. They were so classified that they received lower wages for the same work. They were promoted at a slower rate. President Kennedy made the first attempt to rectify this situation under his Equal Employment Program in 1961, setting up a Committee on Equal Employment Opportunity and directing it, among its duties, to persuade federal agencies to abandon discriminatory practices. President Johnson transferred this function to the Civil Service Commission, keeping the program in force.

The program has been a modest one. Its results have been mixed. Discrimination has been reduced in agencies such as the Post Office and the Veterans Administration where most of the work is routine. Discrimination persists in old-line agencies such as the government departments and regulatory commissions that have business constituencies. More progress has been made with federal establishments in the North and West than in the South. The Negro's employment gains have been greater in unskilled and semiskilled jobs, smaller in the upper echelons. Negroes have been appointed to the Supreme Court, the

Cabinet, and the Federal Reserve Board, and to assistant secretaryships, ambassadorships, and a number of other high posts. But these are exceptions to the general rule.

The overall record is favorable. Negroes constitute 11 percent of the civilian labor force. They number 14 percent of federal employees. They get 20 percent of new federal jobs. More Negroes are being hired as well by state and local governments. Twelve percent of all government employees in the United States are black. Negroes have more than their share of government jobs and less than their share of jobs in private business.[2]

Discrimination by government contractors

The government regularly enters into contracts with thousands of firms under which they engage in construction activities and in the production of other goods, employing millions of laborers to do the work. It is possible to write into these contracts provisions forbidding discrimination in employment, refusing to award contracts to firms who will not agree to accept the provisions and canceling contracts made with firms who fail to live up to them. Government contracts are a source of substantial profit. Potentially, the possibility of their denial or cancellation gives the government power to insure nondiscrimination in employment. Nominally, at least, this power has been exercised by the federal government for many years.

In 1941, on the eve of American entry into World War II, Negroes planned a march on Washington to protest their exclusion from employment in defense industries. President Roosevelt forestalled the demonstration by issuing an executive order directing government agencies to include in their contracts a provision forbidding the contractors to "discriminate against any worker because of race, creed, color, or national origin." The order set up a committee of eminent businessmen and labor leaders, serving without pay, to enforce its terms. The committee issued directives to employers to avoid discrimination and obtained a number of agreements to comply. But the order specified no sanctions for those who failed to do so. The effort was purely educational.

[2] Samuel Krislov, "Government and Equal Employment Opportunity" in Arthur M. Ross and Herbert Hill (eds.), *Employment, Race, and Poverty* (New York: Harcourt, Brace & World, Inc., 1967), chap. xviii.

In 1943, after America's entry into the war, the President issued another order requiring the inclusion of a nondiscrimination clause in all contracts and setting up a new committee with a larger budget and staff to police it. This body received a substantial volume of complaints, investigated them, and sought agreements to comply with the nondiscrimination clause. In less than 1 percent of the cases where agreement was not forthcoming, it issued orders to comply. But it never undertook to enforce an agreement or an order by asking the contracting agencies to cancel a contract. These agencies were more interested in getting construction done and goods delivered to carry on the war than in providing employment opportunities for Negroes. The committee doubtless feared that they would refuse to cooperate. The requirements of the order were therefore defied with impunity. The number of Negroes among employees in defense industries rose from 3 percent in 1942 to more than 8 percent in 1944. But this increase was attributable to the scarcity of labor, not to enforcement of the contract clause.

The Roosevelt program was ended in 1946 when Congress denied it funds. A new order against discrimination was issued by President Eisenhower in 1954, and a Committee on Government Contracts set up to enforce it. This body was authorized to receive complaints and pass them on to the contracting agencies who were then expected to require their contractors to comply. But the agencies did not cooperate. The committee was denied the power and the funds that it needed if the order were to be enforced. No contracts were denied or canceled. Contractors therefore concluded that the order could safely be ignored.

Until the sixties, the nondiscrimination clause in government contracts was never really enforced. The contracting agencies did not believe in it. Employers and unions opposed it. It was without political support. Congress starved the enforcement agencies. These bodies were never able or willing to use the one real sanction in the government's power. As a result, employment opportunity was not improved.

In 1961, President Kennedy issued a new order against discrimination, entrusting its enforcement to his Committee on Equal Employment Opportunity, a function which President Johnson subsequently transferred to an Office of Federal Contract Compliance in the Department of Labor. The order required inclusion in government contracts of a clause compelling contractors to take affirmative action to insure that applicants and employees would be treated without regard to race, creed, color, or national origin, to include a similar clause in their subcontracts, to inform employees regarding their right to file complaints, and to make regular compliance reports. It explicitly empowered the enforcement agency to publish the names of violators, to request the Attorney General to sue them for violation of their contracts, to suspend or terminate such contracts, and to bar the violators from receiving further contracts from the government.

Equipped with a larger budget and a stronger staff than its predecessors, the Committee (later the Office) sped up the processing of complaints, handling more cases in less time. It also proceeded to negotiate compliance agreements. Notable among them was an undertaking by the Lockheed Aircraft Corporation actively to recruit members of minority groups, to provide them with training, and to promote them to salaried jobs. In 1965, the Office imposed the first penalty for contract violation, directing the General Services Administration to award no further contracts to five companies that were engaged in the construction of an office building. Thereafter, it used the possibility of contract cancellation as leverage in obtaining agreements from other firms. In 1968, after protracted negotiations, it exacted an agreement from 18 international unions in the building trades to recruit Negroes for membership and to admit them to programs for the training of apprentices. Observance of such commitments is followed up through a system of compliance reporting and review.

The increase in the percentage of Negroes employed on government contracts is small, but they have been granted access to apprenticeship training and to white-collar jobs. Greater progress should be made in the future with determined enforcement of the nondiscrimination clause.[3]

The Equal Employment Opportunity Commission

Title VII of the Civil Rights Act of 1964, the federal equivalent of the state FEP laws, outlaws discrimination because of race, color, religion, sex, or national origin, specifically forbidding employers to discriminate in hiring, training, compensating, promoting, or discharg-

---

[3] Sovern, *op. cit.*, chap. v; Norgren and Hill, *op. cit.*, chap. vii; *New York Times*, February 14, 1968; and *Business Week*, June 1, 1968, pp. 34, 38.

ing workers, to segregate or classify them, or to discriminate in fixing working conditions or other terms of employment; forbidding unions to exclude, expel, segregate, or classify workers; and forbidding employment agencies to refuse to refer them. The law permits discrimination for other reasons such as seniority and where such characteristics as religion or sex are bona fide qualifications, for example, when a church is employing a pastor or a tenor to sing in a choir. The law does not apply to purely intrastate employment, to educational institutions or private clubs, or to firms with fewer than 25 employees. It sets up for its enforcement an Equal Employment Opportunity Commission with five full-time members appointed by the President.

In part, the Commission's procedure is similar to that of the FEP commissions in the states. It receives and investigates complaints, or where it has reason to believe a violation has occurred, it may file charges on its own initiative. It then seeks to effect settlements through conciliation. If this fails, the procedure provided by the law differs from that followed in the states. Where there is a private complainant, the EEOC informs him of the failure. There are then three possibilities: (1) The complainant may bring suit at his own expense in a federal district court to obtain an order directing the defendant to comply with the law and possibly to employ him and to give him back pay. If such an order is disobeyed, the EEOC can sue to compel compliance. (2) The complainant can ask the Attorney General to intervene. If he agrees to do so, the government carries the burden of the suit. (3) Where the Attorney General finds evidence of a general pattern of discrimination, he can take the initiative in bringing suit. The EEOC was not empowered, as were the commissions in the states, to issue orders to cease and desist. The administration has repeatedly recommended that congress give it this power, but Congress has refused to do so. Enforcement has thus depended upon the policy of the Attorney General in bringing suits.

In its first two years, the EEOC received 16,000 complaints, completed 3,500 investigations, undertook conciliation in 500 cases, and settled 110. An outstanding settlement was that obtained in 1966 with the Newport News Shipping and Dry Dock Company. Here, the Commission's hand in the negotiations was strengthened by the possibility of action by the Office of Federal Contract Compliance and by the Attorney General. The company agreed to favor Negroes in accepting applicants for training and to seek recruits in Negro schools;

to give Negroes promotions and increases in pay on the same basis as those given whites, compensating them for wages that had been held back; and to study the qualifications of the hundred workers last appointed to supervisory posts, putting any Negro with superior qualifications on a preferred promotion list. It also agreed to employ an expert in job evaluation to determine whether any Negroes were improperly classified or working at rates that were arbitrarily set low, and to supervise their upgrading and the equalization of their pay. The agreement thus gave Negroes an opportunity to move into higher job classifications and into supervisory positions as they became available.

Enforcement has continued on several fronts. The EEOC made an industry by industry survey of employment patterns in major cities in 1967, identifying the places where the share of Negro employment was low. It used the information thus obtained as a basis for action, bringing the pressure of publicity to bear on industry leaders and announcing the government's readiness to file enforcement suits. At the same time the Department of Justice launched an enforcement drive, investigating employment practices at plants and offices in 25 states. By the spring of 1968, it had filed 22 suits against employers and labor unions, charging a general pattern of discrimination in each case. When the government has built a record by winning cases in the courts, the commission should find it easier in negotiating agreements to obtain the commitments it seeks.[4]

A word should be said in passing concerning two aspects of the nondiscrimination laws. The prohibition of discrimination because of sex was inserted in the Civil Rights Act by southern congressmen for the purpose of embarrassing the administration. It has added to the burden carried by the EEOC; a third of the complaints filed with the Commission charge discrimination because of sex. Another statute, enacted in 1967, forbids discrimination because of age, save where this is a bone fide qualification for a job. This prohibition is intended to preserve employment opportunities for persons between the ages of 40 and 65. It is enforced not by the EEOC but by the Secretary of Labor, through orders obtained directly from the courts. We shall have no more to say concerning discrimination based on sex or age, since these forms of discrimination raise questions that differ in character from those with which we are here concerned.

---

[4] Sovern, *op. cit.*, chap. iv; and Bullock, *op. cit.*, chap. iii.

The National Labor Relations Board

Under the National Labor Relations Act of 1935, employers are required to grant recognition to labor unions and to engage in collective bargaining. Where more than one union claims to represent the workers in a bargaining unit, the issue is decided by a secret ballot. The law sets up a National Labor Relations Board and empowers it to conduct representation elections. If a union gets a majority of the votes in such an election, the Board certifies it as the exclusive bargaining agent for all of the employees. If a union is refused such certification, the employer will not deal with it. The law also forbids a number of "unfair labor practices" of employers and unions affecting collective bargaining and empowers the NLRB to enforce the rules against these practices by investigating complaints, holding public hearings, and issuing cease and desist orders enforceable upon appeal by the courts.

The National Labor Relations Act was not passed by Congress for the purpose of outlawing racial discrimination. The NLRB was therefore slow to use it for this purpose. But it is now held that such discrimination disqualifies a union for certification as an exclusive bargaining agent, and that the Board may issue orders against discriminatory measures as unfair labor practices. The Board has thus come to serve as an added force against discrimination by labor unions, a field in which the antidiscrimination agencies themselves have not been strong.

In 1944, in the Steele case,[5] where a union had negotiated with a railroad an agreement denying employment opportunities to Negroes, the Supreme Court held that an exclusive bargaining agent was obliged to represent all the members of a group for whom it bargained, whether members of the union or not, "without hostile discrimination, fairly, impartially, and in good faith," and it found that the union had not fulfilled this obligation. This decision was handed down under the Railroad Labor Act, but in the Syers case[6] in 1955, the Court applied the same rule to the National Labor Relations Act. Since that time, in a number of cases where unions had discriminated against Negroes, the federal courts have held that fair representation was denied.

Certification is important to a union only where its status as an

[5] *Steele* v. *Louisville and Nashville R.R.*, 323 U.S. 192.
[6] *Syers* v. *Oil Workers International Union*, 350 U.S. 892.

exclusive bargaining agent is in dispute. It can be ordered to cease and desist from unfair labor practices at any time. The NLRB has held that racial discrimination might be held to violate the law's prohibitions against coercing workers in their decisions concerning union membership, causing employers to discriminate against nonunionists and failing to bargain in good faith. In 1964, in the Hughes Tool case,[7] where a union had segregated its members according to race and had failed to present the grievances of Negro members for settlement, the Board held not only that fair representation had been denied but also that its denial was an unfair labor practice. In 1967, in two cases where a Court of Appeals had upheld the Board in finding racial discrimination to be an unfair labor practice, the Supreme Court refused review, permitting the decisions to stand.[8]

Action under the National Labor Relations Act has marked advantages. Anyone can file a complaint. A case is prosecuted by the General Counsel of the NLRB without cost to the complainant. The Board can issue an order to cease and desist and sue for its enforcement. In the field of discrimination by unions, action under the Labor Relations Act may thus become a powerful supplement to action under the Civil Rights Act.[9]

Prospects for employment opportunity

As yet, the measures adopted to prevent racial discrimination in employment have attained but a moderate success. The rules against discrimination in the armed forces and in the civil service have been effective. It is only recently that the nondiscrimination clause in government contracts has been enforced. The possibilities of action by the National Labor Relations Board are still to be realized. Evidence of the effect of fair employment practice laws is mixed. In general, the laws have had little influence on upgrading and promotion, but they have succeeded in removing barriers to employment, particularly those that were blatant and overt. They have created an atmosphere more favorable to opportunity by overcoming employers' fears that employment of Negroes would lead to adverse reactions by white employees,

[7] *Independent Metal Workers Union Local No. 1* v. *NLRB*, 147 NLRB 166.

[8] *Rubber Workers Local 12* v. *NLRB*, C.A. 5, 363 F. 2d, 12; *International Longshoremens Assn.* v. *NLRB*, C.A. 5, 368 F. 2d, 1010; and 36 *Law Week* 3135.

[9] Sovern, *op. cit.*, chap. vi; and Norgren and Hill, *op. cit*, chap. ix.

by customers, and by the community. Sovern concludes that they have produced an observable reduction in discrimination.[10] Norgren and Hill, comparing the employment of Negroes in 1960 with that in 1950, found a noteworthy improvement in New York, with lesser improvements in New Jersey, Connecticut, and Massachusetts. Comparing employment in New York with that in three industrial states that lacked enforceable FEP laws, they found far greater employment gains for Negroes in New York.[11] Surveys of the results of settlements with employers in banking, insurance, and department stores, all fields traditionally barred to Negroes, showed marked improvement in their number and employment status. Surveys in Philadelphia showed similar gains in banks and in restaurants and hotels.[12] Norgren and Hill conclude that "analysis of experience under these laws demonstrates that enforceable FEP legislation, if properly designed and wisely administered, can be an effective means of combatting racial discrimination in employment."[13]

The proper design and wise administration of FEP laws would satisfy requirements that are not now generally met. There would be a full-time commission with an adequate budget and staff. Civil rights groups, such as the National Association for the Advancement of Colored People and the Urban League, would be permitted to complain against a pattern of discrimination. The commission would be empowered to make investigations and initiate action without waiting for complaints. It would spend less of its time in handling individual cases and more in dealing with general patterns of discrimination by companies and by whole industries. It would not prolong the process of conciliation but would move shortly to formal hearings and the issuance of orders. In agreements, it would seek commitments to take affirmative action: to recruit Negroes, give them training, and promote them. In orders, it would require the employer to hire the complainant and to give him back pay. With unions, as with employers, it would attack general patterns of discrimination. It would insist on access to apprentice training. It would follow up compliance with agreements and orders, making spot checks of employment practices and periodic surveys of employment patterns.

[10] Sovern, *op. cit.*, chap. viii.
[11] Norgren and Hill, *op. cit.*, chap. vi.
[12] Paul H. Norgren, "Fair Employment Practice Laws," in Ross and Hill, *op. cit.*, pp. 551–52.
[13] Norgren and Hill, *op. cit.*, p. 231.

Another means of increasing the employment of Negroes would be to require discrimination in their favor like that involved in compensatory education and in admissions to colleges and universities, counterbalancing the effect of adverse discrimination in the past. In compliance agreements, employers are indeed required actively to recruit Negroes for possible openings. The commissions might go on to establish race quotas which employers would be required to fill. But such an undertaking would be difficult to administer, and it would violate the rule against racial discrimination in the FEP laws.

Other measures are available. Antidiscrimination clauses could be written into contracts awarded by state and local as well as by federal agencies, and all such clauses could be more vigorously enforced. More cases could be brought for action under the National Labor Relations Act. Funds could be withheld by the federal government, under Title VI of the Civil Rights Act, in cases where discrimination was practiced by public or private recipients of federal aid. In cases where firms must be licensed to do business, the licenses of those who discriminate could be revoked. Government has sufficient power to eliminate racial discrimination if such a policy had strong political support.

But equal employment for Negroes is not to be achieved by removing discrimination alone. Steps must be taken to train them for positions at higher levels and for openings demanding new skills. Jobs must be created, insofar as possible, in the areas where they live. The operation of the labor market must be improved. These matters are to be considered later, in Chapters 17 and 18.

12

Political and social opportunity

The last quarter of a century has seen a remarkable succession of governmental actions directed toward the removal of long-standing barriers to equality of opportunity. Congress has passed a series of laws designed to assure equality in education, in employment, in voting, in access to public accommodations and to housing. Nearly 20 state legislatures and 40 city councils have outlawed discrimination in housing; more than 30 states and 50 cities have outlawed discrimination in employment. The federal courts have handed down a number of sweeping decisions banning discrimination in all these fields. The executive branch of the federal government has issued orders against discrimination in the armed forces, in employment by government agencies and by government contractors, and in federally aided housing. It has been vigorous in its enforcement of laws enacted by Congress and decisions handed down by the courts, particularly in the field of education.

Looking at this record, white liberals have reason to feel that great progress has been made. But to the Negro who is still at a disadvantage the progress seems painfully slow. The magnitude of the problem of racial discrimination in the United States is so great that more ambitious measures, pressed with greater vigor, are required. But moves to equalize opportunity still encounter opposition springing from the prejudice of whites. It therefore appears to many Negroes that real improvement of their lot is to be achieved not through voluntary concessions granted by the white community but through the organization and exercise of black power. This approach may be effective, but it raises a serious question concerning our ultimate goal. Should we move toward two societies, separate but equal, or toward a single society where a man is to be judged on his merits, not by the color of his skin?

The two preceding chapters were concerned with opportunities for education and employment. The present chapter describes the remaining measures that attack discrimination: the right to vote, public accommodations, the exercise of civil rights, and the access to housing. It closes with a brief discussion of the prospects for racial equality.

Civil rights

Negroes in the southern states after the Civil War were not only denied equality of opportunity for education and employment but though legally given the right to vote, they were in fact prevented from voting. Under the separate-but-equal rule of *Plessy* v. *Ferguson,* they were denied access to public accommodations. And when Congress and the courts affirmed their rights in all these fields, they were prevented from exercising them by physical violence. Congress moved to enforce the Negro's right to vote through laws enacted from 1957 to 1965, to assure his access to public accommodations under the Civil Rights Act of 1964, and to protect him in the exercise of all his constitutional rights under the Civil Rights Act of 1968. These measures are described in the present section. The provisions of the Act of 1968 that outlaw discrimination in housing are discussed in the next.

The right to vote

The Fifteenth Amendment to the Constitution provided that "The right of the citizens of the United States to vote shall not be denied or abridged by the United States or by any State on account of race, color, or previous condition of servitude." But this provision was flouted by the southern states. Various devices were employed, until they were found or made unconstitutional, to keep the Negro from the polls. It was held that party primaries—the only elections that mattered in the South—were not elections, and Negroes were barred from participation. A man was not permitted to vote unless his grand-father had qualified to vote or unless he had paid a poll tax. Other restrictive qualifications were imposed. Voters were required to pass literacy tests, made easy for whites and impossibly difficult for blacks. Mississippi limited suffrage to persons of good character; and where a person was a party to a common-law marriage, had an illegitimate child, had been convicted of a misdemeanor, or had obstructed a public passage, it found his character to be bad. Access to the polls was obstructed in many places by closed doors, long lines, and slowdowns in voting. As a result, though given the franchise by law, Negroes were disfranchised in fact. In 1960, only 28 percent of the Negro adults in 11 southern states were registered to vote. In 129 counties in 10 states where Negroes were more than half of the adults, less than 10 percent were registered. In 23 counties in five states, there were no Negro registrants.

In 1957 and 1960, Congress empowered the Attorney General to sue for injunctions to enforce the right to vote and authorized the federal courts to appoint voting referees. In the Civil Rights Act of 1964, it barred tougher literacy tests for Negroes than for other voters in federal elections and made a sixth-grade education presumptive evidence of literacy. It authorized individuals to sue election officials for access to the polls, and where a general pattern of discrimination was found to exist, it authorized suits by the Attorney General. In the Voting Rights Act of 1965, Congress provided for the appointment of federal examiners to register Negroes to vote in places where local registrars had failed to do so.

There has been a marked increase in the number of Negroes registered and voting in the South. Of some 5,000,000 Negroes of voting age in 11 southern states, 2,800,000, or 57 percent (compared with 28 percent in 1960), were registered in 1967. In the two years following enactment of the Voting Rights Act, the percentage registered in Alabama rose from 19.3 to 51.6; in Mississippi, from 6.7 to 59.8. In the congressional elections in 1966, votes were cast by 62 percent of the Negro registrants as compared with 70 percent of the whites. More than 1,000 Negroes ran for office in the region and nearly 250 were elected.[1] This was in the deep South. Larger numbers of Negroes have

---

[1] Commission on Civil Rights, *Political Participation* (Washington, D.C.: U.S. Government Printing Office, 1968), Part 2; and Bureau of Labor Statistics, Report No. 332, *Social and Economic Conditions of Negroes in the United States, 1967*, p. 87.

been elected to federal, state, and local offices in the country as a whole.

Negroes still encounter difficulties in voting in the South. There is discrimination in location of the polls and in the choice of election officials, harassment of Negro voters, and interference with Negro poll watchers. Negro names are omitted from voters' lists, and Negro ballots are disqualified on technical grounds. Negro votes are diluted by redistricting and reapportionment and by electing candidates at large. Negroes are prevented from running for office by extending the terms of white incumbents, by substituting appointment for election, by withholding certification of nominating petitions, and by increasing filing fees.[2] If the Negro's right to vote is fully to be assured, the law's enforcement must be continuous and detailed.

Access to public accommodations

Exclusion of Negroes from places of public accommodation was long practiced openly in the southern states and informally but effectively in the North. For half a century, from 1896 to 1946, such discrimination was held to be constitutional under the separate-but-equal rule. Then the law began to change. From 1946 to 1956, the separate-but-equal rule was reversed by the federal courts in a series of decisions outlawing segregation in interstate buses, swimming pools, restaurants, and parks and playgrounds. Statutes forbidding discrimination in public accommodations were enacted by 29 states in the North and West. In many cases, these laws were enforced through the same procedures as those used in attacking discrimination in employment.

In practice, the change in the legal status of segregation had little effect. Noncompliance was easy. Negroes who sought to register at hotels were told that all the rooms had been reserved. Negroes who sought to eat in restaurants found that service was delayed. Those who suffered such discrimination did not file complaints. Public prosecutors did not bring suits. Discrimination was modified in the North; it continued unabated in the South. Then, in 1955 and 1956, Negroes in Montgomery, Alabama, under the leadership of Rev. Martin Luther King, conducted a boycott of the city's bus lines, forcing them to abandon segregation. Thereafter, supported by sympathizers from

[2] Commission on Civil Rights, *op. cit.*, Part 3.

the North, they brought pressure to bear on other places of public accommodation by adopting tactics of nonviolence. They staged sit-ins in restaurants, took "freedom rides" through the South, ignored the segregation of transport facilities, and carried on other peaceful demonstrations of protest. Gradually, under this pressure, refusal of access to public places began to give way.

In 1964, the federal government entered the field. Along with its sections forbidding discrimination in voting, in employment, and in programs receiving federal aid, the Civil Rights Act of that year outlawed exclusion from public accommodations. One provision of the Act forbade commercial establishments such as motels, lunchrooms, filling stations, and movie theaters, where their operations affect interstate commerce, to refuse service because of race or color. For enforcement of this prohibition it called, first, for prosecution by the states; second, for federal conciliation; third, for individual suits for injunctive relief; and fourth, where there is a general pattern of discrimination, for suits by the Attorney General. Another provision of the Act forbade exclusion because of race or color from publicly owned facilities such as libraries, swimming pools, and municipal golf courses. To enforce this provision, complaints can be filed with the Attorney General, and if the complainant cannot afford the cost of litigation, the Attorney General will sue in his behalf.

In a survey of the southern states conducted in 1967, the *New York Times* found compliance with the antidiscriminaton law to be spotty. It found Negroes voting and holding public office, working side-by-side with whites, using the same water fountains and rest rooms, staying at good motels and dining in good restaurants, attending universities and playing on athletic teams. But it found them denied admission to small-town hotels and restaurants and relegated to the balconies in movie houses. It found no Negro clerks in department stores and no Negroes among the congregation in white churches.[3] Desegregation had come a long way; it still had a long way to go.

Freedom to exercise civil rights

The decisions of the federal courts and the enactments of Congress evoked violent resistance in the South. Negroes were threatened and

[3] New York Times, May 29, 1967.

198 Attacks on inequality of opportunity

attacked by whites when they sought to vote, to enroll in universities, to take their children to white schools, to obtain service in restaurants, to use transport facilities, and to enter public parks and libraries. More than a hundred workers for civil rights, both black and white, were murdered within a dozen years. Yet in only four cases were those guilty apprehended, tried, and sentenced to imprisonment. Indeed, the police themselves resorted to violence, attacking peaceful demonstrators with dogs, clubs, fire hoses, and cattle prods, and making mass arrests. In one case, officers of the law were charged with complicity in murder.

To cope with this situation, the Johnson administration introduced bills in Congress in 1966, 1967, and 1968 providing for the imposition of criminal penalties on private individuals and public officials who threaten or attack persons for exercising their constitutional rights. In 1966, such a bill was passed by the House of Representatives but killed by a filibuster in the Senate. In 1967, another bill was passed by the House but not reported out of committee in the Senate. In 1968, a third bill was languishing in Congress, with little prospect of enactment. Then, following the assassination of Martin Luther King, it was quickly passed and signed by the President.

The Civil Rights Act of 1968 makes it a criminal offense to injure, intimidate, or interfere with any person, whatever his race or color, because he was registering, voting, campaigning for office, acting as an election official or a poll watcher, serving on a jury in a federal court, applying for or holding a federal job, or participating in a federal or federally assisted program. It also makes it a criminal offense to injure, intimidate, or interfere with any person because of his race or color, who seeks to serve on a jury in a state court, to attend a public school or college, to work for a state, local, or private employer, to join a labor union, to participate in a state or locally administered program, to use a common carrier, or to obtain access to public accommodations. The law gives protection, as well, to persons who urge or help others to exercise these rights. Violation of its provisions is punishable by a fine of $1,000, imprisonment for a year, or both; in cases of physical injury, it is punished by a fine of $10,000 and 10 years in prison or both; and in cases of death, by imprisonment for life. The federal government is thus equipped to enforce the rights guaranteed by the Constitution where state and local governments fail to do so.

Open housing

The form of racial discrimination that has been most resistant to change is discrimination in housing. White people have been willing to accept equality in other fields—in employment, in public accommodations, even in education—before they would accept it in housing. Segregation in housing long had the support of local, state, and federal governments. The first city ordinance outlawing discrimination in private housing was not enacted until 1957. The first comprehensive state law forbidding such discrimination was not passed until 1959. The federal government did not put an end to discrimination in the rental or sale of federally aided housing until 1962. Congress did not prohibit discrimination in private housing until it passed the Civil Rights Act of 1968.

Government support for segregation

Members of minority groups were excluded from residential areas for scores of years by the way in which local governments administered their zoning laws and building codes and controlled their water and sewerage services. They were also excluded through enforcement by the courts of covenants written into deeds of sale binding the buyers not to resell to persons belonging to specified races, religions, or nationalities. In 1917, a municipal ordinance establishing racially segregated housing zones was found by the Supreme Court to violate the Fourteenth Amendment to the Constitution. In 1948, restrictive racial covenants in deeds of sale were also held to be unconstitutional. A property owner could still refuse to sell to Negroes, and a purchaser could promise that he would not make such a sale. But his compliance with this promise could no longer be enforced by the courts.

In the case of public housing, which was financed for the most part by the federal government and administered by municipal housing authorities, policy governing occupancy was left to these authorities. As a result, most of the projects were initially segregated on a separate-but-equal basis. During World War II, the authorities abandoned this policy, moving toward one of nondiscrimination. But they continued to give preference to families who had been displaced by slum clearance and to other families with low incomes. More Negroes than whites were able to qualify. So public housing continued to have a high proportion of Negro occupancy. Four fifths of such projects are still occupied by a single race; almost always by Negroes.

The Federal Housing Administration insures mortgages, thus encouraging expansion of the supply of credit made available for housing. For many years, the FHA took the position that racial homogeneity was essential to a neighborhood's financial stability. It therefore placed higher valuations on properties in neighborhoods that were white than in those that were mixed. This policy served as a powerful inducement to segregation. After restrictive racial covenants in deeds were held to be unconstitutional, the FHA stopped insuring properties where such covenants applied. But it continued to tolerate discrimination, providing insurance where builders would not sell, mortgagors would not lend, and owners would not rent to Negroes. In 1962, President Kennedy issued an executive order reversing this policy. The order forbade discrimination in the sale or rental of all housing owned or financed by the government. But it applied only to future transactions; existing segregation was not disturbed.

State and local fair housing laws

Fair housing laws have been enacted by some 20 states and more than 40 cities. The earliest laws forbade discrimination only in the sale or rental of publicly owned or publicly aided housing. The present laws ban such discrimination in both public and private housing. New York City enacted the first municipal ordinance against discrimination in private housing in 1957. Colorado enacted the first comprehensive state law against such discrimination in 1959. A fair housing law was passed by the legislature of California in 1963. A constitutional amendment repealing the law and prohibiting such legislation in the future was put on the ballot in 1964 and carried by a vote of two to one. This vote was challenged, however, and was held by the supreme courts of the state and the United States to violate the Fourteenth Amendment. Since the repealer was unconstitutional, the law continued to stand.

The typical fair housing ordinance or statute applies to one- or two-family dwellings not occupied by their owners and to multiple dwellings containing a stated minimum number of apartments, usually from 3 to 10. It outlaws discrimination by owners, brokers, and mortgagors in renting, selling, and financing residential properties. It is administered by the same agency that controls discrimination in employment and enforced through the same procedures. A prospective tenant or purchaser files a complaint. The agency makes an investigation. It first attempts to obtain a settlement through conciliation. Failing this, it may hold a formal hearing and issue an order requiring that a dwelling be leased or sold. In some states, small criminal penalties are provided and a broker convicted of violating the law may have his license revoked. But action is seldom, if ever, carried this far.

In New York City, Negroes who experience discrimination are aided by organizations of private volunteers. If an apartment is advertised for rent and a Negro is told upon applying that it is no longer available, or if a house is advertised for sale and he is told that it has already been sold, he can appeal to such an organization for help. A white volunteer will visit the dwelling, posing as a prospective tenant or purchaser, will arrange to rent or buy it, and will make a deposit. The original applicant will then file a complaint with the enforcement agency. The owner or broker will be called before the agency and confronted by the Negro to whom he refused to rent or sell and by the white volunteer to whom he later agreed to do so. Facing the possibility of criminal prosecution, he may then agree to rent or sell to the Negro. One volunteer organization in New York handles 350 cases a year, obtaining satisfactory settlements in 210. If practiced by the enforcement agency, the process of entrapment by which such settlements are effected would be frowned upon by the courts. But here, entrapment is completed before the agency is notified. The procedure is legal, and it works.[4]

In general, enforcement of fair housing laws is weak. Action by an enforcement agency takes time. Before an order can be issued, the owner may rent or sell the dwelling in dispute. Then all that the agency can do is to order him to offer equivalent accommodations. But these may not be available. In Boston, between 1958 and 1962, complainants succeeded in getting accommodations in only one case out of four.[5] The usual outcome of a discrimination case is a promise in writing to comply in the future with the provisions of the law. But there is no way in which such a promise can be enforced. The process

[4] Edith Iglauer, "A Place to Live," *New Yorker,* September 25, 1966, pp. 188–220.
[5] Commission on Civil Rights, Massachusetts State Advisory Committee, *Housing in Boston,* 1963, chap. iv. See also *Report,* 1961, Book 4, *Housing,* chap. vi.

of conciliation, as we saw in Chapter 11, has been fairly effective in dealing with discrimination in employment. It appears to be much less so under the conditions obtaining in the market for housing.

The federal fair housing law

A section forbidding discrimination in housing was included in the civil rights bills introduced in Congress by the Johnson administration in 1966, 1967, and 1968. As drafted in 1966, the section would have outlawed discrimination in the rental, sale, and financing of all housing, single and multiple. Amended in the House to exempt owners of one-family dwellings, it was killed by a filibuster in the Senate. As presented in 1967, the section called for the application of its prohibitions to different types of housing in three stages. There was a flood of letters against the bill and little pressure for its enactment. It died in committee in the Senate. The fair housing measure was finally enacted into law as Title VIII of the Civil Rights Act of 1968.

The law forbids owners or brokers to indicate a racial preference in advertising a dwelling for rent or sale; to refuse to rent or sell a dwelling to any person because of his race, color, religion, or national origin; to falsely represent a dwelling as unavailable; or to discriminate in the terms or conditions of rental or sale. It forbids brokers to discriminate in providing services, or to engage in "block-busting," inducing owners to sell their homes by telling them that their neighborhood is being infiltrated by persons of another race. And finally, the law forbids mortgage lenders to discriminate in making loans.

Certain types of housing are exempted from these provisions. The law does not apply to persons owning no more than three houses who rent or sell them without the services of a broker. Nor does it apply to "Mrs. Murphy" housing—dwellings of two to four units, one of which is occupied by the owner. Elsewhere, the law is made effective in three stages, about 1.5 percent of the housing supply being covered in 1968, about 30 percent in 1969, and about 80 percent in 1970 and thereafter.

Provisions for enforcement are similar to those contained in other antidiscrimination laws. First, a complainant must seek relief wherever possible from state and local agencies before taking his case to the federal government. Here, as with employment, most cases from the North and West will be handled locally and cases from the South by the federal agency, since no state agencies exist. Second, at his own expense, the complainant may bring suit for relief and damages in a state or federal court. Third, he may file a complaint with the Secretary of Housing and Urban Development. The Secretary will investigate and attempt to effect a settlement through conciliation. If he fails in this, the complainant may bring suit. Fourth, where there is a general pattern of discrimination, the Attorney General may sue for its correction. And fifth, any person who injures, intimidates, or interferes with another on grounds of race, color, religion, or national origin because he has rented or bought a dwelling, or encouraged or aided others to do so, or opposed denial of their right to do so, is subject to criminal penalties. Here, too, responsibility for enforcement lies with the Attorney General.

While enactment of the fair housing law was pending, a black man and his white wife brought suit against the developer of a subdivision outside St. Louis, asking that he be ordered to sell them a house. The plaintiff contended that the developer's refusal to do so was in violation of the Civil Rights Act of 1866, still on the books, which declared that "All citizens of the United States shall have the same right, in every state and territory, as is enjoyed by white citizens thereof, to inherit, purchase, lease, sell, hold, and convey real and personal property." This Act had been passed to implement the Thirteenth Amendment which had freed the slaves. Up to this time, it had been held that the Amendment did no more than prohibit state laws upholding slavery. Now, in a decision handed down only a few weeks after Congress had passed the new fair housing law, the Supreme Court rejected this view. The Thirteenth Amendment it said empowered Congress to enact laws affecting individuals, whether sanctioned by state legislation or not. The Act of 1866 was a valid exercise of this power. Discrimination against a Negro seeking to purchase housing could be enjoined.[6] The prohibition in the Act of 1866 was more sweeping than that in the Act of 1968. It took effect immediately instead of being applied in stages. It covered all housing offered for sale or rent, making no exceptions for Mrs. Murphy apartments or single-family dwellings. But it contained no provisions for enforcement beyond the right to sue for injunctive relief.

Prospects for open housing

Steps have been taken by private groups as well as by governments to promote desegregation of housing. Real estate services have been

[6] *Jones* v. *Mayer Co.*, 36 Law Week 4661.

established to bring together Negroes who are seeking to purchase dwellings outside of colored neighborhoods and whites who are willing to sell to them. White homeowners have been persuaded to welcome colored neighbors. Housing has been developed on a nonprofit basis for interracial occupancy, and efforts made to maintain fixed ratios of blacks and whites. Such undertakings have been carried forward in various places on a modest scale. They serve as demonstration projects, showing the owners of other dwellings that integration can be made to work.

But even if antidiscrimination laws are strengthened and vigorously enforced, even if the efforts of private antidiscrimination groups are redoubled, the concentration and overcrowding of Negroes in substandard housing in the urban ghettoes will not soon disappear. Desegregation encounters obstacles in the attitudes of both whites and blacks. The white homeowner fears that the character of his neighborhood would change. He fears, however mistakenly, that the value of his property, representing a large part of his savings, would decline. By open hostility or by mere unfriendliness, he makes it clear that Negroes are unwelcome. Many Negroes, on the other hand, prefer life in the ghetto among their friends and close to their churches and other organizations to social isolation in the suburbs. Most of them lack the income they would need to rent or buy in mixed communities. The Negroes who move into the suburbs as bars are lowered are families who are northern-born, are well-educated, and have high incomes. As this movement goes forward, they will be absorbed, on a minor but a growing scale. This is an opportunity that should be held open, without regard to race, to those who wish to take advantage of it. But as migration from South to North continues, and as births outrun deaths, the black population of the ghettoes will continue to grow. Something more than removal of barriers to housing will be needed if this larger problem is to be solved.

Toward racial equality

The Negro rebellion of our day is one of the most important movements in the nation's history. Its aims are revolutionary, but they are not radical. In general, the Negro does not seek to change the economic or the political order. He accepts the basic structure of individual enterprise and representative self-government. He asks only to share in its benefits. He demands equality—in opportunity for education and employment, in access to public accommodations, and in a decent place to live. He demands an equal right to vote and to hold office, equal treatment by the police and by the courts, equality in the provision of public services. More fundamentally, he seeks to escape from second-class citizenship and to throw off the stigma of slavery. He asks recognition for his human dignity.

Prejudice and discrimination

There are those who say that the problem of race will solve itself in time. A century ago, the ghettoes of our cities were crowded with immigrants—with Irishmen and Italians, with Russian and Polish Jews. These people were poor, despised, and mistreated, as the Negroes are today. But they moved up and out of the ghettoes and were absorbed by the larger society. The Negro, so runs the argument, will do the same. But the cases are not alike. The immigrants were freemen; the Negroes were slaves. The immigrants differed from the earlier residents in culture; the Negroes differ in race; the taboo against intermarriage is strong. The immigrants had close family ties and high aspirations for their children; the Negro family has been less stable since the days of slavery; its level of aspiration has been low. The immigrants had labor skills and entrepreneurial experience; the Negroes have had neither. The immigrants advanced by serving urban political machines; this route is less open today. The immigrants were absorbed, but the process took three generations; the Negro migration to northern cities has been going on for only 25 years, and the process of absorption has barely begun.

Psychologists tell us that three out of four white American adults are prejudiced against members of minority groups, their attitudes shaped by ethnic stereotypes that are neither reasoned nor open to reason. Such prejudice is not innate; it is acquired during childhood without conscious intent; it governs conduct during adolescence and throughout later life. Discrimination grows out of prejudice. It appears when members of a privileged majority perceive in the emergence of an underprivileged minority a possible threat to their jobs, their families, or their homes. It grows stronger as the minority grows larger and as its situation is improved.

One means of preventing discrimination would be to do away with prejudice. This might be attempted in several ways: by exhortation, by intergroup contact, by education. None of these is really promising. Exhortation is ineffective; evidence and reason leave prejudice unshaken. Intergroup contact may operate to lessen prejudice if people with similar interests meet voluntarily to undertake common tasks. But contact does not necessarily improve understanding or evoke sympathy; where forced or laden with tension, it may increase hostility. Education could prevent prejudice, but it would have to be started at an early age, continued over a wide front for many years, and carried on with sufficient skill to offset a multitude of contrary influences. None of these conditions is likely to be realized.

Discrimination, fortunately, can be reduced though prejudice remains. It can be attacked indirectly by changing the situation out of which it grows. The mechanization of southern agriculture and the migration of Negroes to northern industry undermined the foundations of the caste system in the South and weakened the structure of segregation in the country as a whole. Discrimination can be challenged directly. It can be publicly denounced; it can be forbidden by law. Where opposition is overwhelming, agitation may evoke a backlash, laws cannot be enacted or if enacted cannot be enforced. But here, as with other legislation, complete agreement is not needed. Discrimination can be outlawed if there is a strong enough basis of support.[7]

Integration and black power

There are obstacles to racial integration not only in the attitudes of whites toward Negroes but also in the attitudes of Negroes toward whites. A survey of opinion among Negroes in 13 northern cities in 1967 found three fourths of them feeling that their conditions had been bettered, a fourth feeling they had not; a third feeling friendlier toward white people, a third unchanged, and a third less friendly.[8] Many Negroes feel that progress toward equality has been too slow; that whites have promised much and delivered little, raising hopes they have not satisfied. They feel that southern whites are prejudiced but honest and that northern whites are prejudiced and hypocritical. They are cynical, bitter, and hostile.

---

[7] See George E. Simpson and J. Milton Yinger, *Racial and Cultural Minorities* (3d ed.; New York: Harper & Row, 1965), chaps. xxii, xxiii.

[8] *Fortune*, January 1968, p. 148.

These Negroes reject the goal of racial integration. They fear that it would not produce equality; that integrated institutions would be run by whites; and that blacks would be granted no more participation than needed to keep them docile and subservient. They feel that integration would compel them to deny their cultural heritage—to repudiate their racial identity. Their goal is separate but equal treatment in a dual society. They thus return to the principle that the struggle for equality for a quarter of a century has sought to destroy.

Separatism envisages the existence, side by side, of two economies and two societies, one white and one black. Economically, it holds little promise. The sources of employment opportunity are predominantly white. New plants and offices are being built in the suburbs; to be within reach of them, housing must be scattered and not concentrated in city centers. Negro entrepreneurs will not be granted a monopoly of the Negro market. Negro consumers will be better off if Negro businessmen are compelled to meet the competition of whites. Socially, too, separatism is undesirable. It repudiates the principles of individual dignity and equal opportunity. It requires that men be judged not by their essential qualities but by the color of their skins. It cannot be accepted as the ultimate goal of a democratic society.

In the long run, however, the consequences of integration and of separatism may not be as different as they seem. The door to opportunity should be open to all, whatever their aims may be. Those who have the desire and the ability to pass through it will do so. Those who lack them will not. Negroes who have more education and higher incomes will continue to be assimilated in a mixed society. For the time being, the less educated and the poor will not. But as greater opportunities for employment are provided, as education is bettered, as incomes rise, as housing is improved, the process of assimilation will be expanded. Hopefully the separation of the country into two societies will not survive.

Some Negroes not only reject the goal of racial integration but they also reject the aid of white liberals in their struggle for equality, holding that progress can be made only through the exercise of black power. Black power has various meanings. For some, it means a resort to force. They feel that gradualism has failed; that reform through political processes will be resisted by whites; that violence alone is left. This view is erroneous: the record of progress over recent years is clear; the possibilities of further progress through political action are great. The view is also dangerous. Resort to force may shock the white community into awareness of problems too long ignored. But it can also evoke an angry and repressive reaction. White people have larger numbers and greater power than blacks. Open conflict could leave the Negro worse off than he is today. More progress toward equality is to be made through peaceful processes than through violence.

For others, black power means the organization of economic and political strength and its use in bargaining. It is manifested in strikes and boycotts, in elections, and in pressure on legislatures and on public officials. Through such methods, Negroes can obtain equality of treatment by employers, access to better housing, improved education for their children, and better community services. A majority in many major cities, they can take the reins of local government. This course is consistent with democratic institutions; it can produce results.

In a third meaning, consistent with either of the others, black power is an assertion of black identity and a demand that it be recognized. It frees the Negro from dependence on the white man. It gives him a new sense of belonging. It is a source of self-respect and pride. It is in this meaning that black power finds its principal significance.

PART IV

Attacks on poverty

Minimum wages

In half of the families whose incomes fall below the poverty line, the head of the family is employed. In some cases, he may be employed part-time or for only part of the year. But in others, though he works full-time, his wages are too low to lift his family out of poverty. To meet this situation, at least in part, legislation is enacted making it illegal to pay wages that fall below specified minima. This policy appears to offer a solution to the problem of poverty that is simple and direct. It has widespread popular support. But economists in general are critical. In their view, minimum wage laws are likely to do harm as well as good.

Minimum wage laws

In industrial countries, legislation on behalf of labor had its origin in humanitarian efforts to check the obvious abuses of industrialism. Children had been employed in mines and factories, stunting their growth and depriving them of educational opportunity. Women had been put to work for long hours and at night, under conditions that were harmful to morals and at tasks that impaired their strength. Men, too, had been exposed to industrial accident and occupational disease, working in surroundings that imperiled their safety and their health. Correction of these abuses was the purpose of the early labor laws.

Most of the legislation was concerned with matters other than wages. Child labor was forbidden before a certain age and set at a higher age where work was hazardous; its hours thereafter were limited, and night work prohibited. Employment of women in occupations that would endanger their health, safety, or morals was forbidden, and hours of employment in other occupations brought under control. Where men were employed in hazardous industries, safety regulations were established, and here, too, hours were controlled.

Minimum wage laws were first enacted in New Zealand in 1894, in Australia in 1896, and in Great Britain in 1909. The first minimum wage law in the United States was enacted in Massachusetts in 1912. Fourteen other states passed such laws in the next decade. These laws, however, were applied only to women on the ground that they were unorganized and therefore less able than men to obtain good wages through collective bargaining. Minimum wage protection was not generally extended to both sexes until the federal government entered the field in 1933.

State minimum wage laws

Under the law enacted in Massachusetts, advisory boards representing employers, workers, and the public were established, industry by industry, to recommend wage minima that would cover the cost of living in health and decency and be within the employers' ability to pay. These minima were published, together with the names of employers who were paying less. The only enforcement was through pressure resulting from this publicity. A second law, enacted by Oregon in 1912, also provided for the establishment of minima by joint boards. But employers paying less than the minima were made subject to criminal penalties. Fifteen states and the District of Columbia had minimum wages for women by 1923. In that year, the Supreme Court held the District law to be unconstitutional. This law provided for minima designed to cover the cost of living. The Court held that it violated the Fifth Amendment by depriving women of their right to enter into contracts to work for less than this.[1] As a result, most of the state laws were declared unconstitutional, repealed, or not enforced. By 1927, only five remained. Then, in the early thirties, more laws

---

[1] *Adkins* v. *Children's Hospital,* 261 U.S. 525.

were passed, requiring that minima be fixed to cover not the cost of living but the value of services rendered. In 1936, in a five-to-four decision, the Supreme Court held such a law, enacted in New York, to be unconstitutional on the ground that it violated the due process clause of the Fourteenth Amendment.[2] But in 1937, the same Court, in another five-to-four decision, upheld a law of the state of Washington requiring the establishment of minima to cover the cost of living.[3] The Court now held that states had the power to protect the health and welfare of women because of their weakness in bargaining. The constitutionality of state minimum wage laws for women was finally established.

By 1965, there were minimum wage laws in 38 states and the District of Columbia. Sixteen of them applied only to women; 23 applied also to men. Eight were restricted to a few industries; 31 covered most of the industries in their states. Fifteen provided for the establishment of minima by industry wage boards; 24 established statutory minima. These ranged from 16 cents per hour in Arkansas to $1.75 in Alaska. Those in 10 laws were over $1.25; those in 14 laws were under this amount. The state laws have significance in fixing minima only in small local enterprises. Minima in large establishments and in those engaged in interstate commerce are prescribed by federal law.

Federal minimum wage laws

The federal government first imposed wage controls in 1931, directing government contractors to pay their employees at the rates prevailing in their respective localities. Then, under the National Industrial Recovery Act adopted at the depth of the great depression in 1933, it required that maximum hour and minimum wage provisions be written into the so-called "codes of fair competition" that freed industries from the antitrust laws and permitted them to restrict production and to fix prices. The hour and wage requirement was based on the dubious assumption that a ceiling over hours would increase employment by spreading the work among more employees and that a floor under wages would contribute further to recovery by enlarging purchasing power. The wage minima, determined for each industry by a joint

[2] *Morehead* v. *New York ex. rel. Tipaldo,* 298 U.S. 587.
[3] *West Coast Hotel Co.* v. *Parrish,* 300 U.S. 379.

board and approved by the National Recovery Administration, ran from 12½ cents to 70 cents per hour. They became inoperative in 1935 when the NIRA was held to be unconstitutional in a unanimous decision of the Supreme Court.[4] Thereafter, minimum wages were required in three industries: in bituminous coal in 1935 in connection with the establishment of minimum prices; in the merchant marine in 1936 in connection with the subsidization of shipping; and in sugar beets in 1937 in connection with a producers' subsidy. The minimum wage in bituminous coal was held to be unconstitutional;[5] the minima in the other industries were not challenged in the courts. A comprehensive minimum wage law, and a lasting one, was finally obtained when the Fair Labor Standards Act was adopted by Congress in 1938 and was upheld by the Supreme Court in a unanimous decision in 1941.[6]

The Fair Labor Standards Act has two nonwage provisions. It forbids the shipment in interstate commerce of products of child labor. It fixes maximum hours, setting them since 1941 at 40 per week. This limitation, however, is not absolute. Overtime work is permitted if paid for at one and one-half times the basic rate. The overtime provision is really a means of increasing take-home pay. The other provisions of the law relate to minimum wages.

The Act departs from the pattern of the laws adopted by many of the states. It applies to men as well as to women, being justified not as protecting the weaker sex but as maintaining "the minimum standard of living necessary for health, efficiency, and general well-being." It does not provide for the establishment by advisory boards of different minima for different industries, but since 1945, it has required adherence to a single minimum prescribed for all industries by the law itself.

In the law's early years, the common minimum was approached with caution. It was set at 25 cents an hour in 1938–39, at 30 cents in 1939–44, and at 40 cents beginning in 1945. But provision was made for the appointment of committees, industry by industry, to determine how rapidly each industry could move toward the 40 cents minimum without creating unemployment and to recommend appropriate minima for promulgation by the government. Before this work was com-

---

[4] *Schechter* v. *U.S.*, 295 U.S. 495.
[5] *Carter* v. *Carter Coal Co.*, 298 U.S. 238.
[6] *U.S.* v. *Darby Lumber Co.*, 312 U.S. 100.

pleted, employment was so enlarged and wage levels so raised by World War II that the lowest wages paid exceeded 40 cents long before the date set in the law.

Congress has repeatedly extended the coverage of the Fair Labor Standards Act. At present, the law applies to almost all workers in mining, manufacturing, construction, transport, communications, and utilities and in federal, state, and local governments. It applies to employees of larger firms (those with sales over $250,000 a year beginning in 1969) in wholesaling, retailing, service trades, finance, insurance, and real estate. It applies to farms employing more than 500 man-days of labor per quarter (roughly seven men), perhaps a tenth of all farm labor. The law exempts proprietors and others who are self-employed, executives and administrators, professional employees, outside salesmen, learners and apprentices, and workers who are handicapped. It does not apply to domestic servants; to most employees in agriculture, forestry, and fisheries; or to workers in smaller firms in the trade and service fields. Altogether, in 1967 it covered 50,500,000 of the 62,000,-000 nonsupervisory employees in the United States, leaving 11,500,000 outside its scope.

As it has extended the coverage of the law, Congress has repeatedly raised the minimum wage. It raised the minimum to 75 cents in 1949, to $1 in 1955, and in gradual stages after 1961, to $1.25 by 1963 for those previously covered and by 1966 for those newly covered. The last increase in 1966 raised the minimum for those already covered to $1.40 in 1967 and $1.60 in 1968. It set the minimum for newly covered farm labor at $1 in 1967, $1.15 in 1968, and $1.30 in 1969. For other newly covered labor, it set the minimum at the same levels in these years and at $1.45 in 1970 and $1.60 in 1971. Unless Congress takes further action, there will thus be two minima in 1971: $1.30 for farm labor and $1.60 for all other labor. There is already agitation, however, to raise the minimum to $2.00 an hour.

Minimum wage administration

An effort to fix minimum wages raises a number of questions of principle and procedure. Is it better to establish minima in accordance with the findings and recommendations of advisory boards or to have them determined by legislative bodies and written into the laws? Is it better to establish different minima for different industries and locali-

ties or a single minimum applicable to all? According to what principles should minima be set? Once they are set, how can they be
enforced? These are the questions to which we turn in the section that
follows.

Issues in wage determination

Through painstaking study of conditions in particular industries, it
is possible for an administrative agency to determine how far the
government can go in fixing minimum wages without driving firms out
of business or depriving workers of employment. It is possible, too, for
such an agency in the light of new developments to determine how
soon the minima first established can safely be increased. When a
minimum is set by a legislative body, on the other hand, the figure
chosen is necessarily arbitrary; its impact cannot be foreseen. Its adjustment to changing circumstances is bound to be slow. Administrative
action is therefore superior to legislative action as a means of fixing a
minimum wage.

Whether different minima should be set for different industries or a
single minimum for all industries depends upon the purpose to be
served. Under the NRA, the purpose was to put a floor under wages in
every industry. In this case, different minima were required. A single
minimum would have been uneven in its effects. If set low to raise
wages in the low-wage industries, it would have done nothing for labor
in the higher wage industries. If set high to aid workers in the high-
wage industries, it would have created bankruptcy and unemployment
in the low-wage ones. With the Fair Labor Standards Act, on the other
hand, the purpose is to raise wages only in the low-wage industries,
where labor is poorly organized. It is assumed that wages in other
industries will be set at acceptable levels through collective bargaining.
Here, a single minimum suffices.

Whether different minima should be set for different localities or a
single minimum for the country as a whole also depends upon the
purpose to be served. Under the NRA, the purpose was to raise the
lowest wages in every region. Wages were lower in the South than in
the North. If a single minimum had been set at a level that would have
raised wages without creating unemployment in the South, it would
have had no effect on wages in the North. If it had been set at a level
that would raise the lowest wages in the North, it would have created

serious hardship in the South. Regional differentials were therefore incorporated in the minimum wage provisions of the NRA codes. With the Fair Labor Standards Act, however, the purpose is only to raise the lowest wages in the country. Here, again, a single minimum suffices. The impact of the law is lighter in the North and heavier in the South. In this way, minimum wages influence industrial location. By preserving regional differentials, the NRA encouraged the movement of industry from North to South. By establishing a single minimum, the FLSA discourages this movement.

Where minimum wages are based on recommendations that are made by advisory boards, as is still the case in 15 states, there is need for principles to govern their determination. Three such principles are usually stated: (1) that the minimum should assure a "living wage," one that is adequate for health and decency; (2) that it should assure a "fair wage," one that equals the value of the worker's services; and (3) that it should depend upon the employer's ability to pay. Each of these principles has its difficulties.

The minimum required to provide a living wage is determined by preparing a family budget. But family budgets, as we saw in Chapter 2, can be set at widely different levels, depending on the judgment of the budget makers regarding the goods and services required. On this basis, almost any minimum wage can be justified. A figure may be set, moreover, to cover the living costs of a single person or a family. A minimum for a woman may be fixed on various assumptions: that she gets something from her family and must earn only part of what she needs; that she is fully self-supporting; that she has both herself and dependents to support. Minima may also be fixed for families of varying composition and size. The resulting figures will vary accordingly. None of the minimum wages thus determined can be imposed if the employer is unable to pay. The figure finally adopted will be a compromise between what is held to be desirable and what is found to be possible. It will probably fall below the level that the cost-of-living budget would require.

In fixing a fair wage, an administrative agency can analyze the work performed and compare the wage that is paid for it with wages paid elsewhere. Where work differs in character, it can maintain accustomed wage differentials. Where the character of the work is the same, it can require that wages be brought into line. This is one of the methods that was used by the War Labor Board in approving increases in wages during World War II. But most of the wages with which it dealt were in the upper brackets. The method can be of little help in raising a low wage where the wages with which it must be compared are also low.

A minimum wage may be set, finally, on the basis of the employer's ability to pay. If this is to be attempted, the wage-fixing agency must decide whether the principle is to be applied to the individual ability of each employer or to the average ability of all the firms in an industry. If it is separately applied to each employer, marginal firms will be kept in business, few if any workers will lose their jobs, and few if any wages will be raised. If it is applied to the average wage-paying ability of an industry, firms that cannot afford to pay the average may be put out of business and their employees deprived of jobs. If it is applied to the wage-paying ability of the bulk of an industry's members, it will create hardship only for the small minority of firms and workers who are in its marginal fringe. This would appear to be the best solution. But it requires acceptance, as a matter of policy, of the amount of bankruptcy and unemployment that it may cause. If this approach is adopted, the wage-fixing agency must be given access to the books of all the firms concerned. It must assemble and analyze a large quantity of data. It must take into account all of the adjustments that employers could make in order to stay in business and pay the wages prescribed. While not impossible, the task would be formidable in the extreme.

Enforcement of minimum wages

A worker who has been paid less than the minimum wage prescribed by the Fair Labor Standards Act can bring suit to obtain the rest of the payments due him, plus damages, court costs, and lawyers' fees. Or he can file a complaint with the Wage and Hour Division of the Department of Labor. The Division investigates complaints received from employees, unions, competitors, and employers' associations and also makes investigations on its own initiative. It may sue to obtain an order that will compel an employer to pay the wages prescribed by law and to pay his employees any back wages that may be due. Willful violators are subject to a fine of up to $10,000 for the first offense and to a fine plus six months' imprisonment for the second.

Enforcement of the law is weak. Employers may evade it in various ways. They can falsely claim that workers are in categories that are exempt; the numbers they record as executives and administrators, as learners and apprentices, may be inordinately large. Where payment in kind has been part of the worker's compensation, they may cut it back. In some cases, employers have demanded a kickback, compelling workers to pay them for the privilege of getting and holding a job. Workers rarely bring suits themselves. Nor do they often file complaints with the Division. They may not be informed concerning their rights. They may fear reprisals if they are known to complain. The Division itself can barely begin to enforce the law, its staff being too small to inspect more than a twentieth of the establishments under its jurisdiction in any year. Where it has made inspections, it has found half of the concerns examined to be in violation. And from these concerns, it has collected less than half of the back wages that were due.

Effects of minimum wages

According to economic theorists, there are circumstances under which the imposition of minimum wages will cause unemployment and circumstances under which it will not do so. According to empirical studies of what has happened when minimum wages have been imposed, the minima have operated in many cases to throw people out of work. The magnitude of such displacement has not been great. Its incidence has been concentrated, however, on particular regions, industries, and firms, and on particular groups of workers. There are still important consequences of minimum wages that are unknown. Their most unfortunate effect is their operation as a barrier to the employment of young people who seek an opportunity for self support.

Economic analysis of effects

The economic theorist's analysis of the effect of a minimum wage on the volume of employment can be stated in nontechnical terms: (1) The wage of labor is set, as are other prices, at the level that brings demand and supply into equilibrium. At any lower level, the quantity demanded would exceed the quantity supplied; employers competing for labor would raise the wage. At any higher level the quantity supplied would exceed the quantity demanded; workers competing for jobs would lower the wage. (2) In a competitive market, the individual employer controls too small a part of the demand for labor to influence its wage by reducing the quantity he buys. He must therefore regard the wage as fixed. His only choice is to determine how many workers he will hire. (3) The employer will keep on hiring as long as he can make more money by doing so. He can make more money as long as the added product turned out by an added worker can be sold at a price that exceeds the worker's wage. He would forego a profit if he failed to hire a man who would contribute more to his income than to his costs. He would incur a loss if he hired a man who contributed less to his income than to his costs. He will therefore push his demand for labor to the point where the income resulting from the employment of a marginal worker and the wage paid that worker are in equilibrium. (4) As more workers are employed, the quantity added to output by an additional worker declines. The income that can be obtained by selling this output also declines. At a lower wage, the employer will find it profitable to hire more workers. At a higher wage, he will find it necessary to hire fewer workers. He will lay off men until he reaches the point where his marginal income and his marginal outgo are again in equilibrium. It follows (5) that when the government requires the payment of higher wages, the number of workers demanded will decline. Minimum wages in a competitive market for labor thus result in unemployment. This effect is shown on the accompanying graph.

Where employers do not compete for labor, the effect of a minimum wage is different. Under monopsony, where there is only one employer, he need not take the market wage as given. By hiring fewer workers, he can drive the wage down. He is not compelled by competition to pay an added worker as much as the worker is worth to him. He can thus increase his profits by curtailing the volume of employment. But if the government imposes a minimum wage, it will no longer be possible for the employer to reduce wages by cutting his demand for labor. It will be profitable for him rather to continue hiring as long as the worker's worth exceeds his wages. In this case, minimum wages operate not to reduce employment but to increase it.

These are the theoretical extremes. Actual markets for labor are neither perfectly competitive nor completely monopsonized but are imperfectly competitive. In these markets, economic theorists find several circumstances under which a minimum wage could be imposed without creating unemployment. This would be possible wherever the demand for labor is relatively inelastic, i.e., where an increase in a wage

The competitive employer's demand for labor

The downward-sloping curve shows the quantity of labor that the employer will hire at each of a series of wage rates. When the demand and supply of labor in the market have set the rate at $1.50 an hour, he will hire 300 men. If the government sets a minimum wage at $2, he will hire 250 men. The minimum wage law will deprive 50 men of their jobs.

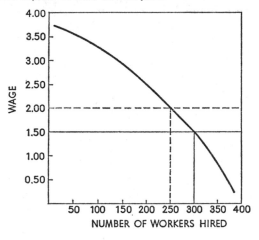

does not cause a proportionate decrease in the number of workers hired. This would be the case (1) where labor cost is so small a part of total cost that an increase in wages can easily be absorbed; (2) where the demand for the employer's product is so inelastic that he can pass the higher wage on to consumers in a higher price; and (3) in the short run, where the substitution of machinery for manpower is technically impossible. Wages may also be raised without creating unemployment (4) where an employer had not been maximizing sales or minimizing costs. Here, the need to pay a higher wage may shake him out of his lethargy and lead him to absorb the rise by increasing his sales effort and improving his managerial efficiency. And (5) employers can pay a minimum wage without reducing employment insofar as it operates to increase the productivity of labor by improving the worker's health, his skill, and his morale. The last of these developments takes time. In the short run, they will not prevent displacement of labor. In the long run, they may do so.

These possibilities are hypothetical; how far they may be actual is unknown. Where a minimum wage is imposed under other circumstances, however, it is clear that labor will be displaced. This will be true where the demand for labor is elastic because (1) labor cost is a large part of total cost, because (2) the demand for the employer's product is elastic, and because (3) machinery can be substituted in the long run for manpower. It will also be true (4) where the possibilities of expanding sales and cutting costs have been exhausted, and (5) where the productive capacities of the workers are not improved.

In the light of economic theory, then, it may be said that there are circumstances under which the imposition of a minimum wage will create unemployment and circumstances under which it will not do so. These circumstances vary from region to region, from industry to industry, and from firm to firm. To assess the effects of minimum wages, we must turn to studies that show what has actually happened when they have been imposed.

Empirical studies of effects

A number of studies have been made of the way in which the imposition of minimum wages has affected the volume of employment. Some of them have had to do with the effects of minimum wage laws enacted by the states. These have examined the influence of such laws on employment by retail stores in Oregon in 1913–14, by laundries in New York in 1933–35, by dry cleaners in Ohio in 1934–35, and by retailers in New York in 1957, and on comparative rates of unemployment since 1950 in labor markets that are covered and in those that are not covered by these laws. Other studies have analyzed the impact of the minimum wages established under the Fair Labor Standards Act in 1938 and by its successive amendments in 1949, 1955, and 1961 on employment in particular industries, most of them low-wage industries in the South.[7] A few studies have appraised the influence of these minima on the mechanization of production and on the structure of industry.

[7] See John M. Peterson, "Employment Effects of Minimum Wages, 1938–1950," *Journal of Political Economy*, Vol. 65 (1957), pp. 412–30; John M. Peterson, "Employment Effects of State Minimum Wages for Women," *Industrial and Labor Relations Review*, Vol, 12 (1959), pp. 406–22; Bureau of Labor Statistics, Report No. 155-1, *Minimum Wage Effects Studies*, 1959; G. Macesich and C. T. Stewart, Jr., "Recent Department of Labor Studies of Minimum Wage Effects," *Southern Economic Journal*, Vol. 26 (1959), pp. 32–35; and N. Arnold Tolles, "The Purposes and Results of U.S. Minimum Wage Laws," *Monthly Labor Review*, Vol. 83 (1960), pp. 238–42. The findings of these studies and the controversies concerning their significance are summarized in John G. Turnbull, C. Arthur Williams, Jr., and Earl F. Cheit, *Economic and Social Security* (3d ed.; New York: Ronald Press Co., 1967), pp. 602–8; and by Jacob J. Kaufman and Terry G. Foran in Sar A. Levitan *et al.* (eds.) *Toward Freedom from Want* (Madison, Wis.: Industrial Relations Research Assn., 1968), pp. 197–205.

The findings of the earlier studies of state minimum wage laws have been disputed. In general, these studies showed that the imposition of the minima was followed by reductions in employment but that the scale of such displacement was small. Colin D. and Rosemary G. Campbell compared the rates of unemployment from 1950 to 1965 in 75 market areas that had minimum wage laws and 71 that did not. They found that the rates were higher throughout the period in the markets that had the laws than in those that did not. But the excess was not great, amounting on the average to only 0.7 percentage points.[8]

The studies of the effects of the minima established under the Fair Labor Standards Act show substantial displacements of labor in particular industries: under the 40 cents minimum after 1938 among pecan shellers, tobacco stemmers, and cottonseed crushers; under the 75 cents minimum after 1949 among oyster canners, cigar makers, and the producers of men's cotton garments and seamless hosiery; under the $1 minimum after 1955 in 9 out of 12 manufacturing industries; and under the $1.25 minimum after 1961 in sawmills and retail establishments. The displacement in the nine manufacturing industries ranged from 3.2 to 15 percent; that in retailing stood at 11 percent. Having examined the effect of the $1 minimum in seven low-wage industries (wooden containers, cigars, textiles, and apparel) from 1955 to 1957, Albert Rees found that 27,600 workers, 3 percent of the labor force, lost their jobs. In 34 industries in 14 states, 11,200 workers, 1.7 percent of those employed were displaced. In 1961, the increase in the minimum wage was smaller and its impact less severe. But from 1960 to 1962, employment in limited-price variety stores declined by 6,900, a drop of 2 percent.[9] In a study of the effects of the federal minima of 75 cents and $1 on mechanization in manufacturing and on the structure of industry, David E. Kaun found that nonlabor inputs had increased at the expense of labor inputs and that the number of establishments operated by individuals and partnerships—presumably smaller enterprises—had declined.[10] The effects of the $1.60 minimum established in 1967 are as yet unknown. More than 10,000,000 persons, nearly a fifth of all non-

[8] Colin D. Campbell and Rosemary G. Campbell, "State Minimum Wage Laws as a Cause of Unemployment" (unpublished manuscript, 1968).

[9] Albert Rees, "Economic Expansion and Persisting Unemployment," Margaret S. Gordon and Robert A. Gordon (eds.), *Prosperity and Unemployment* (New York: John Wiley & Sons, Inc., 1966), chap. viii at pp. 333–36.

[10] David E. Kaun, "Minimum Wages, Factor Substitution, and the Marginal Producer," *Quarterly Journal of Economics,* Vol. 79 (1965), pp. 478–86.

supervisory employees in private industry, were working for less than $1.60 an hour at that time.

It is clear from these studies that minimum wages have operated to create unemployment in fact as well as in theory. The severity of this effect depends upon the level at which minima are set in relation to previous wages and in relation to other wages in the market. If a minimum is set at a figure that covers only, say, the most poorly paid tenth of the workers, it is unlikely to do much harm—or good. If it is set near the median wage, there is greater danger that unemployment will result. The state wage laws set their minima well below the median, raising wages in the bottom quarter of the scale without creating a large amount of unemployment. The minima in the federal law have been set close to the median wage in manufacturing; their effects, accordingly, have been more serious. But there is no evidence that they have caused widespread destruction of small business, whole-sale mechanization of production, or an overwhelming increase in un-employment.

But the studies have their limitations. First, they ignore the fact that the laws have not been vigorously enforced. A law that exists largely on paper cannot be expected to do much harm. Second, the studies do not isolate the influence of the wage laws from that of other factors that are at work. A failure of employment to decline after the mini-mum wage has been increased may be due to the fact that business has expanded and employment in general has grown. During inflation, for instance, a minimum fixed by law may fall below the poorest wages being paid. In such a situation, the law can have little effect. Third, the studies fail to reveal the possible influence of the minimum wage not only in creating unemployment but also in preventing an expansion of employment that might otherwise have occurred. Fourth, the studies are silent concerning the effect of minimum wages in fields that are exempt from coverage. It is possible that workers laid off in covered employments will crowd into uncovered employments, reducing wages there. This will give rise to demands for an expansion of coverage. And as coverage is expanded, the effect of an increasing supply of labor on a contracting free-wage market will be even more severe. Fifth, the studies do not tell us what happens to the workers who are displaced. To what extent are they absorbed by other indus-tries? To what extent must they be supported by charity? Sixth, the studies are silent concerning the effect of minimum wages on wages above the minimum. Where labor is organized, unions will insist that such wages be increased to reestablish preexisting differentials. Employers, moreover, may make such increases voluntarily. Here, too, higher labor cost may lead to mechanization and technological displacement. The upward movement of the whole wage structure may be inflationary in effect. Finally, the studies afford no answer to a question that is fundamental. Is the increase in wages paid to workers who are retained larger or smaller than the wages lost by those who are displaced? In short, is the net effect on the income of labor a gain or a loss? Economists hazard guesses, but nobody really knows.

The incidence of harmful effects

The impact of minimum wages is felt by particular regions, industries, firms, and workers. It destroys the economic advantage of labor-surplus, low-wage areas. It checks the migration of industry to the South and encourages the migration of southern labor to the North. Where an industry is passing out of existence as a result of contracting demand, a minimum wage speeds its demise, making the process of adjustment more painful than it otherwise would have been. Where an industry exists only by virtue of its ability to obtain labor at substandard wages, a minimum wage destroys it, eliminating the service it provides. Within an industry, the impact of a minimum wage is heaviest on the marginal, high-cost firm, possibly forcing it to close its doors. Where such a firm has been farther from the market than its competitors, this creates pockets of unemployment, leaving populations stranded to be supported on relief.

Among workers, the ones who are harmed by the minimum wage are those whose productivity is low: the aged, the handicapped, the unskilled, Negroes, women, and new entrants to the labor force. The law makes it harder for all these people to compete. Some of them lose their jobs; some of them never get jobs. The case of newcomers to the labor market is particularly serious. The law may price them out of the market before they can be trained, refusing them an opportunity to make a start toward self-support. This could be prevented by exempting them from coverage or by making them subject to a lower minimum. But this would add to the difficulty of enforcing the law.

Minimum wage policy

Minimum wage laws have raised the wages of millions who were poorly paid. If applied gradually with discrimination among regions, industries, and workers, and set at moderate levels, they can do some good without doing great harm. If applied swiftly without discrimination and set at high levels, they can do more harm than good, creating hardship for particular workers, industries, and communities.

It is said that the likelihood of these hardships should not deter the imposition of a minimum wage. Minima set at 50 cents to $1.30 an hour under state laws will pay a worker from $1,000 to $2,600 for a 40-hour week and a 50-week year, sums that fall far short of the $3,335 required in 1968 to keep an urban family of four out of poverty. The minimum set at $1.60 by the Fair Labor Standards Act will pay $3,200 which still fails to reach the poverty line. It is said that a region, an industry, or a firm that cannot pay these wages is parisitic in character, existing only by exploiting labor. Such a region should lose its workers to other regions where better wages can be paid. Such an industry should not continue to exist. Such a firm should be put out of business. If consumers do not value its product highly enough to pay its workers a living wage, they should get along without it.

But what is the alternative? It may be that people who otherwise could earn part of their own living are thrown entirely on charity and that youths who otherwise would start on a career of self-support are condemned instead to idleness. Would it not be better to permit these people to produce something, these youths to get a start in life, even though the value of their labor is not high enough to justify a living wage? Employment has some value in itself. It contributes to health, to skills, to dignity, to self-respect. It is clearly to be preferred to enforced idleness.

Where the worker's worth to the employer falls short of the income needed to keep him out of poverty, the dilemma might be resolved in another way. The government could require the employer to pay a living wage, but grant him a subsidy to make up the difference between the worker's worth to him and the wage he would have to pay. Or the government could permit the employer to pay the worker no more than his worth and give the difference between this figure and a living wage to the worker himself. Neither of these measures would afford the worker an incentive to increase his productivity. But neither does public assistance, as we shall see in the chapter that follows. Either measure would be difficult to administer. But so, too, is public assistance. And either one of them would cost less money than would be required to support displaced workers and their families in idleness.

As a general principle, poverty is not best to be attacked by excluding workers from opportunities for employment. This is true, as we saw in Chapters 4 and 11, of discrimination because of race or color or national origin. It is also true of discrimination against those whose labor is worth less than a living wage. Proponents of minimum wages must bear the burden of proof.

Public assistance

Governments in the United States—federal, state, and local—are spending nearly eight billion dollars a year distributing money under public assistance programs to nearly nine million Americans who are in need. Nearly four fifths of a million persons are aided through general assistance programs carried on by the several states. More than eight million are aided through a program that is designed for particular groups and financed in large part by federal grants. Among the recipients of this aid are nearly three million people who are aged, blind, or permanently and totally disabled. This part of the program is generally accepted as desirable and useful. The remaining recipients, numbering nearly five and a third million, include four million dependent children and one and a third million adults—most of them the children's mothers—who care for them. This part of the program has become a storm center of controversy. It is disliked by the legislators who vote the appropriations, by the taxpayers who foot the bill, and by the officials who are responsible for its administration. It is criticized by social workers and denounced by journalists. It is accepted by its beneficiaries with distaste. Here we have charity provided by government on a massive scale. But it would be difficult if not impossible to find its rival for unpopularity. In this chapter we shall review the character of the federally aided assistance program, its inherent problems, its serious shortcomings, past modifications in its operation, and proposals for future reform.

The federal-state assistance program

The federally aided assistance program, as we saw in Chapter 6, is but a part of the effort that is made by federal, state, and local governments to help those who are in need. Inaugurated in the great depression of the thirties, it was based on the assumption that responsibility for charitable relief lay with state and local governments and it was designed to reenforce their efforts by providing federal grants in aid. The program was supposed to be temporary in character, declining in importance as the growth of social insurance took over the burden of assuring security. Instead, public assistance has become a permanent part of the welfare effort and has steadily grown in magnitude and in cost, with the federal government coming to play an ever-increasing role. Today, the program is highly conspicuous, and the problems it raises are central to the welfare effort as a whole.

The pattern of public assistance

The federally aided assistance program provides for aid not to all of those who may be in need but only to those who fall within certain categories: the aged, the blind, the permanently and totally disabled, and the recipients of Aid for Families with Dependent Children (AFDC). This approach was adopted because it makes it easier to obtain support. Legislators are willing to vote funds for aid to persons in one category even though aid to those in another category may be under attack. The approach makes it easier, too, to provide aid on a more generous scale to those in one category than to those in another. The average monthly payments made in December, 1967, were $70.15 for the aged, $80.60 for the disabled, $90.45 for the blind, and only $39.50 for those receiving AFDC. The share of the cost met by the federal government varies from one category to another, standing at 67 percent for the aged, 48 percent for the disabled, 56 percent for the blind, and 55 percent for AFDC. These differences find no justification in the varying needs of the recipients. They are a testimony rather to the prejudices of the legislators.

Another characteristic of the categorical approach has been the absence of a federal contribution toward general assistance, i.e., toward payments by the states to persons who are in need for reasons other than those specified. As a consequence of this omission, such payments are lower than those made to the aged, the blind, and the disabled, averaging $39.40 in December, 1967, with payments ranging from as much as $80.25 in the District of Columbia to as little as $3.70 in Arkansas.

Organization for administration of assistance differs from state to state. In some states, local governments determine the eligibility of applicants and the amounts due them, make the payments, and keep an eye on the recipients, with the states establishing standards, supervising operations, and transmitting federal and state funds. Elsewhere, the program is administered entirely by the states, with local governments taking no part. In both cases, the federal government seeks to make sure that the program is honestly and competently administered. It requires that the program be in operation in every county in the state; that the state itself contribute to its cost; that it be supervised or administered by a single agency; that the employees of this agency be protected by a merit system; that benefits be available to all citizens; that they not be denied by imposing unduly restrictive residence requirements; that assistance be given only to those who are in need; and that applicants be assured fair hearings, the right of appeal, and prompt determination of their claims.

The federal government pays half of the state's administrative costs and three fourths of the cost of certain services rendered to recipients of aid. Its contribution to assistance given in cash is made in accordance with formulas that favor states that have lower per capita incomes and those that make smaller payments. In the case of the aged, the blind, and the disabled, its contribution is $31 of the first $37 per month plus 50 percent of the next $38 where a state's per capita income is above the all-state average and from 50 to 65 percent where it is below that average. In the case of aid for dependent children, the federal government contributes five sixths of the first $18 of a recipient's monthly benefit and 50 to 65 percent of the next $14 depending on the state's per capita income. For the program as a whole, in 1967 the federal government put up 58.6 percent of the cost; the states, 30.7 percent; and local governments, 10.8 percent.

The scope and level of assistance

The payments made under the public assistance program reach only a fourth of those whose incomes fall below the poverty line. Many who would be entitled to assistance do not apply for it. Others who are in need are excluded by requirements that limit eligibility. In many cases, payments are denied to persons who have not been in residence for a year or more. The purpose of this provision, of course, is to discourage migration to take advantage of the assistance offered by states where payments are more generous. But it discourages desirable mobility of labor. And it denies the needy aid that is financed in major part by the federal government. The Supreme Court has agreed to pass on the validity of this requirement in the term beginning in October, 1968. In the case of AFDC, another limitation on eligibility was a federal rule that denied assistance where both parents were at home, even though they were unemployed. This rule was designed to prevent the use of money for payments in cases where there was another potential source of support. But it deprived children of subsistence as long as their parents did not succeed in finding work. This limitation has now been removed, permitting the states to make payments in such cases, but only 22 states had taken advantage of this permission by the end of 1967.

Not only does the program fail to cover most of those who are in need but it also fails to meet the needs of those it covers. In principle, the amount of aid to be provided is that required to make up the difference between the recipient's income and the amount needed for a budget that would enable him to subsist and to satisfy his most urgent needs. The budgetary standards are established by the states, varying widely from state to state. In nearly every state, the level of living which they would permit falls well below the poverty line. In 1961 when a minimum subsistence budget for an AFDC mother with three children called for the expenditure of $2,580 per year, the standards prevailing in the states ranged from $1,255 in Arkansas to $2,213 in Washington. Even at these levels, in general, the payments actually made by more than half of the states fall short of their nominal standards by a third, in some cases by more than half.

There are wide differences in the assistance provided by the several states. In December, 1967, monthly payments to the aged ranged from

$44.70 in South Carolina to $120.55 in New Hampshire; payments to the blind from $45.60 in Mississippi to $136.85 in California; payments to the disabled from $48.50 in Mississippi to $127.20 in Iowa; and payments under AFDC from $8.40 in Mississippi to $60.75 in New York. In general, the payments provide only half of the amounts that are needed for bare subsistence; in some states, only a fourth of those amounts.

The growing burden of assistance

Recipients of public assistance have grown in absolute numbers from 4.6 million in 1940 to 8.1 million in 1967. But they have not changed greatly as a percentage of the population, rising only from 3.5 percent to 4.1 percent. As old-age benefits under the social insurance program have grown, recipients of old-age assistance have remained constant, numbering 2.1 million in 1940 and again in 1967; as a percentage of the population, they dropped by half. The numbers of the blind receiving assistance have declined, standing at only 82,000 in 1967. The numbers of the disabled receiving payments under a newer part of the program have grown from fewer than 400,000 in 1961 to nearly 650,000 in 1967. But the real cause of the increase in the burden of assistance has been the spectacular growth of AFDC.

The numbers receiving payments under AFDC rose from 1.3 million in 1940 to 5.3 million in 1967, from 2.2 percent of those under 18 years of age to 4.8 percent. In New York and California the figure is over 7 percent. In New York City alone, there are more than half a million recipients of AFDC. These numbers are still growing with continued migration from the South and with high birth rates in the ghettoes of the North. If the present trend continues, it is estimated that a tenth of the nation's children will be receiving aid in the early seventies.

When assistance of this sort was first provided by the states, the need the program was intended to meet was that of the widow, usually white, who had been left with dependent children. Today, nearly half of the recipients of such aid are black. A fifth of the mothers have never been married; two fifths have been deserted. A fifth of the children aided—two fifths in some cities—are illegitimate. AFDC has changed in character as it has grown in size.

Administration of public assistance

Among the difficulties that are encountered in the administration of public assistance, there are some that are inherent in the very nature of the undertaking. The activity in which the administrators are engaged is that of giving away money. They must make sure that it is given only to the persons who are entitled to receive it, for the purposes intended, and in the amounts required to satisfy these purposes. For this reason, they must inquire into the needs of the applicant for assistance and the extent to which his resources fall short of the amount required to enable him to meet these needs. In short, they must apply a means test. This is time-consuming and tedious. In practice, it involves an intrusion into the applicant's private affairs. At best, it is distasteful; at worst, humiliating. It creates a relationship between the applicant and the caseworker that makes for tension and dislike.

Even greater difficulties, not inherent in the nature of public assistance, are created by certain characteristics of the program as it exists in the United States. Many of the states deny aid to persons whose character is bad. Here, the caseworker must inquire not only into the applicant's needs but also into his morality. States have cut off aid from AFDC mothers who had men living with them. Investigators have had to search their homes, without warning, to determine whether any men were there. As a result, the relationship between the recipient of aid and the investigator has become one of active hostility. The program, moreover, has had built-in disincentives to orderly family life and to gainful employment. Its staff has been poorly trained, poorly paid, and overworked. Its morale has been low. Its rate of turnover has been high.

Determination of eligibility

Public assistance can be given only to those who are legally eligible. It is therefore necessary to check on each applicant's eligibility. Does he fall into one of the categories covered by the law—is he over 65, blind, permanently and totally disabled, or caring for a dependent child? Has he resided in the state for a year or more? Is he really in need? And, in some states, is he of good moral character?

Determination of need raises several questions of policy. First, if the applicant has any property, should he be required to liquidate it and exhaust the proceeds before he can obtain assistance? If he owns a home, should he be required to sell it? If he has an insurance policy, should he be required to surrender it? If he has securities, a bank account or valuable personal property, should he be required to dispose of them? Since the rent the applicant would have to pay for other quarters might equal the cost of maintaining his home, he is usually permitted to keep it. If the indemnity payable under his insurance policy does not exceed the cost of burial, he is permitted to keep the policy as well. Beyond this, a small sum may be retained. But all other savings must be exhausted before assistance payments will be made. Second, if the applicant earns money or if children living at home earn money, will assistance be denied? If so, parents and children are both discouraged from working and the children are encouraged to leave home. In general, most earnings of the blind and minor earnings of the aged are ignored and children are allowed to keep some part of what they earn. But other earnings reduce or prohibit aid. Third, should relatives be required to contribute to the support of the needy before assistance payments will be made? Should not a son be compelled to support his aged parents or a man to support his wife and children? The answer is not as easy as it seems. The relatives of poor people are likely also to be poor. Even where relatives could help, inquiry into their ability to do so would engender resentment, and efforts to force contributions might so exacerbate family relations that persons entitled to aid would not apply. Nor is it easy to locate and collect from absent fathers. The mothers may not know where they are or, if they know, may be reluctant to tell. If a father is apprehended, he can be jailed for nonsupport. But he will contribute nothing to the family as long as he remains in jail. The cost of enforcing the liability of relatives might well exceed the payments it would save.

A number of states deny aid to persons whose character is bad: to men with criminal records and to women whose morals are loose. This limitation is designed not only to punish the wicked but also to deter the good from falling into evil ways. But there is no evidence that the threat of deprivation will induce the sort of behavior that the state desires. When AFDC payments are denied, moreover, it is the parents who have been wicked and the children who are punished for their wickedness. Until 1968, nineteen states refused AFDC payments to children whose mothers engaged in extramarital sexual intercourse. This rule enabled the states to exclude some 500,000 children from their assistance rolls. In justification, it was argued that a mother who engaged in extramarital intercourse had thus provided her children with a "substitute father" who could be held responsible for their support. Under the provisions of the Social Security Act, the rule was held to be invalid in a unanimous decision handed down by the Supreme Court in 1968.[1]

To determine eligibility, the public assistance caseworker interviews the applicant, his relatives, and others who know him, assesses the truthfulness of his statements, and appraises the evidence submitted in support of his claim. If the process is thorough, more time may be spent in denying assistance than in providing it. If the process is hurried, the decisions to which it leads may be wrong. An applicant who is found to be eligible by one caseworker may be rejected as ineligible by another. Aid may be denied not only to some who are not entitled to it but also to some who are.[2]

Determination of payments

Once it has been determined that an applicant is eligible for assistance, a caseworker must decide how much he is to be paid. The worker makes a separate computation in each case. First, he prepares a budget to cover the applicant's needs. In doing this, he is guided by a standard budget adopted by the state, specifying the amounts to be allowed for each item consumed by each member of a family. Second, the worker examines the applicant's resources, discovering what he owns in the way of housing, furnishings, and clothing, what savings he has, and what his earnings may be. This may require him to inspect the applicant's home, interview his neighbors, and check with his bank. Third, the worker subtracts the applicant's resources from his budget to determine the size of his budgetary deficit. This is supposed to be

---

[1] *King* v. *Smith*, 36 U.S. Law Week 4703.
[2] See Hilary M. Leyendecker, *Problems and Policies in Public Assistance* (New York: Harper & Bros., 1955), chaps. x, xi; Duncan M. MacIntyre, *Public Assistance* (Ithaca, N.Y.: New York State School of Industrial and Labor Relations, 1964), chap. iii; and Elizabeth Wickenden and Winifred Bell, *Public Assistance: Time for a Change* (New York: New York School of Social Work, 1961), pp. 23–33, 72–77; Winifred Bell, *Aid to Dependent Children* (New York: Columbia University Press, 1965), chaps. v, vi.

the figure at which payments will be made. In many states, however, those receiving assistance get only part of this amount.

The process of determining payments is less objective than this description would suggest. The standards established by the states do not cover all contingencies. Special circumstances call for supplementary grants. Should a man be allowed by buy a set of false teeth? Should a woman be allowed to buy a new stove? Should a daughter be allowed to buy a new dress when she graduates from school? In each of these cases, the claimant must plead for a grant. And the latitude given the caseworker in approving or disapproving his request is wide. Decisions regarding intimate matters of personal conduct are thus left to minor officials of the state.[3]

Assistance may take the form of services or of cash. Where medical care is provided, the assistance agency may pay the doctors or other personnel employed. Most payments, however, are made in cash and the recipients are left to purchase the goods and services they need. In 1967, some $2 billion was paid directly to vendors of medical services and more than $5 billion was distributed in cash.

Disqualification for assistance

Families receiving assistance are subject to continued surveillance. Caseworkers may go uninvited into their homes to scrutinize their housekeeping methods and their child-rearing practices. This is done in order to make sure that money being given for care of the needy is serving its intended purpose. Where the money is being wasted or diverted to other uses, the situation can be corrected or the aid can be stopped. Such oversight may be defended as an exercise of prudence. But it invades the privacy of the recipient. It puts him at the mercy of a bureaucrat. It clothes assistance with humiliation.

The method of surveillance that has aroused the greatest objection is that employed in enforcing the "man in the house" rule. If there is no man in the house, the government contributes to the support of a woman's dependent children. If a man is living with her, he is held responsible for their support. But a man may visit the home clandestinely, escaping this obligation and leaving the burden to the state. Where it is known that this has happened, assistance payments are cut

---

[3] Leyendecker, *op. cit.*, chaps. vi, vii; and MacIntyre, *op. cit.*, chap. iii.

off. The way this evidence has been obtained in some places is by making nighttime raids to discover whether a woman has a partner in her bed. This procedure has not been challenged in the courts, but it would seem to violate the constitutional guarantee against unreasonable searches. In any case, it serves to turn dispensers of public charity into policemen and leads the recipients of charity to view them with hostility.[4]

The problem of disincentives

Some of the rules adopted to prevent unnecessary outlays on public assistance have operated as disincentives to family living and to work. In most states, until 1962, no AFDC was given where a man was living with his family, even though he had no work. If a woman had illegitimate children, she received assistance; if she married their father, assistance was stopped. If a man lived with his family, he could watch them go hungry; if he abandoned them, assistance would enable them to eat. The effect of this rule was to encourage promiscuity and illegitimacy, to break up families receiving assistance, and to perpetuate dependency. An amendment enacted in 1961 altered this situation by permitting the states to make assistance payments in cases where a father living with his family was unemployed.

The program has also created a disincentive to work. Where an AFDC parent—usually a mother—had any earnings, it was assumed that her budgetary deficit had been lessened by the same amount, and a dollar was deducted from her check for every dollar she had earned. In effect, this rule imposed a tax of 100 percent on work. In most states, if a recipient of assistance took a full-time job, her assistance checks were stopped. If she was then laid off, it took her some time to get back on the assistance rolls. Employment was uncertain; assistance, once obtained, was not. It would be difficult to imagine an arrangement more discouraging to work. This situation was modified by an amendment enacted by Congress in 1967. Recipients of AFDC are now permitted to earn $30 per month without having their checks reduced; above this figure, the government deducts two thirds of what they earn. At this

---

[4] See Herbert Krosney, *Beyond Welfare* (New York: Holt, Rinehart & Winston, 1966), chap. vi; and Richard M. Elman, *The Poorhouse State* (New York: Pantheon Books, 1966), *passim;* "Welfare's 'Condition X,'" *Yale Law Journal,* Vol. 76 (1967), pp. 1222–33.

level, the tax on earnings stands at 66⅔ percent, still affording a disincentive to work.

The welfare workers

There are around 50,000 caseworkers employed in the administration of public assistance. Nine tenths of them have had no graduate training in social work. Only 1 percent of them have earned a social work degree. Most of them are recent college graduates, though a college education is not needed to prepare them for the work they actually do. They receive little training on the job. Typically, a worker is given a quick orientation, assigned a case load, and turned over to a supervisor who is himself inadequately trained. These young people are called caseworkers and think of themselves as such. But as the term is used by social workers, the designation is unearned.

The caseworker spends four fifths of his time determining eligibility and computing the payments that are due. He spends much of the rest investigating the behavior of those receiving aid. He is a clerical worker submerged by an avalanche of paper forms, a detective apprehending violators of the law. Typically, the worker's case load is heavy. His contact with his cases is necessarily hurried and infrequent, affording no opportunity to become well enough acquainted to develop a bond of sympathy. He would not have time to render social-work services if he were trained to do so.

The relations of those who give assistance and those who receive it are strained. The caseworker is likely to distrust the recipient of aid, to view his dependency with disdain. As an adviser, he may be condescending. As an investigator, he becomes an enemy. The recipient is likely to regard the caseworker with scorn, as one whose function it is to maintain docility among the poor. When requests for supplementary grants are denied, when he is disqualified and aid cut off, his scorn turns into hatred. Between the caseworker and the recipient of aid there is a perpetual state of war. So serious is the situation that workers in some cities have feared for their safety and have refused to conduct investigations unless protected by the police.

Along with the worker's heavy case load, the drudgery of clerical work, and the atmosphere of antagonism have gone low pay, a total absence of prestige, and the lack of any hope of accomplishment. As a result, morale has been low and the rate of turnover has been high. The quality of assistance administration has suffered accordingly.[5]

Relief or rehabilitation?

As originally envisaged, it was the purpose of public assistance to assure a minimum of subsistence for adults who were in need and to provide for the care of dependent children. This was to be done by giving them small amounts of cash. The program was frankly a palliative, not one through which the causes of poverty were to be attacked. In time, however, it came to be argued that the program's emphasis should be shifted from relief to rehabilitation; that its beneficiaries should be made self-supporting; that dependency should be lessened and the need for assistance payments reduced. This approach would give more help in the form of services and less in the form of cash. It was the approach of the social worker who viewed poverty as a matter of maladjustment that was to be corrected through the methods of casework. The view that emphasis should be shifted to rehabilitation was endorsed by Congress in 1962 in a series of amendments to the public assistance law. This enactment was hailed by social workers as a landmark in welfare history. But its influence on the character of the assistance program has not as yet been great.

Cash and services

The welfare effort of federal, state, and local governments includes a great variety of services: educational projects, health care, vocational training, job counseling and placement, protection for abandoned and neglected children, day care for small children, family planning, and the like. Such services are helpful and indeed essential, meeting needs that would otherwise be unfulfilled. But they put no food in empty stomachs. They do not obviate the need for cash.

The comparative merits of services and money as means of helping the needy have long been a subject of popular debate. In support of services, it is argued that recipients of aid may be irresponsible or incompetent; that they may divert the money given them to frivolous

---

[5] Edgar May, *Wasted Americans* (New York: Harper & Row, 1964), chap. vi; and Wickenden and Bell, *op. cit.*, pp. 101–8.

consumption; that services, by contrast, are certain to provide the poor with what they need. In support of money payments, on the other hand, it is argued that they are less paternalistic than services; that they promote responsibility, being used, in fact, for things the family needs; that they permit desirable flexibility in spending; that they are relatively inexpensive to administer. In practice, government must use both forms of aid. Some needs, such as child protection, can be met only by rendering services. Others, such as the need for food and clothing, can be met only by providing cash. The question is not which method is to be used to the exclusion of the other but what the relative emphasis is to be.

Another disputed issue is whether money and services should be provided jointly or separately. Those who favor joint provision argue that applicants for monetary aid can be rendered needed services for which they would not have applied; that monetary aid is more effective when accompanied by services; that services are more effective when accompanied by cash. Those who favor separate provision, on the other hand, argue that services should be provided to all without regard to income, avoiding the stigma attached to aid to those in need; that tying services to money coerces those applying for aid to accept them, whether they want them or not; that the administrative burden of providing monetary aid is so heavy that the service function would be neglected if the two were combined. In practice, administration of public assistance and welfare services has not been sharply separated. And under amendments enacted in 1962, they can be formally joined.

The social work approach

In its earlier years, social work was content to extend a helping hand to the deserving poor, easing their burdens and pointing the way to a better life. Today, the social worker sees himself in a different role. He views the poor as people who are maladjusted—as misfits who are unable to conform. He conceives his function as that of promoting social adaptation. His method is casework, involving psychiatric diagnosis, personal counseling, and emotional therapy. The product of his successful effort is a person who has attained harmonious adjustment to society's demands.

The social worker thinks of himself as a member of a profession, equipped with a unique combination of knowledge and skills acquired through training and experience. He craves professional recognition, asking that social work practitioners be examined and licensed as are physicians, and that administration of welfare programs be confined to licensees. He asks, too, that public funds be provided for social work education so that the supply of trained workers will be large enough to satisfy the demand.

The social worker's conception of his role has not escaped criticism. First, it is said that he accepts society, with all its evils, as given; that he fails to see that dependency is caused not only by shortcomings of the individual but also by the character of his environment; that he diverts attention from the need for social reform. Second, his method is costly in time and money; it requires the devotion of hours of skilled service to every case; it limits help to a small fraction of those who are in need. Third, the social worker's efforts are unlikely to be effective: his cases return to the slums whence they came; the forces that caused their troubles are still at work; improvement, if accomplished, is unlikely to endure.

The social worker's professional pretensions are also criticized. In social work education, there is no discrete body of knowledge and skills. There is nothing in the social worker's training that uniquely equips him to deal with the poor on the public assistance rolls. There is no proof of the efficacy of his techniques.[6]

The 1962 amendments

In the words of President Kennedy, the amendments to the public assistance law enacted by Congress in 1962 embodied "a new approach—stressing services in addition to support, rehabilitation instead of relief, and training for useful work instead of prolonged dependency."[7] Under this legislation, the federal government offered to pay 75 percent of the cost of services proposed by the states for incorporation in their programs of public assistance. These services might take a wide variety of forms, provided they fell within guidelines laid down by the federal Welfare Administration and had the Administration's specific approval. They might be rendered in connection with assistance to the aged, the blind, the disabled, or to dependent children.

[6] See Barbara Wootton, *Social Science and Social Pathology* (London: George Allen & Unwin, Ltd., 1959), chap. ix.
[7] *Social Security Bulletin*, Vol. 25 (1962), p. 10.

They might even be given as a preventive measure to persons who were not already dependent but were in danger of becoming so.

In the case of children, there were two federally aided programs: a program of child welfare services and AFDC. In many states, the former program covered some counties but not others. The new legislation made coverage mandatory by 1975. It required coordination of welfare services and AFDC and ordered the preparation of a "social study and plan for services" for every AFDC child. It encouraged the establishment of work and training programs for AFDC parents who were unemployed. In cases of parental abuse or neglect, it provided for payments to put AFDC children in foster homes.

These amendments were welcomed as a Magna Carta for social work. Their emphasis on rehabilitation rather than relief, on the provision of services along with monetary support, evinced acceptance of the social work philosophy. The amendments were welcomed, too, by politicians, since they appeared to promise more self-help and less dependency, a reduction in assistance rolls, and a curtailment of assistance costs. These hopes, however, are far from being realized. Some states have made progress in providing services, but more have not. The character of the assistance program is unchanged. The funds appropriated are still too small to provide adequate support for those in need. The staff is still too small to do more than manage their distribution. Provision of services along with monetary aid would require large increases in appropriations and in administrative personnel. These have not been forthcoming. The significance of the 1962 amendments has been oversold.

The politics of public assistance

There have been differences within the states between those who have sought to make more adequate provision for the needy and those who have sought to keep taxes down. There have been differences, too, between state and federal governments regarding the administration of federal grants. But, by and large, the public assistance program has not been tainted by politics. Political influence has not been used to put people on the assistance rolls. Politicians have not sought to garner votes by promising larger payments. Congress has not acted in response to pressure from recipients of aid. Through most of its life, the program has encountered little opposition, enjoying broad political support. In recent years, however, the serious problems of AFDC have brought it under attack. And in 1967, this attack led to the enactment of amendments that subjected the program to serious restraints.

The assistance constituency

Most of the groups that benefit from congressional action are organized to exert political pressure. This has not been the case with public assistance. In certain cities in recent years, recipients of assistance have organized to protest alleged inequities in its administration. There have been demonstrations at welfare centers; records have been scattered and destroyed. But there has been no effective organization on a national scale. Annual appropriations running into the billions have nonetheless been made. The program, though still far from adequate, has constantly been enlarged; the federal government's share of its cost has steadily been increased. Congressional action has been almost automatic. Hearings on appropriation bills have usually been perfunctory. Enactment has followed with little or no debate. This seeming miracle has a simple explanation. Senators and representatives are both aware that state officials want the federal government to bear more of the assistance burden so that the states can bear less. And so appropriations grow. Changes in policy have been recommended but seldom urged by Presidents. They have usually had their origin in the public assistance bureaucracy and among its colleagues in the social work field. They have then been considered by Congress, modified in detail, and enacted into law. Recipients of assistance have had no influence on policy. The program has never found a base in a popular constituency.[8]

The revolt against assistance

In recent years, parents of children receiving AFDC have been roundly denounced as undeserving. This part of the assistance program has been condemned on two grounds. It is said to have fostered immorality. It is said to have supported able-bodied men and women in idleness. This attack is grounded in part in racial prejudice. Nearly half of the recipients of AFDC are Negroes. Fifty-six percent of Negro

[8] See Gilbert Y. Steiner, *Social Insecurity: The Politics of Welfare* (Chicago: Rand McNally & Co., 1966), chaps. i, ix.

children receive such assistance at some time during their childhood years. The immorality and idleness of which the critics complain are the alleged immorality and idleness of Negroes.

Two thirds of the recipients of AFDC live in families where the mother has never married or where the father has disappeared. A fifth of the children on AFDC are illegitimate. But it does not follow that the availability of assistance was the cause and illegitimacy the effect. It is to be doubted that women have illegitimate children in order to collect welfare checks. The payments made fall too far short of the cost of rearing a child to make such an enterprise worthwhile. In half of the cases of illegitimacy among AFDC families covered in a study made in 1960, there was only one illegitimate child; in a fourth, there were only two. Only a tenth of the nation's illegitimate children were on the assistance rolls; nine tenths were not.[9]

There are women who are "married to welfare," the public assistance check being the only income they have ever known. There are families in which a daughter brought up on assistance has produced a second generation of children to be supported by the state. But these are the exceptions rather than the rule. The rate of turnover on AFDC is high. In studies made in 1961, it was found that the median length of time on AFDC was 27 months for cases that still were active and 18 months for cases that were closed. Only a tenth of the mothers aided had been receiving assistance for periods as long as nine years. Less than a third of the recipients of aid had grown up in families that had been receiving aid. Welfare in general was not a permanent way of life.[10]

The charge that large numbers of able-bodied adults are being supported in idleness is also open to dispute. In 1965, nearly three million of the adult recipients of assistance were unemployable because they were aged, blind, or permanently and totally disabled. A million of them were parents of dependent children. Of these, only 100,000 were men, some of them disabled, some of them only temporarily unemployed. The men who were employable, some 50,000 in number, were less than 1 percent of the persons listed on the welfare rolls. Most of the unemployed adults on AFDC—900,000 of them—were women. Some of these women were employable. But 40 percent of the fathers

[9] *Illegitimacy and Its Impact on the Aid to Dependent Children Program* (Washington, D.C.: Department of Health, Education, and Welfare, 1960).
[10] *Manpower Report of the President, 1968*, pp. 95–99.

and 75 percent of the mothers could not expect to earn as much when working as they received as welfare grants.[11] Some of the women lacked job skills and work experience but would be employable if trained. But many of them could not accept employment unless there was someone to care for their smaller children while they were at work. This need could be met by establishing day-care centers. But only 5 percent of working mothers have made use of such facilities. The cost of training and day care, moreover, might be greater than that incurred in enabling mothers to care for children in their homes.

The 1967 amendments

In 1967, the attack on AFDC led to the incorporation of a number of restrictive amendments in the public assistance law. Two of these were most important. One was a freeze on federal grants. The other was a provision designed to compel AFDC parents to take work or to take training that would equip them to work.

Under the freeze, in any state, the number of children toward whose support the federal government would contribute was limited to the percentage of the children in that state receiving such support on January 1, 1968. The purpose of this provision was to force the states to curb the growth of their assistance rolls. Its effect was to deny assistance to thousands of children who otherwise would have received it, to reduce the level of payments to those assisted, and to shift a part of the cost from the federal government to the states. The incidence of the limitation was unequal, falling most heavily on those states whose assistance burden was growing most rapidly.

Under the other amendment, the states were required as a condition for obtaining federal grants to deny AFDC payments to any father, mother, or teen-age child deemed able to benefit from work or training if he refused to accept employment and training opportunities that were offered him. In support of this requirement, provision was made for federal grants to finance the establishment of work and training programs and of day-care centers for small children whose parents were enrolled. The purpose of this amendment was to replace de-

[11] Advisory Council on Public Welfare, *"Having the Power, We have the Duty," Report to the Secretary of Health, Education, and Welfare* (Washington, D.C.: U.S. Government Printing Office, 1966), pp. 7–10; and Leonard J. Hausman, "The Welfare Tax Rate," *Conference of New Manpower Researchers* (Washington, D.C.: U.S. Department of Labor, 1967).

pendency, where possible, with self-support. Its effect, in practice, remains to be seen.

Proposals for reform

The acknowledged shortcomings of public assistance should not lead to the conclusion that the program should be abandoned and an entirely different method of meeting the needs of the poor put in its place. Public assistance is indispensable. Income can be provided in some other way to finance current expenditures. But it is only through public assistance that aid involving a combination of monetary support and personal services can be provided and that crises requiring emergency action can be met.

Some of the difficulties encountered in public assistance are inherent in the nature of the undertaking. But most of its shortcomings are consequences of the way in which it is administered. And errors in administration can be corrected. There have been many proposals for reform. These proposals have to do with the pattern of federal-state relationships, with the rules governing eligibility for grants and the size of grants and with the methods used in their determination, with disincentives to marriage and employment, and with the character of assistance budgets and staffs.

1. The categorical structure of federal grants should be replaced by unified support for assistance in all its forms or, failing this, money should be granted to the states to augment the inadequate payments now made to persons receiving general assistance.

2. In its report to the Secretary of Health, Education, and Welfare in 1966, the Advisory Council on Public Welfare recommended that the federal government establish a nationwide standard for assistance payments based on a modest but adequate family budget; that it specify the share of these payments to be made by each state on the basis of an objective measure of its fiscal capacity; and that it finance the part of each state's assistance costs that was not paid by the state.

3. The Advisory Council also recommended that assistance be recognized as a right, and that the only qualification for eligibility be the fact of the claimant's need. Here, the right would differ from that obtaining under social insurance, where payments have been related to contributions and can be claimed without regard to need. Its meaning would be procedural. The claimant would have a right to a prompt and

objective determination of his eligibility; to a hearing by an impartial administrative agency of his appeal against an adverse decision; to be represented by counsel; and to carry his appeal to the courts.

4. There is general agreement that the process of determining eligibility should be simplified. The means test administered by a caseworker should be supplanted by an affidavit made out by the claimant, setting forth the composition of his family, the nature of his resources, and the extent of his need. Such statements should be subject to later sample checks, as is done in the case of income tax declarations and veterans' benefits. This method would doubtless produce some fraudulent claims. But in a large-scale experiment made in New York City, the fraction of claims that was found to be invalid was smaller than under the method usually employed.[12] The simplified procedure would protect the privacy of assistance recipients and preserve their pride. It would reduce the burden of administration and free the welfare staff for more productive work.[13]

5. Flat grants, based on the size and composition of the family, should be substituted for itemized, case-by-case decisions in meeting supplementary needs for furniture and clothing and the like. This has been done in New York City. In this case, too, it should be possible to eliminate a source of irritation, to ease administration, and to put the staff to better use.

6. The disincentive to marry should be removed by abolishing the man-in-the-house rule. A start has been made toward removing the disincentive to work. But over $30 a month, the share of earnings deducted from assistance payments should be reduced from two thirds to one half, permitting the recipient to improve his family's welfare by half of what he earns.

7. Other recommendations are obvious. Assistance budgets should be enlarged. Assistance staffs should be larger and better trained. Work loads should be lighter and salaries higher.

[12] *New York Times*, May 22, 1968.
[13] A proposed rule permitting this procedure was published by the federal Welfare Administration on November 20, 1968. In the absence of objection, it was to be made effective in 30 days. Thereafter, the procedure could be adopted by any of the states.

Income supplements

A number of proposals for the supplementation of income have been advanced in recent years. They have gone under various names: guaranteed incomes, the social dividend, the negative income tax, and children's allowances and family allowances. But all of them have had one feature in common: they would have the government give money to the poor without requiring prior contributions and without imposing a means test. This idea, particularly as it is embodied in the negative income tax, has enlisted a surprising range of support. It has been endorsed by the left-leaning Americans for Democratic Action and by the right-leaning Ripon Society, by the National Association of Social Workers, by more than 1,200 academic economists, and by a committee of business leaders examining the operation of welfare programs. Study of the proposals has been urged by several federal agencies. A Commission on Income Maintenance, consisting of a number of eminent citizens, under the chairmanship of Ben W. Heineman, head of the Chicago and Northwestern Railroad, was appointed by President Johnson in 1968 to conduct an investigation and make recommendations for future policy.

Support for guaranteed incomes has had its origin in three positions that differ radically one from another. First, there are those who believe that automation will raise productivity so rapidly that workers will be laid off in ever larger numbers and growing quantities of goods will not find buyers. In this view, society's need is not employment to produce more goods but money to purchase the goods already being produced. The income required to clear the market must therefore be distributed by the government.[1] This is a view that few persons trained in economics would accept.[2] Second, there are those at the opposite pole who are opposed in principle to what they regard as paternalistic welfare programs administered by bureaucrats. Instead of making grants or rendering services to meet the needs of the poor, they would supply them with money to be spent in the market in any way they pleased.[3] This view, while tenable as a matter of economics, finds little support as a matter of social policy. Third, there are those who are dissatisfied with the uneven coverage and inadequate level of public assistance, with its affronts to human dignity, its disincentives, and its high administrative costs. They see in guaranteed income supplements a way of meeting human needs that would be more effective, more adequate, and more humane—that would preserve desirable incentives and would be less costly to administer. This is the position of most social workers, economists, and other students of welfare programs.

Proposals for income guarantees

The several proposals for income guarantees are alike in many respects. They promise a minimum income to every family. The minimum is related to family size. The plans require no means test. Eligibility is a matter of right. Payments are based on need. Need is measured by the extent to which a family's income falls short of the income guaranteed. The government makes up some part of the shortage. An applicant establishes his right to such a payment by submitting a simple declaration setting forth the size of his family and the size of his income. Payments are financed from general revenues. People with

[1] See Robert Theobald, *Free Men and Free Markets* (New York: Clarkson N. Potter, Inc., 1963); and *The Guaranteed Income* (Garden City, N.Y.: Doubleday & Co., Inc., 1966).
[2] See National Commission on Technology, Automation, and Economic Progress, *Technology and the American Economy* (Washington, D.C.: U.S. Government Printing Office, 1966), Vol. 1, Part 1, chap. ii.
[3] See Milton Friedman, *Capitalism and Freedom* (Chicago: University of Chicago Press, 1962).

large incomes pay taxes as they do now. People with small incomes collect subsidies. Income is openly transferred from rich to poor.

The proposals have another common feature. When the recipient of a supplement earns other money, his need declines. His supplement is therefore reduced. In effect, he pays an offsetting tax. In all of the plans, he is allowed to increase his income by part of his earnings; his tax stands at less than 100 percent. His net benefit is his subsidy minus his tax. At some level of income, his tax will equal the supplement. Here, he breaks even, enjoying no net benefit.

The proposals differ in detail: in the basis and the level of the income guarantee, and in the size of the offsetting tax. They differ, too, in their relation to other welfare programs and in their probable cost.[4]

The minimum income

The income promised under some of the guaranteed income plans is based upon the exemptions and deductions allowed in the income tax law. Under this law, a taxpayer subtracts from his income an exemption of $600 for himself and for each of his dependents and another $600 if blind or over 65. A younger man with a wife and two children subtracts $2,400. He may also subtract $300 for himself and $100 for his wife and each child, or $600 altogether, as a minimum standard deduction (MSD) in lieu of itemized deductions for charitable contributions, local taxes, and the like. His exemptions plus his MSD amount to $3,000. If his income is $3,000, he has no tax to pay. People whose incomes exceed their exemptions plus their deductions pay taxes at rates that rise as income grows. People whose incomes fall short of this amount pay nothing.

The tax law is said to discriminate against the poor. In providing for exemptions, Congress recognized that families of various sizes were entitled to certain incomes on which to live. It made sure that families paying taxes would retain such incomes. But it did not assure these incomes to the poor. With the tax rate in the lowest bracket standing at 14 percent, the $600 per capita exemptions allowed a family of five with an income of $6,000 to reduce its tax by $537 each year. With the rate in the highest bracket standing at 70 percent, the exemption for a

---

[4] See Christopher Green, *Negative Taxes and the Poverty Problem* (Washington, D.C.: Brookings Institution, 1967), chaps. iv–vi.

family of five with an income over $200,000 gives it $2,100. No such
gifts are made to the poor. The exemptions are meaningless for people
who have no incomes or incomes of only $1,000 or $2,000 a year.

The sum of a family's exemptions and its MSD minus its income is
taken as the base that governs the payments made under some of the
plans for a negative income tax. As income declines, need increases and
payments are raised accordingly. More is paid to those earning $1,000
than to those earning $2,000; more to those with no income than to
those earning $1,000. The structure of the income tax becomes sym-
metrical with progressive payments to the poor as incomes fall corresponding to progressive collections from the well-to-do as incomes
rise. This explains why the guaranteed payment has been called a negative income tax. Actually, it is not a tax but a subsidy. The designation,
moreover, is confusing, since two other taxes are involved in the
proposal: the positive tax on income above the exemptions and deductions, and the offsetting tax on incomes earned by the recipients of
subsidies. In order to clarify the discussion that follows, the term will
be dropped.

The use of tax exemptions and taxable income in determining the
base for supplementary payments discriminates in favor of the aged
since their exemptions are twice as large as others and they are allowed
to exclude certain items in determining taxable income. For this reason,
in most plans the income guarantee is based instead on the size and
composition of the family and on the amount required for maintenance
as shown in budget studies. A uniform amount may be allowed per
capita, or more may be allowed for men than for women or for adults
than for children. To discourage higher birth rates, the amount allowed per child may be reduced as the family grows, and a limit may
be set on the payments a family can receive. Allowance could also be
made for differences in the cost of living in different areas. In practice,
these refinements have not usually been undertaken; need has been
measured by family size alone. The budgetary provision for a family,
minus its income, fixes the base on which supplements are paid.

The share of the income deficit that is to be made up by supplements differs from plan to plan. In general, the noneconomists have
promised a larger share and the economists a smaller one. The payments proposed under the former plans would raise the poor above the
poverty line; the payments proposed under the latter would leave them
below it. The noneconomists are willing to incur larger costs and run

greater risks of impairing incentives. The economists seek to hold costs down and to preserve incentives to work.

The offsetting tax

The supplement paid to the poor must be reduced as their incomes from other sources rise. Otherwise people who did not need payments would receive them. People collecting supplements might enjoy incomes as large as those of people paying taxes. The cost of the program would become intolerable. Its equity would be questioned. The taxpayers who were financing it would revolt.

The supplement should not be reduced, however, by the full amount of additional earnings, since this would impose a tax of 100 percent on employment, raising a serious obstacle to work. The proper policy, therefore, is to reduce the supplement by some fraction of added earnings. The problem is whether the offsetting tax should be proportionate to income or change as income rises and what its rates should be. The answer depends upon the effect that a tax on marginal earnings will have on the behavior of the people taxed. But this, unfortunately, is a matter on which it is impossible to speak with certainty.

It is known that high marginal tax rates have had little effect on the incentives of business and professional men in the upper brackets of the income tax. But this may not be true of unskilled laborers or others whose incomes are low. Where net earnings are substantially reduced by taxes, there may be many who would prefer leisure to work. This may be the case with people who are old and frail, with mothers of young children, with men whose work is dirty or exhausting or involves exposure to extremes of weather, and with persons whose jobs are poorly paid. Such people might decide to take it easy if no stigma were attached to idleness and if the rate of the offsetting tax were high.

An ambitious study of the effects of income supplements and tax rates on incentives among the poor was begun in 1968 by Mathematica of Princeton, N.J., under the direction of the University of Wisconsin's Institute for Research on Poverty, financed by a $4,000,000 grant from the Office of Economic Opportunity. Over a period of three years, a variety of income supplements will be given to a sample of 1,200 families in New Jersey cities, varying tax offset rates will be imposed, and reactions will be measured. An effort will thus be made to discover how different methods of supplementing incomes affect work effort and job mobility, consumption patterns and family stability, birth rates, and social attitudes. The results of this study may make it possible to fix the rate of an offsetting tax with greater certainty.

Suprapoverty income guarantees

A forerunner of the current plans for income guarantees was proposed by an Englishwoman, Lady Rhys-Williams, during World War II.[5] Under her proposal, the state would acknowledge its duty to provide all families at all times with all of the necessaries of a healthful life. This provision, known as the social dividend, would take the form of weekly payments based on family size and composition without regard to need. It would be financed by a proportionate tax on other income at a rate as high as 40 percent. It would thus involve redistribution of the nation's income on a major scale.

A second plan involving such redistribution was advanced by Robert Theobald, a publicist, in 1963.[6] Under this plan, the state would guarantee to each of its ctiizens as an absolute constitutional right, an income large enough to enable him to live in health and decency. The income tax exemption would be raised, initially, to $1,000 for each adult and $600 for each child, or $3,200 for a family of four, and later to higher figures. Where a family's income fell below the exemption, the government would make up all of the difference. The cost of the plan would therefore be high. If those receiving payments had other income, they would be allowed to increase it by 10 percent. In other words, additional earnings would be subject to a tax of 90 percent, imposing a heavy penalty on work. This is deliberate, since the author believes that automation is making employment obsolete.

A third proposal of this sort was made in 1964 by Edward E. Schwartz, a professor of social work.[7] Under his plan, income at a certain level would be guaranteed to every family as a right. The

[5] Lady Juliette Evangeline Rhys-Williams, *Something to Look Forward To* (London: MacDonald, 1943); and *Family Allowances and Social Security* (London: Liberal Publication Dept., 1944).

[6] Theobald, *op. cit.*

[7] Edward E. Schwartz, "A Way to End the Means Test," *Social Work,* Vol. 9 (1964), pp. 3–12.

guarantee for a family of four might be set at a maintenance level of $3,000 a year, at an economy level of $4,000, or at a modest but adequate level of $5,000. Where income fell below the figure chosen, the government would make up all of the difference. If other income was earned, it would be subject to an average tax of 60 to 70 percent. Here, again, the cost would be high and the disincentive to employment would be strong.

Infrapoverty income guarantees

The infrapoverty guarantee plans have been produced by academic economists: Milton Friedman of the University of Chicago in 1962,[8] Robert J. Lampman of the University of Wisconsin beginning in 1965,[9] and James Tobin of Yale at about the same time.[10] In general, they use lower bases in computing income deficits than do the noneconomists' plans, call for supplements that make up a fraction rather than all of the deficits, and offset other income at lower rates. They differ in detail.

Under the Friedman plan, the base for the supplement is a family's tax exemptions and MSD minus its other income. The rates of the supplement and the offsetting tax are each set at 50 percent. If a family's exemptions and MSD stand at $3,000 and it has no income, its deficit is $3,000 and its supplement is $1,500. If a family earns $500, its supplement is cut to $1,250, giving it an income of $1,750. Deductions are made at the same rate at higher levels of income as shown in Table 1. It will be noted, however, that total income rises as earnings rise so that an incentive to employment is maintained.

Lampman has produced a number of variants on this type of plan. He uses as the base for his supplement a budgetary allowance for each member of the family minus the family's income. His several versions differ in the amount of the allowance, in the rate of the supplement,

[8] Friedman, *op. cit.*, pp. 192–95.

[9] Robert J. Lampman, "Negative Rates Income Taxation" (unpublished manuscript, Office of Economic Opportunity, 1965); "The Guaranteed Minimum Income: Is It Worth What It Would Cost?" (paper delivered at conference at School of Social Service Administration, University of Chicago, 1966); and "Approaches to the Reduction of Poverty," *American Economic Review*, Vol. 55, No. 2 (1965), pp. 521–29.

[10] James Tobin, "On Improving the Economic Status of the Negro," *Daedalus*, Vol. 94 (1965), pp. 878–98 at pp. 891–94; "The Case for an Income Guarantee," *The Public Interest*, Summer, 1966, pp. 31–41; "Do We Want Children's Allowances?" *New Republic*, November 25, 1967, pp. 16–18; and James Tobin, Joseph A. Pechman, and Peter M. Meiszkowski, "Is a Negative Income Tax Practical?" *Yale Law Journal*, Vol. 77 (1967), pp. 1–27.

Table 1. Friedman plan: income supplements for a family with income tax exemptions and deductions of $3,000

Earned Income	Income Deficit	Amount of Offsetting Tax	Amount of Supplement	Total Income
None	$3,000	None	$1,500	$1,500
$ 500	2,500	250	1,250	1,750
1,000	2,000	500	1,000	2,000
1,500	1,500	750	750	2,250
2,000	1,000	1,000	500	2,500
2,500	500	1,250	250	2,750
3,000	None	1,500	None	3,000

and in the rate of the offsetting tax. In all of them, the level of his guarantee, like Friedman's, falls well below the poverty line. In some cases, the offsetting tax is imposed at a flat rate; in others, at rates that vary with changes in income, as shown in Table 2. In all cases, total income rises as family earnings rise, preserving an incentive to work.

Table 2. Lampman plan: income supplements for a family of four below the poverty line

Earned Income	Amount below Poverty Line	Rate of Supplement	Amount of Supplement	Total Income
None	$3,000	50%	$1,500	$1,500
$ 500	2,500	45%	1,125	1,625
1,000	2,000	38%	760	1,860
1,500	1,500	33%	495	1,995
2,000	1,000	25%	250	2,250
2,500	500	25%	125	2,625
2,800	200	25%	50	2,850
3,000	None	None	None	3,000

Source: Joint Economic Committee, Paper No. 11, *Guaranteed Minimum Income Programs*, 1968, p. 6.

With Tobin, as with Lampman, the base for the supplement is an allowance for each member of the family minus the family's income. The allowance is set at $400 or $600 per capita. The offsetting tax is set at a flat rate of 33⅓ or 50 percent. With a $400 allowance and a 33⅓ percent tax, as is shown in Table 3, a family of five with no income receives a supplement of $2,000. A family with an income of $1,000 has its supplement reduced by $333 to $1,667, giving it a total income of $2,667. And so on. Payment of supplements is continued beyond the poverty line in declining amounts, until a break-even level is reached where the offsetting tax equals the supplement. In our illustration, this occurs at $6,000 where the supplement is $2,000 and the tax is $2,000. Beyond this point, no supplements are paid.

Table 3. Tobin plan: income supplements for a family with a $2,000 allowance and a 33⅓ percent offsetting tax

Family Income before Tax or Allowance	Present Tax Schedule		Proposed Schedule	
	Tax (—)	Income after Tax	Tax (—) or Allowance (+)	Income after Tax or Allowance
$ 0	0	$ 0	$+2,000	$2,000
1,000	0	1,000	+1,667	2,667
2,000	0	2,000	+1,333	3,333
2,500	0	2,500	+1,167	3,667
3,000	0	3,000	+1,000	4,000
3,700	0	3,700	+767	4,467
4,000	—42	3,958	+667	4,667
5,000	—185	4,815	+333	5,333
6,000	—338	5,662	0	6,000
7,000	—501	6,499	—333	6,667
7,963	—654	7,309	—654	7,309
8,000	—658	7,342	—658	7,342

Source: *The Public Interest*, Summer, 1966, p. 38.

One of the difficulties of the other plans is the existence of an abrupt drop, at the point where supplements are no longer paid, from the rate of the offsetting tax to the rate of the individual income tax. A family of five with an income of $3,000 would pay an offsetting tax at a rate, say, of 50 percent. A similar family with an income of $4,000 would pay an income tax in the lowest bracket at a rate of 14 percent. Between $3,000 and $4,000, a small difference in income could produce a large difference in taxation. Tobin has solved this problem by dovetailing the two taxes. Under his proposal, a family would continue to pay the offsetting tax until its income reached a figure where the amounts taken by either tax were the same. In the illustration given in Table 3, this occurs with the rate at 33⅓ percent, at an income of $7,963 per year. Beyond this figure, the rates in the income tax schedule apply.

The plan is pictured in the accompanying graph. The horizontal axis shows income from all sources: wages, interest, dividends, and the like.

Illustration of Tobin's income supplement plan

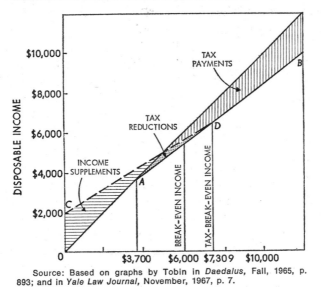

Source: Based on graphs by Tobin in *Daedalus,* Fall, 1965, p. 893; and in *Yale Law Journal,* November, 1967, p. 7.

The vertical axis shows the corresponding disposable income, i.e., the income remaining after subsidies and taxes. If a family received no supplements and paid no taxes, its disposable income would equal its total income and would be shown by the 45° diagonal line. Where disposable income lies above this line, the family is receiving supplements. Where it falls below the line, the family is paying taxes. The line OAB shows the income tax payable by a family of five. The line CD shows the effects of the proposed plan, with supplements paid up to a break-even income of $6,000, with offsetting tax payments continued to $7,963, and with income taxes paid from there on.

Relation to other welfare programs

An income guarantee may be a substitute for other welfare programs or a supplement to them. Friedman proposes the guarantee as a substitute. He would do away not only with public assistance but also with all welfare services and all forms of social insurance. The government would distribute money to the poor. The poor would spend it for anything that they might need. No other form of aid would be required. Lampman and Tobin, on the other hand, regard the income guarantee as a supplement. They would retain public assistance as well as welfare services and the social insurances.

At the level of payments contemplated under plans for an infra-poverty income guarantee, public assistance could be reduced in size but not abolished. The supplements proposed fall below the meager assistance payments now made to families with dependent children in two fifths to two thirds of the states. Substitution of such payments for assistance would leave many thousands of these families worse off than they are today. The supplements would improve the condition of the working poor—people with earnings below the poverty line who now get aid in only one or two of the states. They would not meet the needs of families without a breadwinner: the aged, the disabled, and the fatherless who are now on the relief rolls. Here, assistance payments would be needed to augment the insufficient supplements. If income guarantees were set at a much higher level, public assistance could be substantially reduced. But it could scarcely be abandoned. There would still be emergency needs with which the routine payment of income supplements would lack the flexibility to deal.

Nor would it be possible for the government to abolish welfare services. There are needs that cannot practically be met in any other way. This is true, for instance, of care for abused, neglected, and abandoned children, for the physically and mentally handicapped, the disabled, and the insane. It is true of occupational counseling and placement, of many health services, and of much of education. In cases such as these, money alone would be of little help.

Nor can income supplements, at the levels proposed, be substituted, as advocated by Friedman, for the benefits due under social insurance. The change would reduce the incomes of all single persons and most aged couples now receiving benefits. The insurance beneficiaries, present and potential, have been told for more than 30 years that they are entitled to stipulated benefits, as a matter of right, by the wage and payroll taxes paid on their behalf. They have been assured that payment is guaranteed by funds held in trust for that purpose by the Treasury. To repudiate this pledge, at this late date, would be a breach of faith, morally indefensible and politically impossible.

The two systems of income maintenance—social insurance and income supplements—are based on different principles. If both are to exist, they must be managed independently. How, then, are they to be related? One possibility would be to give no income supplements to OASDI beneficiaries—the aged, survivors, and the disabled. This would leave some of them—people for whom wage and payroll taxes had been paid—worse off than the recipients of income supplements whose earnings had not been taxed. This difficulty could be overcome by raising the lower insurance benefits. But it is unlikely that this would be done without also raising the higher benefits. The cost of the solution might therefore prevent its adoption. Another possibility would be to include insurance beneficiaries in the guaranteed income plan, permitting each of them to elect insurance benefits or income supplements, whichever was higher. Those with the lowest benefits would find it advantageous to elect the income guarantee. Those with high benefits would elect the insurance plan. If the benefits were not taxed, as is the case today, the beneficiaries' incomes would not be affected. But this would give them more favorable treatment under the income guarantee than that afforded recipients of other types of income. If insurance benefits were taxed as is other income, first at the rate of the offsetting tax and then at the rates of the individual income tax, the beneficiaries would have lower incomes, net of taxes, than they had been entitled to expect. The poor would be better off; the well-to-do worse off than without the income guarantee.

The cost of income guarantees

The gross cost of a program of income guarantees depends on the level from which income is deducted in computing the supplements, the rate of the offsetting tax on other income, and under an elective plan, the numbers who elect the supplements. The net cost is determined by subtracting the savings that may be realized by abandoning or reducing other welfare programs. Estimates of cost cover a wide range. The suprapoverty guarantees are more costly, estimates running from $25 billion to $50 billion a year. The infrapoverty guarantees cost less, estimates running, in most cases, between $5 billion and $15 billion. The plans would also affect the economy in ways that cannot be measured: through their influence on incentives and thus on output, through possible savings on expenditures for health and for public safety, and through their impact on the federal budget.

Income guarantees pro and con

A number of arguments can be advanced in support of income guarantees. Some of them are based, however, on the assumption that the supplements will supersede all public assistance. As we have seen, this is unlikely to be the case. In criticism of the guarantee proposals, it must be recognized that the objectives they would serve are inconsistent. The proposals, moreover, present administrative difficulties which, while not insuperable, are serious.

The case for income guarantees

In support of the guarantee proposals, it can be said that they call for inclusive coverage, offering help to all who are in need. They would extend aid to many who do not now receive it, to dependents who are ineligible for other programs, and to workers whose earnings fall below the poverty line. They would do so under a standard that would be objective in character and uniform throughout the country.

The plans are said to call for an integrated system for collecting money from the well-to-do and distributing it to the poor, one that would be much simpler than the complex of programs now in use. If a high income were fully guaranteed, this would be true. But with income subsidies added to welfare services, public assistance, and social insurance, the machinery for attacking poverty becomes more complicated than it was before.

Another presumed advantage of income guarantees is the abolition of the means test, with intrusive investigations ended and administrative discretion giving way to objective rules. But with public assistance retained, a means test will still be needed to determine eligibility. And the income declaration required by the guarantee plan may not be unobjectionable. Types of income excluded under the present tax law, such as gifts from relatives and friends, insurance benefits, and interest on tax-free bonds, would have to be reported to avoid making payments to people who were not in need. Information on savings, as a possible source of support, might also be required. If fraud were to be prevented, declarations regarding such matters would have to be checked and the check would invade the reporter's privacy. This might well be less distasteful than the means test is today. But under public assistance, also, the means test could be modified.

It is said, finally, that an income subsidy plan would do away with the antagonism that now exists between people who are self-supporting and those who subsist on public charity. This seems unlikely. It would be hard to imagine a system that would reveal this conflict of interest in a brighter light than one which draws a line above which people pay money into the Treasury and below which other people draw it out. In 1968, the Gallup Poll reported on a sampling of opinion on a guaranteed income. People with incomes under $3,000 favored the proposal by 49 to 45 percent; those between $5,000 and $7,000 opposed it by 55 to 38 percent; those between $7,000 and $10,000 opposed it by 63 to 30 percent; and those over $10,000 by 68 to 26 percent. Negroes favored the proposal by 66 to 30 percent, and white people opposed it by 60 to 33 percent. Given a clear issue, the population divided into conflicting socioeconomic groups.[11]

Inconsistency of objectives

An income guarantee should satisfy three objectives: (1) It should assure a subsistence income to the poor. (2) It should preserve incentives to work. (3) It should minimize transfers to people who do not need them, holding its cost within the bounds of political feasibility. The three objectives are in conflict. It is necessary, therefore, to compromise among them.

Where a plan promises to pay a supplement that will put incomes at or above the poverty line, as do those of Theobald and Schwartz, it may impose a high tax offset on other income to keep its cost down, thus impairing incentives. Or it may impose a low tax offset to preserve incentives, thus setting its break-even point well above the poverty line. In this event, it will distribute supplements to people who do not need them and its cost will be high.

Where a plan preserves incentives by keeping the tax offset low, it may set its guarantee low to keep costs down. Or it may extend its supplements to people who are not in need. Thus, Tobin holds his tax offset at 33⅓ percent but continues his payments until incomes reach $6,000, a figure that is twice the poverty line.

Where the waste of distributing income to the well-to-do is avoided and incentives are preserved by imposing a tax offset, the level of the income guarantee must be kept low. Thus, Friedman set his guarantee at $1,500 for a family of five; and in his several plans, Lampman promises supplements running from $525 to $2,500, standing at $937.50 in one of them and at $1,875 in two others. All of these figures fall be-

[11] *New York Times*, June 16, 1968.

low the poverty line, and most of them, as we have seen, below the public assistance payments made in many of the states.

Administrative difficulties

It has been suggested that income supplements could be paid in one of two ways.[12] Under the first, the claimant would declare his expected income at the beginning of the year. His employer would withhold the offsetting tax on his wages. The Internal Revenue Service would estimate his remaining benefit and send him a weekly or semimonthly check. If the claimant received more or less income than he had estimated, as would often be the case, he would submit an amended return. The IRS would modify his supplement accordingly. Under the second method, the IRS would mail checks in the full amount of the supplement to everyone covered. Those who did not expect to receive net benefits would refuse them and withdraw from the plan. Employers would withhold the offsetting tax on wages. Claimants would pay the tax on other income each quarter. Final adjustments would be made, under both methods, after the end of the year. Overpayments would be recovered and underpayments made up.

If the Internal Revenue Service were given full responsibility for administration of the program, the added burden imposed upon it would be a heavy one. Millions of people with little education, many of them people who had never made out a tax form, would now have to report on their estimated income at the beginning of the year, on changes in income during the year, and on realized income at the end of the year, with all the detail that might be required. It would be necessary to give these people help in preparing their returns. The definition of income used in computing the income supplement should differ, moreover, from that employed for the personal income tax. To avoid discrimination in favor of farmers, for instance, it should include the value of food produced and consumed on farms. To avoid discrimination in favor of homeowners, it should include the rental value of owner-occupied homes. It would be necessary, then, to check on underreporting of farm consumption, on undervaluation of housing, and on other possible fraud. The IRS could be relieved of part of this burden by assigning to some other agency the duty of assisting appli-

[12] Tobin, Pechman, and Meiszkowski, *op. cit.*

cants for income supplements in the preparation of their claims. The IRS could then confine itself to the business of collecting taxes, mailing out checks, and preventing claimants from obtaining excessive supplements through fraud.

The burden of administering an income supplement would be heavy. But the burden of administering public assistance is even heavier. And this burden should be substantially lightened as the income supplement took over a major part of the assistance load.

Children's allowances

Income guarantees and children's allowances (also called family allowances) have both been advocated in recent years as substitutes for public assistance. They have also been debated as if they were alternatives, the proponents of each attacking the other. Actually, the two programs differ, both in purpose and in coverage. The guarantee proposals aim to reduce poverty; the allowance proposals aim to improve child welfare. The income supplements are paid to all poor families, including those who are childless and those whose children are grown; the allowances are given only to families with minor children. The supplements are paid only to families who are poor; the allowances are given to the rich as well. The children's allowance is a form of demogrant, a payment made solely on the basis of demographic status without regard to need or income. The size of a family's allowance is determined by the number and the ages of its children.

Allowances in other countries

Children's allowances are paid in more than 60 countries, including all western countries but the United States. The first laws providing for such allowances were enacted in New Zealand in 1926, in Belgium in 1930, and in France in 1932. The programs in the English-speaking and Scandinavian countries cover all children and are financed from general revenues. Those in most other European countries are part of the social insurance systems, are limited to the children of insured workers, and are financed in the main by taxes on employers. The allowances are usually paid to the mother. Twelve programs pay nothing for the first child; three place an upper limit on the number for whom payments are made. Under some of the programs, allowances are the same for all of the children in a family; in most, they vary with the order of birth or age. Most programs pay more for earlier children than for later ones or for older children than for their younger siblings; none pay less as ages rise. Allowances are usually paid until the age of 16, with possible extensions for children who are still in school.[13]

In few cases are allowances high enough to cover the cost of rearing a child. In France, where payments are comparatively high, they vary with the ages and numbers of children in a family and with the regions in which they live. In Paris in 1967, the average payment to a family with three children was $432 per year, adding 28 percent to the income of the average worker. The family also receives allowances for prenatal care, for maternity, and for housing.[14] In Great Britain, on the other hand, with nothing paid for the first child, 18 shillings a month for the second, and one pound a month for later children, the allowance amounts to only $237 a year for a family with three, adding only 6.2 percent to the average worker's income.[15] In Canada, the allowances are even lower, standing at $72 a year for children under 10 and at $96 for those between 10 and 16. There is also an allowance of $120 for 16- and 17-year-olds who are still in school.[16]

Allowance proposals in the United States

The United States already affords advantages to families with children. Benefits under the OASDI and Railroad Retirement systems and under some of the workmen's compensation and unemployment insurance programs are related to the number of dependents. Allowances are made for the dependents of enlisted men. Elementary and secondary education are provided without charge. Payments are made on behalf of needy children under the public assistance laws. In some

[13] Department of Health, Education, and Welfare, *Social Security Programs Throughout the World, 1964* (Washington; D.C.: U.S. Government Printing Office, 1964); and James C. Vadakin, *Children, Poverty, and Family Allowances* (New York: Basic Books, 1968), chap. iii.

[14] Eveline M. Burns (ed.), *Children's Allowances and the Economic Welfare of Children* (New York: Citizens' Committee for Children of New York, 1968), pp. 76–89; and Joint Economic Committee, *Guaranteed Minimum Income Programs* (Washington, D.C.: U.S. Government Printing Office, 1968), chap. ii.

[15] Burns, *op. cit.*, pp. 90–114; and Joint Economic Committee, *op. cit.*, chap. iii.

[16] Burns, *op. cit.*, pp. 61–75; Joint Economic Committee, *op. cit.*, chap. v; and Vadakin, *op. cit.*, chap. iv.

cases, medical services and school lunches are provided to poor children and housing is subsidized. A $600 exemption is allowed under the income tax for each dependent child. This provides no income to the poor, but it gives a children's allowance to those who are not poor, running from $84 for those in the bottom bracket to $420 for those at the top.

There are now proposals that these arrangements be supplemented or supplanted by a system of children's allowances. James C. Vadakin, an economist, has proposed that an allowance be provided for every child at a flat rate of $120 per year.[17] Daniel P. Moynihan, director of the Joint Center of Urban Studies at Harvard and M.I.T., has proposed that $96 per year be paid for each child under the age of 8 and $144 for each child between 8 and 17.[18] Alvin L. Schorr, of the Department of Health, Education, and Welfare, has proposed an allowance that would be limited to preschool children. Under his plan, $600 a year would be paid for each child under the age of six. Schorr regards the preschool years as crucial. He would pay no allowances for children over six, but believes that they would benefit from the fact that AFDC could spend its savings on younger children in paying more to older ones; that welfare services for older children could be expanded; and that these children would benefit indirectly from the allowances paid their younger siblings.[19]

The case for children's allowances

Those who advocate children's allowances give the welfare of children priority over other welfare needs. It is the child whose need is greatest, who is least able to help himself, and who is least well cared for by the state. It is the child, too, whose development is most important for the future. His opportunities should be assured before the needs of older folks are met.

The logic of children's allowances is persuasive. The father's wage depends upon his worth to his employer. It is not related to his children's needs. The mother's job is that of raising children. Her proper performance is vital to the community. Her ability to render this

[17] Vadakin, *op. cit.*, chap. 7.
[18] Daniel P. Moynihan, "The Case for a Family Allowance," *New York Times Magazine*, February 5, 1967, pp. 13 ff.; and "The Crisis in Welfare," *The Public Interest*, Winter, 1968, pp. 3–29.
[19] Alvin L. Schorr, *Poor Kids* (New York: Basic Books, 1966), chap. ix.

service should not be limited by her husband's wage. It should be assured by the state.

Some of the advocates of children's allowances argue that a large family is as much of a hazard as old age, disability, unemployment, and survivorship and that protection should be afforded against this hazard as against the others through a social insurance program. The risk of having children is said to be predictable; rates could therefore be fixed to cover its cost. But this contention is open to criticism. Protection is provided in the other cases against contingencies for which the individual cannot plan and save. Large families, on the other hand, are not inevitable: childbirth can be controlled. It is not properly to be regarded as an insurable risk.

The children's allowance does have one great advantage. It carries no stigma, being paid to rich and poor alike. It does away with the means test, requiring no questions regarding need or income. Determination of eligibility would be a simple clerical operation. The cost of administration would be low.

The case against children's allowances

Opponents of family allowances fear that they would lead to an increase in the birth rate. There is no evidence that the allowances paid in other countries have had this effect. France with its larger allowances has a birth rate that is lower than in neighboring countries with smaller allowances. In Canada, with allowances, the trend of the birth rate has been the same as in the United States with none. In general, however, the payments have been small and other factors have been at work. If the sums paid were larger, their influence might be seen. At the level proposed by Schorr, a mother with three children under the age of six would get $1,800. As each child reached six, she would lose $600. But she could offset this loss by having another child. It cannot be lightly assumed that this incentive would be without its effect. But such an influence could easily be weakened by reducing the allowance per child as families grew and by limiting the number of children for whom allowances would be paid.

A second fear is that parents would use the allowances for purposes other than the care of their children. This is an objection that has not been raised against the dependents' exemptions provided under the income tax. Experience abroad affords little evidence on the point. But trained observers are inclined to give it little weight. Family income, they say, is pooled; the allowances are not earmarked. But when the family spends, the children's needs get first priority.[20]

The allowances in general are pitifully small. Those provided in most cases fall below the average payment made under AFDC in the United States. Those provided in Canada are lower than AFDC payments in Mississippi. The allowances proposed by Vadakin and Moynihan are set at 20 to 30 percent of the average payment under AFDC. Even the $600 allowance proposed by Schorr falls below AFDC payments in five of the states.

Even at these levels, the proposals entail substantial costs. Vadakin's proposal would cost $8 billion; Moynihan's proposal, $9 billion. An allowance of $25 a month to all children under 18 would cost $20 billion. An allowance of $50 to those under 6 and $10 to those between 6 and 18 would cost a similar amount. These figures are to be compared with the $5 billion to $15 billion cost of an infrapoverty income guarantee. The two programs may serve different purposes but they are clearly budgetary rivals.

The principal defect of the children's allowance proposals is the fact that most of the payments would go to people who do not need them. Not only would they be of little help to the poor but they would be a windfall for the well-to-do. If a monthly allowance of $25 were provided for each child under 18, three fourths of the money paid out would go to families above the poverty line. If $50 were allowed for each child under 6 and $10 for each child between 6 and 18, five sixths of the payments would go to the nonpoor. Part of the money paid to those in the upper brackets of the income tax could be recovered by eliminating children's exemptions and deductions and treating the allowances as income to be taxed at progressive rates. But under the $25 allowance, two thirds of the benefits after taxes—and under the $50–$10 allowance, three fourths of such benefits—would still go to families that were not in poverty.[21] Harvey Brazer has suggested that families in the upper brackets be required to add some part of the allowances received not only to taxable income but also to the tax liability itself.[22] A larger part of the unnecessary payments could thus be recovered.

[20] Burns, *op. cit.*, pp. 14–15: Vadakin, *op. cit.*, p. 86; and Schorr, *op. cit.*, p. 162.

[21] Mollie Orshansky, "The Shape of Poverty in 1966," *Social Security Bulletin*, March, 1968, pp. 3–32 at pp. 22–26.

[22] Burns, *op. cit.*, pp. 140–49.

But the government would still be distributing money, running into the billions, to people who did not need it and then undertaking to get part of it back through taxation. The problem could be solved more simply by confining children's allowances to families with low incomes. This would cut the cost of the program by three fourths or more. It would eliminate the waste involved in sending money out only to call it back. But the allowance would no longer be a simple demogrant. A test of income would be needed to determine eligibility. The cost of administering the program would be higher. The recipients of allowances would be stigmatized.

How support incomes?

The first line of defense against poverty among the aged, the disabled, survivors, and the unemployed is to be found in social insurance. These programs provide benefits in a manner that is objective and relatively free of controversy. They are well established, well administered, and generally accepted. Where their coverage is incomplete, it can be extended. Where benefits are inadequate, they can be raised.

Even when this is done, there will be residual need for families who are ineligible for insurance, families without breadwinners, and families whose earnings leave them below the poverty line. Here, the rivals for the task of providing aid are public assistance, income supplements, and children's allowances.

With all their merits, children's allowances have serious shortcomings. As proposed, they distribute the bulk of their benefits to families who are not in need. This defect could be remedied by confining them to the needy. But another would remain. Children's allowances would afford no aid to families who were childless, however great their need.

If the goal of a guaranteed income is set at the poverty line or higher and the income deficit fully made up, this program, too, would be open to objection. It would either impair incentives or distribute benefits to people who were not in need. If the goal of such a plan is set at a lower figure, however, and the income deficit only partly made up, incentives can be preserved and the distribution of benefits to those not in need can be minimized. On this basis, the income guarantee has a useful function to perform. It can extend aid to needy families who do not now receive it—families whose earnings fall below the poverty line. It can provide aid, also, to families now receiving public assistance, and do so in a less objectionable way and at a lower cost.

But income supplements, at any level that is likely, cannot do away with public assistance. There will still be families in need for whom the payments will not suffice, such as large families whose breadwinners are dead, disabled, or departed, and families facing extraordinary burdens in emergencies. Here, public assistance must meet the need that remains. Its task will be lightened by virtue of the payments that income supplements will have made. Its performance can be improved by raising its standards and making them uniform, by simplifying its determination of eligibility, and by removing its disincentives to marriage and to work.

Housing

Next to health and education, the product that is most important to the poor is housing. It determines the character of their environment, the quality of their lives, the nature of their opportunities. Yet housing is the field in which private enterprise has turned in its sorriest performance. It is a field in which one of the largest, most varied, and most costly efforts made by government has been rewarded with the least success. Attempts to halt the decay of the cities and to restore the quality of the urban environment have done little or nothing for the poor. Attempts to provide low-rent housing on a substantial scale have ended in failure. But the effort goes on. New programs are devised; new monies appropriated. Intractable as it seems, the problem may yet be solved.

Private enterprise in housing

In fields other than housing—in mining and manufacturing, in transport and utilities, in wholesale and retail distribution, in the building of business structures, highways, bridges, and dams—private enterprise has made striking progress in cutting costs and increasing output. In the provision of housing, its record of accomplishment is small. Here, it has been handicapped by the peculiarities of the product, by the character of the market, by antiquated technology, by restrictive regulations, and by disorganization in the housebuilding industry. In the face of urban decay, unless assisted by government, private enterprise has been impotent.

The housing market

As a marketable product, a house has its peculiarities. It is rooted to the ground; if houses are scarce in Boston, empty houses cannot be moved in from Baltimore to add to the supply. The purchase of a house is part of a package deal, involving acceptance of its surroundings—churches, schools, and shops, transport facilities, and the neighborhood as a whole—and involving also the purchase of land and arrangements for credit. Of some 60 million dwelling units in the country, only 3½ percent are available for purchase or for rent at any one time. And of those available, only 3 percent are new; 97 percent are secondhand. Little or no new housing is built for the lower income groups and little or none is built to rent. New houses—most of them free-standing, single-family dwellings surrounded by land in the suburbs—are built for the well-to-do. Most purchasers or renters must content themselves with castoffs, dwellings built some time ago to suit some other person's tastes, dwellings requiring redecoration and structural repairs. In a few years time, a used automobile winds up on a junk heap; a used house, whatever its age and its limitations, remains a unique part of the housing supply.

Because of the peculiarities of the product, the market for housing differs from that for other goods. There are no comprehensive market data. Negotiations are carried on in secret. Each of them is unique. Sellers and buyers are largely inexperienced. Bargaining is prolonged. Transactions are complicated. The purchaser must obtain not only a deed conveying ownership but also a contract of sale and an abstract and insurance of title. He usually must borrow a large part of the property's value, giving the lender a mortgage. He must buy property insurance and pay the taxes and assessments that are due for the rest of the year. He must not only pay the price of the house and lot but also a commission for the broker who arranged the sale, a fee for the lawyer who drew up the contract and the deed, a fee for the clerk who abstracted the title, a fee for the notary who witnessed the signatures, and a fee for the county's recorder of deeds—these charges amounting to a tenth of the cost of his home. Then, if he keeps up payments on his mortgage, he need only face the risks of fire and other disasters, of depreciation and obsolescence, and the recurring costs of insurance, taxes, and repairs. In no other purchase will he have to surmount such obstacles.[1]

The housebuilding industry

There have been advances in the technology of house construction. The methods of mass production have been employed, particularly in building subdivisions, on a major scale. Designs have been standardized, new materials used, components prefabricated and assembled on the site. But such construction accounts for a small minority of new housing. And it is produced for sale at an increasing price: in 1947, mass-produced houses in the Levittowns sold for $7,500; in 1968, with higher costs for land, labor, and materials, for $17,500 and more. The one place where industrialization is reducing costs and prices is in the production of mobile homes. Here, standardization, new materials, and factory assembly have cut the cost of a 12-foot by 60-foot unit to $8 per square foot compared with $13 for houses that are custom-built, and have made possible the sale of a two-bedroom, aluminum-sided dwelling for as little as $4,500. The mobiles now account for a fourth of the single-family homes produced each year. Zoning restrictions in many cities and suburban areas stand as an obstacle to even greater sales.[2]

In general, a house is not a standard product. Different designs are demanded by different buyers. Different materials and methods of construction are required by the building codes in different cities. This diversity affects the technology of house building and the organization of the house-building industry.

In the main, houses are made to order from materials bought in special lots and sizes and by handicraft methods involving cutting and fitting on the job. The work is done at the site, much of it in the open; it is therefore seasonal and is interrupted by bad weather. It is interrupted, too, by delays in the delivery of materials and in the arrival of craftsmen. Modernization is obstructed by the conservatism of buyers, by the opposition of labor unions, and by the provisions of building codes. As a result, houses cost more than need be. Technical innovation

[1] Martin Meyerson, Barbara L. Terrett, and William L. C. Wheaton (eds.), *Housing, People, and Cities* (New York: McGraw-Hill Book Co., Inc., 1962), chap. iii.
[2] *New York Times*, August 28, 1968.

could cut the cost of the structure itself. But the cost of land, of financing, of interior finishing and equipment would remain. The total would still be high.

The housebuilding industry is not a separate entity but is a minor part of the general construction industry. It includes a few thousand large-scale builders of subdivisions and apartment houses and hundreds of thousands of small builders operating with little capital, scant credit, and few employees. The construction of multiple dwelling units is initiated by large investors, real estate operators, and speculative builders; the construction of single-family housing by speculators, subdividers, and potential owners. The initiator buys the land, hires an architect and a general contractor, inspects the work, and makes payments as it proceeds. The general contractor may do part of the work himself. But in the main, he hires it done by subcontractors who employ the craftsmen in scores of different trades (excavation, masonry, carpentry, plumbing and heating, wiring, lathing and plastering, tiling, glazing, painting, landscaping, and so on), provides them with equipment, and directs their work. The relationship between the general contractor and the subcontractors is constantly shifting. The industry has no permanent organization. Each house is a separate job. Bringing some order out of this chaos, there is a pervasive pattern of restraints—bidding rings operated by subcontractors, boycotts conducted by materials dealers to control the channels of trade, union contracts governing hours and wages, union rules restricting changes in technology, and restrictions in building codes—that reserve the local market for local contractors, materials dealers, and laborers.

This gives but a glimpse of the anarchy that characterizes the housebuilding industry. But it should serve to explain why the industry has done so little to provide a supply of housing that would be within the reach of people who are poor.[3]

The decay of the cities

The automobile and the modern highway have brought about a mass migration from the cities to the suburbs. Urban residents have moved to suburban homes. Urban industries have built new plants in suburban areas. Stores and shops have followed homes and jobs. Left behind, the center of the city still survives, with its corporate offices,

[3] Meyerson, Terrett, and Wheaton, *op. cit.*, chaps. vii–x incl.

its financial and professional services, its department stores and specialty shops, its hotels and recreational facilities, its public institutions, and its luxury apartments for the rich. But stretching from the city center to the city line, where once the well-to-do resided, there is an area of blight, with streets decaying, houses deteriorating, and property values going down. Here is the slum, the ghetto, the housing of the poor, of racial and national minorities.

Here, there may be profits for the slum lord. He mines his property, refuses to maintain it, overcrowds it, and continues to collect the rent. But there is trouble for city government. The need for municipal services—for police and fire protection, for health and welfare—increases and their costs go up. Property values and, with them, the value of the tax base and the yield of taxes go down. Municipal services suffer. The quality of slum life goes from bad to worse.

In the face of this devastation, the private builder is helpless. He cannot stop the flight from the city. He cannot restore the blighted area. He cannot do the large-scale planning that the job demands. He cannot assemble land in sites as large as needed. He cannot meet the enormous costs. If the spread of blight is to be halted and the urban environment renewed, responsibility must be taken by government. And a large share of the cost must be borne by government. Here, again, private enterprise cannot go far, unaided, toward housing the poor.[4]

Government housing policy

Government has intervened in housing in a variety of ways. It has regulated private housing through zoning laws, building and housing codes, and rent controls. It has promoted the construction of private housing by increasing the supply of credit. It has subsidized the renewal of blighted areas by private builders. It has itself gone into the business of building and operating rental housing.

Regulation of private housing

All municipalities have city plans which guide public development, determining the layout of streets, the location of civic centers, and the

---

[4] Carter MacFarland, "Urban Renewal" in William L. C. Wheaton, Grace Milgram, and Margy E. Meyerson (eds.), *Urban Housing* (New York: The Free Press, 1966), pp. 428–41.

reservation of land for recreation. They have zoning regulations which restrict private development, controlling the uses to which different areas may be put. These regulations specify the sites that may be used for industry and commerce, for multiple family dwellings, and only for single residences. They prevent construction that is not desired. But they build no houses.

All cities have building and housing codes. The building codes are concerned with structural safety. They specify the materials and the methods of construction that may be used. New buildings that would be unsafe cannot be built. Old buildings that are unsafe may be condemned. The housing codes are concerned with sanitation, ventilation, and the like. New rental housing must conform to the standards they provide. Old rental housing may be inspected and repairs prescribed. Enforcement, however, is minimal, being undermanned and subject to political pressure. The housing codes construct no houses. Their vigorous enforcement might even reduce the supply of houses and raise their rents.[5]

In wartime, the demand for housing in the vicinity of military installations and defense plants rises. But building materials and labor are diverted to military use, and the supply of housing is not increased. With demand growing and supply frozen, rents soar. In this situation, government has acted to bring rents under control, holding them at prewar levels, forbidding landlords to raise them without permission, and prohibiting the eviction of tenants who will not pay more. It has done so to protect tenants against exploitation, to aid in the recruitment of workers for war plants, and to restrain widespread inflation. Ceilings on rents have often been evaded. Maintenance of rental housing has been neglected. But on balance, rent control has worked.

Rent control is popular with tenants, and thus has strong political support. But control is unfair to landlords, holding them to a smaller return than that received on funds invested in other fields. It brings about malallocation of dwelling space, since families who grow smaller hold on to large apartments where the rents are fixed. It discriminates among tenants, favoring those already located as against newcomers who are seeking space. In the long run, it injures the very group it is supposed to aid, since it prevents the supply of rental housing from increasing and may even cause it to decline. Rent control may be

[5] Alvin L. Schorr, *Slums and Social Insecurity*, Research Report, No. 1 (Washington, D.C.: Social Security Administration, undated), chap. iv.

needed in a time of acute emergency. As a permanent policy, it is likely to do more harm than good.

Promotion of private housing

During the great depression of the thirties, homeowners in large numbers, unable to keep up payments on their mortgages, were threatened with foreclosures on their homes. Mortgage lenders were threatened with illiquidity or with substantial losses on their loans. To ward off these disasters, the federal government entered the field, setting up a Home Owners Loan Corporation which refinanced the mortgages, rescued the lending institutions, and saved thousands of homes. This operation built no houses. But it brought the government into the business of housing finance.

Since the thirties, through the Federal Housing Administration and the Veterans Administration, the government has sought to promote the construction of housing by private builders and to encourage homeownership by increasing the availability of credit and easing its terms. By granting federal charters to savings and loan associations and insuring their deposits, it has increased the volume of savings flowing through these agencies. By insuring payments on housing loans, it has enlarged the supply of mortgage money. By creating a secondary market for mortgages, it has assured the liquidity of lending institutions and freed their funds to make more loans. Not only has government enhanced the supply of housing credit but it has eased its terms. It has made loan ratios higher, down payments smaller, maturities longer, and interest rates lower. All this has operated to produce more houses. But the program has emphasized homeownership, doing relatively little to enlarge the supply of houses for rent. And its benefits have gone, almost entirely, to people in the middle income groups. It has done little or nothing to rehouse the poor.[6]

Public housing

In the United States, public housing is housing that is designed by private architects and constructed by private builders under contracts with public authorities and is subsequently owned and operated, on a

---

[6] Paul F. Wendt, *Housing Policy* (Berkeley, Calif.: University of California Press, 1962), chap. vi; and Meyerson, Terrett, and Wheaton, *op. cit.*, chap. xiii.

rental basis, by such authorities. The first public housing in the country was built by the federal government during World War I to provide quarters for military personnel and for workers in defense plants. Housing was next built by the Public Works Administration during the great depression as a means of providing employment and stimulating business recovery. The 50 projects constructed in some 30 cities during this period were later transferred to municipal housing authorities. Construction of public housing as a permanent policy dates from the Housing Act of 1937. Here, the purpose was not only to promote recovery but also to provide better dwellings for the poor.

As amended in later years, the Act of 1937 authorizes the federal government to extend financial aid to state and local governments in providing low-rent housing to low-income families. The law calls for the creation of municipal housing authorities whose function it is to assemble the land required for new housing developments, design the structures, let contracts for their construction, and own and operate the finished dwellings. Such authorities have been created in more than 1,500 communities in all but three of the states: Oklahoma, Utah, and Wyoming. The federal government approves the sites selected, helps in planning the projects, sets and enforces standards governing the quality and cost of construction, and makes loans and grants to the local authorities.

Local governments are required by the law to contribute 10 percent of the capital invested in each project. They raise this money by selling bonds whose interest is exempt from the federal income tax. Their contribution thus includes a federal subsidy. The federal government is authorized to put up 90 percent of the capital required. Its contribution may take the form of an outright grant or an annual payment. In practice, it has been the latter. The federal payments are made each year for 40 years. They cover the cost of interest and amortization on the local bonds. The local authorities collect the rents from the projects and meet their operating costs. They exempt the projects from property taxes but their losses here are offset by payments in lieu of taxes made in practice at federal expense. In effect, the federal government contributes virtually all of the capital required for a project. The local government breaks even on the operating costs.[7]

In its earlier form, the law favored demolition of substandard

[7] Robert M. Fisher, *Twenty Years of Public Housing* (New York: Harper & Bros., 1959), chaps. iv and v; and Wendt, *op. cit.*, pp. 190–202, 217–24.

housing and reconstruction rather than renovation. It was a "slum clearance" law, requiring that an old building be destroyed for every new one built. It thus added nothing to the quantity of housing. This limitation was subsequently dropped. The law also required that new quarters be found for tenants displaced by demolition. This requirement has been retained.

The annual number of public housing starts depends upon congressional appropriations. It has run around 35,000 dwellings a year. There were 680,000 public housing units in existence and 55,000 under construction at the end of fiscal 1968, a total of 735,000. Congress has authorized the construction of 425,000 more units by the end of fiscal 1971.

Urban renewal

In 1949, the emphasis in public housing policy shifted from the construction of new dwellings to the rehabilitation of whole neighborhoods—from the housing of the poor to the restoration of property values and tax yields. The thrust of the program came to be that of arresting urban blight, demolishing decaying structures, and developing new communities. Industry and commerce were to be attracted, the well-to-do lured back from the suburbs, the urban environment restored. Housing came to be incidental to the larger design.

Urban renewal is the product of a joint effort by municipal and federal governments and private developers. Under the Housing Act of 1949 and its amendments, a renewal project must be initiated by some sort of local public agency. First, there must be a finding that the section to be renewed is a slum or a blighted area. This is usually taken to be an area containing a concentration of substandard buildings, though the terms are not defined in the law and the decisions made are highly subjective. Second, a renewal plan is adopted by the local public agency. In preparing the plan, the LPA is assisted by an advisory planning body and by the Urban Renewal Administration. It submits the proposed plan for consideration by a citizens' advisory committee and at public hearings. It then makes such modifications as seem desirable and presents the plan for approval by the local government. Third, the government submits the plan to the URA together with a "workable program" for its effectuation. This program must detail the condition of the properties that are to be taken, the nature of the reconstruction that is proposed, and the way the project fits into a comprehensive plan for the city's development. It must show that the city's building and housing codes are adequate to insure the safety and health of residents in the renewal area; that housing will be available for the relocation of those who are displaced; that the city has an administrative organization that is capable of carrying out the program; and that its financial resources are sufficient to enable it to meet its share of the costs. In practice, the URA has not always insisted that these requirements be fully satisfied. When that body gives its approval, the LPA proceeds, fourth, to acquire the land included in the project through voluntary sale or the exercise of eminent domain. Then, fifth, it evicts the occupants of structures on the site, razes the poorer buildings, and makes improvements, laying out new streets and providing needed facilities. And finally, sixth, it sells or leases the site to a private developer.

These operations are financed in large part by the federal government. There are loans for the preparation of plans, the purchase of land, and the provision of working capital. There are grants to cover the cost of relocating displaced residents and businesses, to meet half of the cost of water and sewer facilities and two thirds of the cost of health and recreation centers. But the major federal contribution is a capital grant toward the cost of the undertaking as a whole. The price that the city gets when it sells the project to a private developer will be much lower than the cost it incurred in buying and improving the site. The developer will be heavily subsidized. He may get the site for around 30 percent of its cost. The city will sustain a loss amounting to 70 percent. A third of this loss must be borne by the city itself (a fourth if the city is held to be economically depressed). It may make this contribution in the form of land or of streets, utilities, schools, or other improvements on the site. The federal government will shoulder two thirds of the loss (three fourths where cities are depressed).[8]

Problems of urban renewal

The urban renewal program has been attacked on many fronts. The planning process is said to be defective; the resulting plans inadequate.

[8] Martin Anderson, *The Federal Bulldozer* (Cambridge, Mass.: M.I.T. Press, 1964), chap. ii; Scott Greer, *Urban Renewal and American Cities* (Indianapolis: Bobbs Merrill Co., 1965), chap. i, ii; and William L. Slayton, "The Operation and Achievements of the Urban Renewal Program" in James Q. Wilson (ed.), *Urban Renewal* (Cambridge, Mass.: M.I.T. Press, 1966), chap. vi.

At the city center, commercial interests profit. Elsewhere, even with sites provided at a bargain, private developers may not find it economical to build. Great hardships are imposed on the people who are evicted from the renewal areas. Luxury apartments are subsidized. The supply of housing for the poor is cut; their rents go up.

Planning for renewal

A local public agency responsible for a renewal program is advised by a citizens' advisory committee. Such a committee is supposed to include in its membership residents of the renewal area. This representation may be difficult to obtain. Most of the people concerned are poor. They are ignorant of the issues involved and inexperienced in negotiations. They are unlikely to be organized. In those cases where the poor are represented, their participation may be regarded as an obstacle. Their interest is not in the ultimate transformation of the city as a whole but in the immediate effects of the program in their neighborhoods. They ask for better municipal services. They oppose reconstruction that would compel them to move. For this reason, they may not be invited to participate. The advisory committee will consist, instead, of civic notables who will lend the program their prestige.

The renewal plans adopted are limited in scope. They are confined to the city limits, being unrelated to the needs of the metropolitan area as a whole. They may even be confined to particular neighborhoods without relation to a city plan. Renewal planning is not coordinated with highway planning. Roads may be driven through slums and blighted areas without regard to the requirements of renewal plans. Where the two are in conflict, highway plans will usually prevail.

The projects chosen by the planners, instead of being those most needed by the people, are likely to be those that restore middle-class amenities and embellish the city center, making the greatest show. The influence determining their choice will be that of the business interests, the real estate operators, and the private developers. The human values at stake will get short shrift. The pattern of renewal favored will be the one that is commercially most promising.[9]

[9] Jewell Bellush and Murray Hausknecht (eds.), *Urban Renewal: People, Politics, and Planning* (Garden City, N.Y.: Doubleday & Co., 1967), pp. 287–301; Greer, *op. cit.*, chaps. iii and iv; and Meyerson, Terrett, and Wheaton, *op. cit.*, chap. xv.

Relocating residents and businesses

When an area is chosen for renewal, its occupants are evicted. The law requires that they be offered safe and sanitary housing, in good locations, at rents they can afford. It provides for modest payments to help them with their moving costs. Ideally, relocation should be administered by a staff of social workers. The need for relocation should be explained, questions answered, aid given in finding and preparing new quarters, help provided in moving, and payments made to cover its costs. In practice, the people who do this work are usually untrained, poorly paid political appointees. The amount of help provided is far from adequate. The fraction of those evicted who receive it is small.

There has been extensive controversy as to whether those displaced by renewal have been properly rehoused. Administrators of the program say they have. Its critics say they have not. Studies made in particular cases show that experience has differed, depending upon the character of the group in question and the availability of suitable vacancies. Some of those who are evicted disappear; investigators do not know how they are rehoused. Others get new quarters that are inferior in quality to the old. Still others get quarters of good quality but have to pay larger amounts of money and higher fractions of their incomes in rents. Few, if any, of the residents who are displaced will be able to return to an area after it has been rebuilt; the rents then charged will be too high for them to pay.

More than half of the people displaced by urban renewal are Negroes. Indeed, slum clearance is often called "Negro clearance." Here, relocation is particularly difficult. Negroes do not want to be scattered. But efforts to move them in masses are resisted by the neighborhoods to which they go.

As the slums are emptied, their residents move into surrounding areas, overcrowding the dwellings found there, creating new slums, and spreading blight. These areas are next marked for renewal, their housing condemned, the tenants evicted to move again. So people are pushed around, from one slum to another, the bulldozers following on their heels.

There is a possible alternative. Demolition of old dwellings could be delayed until new housing was assured. New dwellings could be made ready for occupancy before people were evicted from the old. The spread of blight could be retarded, and the relocation of tenants eased. But this is not the way things are done.

Particular hardships are imposed on the owners of small-scale neighborhood businesses. Forced relocation separates them from their markets. Their sales may decline. Their rents may rise. The basis of their livelihood may be destroyed. The government contributes to the cost of moving. But it does not compensate for the loss of income.[10]

Results of urban renewal

At the city center, the results of urban renewal are impressive. There are open plazas, green parks, broad boulevards, towering apartment buildings, and massive commercial structures of steel and glass. Unseen but even more important are the profits of developers and builders, the gains of downtown businesses, the rise in property values, the growth of the tax base and the tax yield. But between the city center and the city line, the prospect is less bright. Decay persists. Developers are indifferent. Land can be made available at a fraction of its cost. But the saving on land would be only a tenth of total cost. If a market were assured, this subsidy would not be needed. Eminent domain and abundant credit would suffice. But without a market, renewal will not pay off. The program will rebuild the city center. It will not do away with the encircling blight.

The land that is cleared for renewal is more than four fifths residential. The new structures reared on it are around two-fifths nonresidential and only three-fifths residential. The program has destroyed twice as many dwellings as it has built. The dwellings built, moreover, are largely apartments for the rich. These are the tenants who are subsidized. The program has reduced the quantity and raised the rents of housing for the poor.[11]

Problems of public housing

Public housing, like urban renewal, has come in for criticism. Its cost has been high. Its design has been standardized and cheerless. Its

[10] Anderson, *op. cit.*, chap. iv; Schorr, *op. cit.*, chap. iii; and Bellush and Hausknecht, *op. cit.*, pp. 314–51.
[11] Bellush and Hausknecht, *op. cit.*, pp. 485–595; and Wilson, *op. cit.*, chaps. xx, xxiii.

management has been paternalistic. Rules governing occupancy have been intrusive and prejudicial to incentive. Rules regulating behavior have been meddlesome. The housing has not improved the character of its occupants. It is politically unpopular. It is heavily subsidized and heartily disliked.

The cost of public housing

Decent new housing has not been produced to rent at a price that the poor can afford to pay. Even with the cost of capital largely written off and with taxes partly abated, the cost of an apartment in a new multifamily urban structure runs to $150 a month. Half of the families in the slums can pay only $56 to $110, and half can pay only $35 to $60.[12] The average cost of operating a unit in all types of public housing in 1964 was $70 per month; the average rent was $44. Families who live in such housing are subsidized to the extent of $500 a year.

Within limits, costs could be cut and subsidies reduced. The price of land located in the slums is high. Overcrowded structures yielding large rents must be purchased and demolished before construction can begin. In some places, it may be possible, instead, to build on nearby vacant land such as abandoned railroad yards or market areas. The housing built here can depopulate the slums. The slum land can then be acquired at a lower price. The cost of the site influences the cost of the buildings erected on it. Where the price of land is high, it must be crowded with massive structures, and these are costlier to build. Where it is possible to build on cheaper land, there can also be savings in construction costs.

There are other ways in which these costs might be cut. It would be possible to renovate existing structures instead of building new, but the savings that could be realized do not appear to be great. It would be possible to reduce standards, providing fewer elevators, smaller rooms, and closets without doors, but this would perpetuate the slums. There might be further innovations in materials and methods of construction, though the possibilities here have largely been realized. There is one method of cutting costs, however, that has proved to be effective. Under the "turnkey" program launched in 1966, responsibility for providing public housing is turned over to private developers. A developer enters into an arrangement with a local housing authority in

12 *Business Week,* February 3, 1968, p. C-11.

which the authority provides him with specifications for a housing project and agrees to purchase the project, when completed, at a price that will cover his costs and yield him a reasonable profit. He then acquires a site, draws up his own plans for its development, arranges his own financing, constructs the buildings, and turns the key for the finished project over to the authority. The method frees him from complicated procedures that were formerly required. It enables him to complete the work in half the former time. It cuts the cost of a project by 10 to 15 percent. This saving is not large enough to obviate the need for subsidies. But it is large enough for costs and subsidies to be reduced.[13]

Occupancy of public housing

The supply of public housing falls far short of the demand. It could be rationed by raising the rents. But this would defeat the purpose of providing low-rent housing to the poor. The rationing is therefore done administratively. Certain conditions are laid down to govern eligibility. The applicant must be a citizen. His income may not be more than five times the rent. He must now be living in substandard housing. Preference is given to those with the most urgent needs: to families with children and to those displaced by clearance of slums. Admission may be denied to applicants who pose potential problems: to those whose irregular employment and frequent relocation raises questions concerning their ability to pay the rent; to those whose record of property destruction or unsafe housekeeping suggests that they would damage the buildings; to those who would endanger other tenants because of contagious disease, mental illness, drug addiction, sexual deviation, or liability to violence. Admission is also denied to persons who are judged to be immoral: to men who have been convicted of a crime; to women with illegitimate children; to the partners in a common-law marriage. In its administration of these rules, the staff of the housing authority must invade the privacy of the applicant for housing in much the same way in which the welfare worker pries into the affairs of the applicant for relief.

The occupants of public housing are not the poorest of the poor, since they could not pay even the subsidized rent. They are rather the

[13] "Turnkey Public Housing," *Journal of Housing*, January, 1968, pp. 15–24.

next-to-the-lowest income group. The median income of tenants is less than $2,500 a year. A quarter of them are recipients of public assistance. A quarter are over 65 years of age. Many are broken families. Half are Negroes. These categories overlap. A typical tenant is a black woman, without a husband, supporting a family with help from AFDC.

Public housing is for the poor. As a family's income rises, it must report that fact to the housing authority. When its income has risen as much as 25 percent, it must move to other quarters. Thus, if a family that earned $2,400 when admitted is now making $3,000, it must leave. The family then returns to the slums, living in worse quarters and paying a higher rent. It therefore has a strong incentive to lie about its earnings. The housing staff, on the other hand, must check on the family's income. Here, again, the relation between the two is an unhappy one. The rule requiring eviction, finally, acts as a disincentive to working harder and earning more.

Life in a housing project

Public housing projects differ in design. Some are two-story row housing in outlying areas. Others are elevator apartments on super-blocks near the center of town. All of them provide dwellings with several rooms, central heat, kitchen, bath, and closets. Some of them provide laundries, nurseries, playgrounds, and other amenities. They afford the only safe, sanitary, and decent new housing that is built for families with low incomes. But the design of these structures—particularly that of the massive apartment buildings—has been strongly criticized. They are said to be monolithic, monotonous, institutional, and impersonal. They lack the diversity of use that characterizes the buildings in the slums. They inhibit neighborhood life. Their hallways and elevators are unsafe. They concentrate violence and crime. They become new ghettoes, where life is worse than in the slums that they replaced. There is, in this attack, a measure of nostalgia for a romantic past. But there may be, as well, a measure of truth.[14]

The manager of public housing determines admissions, maintains the structures, checks vandalism, handles complaints, settles disputes, col-

[14] See Jane Jacobs, *The Death and Life of Great American Cities* (New York: Random House, 1961).

lects rents, and evicts tenants who earn too much or misbehave. He also makes rules to govern tenant conduct: no pets, no overnight guests, no painting or remodeling, no nails in the walls, no shaking mops out of windows, no bikes on sidewalks, and so on. In enforcing these rules, he may enter and inspect any apartment at any time. His relation with the tenants is one of mutual distrust and dislike.

Control of a housing project is bureaucratic and impersonal. There is no community and no tenant self-government. Residence in such a project is a badge of inferiority. Maintenance of the project is not a matter in which its tenants take pride.[15]

The failure of public housing

The volume of public housing is small. It shelters 7 percent of the families in New York, but little more than 1 percent in the country as a whole. It accounts for only 1½ percent of the stock of urban dwellings and for only 2 percent of the housing starts. Only a tenth as many dwellings have been built for the poor under the public housing program as have been built for the middle income groups with aid from the FHA.

Public housing has been supported by housing officials, social workers, labor unions, Negroes, and city governments. It has been opposed by property owners, realtors, builders, and lenders, being viewed as a competitive threat. It has never been popular with Congress. To the congressman, homeownership is a virtue; it is properly to be promoted at public expense. Residence in public housing, on the other hand, is identified with shiftlessness and immorality; it is not to be encouraged by men of substance and probity. The public housing program has therefore been given a pittance in relation to the need. It has not been killed; it has never really been brought alive.[16]

New approaches to housing

The Housing and Urban Development Act of 1968 has been hailed as the most comprehensive and far-reaching housing legislation since 1949. It makes a good start toward carrying out the Johnson administration's ambitious proposal to provide six million new dwellings for

[15] Schorr, *op. cit.*, chap. v.
[16] Bellush and Hausknecht, *op. cit.*, pp. 451–61; and Meyerson, Terrett, and Wheaton, *op. cit.*, pp. 345–51.

low and moderate-income families in the next 10 years, a number 10 times as great as that recorded in the past decade. The Act extends familiar programs such as public housing and urban renewal. It strengthens newer programs such as demonstration cities and rental supplements. It introduces two important innovations: a federal guarantee of payments on securities issued to finance the creation of new towns, and an interest subsidy for homeowners in the next-to-lowest income group and for owners of housing rented to tenants in this group. There are fresh approaches to urban renewal in the demonstration cities and new-towns programs, to homeownership and rental housing in the plan for interest subsidies, and to low-rent housing in the subsidization of rents. The law authorizes bold action. Whether Congress will appropriate the sums required, year after year, to carry out its provisions remains to be seen.

Demonstration cities

It is the purpose of the demonstration cities program, adopted in 1966, completely to transform a number of the country's most severely blighted urban areas. The program is not a substitute for urban renewal. It is intended rather as a supplement, as a means of showing what can be accomplished, in particular neighborhoods, by an all-out effort to rehabilitate the total environment. It recognizes that the problems of the slums—employment, education, health, and social services, along with housing—are interrelated. It holds that their solution requires a simultaneous and coordinated attack. It concerns itself not only with the renovation, demolition, and construction of buildings but also with the provision of community facilities and services. By marshalling all the resources of public and private agencies, it seeks to provide the setting for a better life.

Such is the concept. Sites in 63 cities have been approved for demonstration projects. Grants to cover the cost of planning have been made. A billion dollars has been authorized for grants in fiscal 1970. The program is getting under way. Its outcome remains to be seen.

New towns

Continued growth of population, with increasing urbanization, is packing more people into metropolitan areas and impairing the quality of urban life. Relief from this pressure is offered by the proposal to build new towns on the periphery of existing cities. These would be complete communities, accommodating 50,000 to 100,000 people, planned and built from the ground up. They would be economically and socially integrated, providing for all income groups. They would have work places close to homes, with shopping centers, schools, and libraries, clinics and hospitals, open spaces and recreational facilities. They would be functionally efficient and aesthetically pleasing.

The creation of such communities would require huge expenditures. Unaided, private enterprise would be unlikely to assume the risks. If new towns are to be built, their construction must be aided by the federal government. This aid might be provided in a variety of ways: by giving vacant land—abandoned military installations and the like— to serve as sites; by making grants to pay for water and sewer systems, park lands, and recreational facilities; or as provided by the Act of 1968, by guaranteeing payments on securities issued by private developers.

The creation of new towns has been opposed by property owners in the cities who fear that their competition would cause property values to fall, and by city officials who fear that they would divert funds from urban renewal and prevent improvement of the tax base and the tax yield. In the absence of offsetting pressure from groups who might gain from new towns, Congress has been slow to act.[17]

Interest subsidies

Under the Act of 1968, the federal government is empowered to subsidize the payment of interest as a means of encouraging the ownership of homes by families in the next-to-lowest income group and the provision of rental housing for families in this group. This aid is limited to families with incomes that do not exceed the limit set for residents in public housing by more than 35 percent. Such a family must devote a fifth of its income to payments for amortization of a mortgage running for as long as 40 years, for interest, and for taxes and insurance. If it then fails to meet the charges that are due, the government can contribute the difference between the contractual interest and a rate of 1 percent. Thus, where the monthly payments due on a

---

[17] Adela Adam Nevitt, (ed.), *The Economic Problems of Housing* (New York: St. Martin's Press, 1967), chap. xi; Bellush and Hausknecht, *op. cit.*, pp. 536–42; and Greer, *op. cit.*, chap. vii.

$12,000 house at 6¾ percent amount to $99.66 and where a family earning $300 a month pays $60 of this charge, the government can contribute the remaining $39.66. In the case of rental housing for tenants with incomes falling within the same limit—too high to be eligible for public housing and too low to pay commercial rents—the government, again, can contribute, for 40 years, the difference between the landlord's contractual interest and 1 percent. This should help the tenant by enabling the landlord to reduce his rent. These subsidies should bring homeownership and adequate rental housing within the reach of families with incomes just above the poverty line. In neither case do they contribute to the housing of the very poor.

Rent supplements

Under a program initiated in 1965, rent supplements are paid for quarters in housing provided by nonprofit groups such as churches, social agencies, labor unions, and the like. They are paid on behalf of tenants whose incomes are low enough to make them eligible for public housing but who are unable to obtain decent housing by paying a quarter of their incomes in rent. The landlord charges a "fair market rent," one that enables him to cover his costs. The tenant contributes a fourth of his income toward this rent. The government makes up the difference between the two. As his income rises, the tenant pays more and the government less. When a fourth of the tenant's income equals the fair market rent, the government's contribution comes to an end.

Rent supplements present administrative problems. The tenants who are to receive the supplements must be selected. Their incomes must be checked to determine the amount of rent that they can pay. The housing must be inspected to make sure that it conforms to prescribed standards and is properly maintained. The fair market rent collected by the landlord must be audited to make sure that the government is not overcharged. Disputes between landlords and tenants must be settled and evictions controlled. But these difficulties, however serious, are less than those encountered in the administration of public housing.

Rent supplements have a number of advantages. They cost less than public housing. They scatter subsidized tenants throughout the city instead of concentrating them in huge housing projects. They avoid the institutionalization that characterizes public housing and the stigma that is attached. They do not require eviction of the tenant if his income rises. They do not impair his incentive to work.[18]

Despite their merits, rent supplements have been politically unpopular. The appropriations made for their payment have been meager. The program has been small in scale.

[18] Charles Abrams, "The Subsidy of Housing," *Journal of Land and Public Utility Economics,* Vol. 22 (1946), pp. 131–39; and Bellush and Hausknecht, *op. cit.,* pp. 508–19.

Job creation and area
development

So far in our discussion of the attack on poverty, we have been concerned with programs and proposals that provide poor people with
money or with services that lighten the burdens they must bear: with
public assistance, rent suplements, guaranteed income, and children's
allowances; and with welfare services and public housing. Such measures are necessary, but they are only palliatives. They do not attack
the causes of poverty; they do not prevent its occurrence or recurrence. But government has also adopted measures that attack causes
and look toward prevention: measures that are designed not only to
support the unemployed but to enlarge the volume of employment;
not only to extend relief to impoverished farmers but to increase their
mobility and productivity; not only to maintain welfare services in
depressed areas but to provide these areas with a basis for development.
It is to such measures that we turn in this chapter and the next.

Job creation

Government has undertaken to expand employment in three principal ways. First, it has sought to enlarge the number of jobs by adopting
monetary and fiscal policies that operate directly to increase the aggre-

gate demand for goods and services and indirectly to increase the demand for labor. Second, it has sought, through persuasion and through subsidization, to induce private business to create new jobs and hire the unemployed to fill them. Third, it has itself created jobs to provide employment for the unemployed. It did so on a large scale during the great depression of the thirties. It has done so on a smaller scale during the sixties. It has now been proposed that government should guarantee employment as a matter of permanent policy to anyone who cannot find it elsewhere—that it should serve, in the current phrase, as an "employer of last resort." Each of these approaches has succeeded in putting people to work. But each of them presents problems that give ground for concern.

Increasing aggregate demand

It is a commonplace of economics that government can increase the total demand for goods and services by giving people more money to spend. It can do so by making it easier to get credit, by cutting taxes, and by enlarging public expenditures. The increase in demand will operate in turn to increase employment. By raising the rate of growth in demand to 5 percent or more per year, government can reduce the rate of unemployment to 3 percent or less. And a reduction of unemployment will bring about a reduction of poverty.

In a tight labor market, former obstacles to employment will tend to disappear. Employers will have to compete for labor. To get it, they will hire more young people and more members of minority groups. Where workers lack training, employers will train them. Wages will rise, hours will be lengthened, overtime earnings will be increased. More workers will join the labor force, with two or more members of a family taking jobs. Family incomes will grow. And with adequate incomes, many of the problems associated with poverty will be solved.

Beginning in 1961, monetary and fiscal policy were consciously and actively employed to promote prosperity. As a result, the economy experienced the longest and strongest expansion in its history. From 1961 through 1967 the gross national product grew at the rate of 5.2 percent per year. The volume of employment increased from 65 million to 75 million. The rate of unemployment dropped from 6.7 percent of the labor force to 3.8 percent. From 1959 through 1966 the portion of the population in poverty declined from 22.1 to 15.4. Nearly 10 million people were lifted above the poverty line. The effectiveness of monetary and fiscal action was demonstrated beyond dispute.[1]

There are economists who argue that maximization of demand is all that is needed to do away with poverty. This view is not to be accepted. Certainly, unemployment is a major cause of poverty and monetary and fiscal policies that will increase opportunities for employment must play a large part in any effort to reduce poverty. But such policies have their limitations and their risks.

Unemployment is to be attributed not only to a deficiency in the aggregate demand for goods and services but also to structural changes and rigidities in the market for labor. Men are thrown out of work as tastes change and the demand for particular goods declines, and as technology changes and the demand for workers with particular skills declines. Jobs disappear as the resource base of a region is exhausted and industry moves away. New jobs are created in different places, in different industries, requiring different skills. Movement of labor from areas of surplus to areas of shortage is not frictionless. Workers are uninformed concerning openings elsewhere and are not always able or willing to move. Blue-collar workers are not readily hired for white-collar jobs, nor are youngsters hired for jobs requiring experience or Negroes for jobs where employers observe a color line. It takes something more than enlargement of demand to move workers into vacancies. Government must make sure that barriers to mobility are lessened, that training is provided, and that racial discrimination is overcome. It is only within the context of such a program that enlargement of demand can bear full fruit in the creation of employment.

When it occurs, expansion of employment will bring income only to families who have a member in the labor force. But two fifths of the poor do not. The aged, the disabled, and women left with dependent children must be cared for outside the labor market. Some poverty, too, is due to the fact that the earnings of workers, even when employed, are too low to lift them above the poverty line. In 1966, a fourth of all poor families, 1.5 million in number, were headed by a man who had worked 40 hours a week for 50 weeks or more.[2] Mea-

---

[1] *Economic Report of the President, 1968*, pp. 59, 130.
[2] *Ibid.*, p. 145; and Mollie Orshansky, "The Shape of Poverty in 1966," *Social Security Bulletin*, March, 1968, pp. 3–32 at p. 14.

sures in addition to the creation of employment opportunities are thus required for the amelioration of poverty.

If expansionist policies could create enough demand and thus provide enough jobs nearly to do away with poverty, they might also set off an inflationary spiral. Indeed, unemployment could not be cut much lower than 3.5 percent without serious inflation. Expansion would then be dissipated in rising prices. The higher prices would cut the real income of the poor. The problem of poverty would remain. The higher prices would operate, too, to produce an adverse balance of international payments. Imports would rise; exports would fall; monetary reserves would decline. Inflation could be checked by imposing administrative controls. But this would require the government to fix prices and wages; to ration consumers' goods and allocate materials and manpower as it did in World War II; and to establish import quotas and control the use of foreign exchange. The cost of such an undertaking would be enormous. Made permanent in peacetime, it would put the economy in a straitjacket. It would give rise to violent political conflict. It would change the character of the society.

In short, the maximization of aggregate demand is a powerful and an essential measure in the attack on poverty. But it is not sufficient in itself. And it cannot be pushed too far without inviting inflation and all the evils it entails.

Jobs in the private sector

In the sixties, the country has been confronted by the spectacle of unemployment amidst prosperity, of poverty amidst affluence, of violence in the ghettoes of its cities. Recurring riots have been attributed in large part to unemployment among Negro youths and to the persistence among their elders of a hard core of the unemployed. In this situation, the government has exhorted business enterprises to enlist in an attack on these problems as a matter of social responsibility, appealing to them to provide training for the unskilled and jobs for the unemployed, and urging them to build plants in the ghettoes to create jobs there.

There have been many obstacles to a favorable response. Most of the hardcore unemployed have never developed work habits and have been idle for years on end. Most of the youths are lacking in training and experience. In both groups, motivation is weak. Among such workers, the rate of absenteeism is high, the problem of discipline serious, and the quality of workmanship low. Much counseling is needed, at a substantial cost. It is understandable that businessmen prefer to hire workers whose training, experience, and motivation are assured. So, too, with the location of enterprises in the ghettoes. The qualifications of workers found there may be low, the cost of employing them high. It may be difficult to persuade supervisory and clerical personnel to come to work in these areas. With riots recurring, the money invested in new plants may be lost. It is understandable, again, that businessmen prefer to build these plants on land that is available in suburbs and small towns. Private enterprise, it should be recalled, is legally obligated to serve the interest of its stockholders. It is not its duty to function as a welfare agency. If government, as a matter of public policy, desires to use business as an instrument in providing training and employment, it is government, not business, that must meet the cost.

The federal government has recognized this fact. In a number of programs inaugurated in 1967 and 1968, it contracted or offered to contract with private firms to train and employ several thousand disadvantaged workers, making payments running to $3,000 per worker to cover their costs. In one experimental project, designed to provide training and jobs in the ghettoes of five cities, it agreed to pay $5,000 per year for every worker trained and hired. The most ambitious of these programs—Job Opportunities in the Business Sector (JOBS)— was launched in 1968. It was designed to engage 100,000 of the hardcore unemployed in 50 cities by mid-1969 and 500,000 by mid-1971, with government meeting the cost of training and making up for losses of productivity, its payments running to $3,500 per person per year. A National Alliance of Businessmen, under the leadership of Henry Ford, undertook to enlist the cooperation of business enterprises, setting up quotas for each major city and for each large firm and urging participation in the plan. At the end of 1968, the Alliance reported that 12,000 employers had hired 84,000 workers of whom 61,000 were still on the job.

Job creation in the thirties

Faced with unemployment averaging 10 million—around a fifth of the labor force—during the thirties, the federal government devised a number of programs for the purpose of creating jobs. It increased the volume of public works, employing additional laborers in the construction of highways, dams, schools, hospitals, and the like. These projects were slow in getting under way. Four fifths of the jobs they created were for construction workers. Their influence on the volume of employment was small. To provide jobs more rapidly for larger numbers, the government set up a Civil Works Administration in 1933. This agency gave temporary employment to four million workers, at regular wages, on projects that would not compete with private business. It was superseded by a Works Progress Administration in 1935. WPA employment was limited to persons who were on relief, the program being based on the view that aid should be provided in the form of jobs rather than cash. Less than half of those who were eligible were ever employed, the number on the rolls amounting to about two million at any one time. Here, again, the unemployed were put to work on projects that would not compete with private enterprise: cleaning up parks, for instance, and preparing card catalogs for libraries. The standards of performance on some of the work were low. Opponents of the program denounced the projects as unneeded, calling them "leaf-raking" and "boondoggling," and pictured the workers leaning on their shovels. But the services provided were useful, and work on almost any basis was preferable to continued idleness.

Two other programs were designed for youths who were unemployed. Under a Civilian Conservation Corps, 1,500 camps were set up in the forests, each of them employing 200 young men on conservation projects, providing them with maintenance and paying them $30 a month. More than two million youths passed through these camps before the end of the decade. Their work was useful; their work experience was valuable. An opportunity to provide them with basic education and vocational training was largely missed. Under a National Youth Administration, part-time jobs, paying around $15 a month, were provided to enable students to remain in schools and colleges; by 1940, one and a half million young people were being aided in this way. Work relief was extended during the period to another million who were not in school: they were given jobs on part-time construction, sanitation, and clerical projects, at around a quarter of the WPA wage. Here, again, an opportunity to provide effective vocational training was lost.

Job creation in the sixties

Job creation by government, neglected in the forties and the fifties, was attempted again in the sixties. This time, it was a product of concern with the problems of depressed areas, of dissatisfaction with the operation of the public assistance program, and of determination to launch a general attack on poverty. The movement comprised a variety of programs, patterned after those originated 30 years before. An effort was made to increase employment in the depressed areas by stepping up expenditures on public works. A few thousand chronically unemployed adults were put to work on WPA-like projects, beautifying highways, parks, and recreational areas, rehabilitating facilities in blighted urban neighborhoods, providing day care for children of working mothers, and serving as aides to professional workers in education, recreation, and public health. A number of programs combined employment and training. The emphasis in the Manpower Development and Training Program and in the Job Corps was on training; these are to be discussed in Chapter 18. The emphasis in the Work Experience and Training Program and in the Neighborhood Youth Corps was on providing jobs.

The belief, which we encountered in Chapter 14, that employable people were living on public assistance led to proposals to substitute work relief for cash relief. Such action was taken by a number of states, some 400 communities putting 30,000 recipients of assistance to work as janitors, watchmen, and maintenance men. Congress also responded, when it amended the Social Security Act in 1962, by providing that aid to parents with dependent children could be given in the form of payments for work. A work and training program was inaugurated by the welfare authorities with the federal government first meeting half and later all of the costs. Employment was provided to heads of families who were able to work but had no jobs. By 1967, there were 150,000 engaged, half of them women and three fourths of them on the assistance rolls. These people were put to work by state and local agencies and private nonprofit organizations. The projects adopted, mostly involving unskilled labor, provided little in the way of useful work experience or training, having the character of old-fashioned work relief. Under the law, those enrolled in the program were to receive payments to cover their basic needs as determined by the standards set by the states; in practice, two thirds of them got less than this. The average participant dropped out of the program within five months. His employment record after participation was no better than before.[3] There was no incentive for recipients of assistance to take part in the program, payments to persons who did so being no larger than payments to those who did not. This situation was changed by the amendment adopted in 1967 disqualifying adults from receiving AFDC payments if they should refuse to accept employment or to enroll for training. This made for a much larger program. But there was no reason to suppose that it would differ in character or in results from the earlier one.

In the sixties, as in the thirties, jobs were also created for youths between the ages of 16 and 21. Under a work-study program, mentioned in Chapter 10, institutions of higher learning were enabled to pay needy students for work done during summer vacations and during the academic year, with the federal government meeting nine tenths of the cost. The Neighborhood Youth Corps, set up in the Department of Labor in 1964 and financed entirely by the federal government, initiated three programs to provide employment to disadvantaged youths. Under one, schools provided part-time jobs to enable students to continue with their schooling. Under a second, government and private nonprofit agencies provided full-time jobs, affording an "ageing vat" for entrants to the labor force. The third gave employment during the summer; it was supposedly designed to insure against riots. Those employed in the three programs were paid the minimum wage prescribed by federal law. The programs, taken together, provided jobs for 500,000 youths each year. The Youth Corps was popular with employers, who were supplied with labor free of charge. It gave the youths enrolled an opportunity to acquire work attitudes and habits. It offered little in the way of vocational counseling or training.[4]

---

[3] Sar A. Levitan, *Antipoverty Work and Training Efforts* (Ann Arbor, Mich.: Institute of Labor and Industrial Relations, University of Michigan, 1967), chap. iv; and Worth Bateman, "An Application of Cost-Benefit Analysis to the Work Experience Program," *American Economic Review*, Vol. 57, No. 2 (1967), pp. 80–90.

[4] Levitan, *op. cit.*, chap. iii.

"Employer of last resort"

A National Commission on Technology, Automation, and Economic Progress, reporting to Congress in 1966, recommended "a program of public service employment, providing, in effect, that Government be an employer of last resort, providing work for the 'hard-core unemployed' in useful community enterprises."[5] And a National Advisory Committee on Rural Poverty, reporting to the President in 1967, recommended that the government "stand ready to provide jobs . . . to every employed person willing and able to work."[6] Under this proposal, the government would hire all the surplus labor that was offered just as it has purchased surpluses of agricultural commodities. The proposal has been widely endorsed. When the Gallup Poll sampled national opinion on a guaranteed income, it found 36 percent of the respondents for it and 58 percent against. But when it asked for opinions on guaranteed employment that would yield the same income, it found 78 percent of the respondents pro and only 18 percent con.[7]

Proponents of guaranteed income and of guaranteed employment have had little to say concerning the relation of the two. Presumably, they would be supplementary rather than substitutes, one for the other. The guaranteed income would be paid to persons who were not in the labor force. It would be paid to persons at work whose wages were low. It would be paid, also, to persons who preferred to live in idleness. Refusal to accept guaranteed employment would not disqualify an applicant for guaranteed income. But the structure of the income guarantee would be such that the worker would gain by accepting employment at a guaranteed job. The incentive to work would be preserved.

An alternative to government employment would be government subsidization of employment by private enterprise. But this would not fully satisfy the need for jobs. Provision of employment for disadvantaged workers is not a private responsibility. Government is in-

---

[5] National Commission on Technology, Automation, and Economic Progress, *Technology and the American Economy,* Vol. 1 (Washington, D.C.: U.S. Government Printing Office, 1966), p. 110.

[6] National Advisory Commission on Rural Poverty, *The People Left Behind* (Washington, D.C.: U.S. Government Printing Office, 1967), p. 19.

[7] *New York Times,* June 16, 1968.

escapably concerned with the welfare of the unemployed; business is not. Government may induce business to provide training for workers who are potentially productive, but not to give jobs to all who may come. Government, moreover, can create employment where business cannot. It can put people to work producing useful goods and services for which no private market exists: flood control, for instance, and public health work. Business is limited to the production of goods and services for which it can collect a price. If jobs are to be provided in other fields, this must be done by government.

Another alternative to government employment is public assistance. For a number of reasons, employment is to be preferred. It avoids the waste of manpower and provides the community with goods and services it would not otherwise enjoy. It instils job habits, imparts and preserves job skills, and maintains morale. Where public assistance is demoralizing, employment contributes to self-respect. Employment may cut the costs of illness, delinquency, and disorder. Work for wages is better for the community and better for the worker than idleness on relief.

Problems of guaranteed employment

The administrators of a government guarantee of employment would be faced by a number of problems: how to select workers among those applying, what sorts of jobs to provide, where to set wages, and how to supervise the work. Those who advocate such a guarantee propose that the government hire all comers. But it might not be possible to do so. Impoverished farmers would head for the cities, seeking the guaranteed jobs. Workers receiving wages lower than those paid for such employment would quit and apply for these jobs. It is estimated that three million workers would demand employment and that the cost of hiring them would run to $12 billion a year.[8] It is unlikely that any such sum would be appropriated for the purpose. Some way would have to be found to keep down the numbers and the cost. One possibility would be to limit employment to those in the greatest need. For this purpose, however, a means test would have to be used. The program would assume the unhappy aspect of work

---

[8] Garth L. Mangum, "Government as Employer of Last Resort," in Sar A. Levitan *et al.* (eds.), *Towards Freedom from Want* (Madison, Wis.: Industrial Relations Research Assn., 1968), pp. 135–61, at pp. 152–53.

relief. If not need, what should the criterion be? Should the jobs be reserved for the hardcore of the unemployed—for those who show the least promise of finding other work? or should they be given to those more likely to benefit from work experience—to those who will move on to better jobs? The answers depend upon the purposes the program is supposed to serve.

If the labor employed is not to be wasted, its product should be useful. But government is handicapped in providing useful work. It cannot employ people to turn out goods and services that are already produced by private enterprise. If it does so, it will be charged with engaging in unfair competition and destroying private jobs. It must therefore put its employees to work producing goods and services that cannot be sold in the market. But they must still be useful. The possibilities, however, are great. There are many services, long needed, that are not performed. There is work to be done in improving the environment: conserving resources, rehabilitating structures, beautifying roads and parks. There are services that are inadequately supplied: mail delivery, street cleaning, trash removal, and the care of open spaces. It would be possible to employ the poor in larger numbers to meet the needs of the poor: providing day care for children and help for the aged and infirm. It would be possible, too, to develop a class of subprofessionals to serve as aides in health, in education, and in other fields where professional personnel is in short supply. In short, there is no end of noncompetitive, useful work that competent people could be employed to do.[9]

In the interest of the worker, the employment provided should be at real jobs: jobs that are full-time and exacting, and jobs that command respect. For older people and for those who lack the capacity for improvement, it is not necessary to provide employment that will give training and develop skills. Here, work is an end in itself; employment in unskilled occupations will suffice. For younger people, however, where there is capacity for growth, the jobs provided should lead to something better, affording progression through training, experience, and promotion. In none of the work programs of the past have these requirements been satisfied. Standards of performance have been low. Workers have been placed in dead-end jobs, with little training or carry-over of experience. The work has borne the stigma of charity.

---

[9] See Arthur Pearl and Frank Riessman, *New Careers for the Poor* (Glencoe, N.Y.: Free Press, 1965).

Government must do better in the future if heavy investment in guaranteed employment is to be justified.

At what level should wages be set? Here, in the case of work relief, WPA faced a dilemma. It could require a man to work full time to earn the payment made to people on relief. If it did so, labor would be exploited; the wages paid per hour would be shamefully low. Alternatively, WPA could pay the market rate of wages for full-time work. If it took this course, the cost of work relief would be impossibly high. Its first solution was to pay the market rate of wages but require employees to stop work when their relief incomes had been earned. As a result, the length of the workweek varied from man to man, in no case being long enough to preserve work habits or to maintain skills. The final solution was to pay a "security wage," setting it at a level higher than relief payments and lower than market wage rates, the purpose being to provide an incentive for workers to return to private employment as business improved.

Currently, proponents of guaranteed employment are not concerned with recovery from depression but assume that such employment will be needed in good times as well as in bad. They propose that wages for this work be set at the level required by the minimum wage law. If this should be done, workers not covered by the law and receiving less than the minimum would quit their work and apply for the guaranteed jobs. Whenever the minimum wage was raised, moreover, the workers displaced would apply for these jobs. This movement from private to public employment would add to the program's cost.

And finally, it would be particularly difficult to supervise workers on guaranteed jobs. Other employers, private and public, would hire the more productive labor. The guaranteed employment program would get those who were left, most of them people of lesser ability, lacking in skill, experience, and motivation. These people could not readily be fitted into many of the jobs the program had created. Much effort would have to be devoted to placement and training, to supervision and discipline. The standards of performance would be low.

The objectives of creating jobs and minimizing production costs are inconsistent. It would doubtless be cheaper to maintain some of the poor in idleness than to incur the costs involved in putting them to work. But work is to be preferred to idleness, even though costly. And where the productivity of labor can be raised through work experience, the undertaking may justify its cost.

Rural rehabilitation

One fourth of the people living in rural areas in the United States in 1965 were in poverty. One fifth of the rural poor were Negroes; four fifths were white. One fourth lived on farms; three fourths in towns and villages.[10] The rural poverty was concentrated in certain regions: in Appalachia, the deep South, and the Ozarks, among Indians and Mexican Americans in the Southwest, and in scattered pockets in the lake states and on the western plains. The impoverished regions were characterized by dilapidated housing, poor schools, and poor health and welfare services. Their people suffered from inadequate diets, high rates of morbidity, and low levels of education. They were as much in need of help as the urban poor.

Between 1933 and 1968, the federal government spent around $80 billion extending aid to farmers. Its efforts were directed in the main toward raising the prices the farmers got for their crops. It did so by restricting output, by taking surplus commodities off the market, and by paying farmers the difference between prices fixed by the market and those fixed by law. The gains realized by farmers were proportionate to their sales. The greater part of these gains went, therefore, to large operators, amounting in some cases to hundreds of thousands of dollars per year. The gains realized by small farmers were insignificant. The program was not designed to lessen rural poverty.

Residents of rural areas have benefitted from welfare programs that were nationwide in scope: social insurance, public assistance, federal grants for the construction of hospitals, and federal aid for local schools. The government has also adopted programs, over the years, to help farmers who were poor. But these have been less popular with politicians, less well financed, and less important than the ones that subsidize the well-to-do.

Aid to small farmers

Small farmers are poor because their productivity is low. Some of them are cultivating infertile soils. Most of them have farms that are too small and capital that is too limited. Many of them are incompetent; they are poorly educated, unskilled, aged. They have not been

[10] National Advisory Commission on Rural Poverty, *op. cit.*, pp. 3–5.

reached by the agricultural extension services and are not aware of changes in agricultural technology. Low productivity can be attacked in either of two ways. Poor farmers can be encouraged to move out of agriculture into industry. Or they can be helped to raise their efficiency. A large-scale exodus from agriculture has been under way for three decades. It could be accelerated by providing the farmer with information on openings in urban industry, by training him to fill such openings, and by helping him to move. It could be promoted, too, by encouraging industries to locate in rural areas. But many farmers are unable or unwilling to move; they are too ignorant, too handicapped, too old, too reluctant to change their way of life, and too afraid to take on new responsibilities. These people can be helped, however, to increase their productivity. They can be instructed in methods of cultivation and farm management, and assisted in financing enlargement of their farms and acquisition of larger amounts of capital. Their greater efficiency hopefully will bring them incomes that will lift them out of poverty.

The first of these approaches has been taken by a rural development program that was first set up in the Department of Agriculture in 1955. Under this program, local committees are formed in rural areas to study resources and needs and formulate plans for development. Such plans may include training for employment off the farms and measures designed to attract new industries. They are financed by local governments with various forms of federal aid. The concept is sound, but the program has been small; its achievements insignificant.

The second approach was first taken in 1937 by the Farm Security Administration and has been carried forward since 1946 by its successor, the Farmers Home Administration. This agency makes loans to rural communities, to farm cooperatives, and to individual farmers, and insures repayment of loans that are made by private lenders. Its loans to local governments finance the construction of water and sewer systems, housing, and recreational facilities. Its loans to cooperatives finance irrigation and drainage projects, the erection of grain elevators and the acquisition of heavy equipment. Its loans to the farmers themselves serve a number of purposes. There are long-term loans to enable the farmers to buy land and to enlarge their holdings, to construct farm buildings, and to develop soil and water resources. There are loans, for shorter terms to enable them to buy farm equipment, livestock, feeds, seeds, fertilizers, and insecticides. These loans are made on easy terms, with long maturities and low interest rates. But most important is the fact that their use is supervised in order to make sure that their intended purposes are served. Members of the FHA staff visit the borrowers, help them to prepare farm plans, advise them on their choice of crops and methods of cultivation, make recommendations on farm management, and work out a schedule for repayment of the debt. In this way, the agency has put hundreds of thousands of small farm families on their feet. Given the economic level of the borrowers, the record of repayment is remarkably good. Nine tenths of them have made their payments on schedule. Loans written off as losses have been less than 1 percent of those made. In execution as well as in conception, this program must be adjudged a success.

Farm labor

Poverty is extreme among those who work as laborers on farms. Their numbers have run around a million in recent years. Their wages are low, amounting during the sixties to less than a dollar an hour. They are employed for only part of the time, working for about 140 days a year. Their annual incomes are less than $2,000; some of them as low as $1,000. A half million are migrants, moving from South to North each year with the ripening of the crops, some of them under contracts with farmers, some picking up work as they go along. These workers, mostly unskilled young Negroes, take their families with them, crowding into miserable quarters with inadequate sanitation— the school-age children working after hours or in violation of the law, and the younger children shamefully neglected. Farm laborers are covered by little of the nation's welfare legislation. One tenth of them, working on farms with seven or more employees, are covered by the federal minimum wage law; nine tenths of them, working on smaller farms, are not. The workers in three states are insured against industrial accidents; those in 47 states are not. None are insured against unemployment. Workers who remain long enough with a single employer attain eligibility for old-age, survivorship, disability, and medical benefits under the federal law; the migrants, constantly on the move, do not. Those who remain in a single state are eligible for public assistance; the migrants, not meeting the residence requirement, are not.[11]

[11] See Richard L. Tobin, "One Million Migrants," *Saturday Review,* August 17, 1968, pp. 12 ff.

Steps have been taken to help farm labor. Some of the states that depend on migrants have set up summer schools and playgrounds to care for their children. Under the federal housing law, funds have been made available on liberal terms for the construction of housing for migrants; but farmers have been reluctant to borrow for such projects, so little housing has been built. Under the Migrant Health Act of 1962, the federal government makes grants to public and nonprofit agencies to cover part of the cost of operating health clinics for migrants and their families; such services are now provided in many of the states. Under the Economic Opportunity Act of 1964, the government makes loans to finance programs of housing, sanitation, and education for migrants and to provide day care for their children. By 1967, 150,000 migratory workers in 35 states had benefitted from the services provided in this way.

Area development

There are regions in the United States that suffer from pervasive poverty. Their resources have been exhausted; the demand for their products has declined. Industries have moved away; their economies are stagnant. As a result, their rates of unemployment are high; the average incomes of their families are low. Such regions are found in New England, in the Appalachians, on the coastal plains, in the Ozarks, and along the upper Great Lakes. These areas have not shared in the country's prosperity since World War II. Their welfare burden is heavy; their tax bases limited; their social services inadequate. The productive capacities of their people are impaired.

Given time, the problem of poverty in these areas should disappear. With opportunity elsewhere, people will move out. Workers will find employment at good wages; their families will be given better care. The declining region will be left to die. But this solution is not easy to accept. Younger people may leave, but the older ones will stay; the burden of public assistance will remain. People are not content to see their home communities decline. Instead of sending workers out to seek employment, they prefer to provide employment at home by moving industries in. And this solution may be both economically feasible and socially desirable. With modern transport, the depressed areas are less remote from urban markets. With open space, they offer less congested areas in which to work and live. So public policy, in recent years, has turned to area development.

Early development efforts

Private industry may be induced to locate in depressed areas in either of two ways. First, government can make these areas more attractive by investing in social capital: in roads that will increase accessibility and reduce transport costs; in water systems needed for industrial operations; in schools and health facilities that make communities more livable. It can invest, too, in human capital, giving vocational training and developing labor skills. Second, government can offer subsidies to business: it can guarantee private loans; make public loans on easy terms; make outright grants. It can prepare industrial sites and provide them at a loss or free of charge. It can offer a variety of escapes from federal, state, and local taxes. It can let contracts to favored plants.

Following both of these approaches, development efforts have been made over the years by a variety of private and public agencies; by chambers of commerce, banks, railroads, public utilities, and community development corporations; and by port districts and departments of state governments. The role of the federal government has been a growing one. Its most notable achievement has been the development of the Tennessee Valley, designed in the thirties to control floods, promote navigation, and develop the hydroelectric potential of the Tennessee River system; and extended in the forties to produce materials for warfare—aluminum for aircraft and atomic fuels. Area development was next undertaken by the Kennedy administration as a means of countering a business recession. Under the Area Redevelopment Acts of 1961 and 1962, the federal government made loans to local governments and to private businesses in areas where the unemployment rate was high, putting up as much as 86 percent of the cost of public improvements and 65 percent of the cost of private plants. By mid-1964, it had obligated $225,000,000 for loans on 470 projects that were expected to create 67,000 new jobs. The government undertook to promote development on a larger scale and for a longer period when Congress passed the Appalachian Regional Development Act and the broader Economic Development Act in 1965.

Appalachia

The region known as Appalachia, stretching through 11 states from Pennsylvania to Alabama, is the most extensive of the depressed areas. Here, the land has been despoiled: the first growth of timber cut off, the earth laid bare by strip mines, the hillsides eroded by careless cultivation, the streams polluted, the valleys ravaged by floods. Here are widespread and protracted unemployment, low incomes, human deterioration, and swollen welfare rolls. But here, too, are potentials for development: a second growth of timber, remaining deposits of coal, pasture lands, recreational resources, sites for hydroelectric installations, and a labor force that could be trained for factory work. To promote the redevelopment of this region, Congress set up an Appalachian Regional Commission, its membership including the governor of each of the 11 states or his appointee and a representative of the federal government—its work to be supervised by an executive director. This body was to prepare a comprehensive development plan, provide technical assistance to state and local governments, and coordinate their development programs. The cost of the enterprise was underwritten by the federal government, the law authorizing loans to cover 50 percent of the cost of improving timberland and grants to cover 70 to 80 percent of the cost of constructing highways, filling and sealing abandoned mines, providing pasturage and controlling erosion. The total expenditure authorized through 1971 was $1,100,000,000. Of this, $847,600,000 was for highways and $252,400,000 for all other purposes. The region's greatest need, in the judgment of Congress, was for roads to overcome its isolation and open it to development.

Three years later, there was evidence of progress. Unemployment was down; income was up. But this was attributable to a rise in the demand for coal. The highways were being built. New industry was trickling in: small plants were making tufted bedspreads, ceramic tableware, and parts for wooden toys, each employing from 10 to 40 men. Altogether, 4,500 jobs were said to have been created by mid-1967. There were signs of improvement in the towns: streets had been paved, housing rehabilitated, a few hospitals built. There were vocational training programs and new marketing cooperatives. But the poorer communities showed little change. New programs were resisted. Welfare workers were denounced as radical agitators and driven away. There was little indigenous development. The economy had come to depend increasingly on the federal government. Such gains as were realized had been purchased at a high cost.[12] But the effort had only begun; judgment should be suspended until the final evidence was in.

The Economic Development Program

The broader program inaugurated in 1965, under an Economic Development Administration in the Department of Commerce, extends aid to places in three categories, identified as development areas, districts, and regions. A development area falls within the boundaries of a county, a labor market, or a large city. A development district includes a number of counties, usually 5 to 10, containing two or more development areas and at least one development center—a city with a potential for further growth. Development regions include parts of two or more states, Appalachia being the prototype. These places become eligible for aid when it is found that they have been dependent on one or two declining industries; that their unemployment rates are above and their per capita incomes below the national average; that their housing and facilities for health and education are substandard; that they have had substantial emigration.

Organization and procedure in the development regions are like those in Appalachia. The states concerned set up a regional commission with state and federal co-chairmen. This agency employs a planning staff with the federal government meeting first all and then half of the cost. It initiates long-range programs, makes recommendations to the governments concerned, and coordinates their development activities. Federal aid beyond the administrative costs requires specific action by Congress. Five regions have been recognized in addition to Appalachia: New England, the Coastal Plains, the Ozarks, the Upper Great Lakes, and the Four Corners where Utah, Colorado, New Mexico, and Arizona meet.

In area or district development, a comprehensive program is prepared by a local committee and approved by the state governments and the EDA. Projects included in the program are then eligible for federal aid. The federal government makes grants to cover three fourths of

[12] Peter Schrag, "Appalachia," *The Saturday Review*, January 28, 1968, pp. 14–18.

the cost of planning and administering the program and half to four fifths of the cost of public facilities. It makes grants to small cities, not themselves depressed, that may serve as centers to promote development in the hinterland. Where private firms cannot obtain capital elsewhere, the government makes long-term low-interest loans to cover two thirds of the cost of their projects. Congress authorized the expenditure of $3,350,000,000 on these grants and loans from 1965 to 1970.

The aid provided on 142 projects listed by EDA in August of 1968 varied in scale from $32,500 to help establish a firm in the Zuni Indian Reservation to employ 28 Indians in the manufacture of electrical components to $10,000,000 to help build an aluminum plant in Goodnoe, Washington, to provide employment to 500 people. The average loan or grant was for less than $1,000,000. Sixty-five were for water or sewer systems, 23 for industrial enterprises, 13 for vocational training centers, 12 for factory sites, 10 for highways and airports, 9 for tourist facilities, and 10 for a variety of other purposes.[13] Altogether, the aid extended by EDA to mid-1967 was said to have created about 15,000 permanent new jobs.[14] The record is not an impressive one. But here, again, final judgment should be withheld.

The prospects for development

What is the likelihood that industry can be induced to locate in depressed areas? Some factors are favorable. The markets for consumers' goods are more widely scattered than formerly. Many new materials and products are smaller in bulk, lighter in weight, and easier to ship. The modern highway and the truck have increased accessibility. Changes in the structure of railroad rates have removed the obstacle of discriminatory freight costs. The diesel engine and the growth of electric transmission have broadened the availability of power. Wages are lower and unions weaker in the depressed areas than in more prosperous ones. The new skills needed can be taught. Those making decisions on industrial location have greater freedom of choice than was once the case. But difficulties remain.

Between 3,000 and 4,000 decisions on plant location are made in the United States each year. Some of these involve the relocation of exist-

[13] *Economic Development*, August 1958, pp. 4–12.
[14] Economic Development Administration, *Annual Report, 1967*, pp. 34–35.

ing establishments, others the building of branches, still others the creation of new concerns. When big companies relocate or build branches, they weigh a number of factors: markets, materials, and transport; labor, wage rates, and community facilities; the cost of sites; the character of street, water, and sewer systems; and local taxes. Their decisions are calculated and deliberate. When new firms set up small plants, they usually produce for local markets, locating in the community where the founder lives. Here, careful analysis of locational advantages is not the rule. Public policy may sometimes influence decisions on plant location, but it will seldom be determining.[15]

Where government provides the social capital that is needed by industry—roads, highways, water and sewer systems, hospitals, schools, and the like—it makes development possible. But there is no assurance that development will actually occur. The highways of Appalachia will make the region accessible. But they may never be crowded with the traffic that would bring prosperity.

New plants may be attracted by subsidies—by free sites, tax concessions, and long-term, low-interest loans. But the plants that respond to such inducements may not be worth having. Some of them may be vagabonds, moving from place to place to take advantage of public favors. All of them are certain to be dubious risks, since firms whose prospects are good enough to enable them to borrow from commercial lenders will not be eligible for the government's soft loans. The new plants, finally, are likely to be small in scale, in competitive fields, providing few jobs, and promising little growth.

The development program has other disadvantages. Many areas will compete for federal funds. The program could become a congressional pork barrel, like the annual rivers and harbors bill, with votes traded to get appropriations and total expenditures steadily inflated. But with so many areas participating, the money may be spread too thin to have a significant effect. With so many areas competing, moreover, their efforts to attract new industries will tend to cancel out. Communities that have invested heavily in the development effort may someday be in trouble. Encumbered with debt, they will find their borrowing more costly later on. Development is a gamble that may—or may not—pay off.

[15] Management and Economics Research, Inc., *Industrial Location as a Factor in Regional Economic Development* (Washington, D.C.: Economic Development Administration, undated).

Labor markets and manpower development

Structural unemployment may be attacked by programs of area development and job creation. It may also be attacked by improving the operation of the labor market and by providing the unemployed with needed skills. Where a worker is excluded from employment by racial discrimination, he may be helped to obtain it, as we saw in Chapter 11, through fair employment practice laws. Where he has lost his job through area depression, he can be aided in finding another not only by attracting industry into the area but also by helping him to move out. Where he has lost his job through a decline in demand for his product or a change in the technology of production, he can be given training for different work. Where a young person has never found employment and where an older person has long been unemployed, he, too, can be given guidance and training. This approach requires the provision of information concerning job opportunities and the matching of workers to jobs through a system of employment exchanges. It may require assistance for the worker in moving from place to place. It calls for basic education, for habituation to work, and for vocational training and retraining to equip the worker with skills that are in demand. If it is to provide help to those who need it most, it must seek out the needy, discover the nature of their needs, and fashion services to meet them.

Some of this activity has been carried on for many years. The first nationwide system of public employment offices was set up during World War I. Federal aid for vocational education dates back to 1917. But it was not until the sixties that efforts were made to change the employment office system into an agency for comprehensive manpower planning and development, and to provide training to school drop-outs and to workers past school age, reaching out to serve the disadvantaged and the hardcore unemployed—those who lack job skills, have not been able to hold a job, and work only occasionally if at all. At the same time, steps were taken to reform, expand, and strengthen the labor-market services that had long been carried on.

Improving labor market operations

The market for labor is a complex of individual markets, some specialized by the type of labor involved and some by the area from which they draw. There are markets for blue-collar workers and for white-collar workers; for executives, professional people, and technicians; and for skilled and unskilled laborers. There are markets that are purely local, others that are regional, still others that are nationwide or international. The market for unskilled labor is likely to be local; that for skilled labor or technicians regional or national; that for executives and professional workers nationwide or international. The employer who seeks a bassoon player or a deep-sea diver is unlikely to stop at regional or even national boundaries.[1] The boundaries of labor markets tend to be broadened in prosperity and narrowed in depression.

In the United States, there is a substantial degree of labor mobility among occupations, among employers, and among geographic areas. Transfers from one occupation to another are usually initiated by the employer, and those from firm to firm or from place to place by the worker. One move in five is induced by unemployment; four in five by a desire for betterment. In a survey reported in 1964, only 35 percent of the workers interviewed were living where they were born; 22 percent were living more than a thousand miles away. Nearly 30 percent had moved since 1950, half of them for 200 miles or more. The

[1] Albert Rees, "Information Networks in Labor Markets," *American Economic Review*, Vol. 56, No. 2 (1966), pp. 559–66.

highest mobility was found among technical, professional, and managerial workers; among younger people; and among those with college degrees. Forty percent of the family heads between 18 and 24 years of age and 45 percent of the college graduates under 35 years of age had moved within the past five years. By comparison, the mobility of blue-collar workers, of farmers, and of the self-employed was low.[2] The matching of workers to jobs in the upper occupational levels may largely take care of itself; it is at the lower levels that the aid of a system of employment exchanges is most urgently required.

Variety of market channels

Employers find workers and workers find jobs in many different ways. Some are informal. Workers apply directly; they walk in at the hiring gate; in 1960, more than a third of all placements were made in this way. Relatives and friends are referred by present employees; this accounts for nearly a fourth of the positions filled. Other channels are formal. A tenth of those employed in 1960 were located through newspaper advertisements. Others were found through college placement bureaus and union hiring halls. About 4 percent were hired through private employment agencies.

The private agencies grew rapidly in the forties and the fifties, numbering nearly 4,000 in 1958. They are more active in placing technical and professional personnel than in finding jobs for skilled or unskilled laborers. They charge substantial fees for a service that public employment offices render free. Some employers are satisfied with their service, particularly in recruiting clerical employees. Others complain that they do not adequately screen the workers they refer. In the past, such agencies have been found to engage in practices unfair to labor. They have misrepresented wages and working conditions to applicants for jobs. They have bribed foremen to discharge workers so that they might collect additional fees from new recruits. When jobs have been scarce, their charges have been extortionate. Employment agencies have therefore been subjected to public control. Most states require such agencies to obtain licenses and to post bonds that will assure their responsibility in the event of suits for damages. Many states regulate agency operations, forbidding misrepresentation, requir-

[2] John B. Lansing and Nancy Barth, *The Geographic Mobility of Labor* (Washington, D.C.: Area Redevelopment Administration, 1964).

ing full disclosure, and demanding the return of fees where jobs do not materialize and where workers are shortly discharged through no fault of their own. And some states have fixed the fees an agency may charge. Such a law was held to be unconstitutional in 1928, but this position was reversed in 1941. The states now have unquestioned power to regulate.[3]

The system of public employment offices accounted for 16 percent of the placements made in 1960, as compared with 25 percent for the public system in Great Britain, 33 percent in the Netherlands and Sweden, and 40 percent in West Germany. Its volume was four times that of the private agencies. Its efforts were more largely directed to meeting the needs of the blue-collar groups.

USES: origin and growth

Public employment offices were first set up by some of the states toward the end of the last century, beginning with Ohio in 1890. A nationwide public employment service established during World War I found jobs for demobilized veterans but was allowed to languish during the twenties. The present employment service had its beginning in 1933 under the Wagner-Peyser Act. This law offered federal grants on a 50–50 matching basis to promote the creation of employment offices by the states and set up the United States Employment Service (USES) to cordinate their activities. Half of the states had created such offices by 1935 when Congress, in the Social Security Act, required all the states enacting unemployment insurance laws to have such offices for their administration and offered to meet their entire costs from the proceeds of the federal payroll tax. With enactment of unemployment insurance laws by all the states, the federal-state employment service became complete.

The USES has always functioned as an employment exchange, responding to requests from employers by referring applicants for jobs. A number of other tasks have been assigned to it from time to time. During the thirties it devoted most of its energies to determining the eligibility of claimants for unemployment insurance and screening applicants for work relief. During World War II the Service was federalized and was used to allocate labor among defense activities. After the

---

[3] *Ribnik* v. *McBride,* 277 U.S. 350; and *Olsen* v. *Nebraska,* 311 U.S. 236.

war, the offices were returned to the states and were used once more in finding jobs for veterans. During the recessions of the fifties, they again were busied with unemployment insurance claims. Their other work declined.

During the sixties, USES was given new responsibilities and its budget and staff were enlarged. Today, it comprises autonomous employment office systems in 54 jurisdictions, all of them financed entirely by federal grants. These systems have some 2,000 local offices, a budget approaching $300,000,000, and a staff of more than 30,000. They placed more than 10,000,000 applicants in jobs in 1967.[4]

From employment exchange to manpower agency

An employment exchange serves as a meeting place where employers register their needs for workers and workers register their desires for jobs. It collects, analyzes, and disseminates information on the demand for labor in its market and on the available supply. It may publish lists of vacancies, identify markets where demand is growing and skills where supply is short. It serves employers by screening workers and referring those who are best qualified. It serves workers by counseling them on the character of jobs that are available and by referring them for vacancies. Employers need not accept the workers who are recommended; workers need not accept the recommended jobs. The system facilitates the operation of free markets. It increases labor mobility.

The USES performance of its employment exchange function has had its shortcomings. The Service does not know where job vacancies in general exist or where the workers who could fill them are to be found. It knows only about those vacancies that have been listed with it by employers and about those workers who have chosen to register. Employers have filed a small fraction of their vacancies, hesitating to use the service because its image—largely a consequence of its function in handling claims for unemployment insurance—has been that of an agency that deals with workers who are inferior in quality. Workers, too, are reluctant to use the Service because of the stigma that is attached. USES has been most seriously handicapped in dealing with interstate placements. It is not well informed concerning vacancies that

[4] "Public Employment Service in the Nation's Job Market, 1933–1963," *Employment Security Review*, June, 1963.

exist, even within a local labor market, across state lines. It has no lists of workers available in other states. The state systems are supposed to share such data but they are slow to do so, and the information is stale by the time it is received. Until the sixties, finally, the attitude of the Service was passive. It waited for employers to register their vacancies, then referred the workers on their lists who were best qualified. But it did not seek out those who needed its services in order to promote their wider use.[5]

During the sixties the concept of the Service's function was radically changed and its efforts were directed toward new goals. More than an employment exchange, it was to become a comprehensive manpower agency, engaged in manpower planning and development. As a planner, it was to take a long perspective, analyzing trends in the demand for labor and estimating future needs, surveying present labor skills and projecting future supplies, discovering probable openings for which labor should be trained, and designing educational programs to prepare future workers for growing careers. As a development agency, USES was to search out all those who needed help in getting jobs—the poor, the youths, the older workers, members of minority groups, the handicapped, the disadvantaged, the hardcore of the unemployed. It was to provide these people, through local manpower centers, with a broad range of services, such as testing their capacities; advising them on future careers; referring them for medical care, for remedial education, for training in institutions or on the job; arousing their ambitions; effecting their rehabilitation, increasing their employability; and finally placing them in vacancies and following up on their performance. Such a responsibility would be heavy and its fulfillment costly. It envisaged a more ambitious role for USES than it had played before.[6]

USES in the sixties

USES has improved its traditional operations over the past decade. It has set up a number of attractive and well-located offices, some of them specializing in professional and commercial placements and

[5] E. Wight Bakke, *A Positive Labor Market Policy* (Columbus, Ohio: Charles E. Merrill Books, Inc., 1963), chap. v; and Richard A. Lester, *Manpower Planning in a Free Society* (Princeton, N.J.: Princeton University Press, 1966), pp. 68–81.
[6] "Employment Service Task Force Report," *Employment Service Review*, February, 1966; and Lester, *op. cit.*, chap. iii.

others in industrial occupations and the service trades. To improve its popular image, it has separated its employment exchange function from its unemployment insurance function in the larger cities. Its volume of applications and placements, however, has declined. At the same time, the state systems have been assigned a variety of new functions, without prior consultation, without regard to competence, and without adequate implementation. In 1962, the Service was directed, under the Manpower Development and Training Act, to recruit unemployed heads of families who had long been attached to the labor force and to make arrangements to train them for new occupations. In 1965 under the Human Resources Development Program, a pilot project set up in six cities, it was asked to seek out disadvantaged workers in rural pockets of poverty and in city slums and to provide them with counseling and training to increase their employability. In 1967, it was directed to undertake the rehabilitation of youths who had been rejected by Selective Service and to provide work experience and training for parents of children on the public assistance rolls. But the Service has not completely accepted the new concepts regarding its objectives. It has its own traditions and is resistant to change. It still functions, primarily, as a job exchange.

In 1964, USES did take the initiative in providing for the development of youths between the ages of 16 and 22, setting up a nationwide network of Youth Opportunity Centers, separate from its employment offices and adjacent to city ghettoes. It had established 170 such centers by 1967. Here, it gave intensive counseling to youths referred to it by local schools, draft boards, and other community agencies, placing them in training programs that would start them on the road to jobs. It handled more than a million such cases during the fiscal year. The results of this undertaking are unknown. Data are not yet available to prove or to disprove the value of the counseling that has been done. In the meantime, its usefulness is accepted on faith.[7]

Aid in relocation

The geographic mobility of labor has been facilitated through programs existing for some years in a number of European countries. Workers with little hope of steady employment at home are assisted in

---

[7] Arnold L. Nemore and Garth L. Mangum, *Reorienting the Federal-State Employment Service* (Ann Arbor, Mich.: Institute of Industrial and Labor Relations, University of Michigan, 1968), pp. 11–14.

shifting to new locations, being given loans or grants to cover the costs of traveling for interviews, moving household goods, temporarily maintaining two residences, commuting between home and job, and supporting the family until the first pay check is received. A similar program was set up in the United States on an experimental basis under legislation enacted by Congress in 1963. Administered by USES, it makes federal loans and grants to workers in depressed areas who have no prospects for jobs at home but do have definite offers of employment elsewhere. The Service extended such aid to 6,500 workers in the fiscal years 1965–67. The average cost of a move was as little as $400, but the rate of defaults on the loans that were made was high. Even so, the cost of the program was less than that of maintaining as many families, at their old locations, on relief.

The experiment has shown that the availability of assistance does increase mobility, effecting moves that would not otherwise have been made to jobs that would not otherwise have been filled and easing adjustment to new surroundings. Younger workers are more willing to move than older ones; skilled workers more willing than the unskilled. Workers are readier to move when no work is available and local prospects are poor and less ready when there is seasonal work to be had and when local prospects are at all promising. Of those who moved during the first three years of the program, a fifth returned, a fifth lost their new jobs but did not return, but three fifths stayed put. Aid for relocation produces the desired results. The program should be made permanent, and its application extended to other areas.[8]

Proposals for reform

A fundamental obstacle to efficiency in USES is the division of the service into more than 50 autonomous systems. The boundaries of labor markets, particularly those for high-level personnel, do not follow state lines. Some states are too small to permit effective operation. And interstate placements are sporadic and slow. Control by the states also makes for inferior service. In some states, the quality of the employment office staff is high; in most states it is not. The salaries paid are too low to attract people of great ability. Training programs are inadequate. Opportunities for advancement are limited. Morale is

---

[8] *Report of the Secretary of Labor on Manpower Research and Training, 1966,* pp. 45–50; Bakke, *op. cit.,* pp. 65–68; and Nemore and Mangum, *op. cit.,* pp. 14–15.

poor, and turnover is high. With the responsibilities now assigned it, USES needs a staff with greater competence and dedication than it is able to command.

The obvious way to overcome these deficiencies would be to feder- alize the Service, unifying the several systems and imposing common standards under strong central leadership. But such a move would encounter determined resistance. The state systems are well en- trenched and politically powerful. It is argued, moreover, that their staffs are better informed on local conditions than federal officers would be and that their services are better adapted to local needs.

Short of federalization, USES could be strengthened by exerting stronger leadership. Guidelines could be promulgated, and priorities assigned. The number of offices could be increased, their staffs en- larged, and their personnel better trained and paid. All this and more could be accomplished through the power of the federal purse on which the Service depends for its support.

To improve performance of its placement function, USES should make every effort to persuade employers to list more vacancies, to give advance notice of imminent layoffs, and to forecast probable openings. It should computerize its data on vacancies and manpower to permit immediate accessibility. It should facilitate intermarket placement by setting up a nationwide electronic job and manpower data bank, with information fed in by employers, unions, and employment offices, and making knowledge of all existing openings and all qualified workers available instantaneously. With service thus speeded, wider participa- tion by employers and by workers should be assured.[9]

Increasing employability

A generation or more ago, the work done by much of the labor force required no special training. Today, with advancing technology, the occupational structure of the labor force has changed; the share of professional, technical, and other skilled jobs has grown; and the share of common labor has declined. Those who lack training are handi- capped in finding work to do; they are more likely than those with training to be unemployed. There is increasing need, therefore, for training in occupational skills.

Vocational training is needed by three different groups: by youths

[9] Bakke, *op. cit.*, chap. x; Lester, *op. cit.*, chap. ix; and "Employment Service Task Force Report," *op. cit.*

preparing to enter the labor force; by persons suffering handicaps that must be overcome; and by persons whose former skills are no longer in demand. Both private and public agencies have long been active in the field. Employers have given training on the job. Unions in the skilled trades have given training to apprentices. Local governments have provided vocational education through the public schools. State governments have maintained programs for the rehabilitation of the handicapped. The federal government has given vocational training to men in the armed services. It has subsidized vocational education in the schools since 1917 and vocational rehabilitation by the states since 1920. During the sixties, its activities in the field have increased manyfold. Under the Area Redevelopment Act of 1961, it attempted to create supplies of skilled labor as a means of attracting industry into depressed areas. Under the Manpower Development and Training Act of 1962, it undertook, initially, to retrain unemployed heads of families who had been attached to the labor force, later extending its efforts to training the disadvantaged, both adults and youths. Under the Economic Opportunity Act of 1964, finally, the government set up a Job Corps with residential centers where training was given to youths between the ages of 16 and 21 who were unemployed. Taken together, the federal programs provided training to close to a million persons in 1967.

Vocational education

In 1917, Congress appropriated $7,000,000 for use in matching grants to encourage public schools to offer courses in agriculture, home economics, industry, and trade. By 1963, it had increased its appropriation to $55,000,000 and added fisheries, distribution, practical nursing, and technical fields. One fifth of high school students and 2 percent of the 18–21 age group were enrolled. The training offered bore little relation to employment opportunities. Two thirds of those enrolled were in agriculture, a field where employment had long been declining, and in home economics, a field that offered preparation for marriage but not for jobs. Little effort was made to discover the sort of skills that would be demanded by employers or to direct vocational curricula toward providing them. And even where instruction in industrial occupations was offered, the methods taught were often obsolete.

In 1963, a panel of consultants recommended expansion of the program to serve all people in need of training: new entrants to the labor force, older workers, those upgrading their skills, and those suffering special handicaps. It also called for the construction of vocational schools to serve wide areas, for cooperation with employment offices to determine the skills most needed, for expansion of vocational curricula to cover added fields, for employment counseling and guidance, and for better training and supervision of teaching staffs. Funds to carry out these recommendations were provided under the Vocational Education Act of 1963, the appropriation being raised by 1968 to $250,000,000 a year.

The reforms recommended in 1963 have been but partly realized. Area schools have been constructed. Enrollments have grown, comprising a fourth of high school students and 4 percent of the 18–21 age group in 1967. But little has been done to attract the disadvantaged who are most in need. Expansion of curricula has proceeded along traditional lines. Agriculture and home economics still dominate the offerings, with training for new occupations accounting for but a tiny fraction of the whole. There has been cooperation with employment offices in some places but not in others. There has been little expansion of counseling and guidance. This disappointing response is attributable to the fact that the new directions given in the Act of 1963 were permissive rather than mandatory, the uses to which the added funds might be put being left to the states. With bureaucratic resistance at the local level and without strong leadership from federal authorities, progress has been slow.[10]

Vocational education operates under serious handicaps. Four fifths of its students come from the lower income groups; half of them from the lowest quarter of students in ability. Vocational courses have come to be regarded as a dumping ground for those who cannot meet the standards of the academic curriculum. Vocational teachers are accorded a lower status than instructors in academic fields. In the suburbs, in smaller cities, and in rural areas, instructional facilities and equipment are generally adequate. In the city slums where needed most, they are inferior.

It is impossible to say how successful the school vocational pro-

---

[10] Garth L. Mangum, *Reorienting Vocational Education* (Ann Arbor, Mich.: Institute of Labor and Industrial Relations, University of Michigan, 1968); and Jacob J. Kaufman and Carl J. Schaefer, *The Role of Secondary Schools in the Preparation of Youth for Employment* (Institute for Research on Human Resources, Pennsylvania State University, 1967).

grams have been in preparing students for jobs. The rate of drop-outs has been high. A minor fraction of those trained make use of the skills they have learned. Graduates from vocational courses do get jobs and for a few years earn more than do graduates from academic programs. But they might have had jobs and have earned as much if they had taken different courses—or none. Vocational education may increase employability, but this cannot be proved.[11]

Experts on vocational education would change the present program in many ways. Pupils in the earlier grades and in junior high school would be taught the character of different occupations and the choice of possible careers. Courses would be adapted to future manpower needs; training given for occupations that offered expanding opportunities. Instruction, however, would not be limited to narrow specialties but would afford a broad base of skills that could be used in many occupations, some of them, perhaps, as yet unknown. Students would be counseled on their choices of careers, placed in jobs, and followed up until adjustment was assured. Formal vocational training would also be offered to adults, and remedial courses provided for those with special needs. Federal leadership would be asserted and federal grants so administered as to afford incentives for desired innovation and improved performance. The budget required to make such grants, instead of the present $250,000,000, would run to $1.6 billion a year.[12]

---

[11] Alice M. Rivlin, "Critical Issues in the Development of Vocational Education" in William G. Bowen and Frederick H. Harbison (eds.), *Unemployment in a Prosperous Economy* (Princeton, N.J.: Princeton University, 1965), pp. 153–66; and Gerald G. Somers and Graeme H. McKechnie, "Vocational Retraining Programs for the Unemployed," Industrial Relations Research Association, *Proceedings of the Twentieth Annual Meeting, 1967*, pp. 25–34.

[12] Mangum, *op. cit.*, pp. 44–56. Substantial progress toward this goal is now made possible by the Vocational Education Amendments of 1968. Under this legislation, federal grants are authorized, rising from $355 million in 1969 to $675 million in 1971, to encourage the states to improve and extend their efforts in this field. These grants may be used to support programs for pupils in high schools, for unemployed high school graduates and drop-outs, and for people in the labor force who are in need of training. They may be used for a variety of purposes: to broaden and strengthen traditional programs, to set up experimental and demonstration programs, to finance cooperative programs combining vocational training with experience in private employment, to finance programs combining such training with self-supporting employment in public or nonprofit agencies, and to build, equip, and operate residential training schools for youths between the ages of 15 and 21. The legislation calls for cooperative arrangements with public employment offices to obtain information on job opportunities and for intensification of occupational guidance and employment counseling. It provides for aid in the planning of vocational curricula, the preparation of instructional materials, the training of teachers, and the evaluation of programs.

Vocational rehabilitation

Vocational rehabilitation for the handicapped is also administered by the states and financed in part through federal grants. But it differs from vocational education both in methods and in results. The program began with services offered to disabled veterans at the end of World War I. It was extended in 1920 to persons disabled in industry, and was further expanded after World War II. In its present form, the program dates from 1943. Its purpose is to prepare the handicapped for employment. To this end, rehabilitation services are offered by 90 different agencies administered by the several states, with the federal government putting up 75 percent of the cost of regular operations and as much as 90 percent of the cost of innovations but exercising little supervision over performance.

Persons are eligible for rehabilitation if they have physical or mental difficulties that are substantial handicaps to employment and if these handicaps can be overcome. Of those eligible, estimated at 4,000,000 to 6,000,000, around 700,000 are receiving help at any one time. The rehabilitation agencies do not recruit their clients but wait for them to come. People are referred by doctors and hospitals, by educational institutions, by friends and relatives, or come of their own accord. Most of them are from the lower income groups but not from those in deepest poverty.

The unique element in the program is the relationship that is developed between the handicapped client and a trained counselor whose responsibility it is to analyze the client's trouble, prepare a rehabilitation plan, and obtain whatever services may be required. This may involve surgery, hospitalization, the provision of prosthetic devices, and related therapy. It may also involve vocational training, work experience, job placement and follow-up, and provision of equipment and tools for the self-employed. These services may be rendered in hospitals, vocational schools, business colleges, or on the job. The median time devoted to a case is a little less than a year.

The program enjoys popular support. Its staff is usually competent; its work highly effective. Three fourths of those discharged in 1966 had been successfully rehabilitated. Of these, four fifths were placed in paying jobs at wages higher than those earned before. Of those discharged up to 10 years earlier, four fifths were still employed. Reviewing the program, Mangum and Glenn find that its comprehensive, flexible, personalized approach is costly in money and manpower and therefore not for general application. But they conclude that the approach "has proven its ability to serve the physically and mentally handicapped and its methods appear equally applicable to the economically, educationally, and culturally handicapped."[13]

The Job Corps

It has been the purpose of the Job Corps to increase the employability of disadvantaged young men and women by providing them with remedial education and job training in a number of large residential training schools. Creation of the Corps was authorized by the Economic Opportunity Act of 1964; its administration was entrusted to the Office of Economic Opportunity. Congress required that two fifths of those enrolled be trained in conservation centers modeled on the camps set up by the Civilian Conservation Corps in the thirties. Ninety such centers were established; their administration being delegated to the departments of Agriculture and the Interior. This part of the program affords little preparation for urban jobs. But 28 urban centers were set up, ranging in size to as many as 3,000 enrollees and operated under contract by universities and corporate enterprises. Enrollment in the program at any one time has run around 40,000.

The first of those enrolled, most of them 18 to 20 years of age, were hastily screened by USES. More than half were Negroes. The average entrant was at the eighth-grade level in school but at the fifth-grade level in reading and mathematical ability. A third of those accepted could not read a simple English sentence or solve a second-grade problem in arithmetic. The program had trouble getting started. Its administration was chaotic, its centers unfinished, and their staffs overworked. The entrants found themselves subject to unexpected discipline. Many dropped out within a week or 10 days. Life among those who stayed was rough and tough. Gangs were organized, and enrollees exploited and abused. There was drunkenness, fighting, and rioting in the centers; and disturbances, vandalism, and crime in the surrounding communities. The Corps' public image could hardly have been

[13] Garth L. Mangum and Lowell M. Glenn, *Vocational Rehabilitation and Federal Manpower Policy* (Ann Arbor, Mich.: Institute of Labor and Industrial Relations, University of Michigan, 1967), p. 56.

worse.[14] In time, however, the worst of these difficulties were over-come. The screening of entrants was tightened, their age reduced to include 16- and 17-year-olds, incorrigibles excluded, discipline sharp-ened, and community relations improved.

The Corps' record of accomplishment is favorable but not impres-sive. The rate of drop-outs has been high. A stay of two years was authorized by law. But in 1967, only one entrant in nine had stayed as long as a year. A third had left within three months, and another third within six months. There were gains in educational performance for the ones who stayed. Those who were in the Corps as long as nine months raised their reading ability by 1.5 grades, their arithmetical ability by 1.8 grades, and improved their work attitudes and skills. A survey of 75,000 enrollees who left the Corps before May, 1967, found 53 percent of them employed, 10 percent back in school, and 7 per-cent in the armed services. The average hourly wage of those em-ployed was $1.19 before enrollment and $1.51 afterward.

These gains were realized at a considerable cost. Yearly expendi-tures per entrant stood around $8,500 in 1966, around $7,000 in 1967—figures that far exceeded the cost of a year at a college in the Ivy League. The benefits realized through the program were found by one study to exceed its costs. But the estimate was open to question: the trainees might have found jobs and earned higher wages without en-listment in the Corps, and there was no assurance that the gains they had realized would be retained. In the judgement of Sar A. Levitan, "no conclusive case has yet been established to justify the Job Corps on the basis of past performance. . . . There is need for more convincing data to prove that the expensive . . . program is justified."[15] Cer-tainly, the disadvantaged youths for whom the Job Corps was estab-lished need help to increase their employability. But help can doubtless be provided in a more effective and a less expensive way.

Manpower development and training

The Manpower Development and Training Program (MDT) was the first nationwide program created for the purpose of training the

---

[14] Christopher Weeks, *Job Corps* (Boston, Mass.: Little, Brown & Co., 1967).
[15] Sar A. Levitan, *Antipoverty Work and Training Efforts* (Ann Arbor, Mich.: Institute of Labor and Industrial Research, University of Michigan, 1967), p. 37.

unemployed. As first set up, under legislation enacted by Congress in 1962, it was designed to provide instruction in the main to experienced adults—heads of households who had been attached to the labor force for two or more years—whose skills had been rendered obsolete by technological change. As employment improved, its emphasis shifted to training the disadvantaged, particularly Negroes, persons with little education, and jobless youth. Its services were enlisted in the war on poverty.

Those who are to be trained under MDT are selected by state employment offices. The instructional program is administered by the states' vocational education authorities. Training is given through public and private institutions and on the job. Some of it is offered by vocational teachers in the public schools. But this approach is ill adapted to the needs of older workers who are seeking skills that lead to immediate employment. Much of the instruction is therefore given in large skill centers that are independent of the public schools, and by instructors recruited from industry. A program may run as long as two years and may include remedial work, when needed, in basic education and general occupational instruction as well as preparation for specific jobs. Training is given for more than 600 different occupations, half of them demanding industrial skills, the other half in the clerical, sales, and service fields. Trainees who need it—four fifths of the total—are given a weekly allowance to cover the costs of transport and subsistence, amounting for adults to around $50 a week. The costs of the program are met in their entirety by the federal government. Some 600,000 people had been enrolled either for institutional or on the job training by the beginning of 1967, nearly 100,000 of whom were receiving instruction at that time.

Half of those enrolled in the program are trained, as described, in institutions; half are trained on the job. These trainees are selected by their employers and are paid for the work they do, the government reimbursing the employers for their training costs. Some 6,000 firms are participating in the program, providing instruction in 700 different occupations. On-the-job training has a number of advantages. The trainee is subjected to the atmosphere and discipline of the workplace. He earns while he learns. He acquires skills that are immediately salable. The chances are 9 out of 10 that he will be kept on the job when his training is completed. His motivation is therefore strong. There is no need to duplicate heavy equipment. Supervisors can double as instructors. The cost of instruction per trainee is only one fourth as great as where it is given in institutions. But there are also disadvantages. On-the-job training is likely to be narrowly specialized, adapted to the needs of the employer rather than those of the employee. It tends to ignore deficiencies in basic education and to neglect theoretical concepts and general skills. Employers are also likely to skim the cream of MDT manpower, rejecting disadvantaged applicants and selecting those who are best qualified. They may thus be paid by the government to train workers they would have been willing to train without a subsidy. It is only when the employer provides instruction as a social service that subsidization is justified.

Results of job training

Judged by its results, MDT has been highly successful. Nine tenths of the on-the-job trainees were still employed when last interviewed. Three tenths of the institutional enrollees did not complete their training. But one tenth left to take jobs, only a fifth for other reasons. Of those who completed their courses, nine tenths were employed during their first year out; seven tenths for three fourths or more of the time. Four fifths were at work when interviewed in later months. Three fourths were employed at work related to their training. Those employed had worked more hours during the year after the training than during the year before and had earned more money per hour; their incomes had therefore risen, the average gain running around $750 a year. The program was least successful in increasing employment and raising wages for the disadvantaged—for Negroes, for older workers, and for youths. But here, too, workers who had had the training did better than those who had not.[16]

The yearly cost of the program per trainee has run around $2,000 in institutions and $500 on the job. A number of sample studies find these costs to be more than recovered in benefits. One study shows government getting its money back within five years through savings in unemployment insurance benefits. Another shows it recovering its outlay in five years from increases in the yield of the income tax. A third study puts the benefit to government at nearly twice the cost of

[16] Garth L. Mangum, *Contributions and Costs of Manpower Development and Training* (Ann Arbor, Mich.: Institute of Labor and Industrial Relations, University of Michigan, 1967), pp. 12–17.

instruction in institutions and more than three times the cost of instruction on the job. The benefit of training to the worker during his lifetime is estimated at five times its cost.[17] After surveying this evidence, Garth Mangum concludes that "the overall contributions of the program have exceeded its costs by a margin which not only merits support but justifies expansion."[18] He recommends that the life of MDT, due to expire in 1969, be made permanent, that on-the-job training be expanded, and that funds for institutional training be doubled.

Potentialities of labor market action

Programs to improve the operation of the labor market and to increase the employability of labor contribute importantly to social welfare. They can add to the total volume of employment. By increasing mobility they can promote a better allocation and a more efficient use of manpower. And by providing new skills they can enhance productivity. Such programs also contribute to individual well-being. They enlarge opportunity. They raise the level of living. They afford greater security.

The workers who profit most from labor market action are those who have capacities for gainful employment; who are located in areas where their skills are no longer needed but are willing to move; and who are lacking in salable skills but are willing to learn. These people can be selected from among the unemployed and given help in acquiring skills and finding jobs. In such cases, labor market programs are almost certain to succeed. But there are others for whom the outcome is less clear. Those whose basic training was deficient, whose work experience has been sporadic, who are lacking in hope and in ambition, may be slow to respond, even though they are offered the same opportunities. The costs incurred in helping them will be higher and the benefits derived will be lower than with the more ambitious group. But these are the people who are in greatest need. These are the ones who must be lifted out of poverty and dependency and set on the road to self-support. The task is but barely begun. It merits the highest priority.

[17] *Ibid.*, pp. 66–71.
[18] *Ibid.*, Summary. See also Somers and McKechnie, *op. cit.*

Birth control

Important among the causes of poverty is the fact that people who are poor have larger families than they can adequately support and more children than they can give a proper start in life. Important among the methods of reducing poverty is the practice of birth control. In this chapter, we examine the relationship between poverty and family size, review public policy toward birth control, and consider the sort of family planning program that is needed for the reduction of poverty.

Family size and poverty

There is an inverse correlation between the socioeconomic status of families and their size. Birth rates are higher where incomes are small than where they are large, where parents have little education than where they are well educated, among laborers than among businessmen, among Negroes than among whites, in rural than in urban areas. With larger families at the lower socioeconomic levels, there are more dependents to be cared for and more children growing up in poverty. There is less adequate provision for present needs and less adequate preparation for the future.

330

Socioeconomic status and reproduction

The inverse correlation of socioeconomic status and rates of reproduction has been observed for many years. A survey made in 1935 found higher birth rates where incomes were low, where mothers were poorly educated, in lower occupational groups, in rural areas, among Negroes, and among the foreign-born.[1] Many of these differentials narrowed during the forties; the difference between the native population and the foreign-born virtually disappeared. But the other differences persisted, and in the fifties, they even increased.[2]

Data on class differences in rates of reproduction in 1960 are abundant. Some of them may be summarized:

The number of children ever born to the average wife aged 30 through 39 was 2.5 where the family income was over $7,000; 2.9 where it was between $2,000 and $7,000; 3.7 where it was under $2,000.[3]

The annual rate of reproduction among 1,000 women aged 15 through 44 was 98.1 among the non-poor and 152.5 among the poor and the near-poor. The number of births during the child-bearing period was 2.9 for women who were not poor and 4.6 for women who were poor and near-poor.[4]

The number of children ever born to women aged 30 through 39 was 1.5 for university graduate students, 2.2 for college graduates, 2.3 for high school graduates, 2.6 for high school dropouts, 2.8 for elementary school graduates, 3.2 for those who dropped out of the fifth, sixth, or seventh grades, and 3.5 for those who dropped out of the first four grades.[5]

The number of children born each year to 1,000 women aged 15 through 44 was 91 for whites and 134 for non-whites.[6]

The number of children ever born to non-white mothers aged 35

---

[1] Clyde V. Kiser, *Group Differences in Urban Fertility* (Baltimore, Md.: Williams & Wilkins Co., 1942), chaps. iii-v.

[2] National Bureau of Economic Research, *Demographic and Economic Change* (Princeton, N.J.: Princeton University Press, 1960), pp. 77–113.

[3] Kingsley Davis, "Demographic Aspects of Poverty," in Margaret S. Gordon, *Poverty in America* (San Francisco, Calif.: Chandler Publishing Co., 1965), pp. 299–319 at p. 301.

[4] Arthur A. Campbell, "Family Planning and the Reduction of Poverty in the United States," in Oscar Harkavy, *Implementing DHEW Policy on Family Planning and Population* (Washington, D.C.: Department of Health, Education, and Welfare, 1967), Attachment A, p. 6.

[5] Davis, *op. cit.*, p. 309.

[6] Bureau of Labor Statistics, Report 332, *Social and Economic Conditions of Negroes in the United States*, 1967, p. 77.

through 39 was 2.7 where income was over $7,000, 3.28 where income was between $2,000 and $7,000, and 4.43 where income was under $2,000.[7]

The average number of children ever born to women aged 40 through 44 was 2.5; for white women on farms it was 3.7; for non-white women on farms it was 5.4.[8]

It would appear to be established beyond dispute that low income, inadequate education, membership in racial minorities, and residence in poor communities all make for high birth rates.

A sample of the data on the relation between family size and poverty may also be given:

In 1965, the portion of families living in poverty was 11 percent where there were one or two children, 15 percent where there were three, 21 percent where there were four, 33 percent where there were five, and 43 percent where there were six or more.[9]

In 1966, half of the children in poverty were in families where there were five children or more. Such a family was three and one half times as likely to be in poverty as a family with one or two.[10]

In 1964, the portion of non-white families in poverty was 32 percent where there were one or two children, 54 percent where there were three or four, and 76 percent where there were five or more.[11]

Large families make for poverty. The budgets that determine the poverty line are adjusted for family size. People whose earnings would put them above the poverty line if their families were small fall below it because their families are large.

Large family size increases the burden of dependency. In 1965, the number of children under 18 years of age for every 100 adults was 62 among the nonpoor, 101 among the near-poor, and 130 among the poor.[12] The poor family, in other words, had twice as many children to support as did the family that was not poor. In such a situation, parents are unable to supply their children with the proper quantity and quality of food, clothing, housing, and medical care. Themselves

---

[7] Davis, *op. cit.*, p. 311.

[8] President's National Advisory Commission on Rural Poverty, *The People Left Behind* (Washington, D.C.: U.S. Government Printing Office, 1967), p. 6.

[9] Harold S. Sheppard, "Effects of Family Planning on Poverty in the United States" in U.S. Senate, Committee on Labor and Public Welfare, *Examination of the War on Poverty* (Washington, D.C.: U.S. Government Printing Office, 1967), Vol. 3, pp. 717–35 at p. 718.

[10] Mollie Orshansky, "The Shape of Poverty in 1966," *Social Security Bulletin,* March, 1968, pp. 3–32 at p. 9.

[11] Sheppard, *op. cit.*, p. 720.

[12] Campbell, *op. cit.*, p. 4.

lacking in education, they cannot provide the cultural background or
the intellectual stimulus that fosters educational attainment. The consequences are all too clear. There is impairment of health, as is shown by
rejections for military service on account of physical or mental
defects. Only a third of the nation's children are in families where
there are four or more, but 70 percent of the young men rejected for
service came from such families; only a tenth of the children are in
families where there are six or more, but half of those rejected came
from families of this size.[13] There is impairment of educational performance and employment opportunity. Children from larger families
are more likely to become school truants, to fall behind their grades, to
drop out, to get poor jobs, to be unemployed, to become delinquent.
Their chances of breaking out of the cycle of poverty are small. There
are also social costs. With excessive procreation, the burden of dependency and delinquency grows heavier. The accomplishments of
programs designed to lessen poverty are offset in some part by the
increasing numbers of the poor. Much of the money spent on welfare
is swallowed in a bottomless pit.

Causes of differential reproduction

If the poor have more children than the well-to-do, it is not because
they want more. Several studies made in recent years of the numbers
of children wanted by American wives show that the number wanted
by women in the lower socioeconomic groups is no larger than the
number wanted by women in the upper groups. Wives in families with
small incomes wanted no more children than did wives in families with
large ones. Wives of blue-collar workers wanted no more children
than did wives of white-collar workers. Colored women wanted fewer
children than did white women.[14] But the women in these studies had
had or expected to have more children than they wanted. And here

[13] President's Task Force on Manpower Conservation, *One Third of a Nation:
A Report on Young Men Found Unqualified for Military Service* (Washington,
D.C.: U.S. Government Printing Office, 1964), pp. 18–20.
[14] Charles S. Westoff *et al., Family Growth in Metropolitan America* (Prince-
ton, N.J.: Princeton University Press, 1961), chap. viii; Pascal K. Whelpton,
Arthur A. Campbell, and John E. Patterson, *Fertility and Family Planning in the
United States* (Princeton, N.J.: Princeton University Press, 1966), pp. 92–124;
Frederick S. Jaffe, "Family Planning and Poverty," *Journal of Marriage and the
Family*, November, 1964, pp. 467 ff; and Judith Blake, "Income and Reproductive
Motivation," *Population Studies*, Vol. 31 (1967), pp. 185–206.

there were differences among the socioeconomic groups. Among the women who had had three or more children, 45 percent said that the last one was unwanted. Among the white wives 17 percent and among the nonwhite wives 31 percent had had unwanted children. Among those who had not finished high school, 32 percent of the white wives and 43 percent of the nonwhite wives had had such children.[15] In the upper socioeconomic groups, the excess of children expected over children wanted was small; in the lower groups, it was larger. Wives with a college education expected 15 percent more children than they wanted; wives with a high school education expected 38 percent more.[16]

The poor have more children than the well-to-do, not because they want them but because they fail to prevent their coming. Birth control is practiced at all levels of income, but its practice is less frequent in the lower income groups. Among all families, in 1960, contraceptives were used by 86 percent. Among white families where the mother had no more than a grade school education, the figure was 72 percent. Among Negroes, it was 57 percent. The portion of families practicing contraception was lowest in the rural South.[17]

One circumstance in which birth control has not been attempted is that of premarital conception, leading to illegitimate birth or to forced marriage. Here, again, there are differences among socioeconomic groups. The incidence of illegitimacy is higher where incomes are low. It is estimated that 6.2 percent of the children born in the United States are illegitimate. For the poor and the near-poor, the figure is 15.7 percent.[18] Of white births, 3.1 percent are illegitimate; of nonwhite births, 23.6 percent.[19] The rate of forced marriages is said to be more than twice the rate of illegitimacy.[20] In both cases, the child is unwanted and resented. Where illegitimate, he is handicapped. Even where legitimatized by marriage, he is disadvantaged. The youthful parents are forced to assume responsibility before they are ready, psychologically or financially, to do so. The child is not likely to be given proper care.

[15] National Academy of Sciences, *The Growth of United States Population, 1965*, p. 10.

[16] Whelpton, Campbell, and Patterson, *op. cit.*

[17] National Academy of Sciences, *op. cit.*

[18] Campbell, *op. cit.*, p. 13.

[19] Department of Health, Education, and Welfare, *White–Non-white Differentials in Health, Education, and Welfare* (Washington, D.C.: U.S. Government Printing Office, 1965), p. 11.

[20] Davis, *op. cit.*, p. 317.

The failure of many in the lower income groups to practice contraception is due in large part to ignorance of its possibilities and to inaccessibility of family planning services. The character and significance of birth control are not taught in the schools. The well-to-do get information from their family doctors; the poor have no such personal relationship. Until recently, welfare officials and social workers refused to give them information or to refer them to agencies where it could be obtained. Many hospitals that deliver children for mothers who are poor have not provided contraceptive services. Where such services have been offered, they have often been given at inconvenient times and places, in unattractive and overcrowded quarters, and in an atmosphere of personal indifference or hostility. The Planned Parenthood Federation, the only agency promoting family planning for the poor, had 175 clinics in 101 cities in 1963, reaching 230,000 women, less than 5 percent of the number held to be medically indigent. In New York City in 1967, half of such women had access to contraceptive services; in Philadelphia, only a fifth.[21] In rural areas, few, if any, women in the lower income groups have access to such services.[22]

Even where knowledge is available and services accessible, many who are poor may fail to practice birth control. Their attitudes may be unsympathetic. They may view large families as part of an accepted way of life. They may be fatalistic, seeing no hope or meaning in the future, no point in giving their children better care. So they are apathetic, irresponsible.[23]

And finally, poor families who do practice contraception may use methods that are relatively ineffective. They may do so because the more effective methods cost more money, because they are less convenient, because they interfere with spontaneity or detract from pleasure, or because they are frowned on by the church. So contraception ends more often in failure, and the birth rate goes up.

Public policy toward birth control

Among the methods of preventing childbirth, there are three—abortion, sterilization, and contraception—that are subject to legal restraint. The three differ in character. Abortion and sterilization in-

[21] *Philadelphia Evening Bulletin,* September 6, 1967.
[22] President's National Commission on Rural Poverty, *op. cit.,* p. 75.
[23] Lee Rainwater and Karol K. Weinstein, *And the Poor Get Children* (Chicago, Ill.: Quadrangle Books, 1960).

volve the use of surgical procedures; contraception does not. Abortion destroys incipient life following conception; it raises moral and religious questions that differ from those raised by the other two.[24] Sterilization prevents conception from taking place. It interferes with the physical integrity of the body, destroying the capacity to procreate new life. Contraception does not alter the body; it does not destroy the capacity to reproduce.

Abortion has generally been forbidden by law except where necessary to save a mother's life. It is only recently and in a few states that this prohibition has been relaxed. Where voluntary, sterilization has generally been tolerated by the law. But contraception, a far less serious matter, has long been subjected by both state and federal governments to a variety of restraints. In recent years, however, public attitudes have changed and many of these prohibitions have been relaxed.

The law on abortion

Until 1967, statutes making it a criminal offense to commit an abortion except to save a mother's life were in force in all the states. In no other country was the law more strict; in many, it was permissive. In the Scandinavian countries, abortions might be obtained, subject to medical approval, on socioeconomic grounds. In Japan and in the communist countries, they could be obtained at the mother's request.[25]

The number of abortions performed each year in the United States is unknown. There is no central registry for legal abortions; it is estimated that they number about 8,000 a year. Guesses as to the number of illegal abortions run between 200,000 and 1,200,000. Few legitimate physicians will consent to perform such operations. They are therefore performed by irresponsible practitioners, many of them under conditions involving risk to life and health. Such operations are said to result in some 500 deaths each year. The laws against abortions are indifferently enforced. The only violators prosecuted are those

[24] *The Terrible Choice: The Abortion Dilemma,* based on the proceedings of the International Conference on Abortion sponsored by the Harvard Divinity School and the Joseph P. Kennedy, Jr. Foundation (New York: Bantam Books, 1968), chap. viii.

[25] *Ibid.,* chap. v; and Ruth Roemer, "Abortion Law: the Approaches of Different Nations," *American Journal of Public Health,* Vol. 57 (1967), pp. 1906–22.

specializing in the practice. And the only occasion for prosecution is where abortion results in injury or death.[26]

Public policy regarding abortion discriminates in effect against the poor. Abortions are costly; the poor get fewer than the well-to-do. In New York City, abortions per 1,000 deliveries have amounted to 3.9 in proprietary hospitals, to 2.4 in the private patient services of nonprofit hospitals, to 0.7 in the wards of such hospitals, and to 0.1 in public hospitals. The rate of abortion among whites has stood at 2.6; among Negroes at 0.5. Not only are abortions less frequent among the poor but they are also less safe. In New York City in 1960–62, the death rate from abortions per 10,000 live births was 1.0 for white women and 8.0 for Negroes.[27]

Some of the laws prohibiting abortions have been modified in recent years. A model statute, prepared by the American Law Institute and endorsed by the American Medical Association, would permit abortion, when approved by medical authorities, not only to save a mother's life but also to preserve her physical or mental health, to prevent the birth of a defective child, and in cases of incest or rape. In 1967 and 1968, five states (California, Colorado, Georgia, Maryland, and North Carolina) amended their laws to conform, in general, to this pattern. Comparable bills were introduced in the legislatures of a dozen other states. None of these measures would permit abortion to prevent the birth of an illegitimate child or to limit family size. In New York, however, a bill proposed by a state commission would have permitted abortion not only under the circumstances given in the model statute but also where a mother's physical or mental condition was such as to prevent her from caring for a child when born, and where a mother already had four living children. The last of these conditions was disapproved by the governor; the bill as a whole was rejected by the Assembly.

The law on sterilization

Sterilization may be compulsory or voluntary. Compulsory sterilization is a eugenic measure, designed to prevent the transmission of hereditary defects. Between 1907 and 1937, 32 states enacted laws empowering their governments to order the sterilization of persons having

[26] *The Terrible Choice*, chap. iv.
[27] *Ibid.*, pp. 44–45.

such defects. These laws applied in the main to inmates of state mental institutions—to the feeble-minded and to persons suffering from various psychoses. But they were extended in some cases to cover epileptics, where inheritance of a defect was dubious, and sex offenders and habitual criminals, where such inheritance did not exist. In general, the courts have upheld the application of the laws to mental defectives but not to the other groups. The power to order sterilization is not extensively used, with the number of cases reported amounting to only 500 a year.

Voluntary sterilization is nowhere completely forbidden. In Connecticut, Kansas, and Utah, it is restricted to cases of medical necessity. In North Carolina and Virginia, it must be approved by two physicians. In most states, it is permitted if the spouse gives his or her consent. In 22 states, the law is silent; sterilization is not restrained. The number of such operations, however, is relatively small: around 100,000 are performed each year.

Under present circumstances, sterilization has little significance as a method of controlling family size in the United States. People in the lower income groups may be unaware of the possibility, or if they know of it may fear, mistakenly, that it would impair their sexual activity, or they may be unwilling to sacrifice their procreative powers. Physicians, moreover, are reluctant to perform the operations. And where they do so, they may charge more than the poor can pay.[28]

The law on contraception

Legislation regarding contraception had its origin nearly a century ago as part of a national drive against obscenity. The first federal law, enacted in 1873, prohibited the importation of contraceptives, along with that of obscene literature, excluded them from the mails, and forbade their shipment across state lines. This measure touched off a burst of legislation by the states. Almost all of the states enacted laws against obscenity. More than half of the laws explicitly limited the distribution of contraceptives. The rest could be construed to do so.

As late as 1930, the laws of 31 states made it a crime for anyone but a physician to give information on birth control. Twenty-six states

[28] Alan F. Guttmacher, "Sterilization," *The Nation*, April 6, 1964, pp. 344–47.

made it illegal to advertise or display contraceptives. In most states, sales could be made only on a doctor's prescription or for the prevention of disease. Wisconsin forbade physicians to provide contraceptive information or devices to unmarried women. Massachusetts forbade them to give such information or devices even to couples who were married. Connecticut forbade anyone, including married couples, to practice contraception. The laws of these two states were unsuccessfully challenged in their courts. Repeated efforts to repeal or amend them met with failure.[29]

The laws against contraception were never really enforced. Contraceptive devices of certain types were generally available. Contraception was widely practiced, as the statistics of reproduction made clear. A woman who made no effort to prevent conception could produce 15 children by her 45th year. Among couples of that age who never practiced contraception, the average number of children was actually around 10.[30] But the average number of children ever born to all women aged 40 through 45 was not 15 or 10 but 2.5. The birth rates in Massachusetts and Connecticut, the two states with the strictest laws, were among the lowest in the nation.

Changing attitudes

The legislation condemning birth control originated in the puritanical tradition of Protestantism, in the belief that sexual indulgence was wicked, that removal of the risk of pregnancy would encourage promiscuity, that morality should be enforced by law. As Protestants came, in time, to abandon this position, defense of restrictions on birth control was taken over by the Roman Catholics. In the view of the church, frustration of conception was intrinsically evil, a violation of natural law. In support of this view, the church undertook to control not only the sexual behavior of its own communicants but also that of Protestants, Jews, and persons with no religious faith. It brought pressure to bear on Congress and on the legislatures of the states to prevent repeal or amendment of the anticontraception laws. It exerted pressure, too, on public health and welfare agencies. Where doctors in public

[29] A. H. Sulloway, "Legal and Political Aspects of Population Control in the United States," *Law and Contemporary Problems,* Summer, 1960, pp. 592–613.
[30] Joseph W. Eaton and Albert J. Mayer, *Man's Capacity to Reproduce* (Glencoe, Ill.: Free Press, 1954), p. 20.

hospitals undertook to give contraceptive information and where workers in public welfare agencies sought to do so, they were threatened
with budgetary cuts. Where private hospitals and social agencies
provided such services, they were threatened with loss of private
financial support. In many cities, family planning clinics were excluded, under Catholic pressure, from the fund-raising efforts of the
united charities. With public officials thus intimidated and private
agencies handicapped, the church restrained the growth of birth control. The situation had one clear effect: contraceptive information and
devices were readily available to the well-to-do; they were withheld, in
large part, from the poor.

In the fifties and the sixties, the tide of opinion turned. The notion
that conformity to desired standards of sexual behavior could be assured by law came increasingly to be recognized as fallacious. The
need for birth control, particularly in the underdeveloped countries,
was demonstrated by a worldwide explosion in population. The need
for control at home was seen in a mounting burden of welfare costs.
New techniques for preventing conception were widely publicized.
Respected national organizations of scientists, physicians, public health
officials, and businessmen passed resolutions favoring birth control.
Eminent Protestant and Jewish clergymen and bodies representing
their communions issued statements holding contraception to be moral
and recommending the wider availability of contraceptive services.
Polls of public opinion showed that nine tenths of the people believed
that information on contraception should be given to any married
person who asked for it; that three fourths believed that such information should be given to any adult, whether married or not; and that
more than half believed it should be given to students in high schools.

Along with this shift of opinion came changes in the position of the
Catholic church. The desirability of family planning was accepted,
and the church's opposition confined to the use of mechanical and
chemical agents to prevent conception, as opposed to reliance on the so-
called rhythm method, which the church approved. The former opposition to public birth control programs was relaxed; provision of information by public hospitals and welfare agencies was accepted as
long as the practice of contraception was voluntary and the method
approved by the church, among others, was taught. In 1967, following
five years of debate, a commission appointed by the Vatican to review
church policy on the subject made its report, the great majority of its

members recommending that the traditional opposition to contraception be reversed. Then in 1968, Pope Paul VI issued an encyclical rejecting the commission's recommendation and reiterating the traditional view. The encyclical denounced contraception involving artificial methods as a mortal sin, appealed to legislative bodies to forbid it, and urged physicians to discourage patients from its use. The papal position was promptly rejected by many Catholic theologians, physicians, and social scientists; by half of the priests and by 95 percent of the curates covered in a study made at Notre Dame;[31] by more than half of the Catholic communicants questioned in a public opinion poll; and by four fifths of those under the age of 30. The American Conference of Catholic Bishops, in an ambiguous pronouncement, endorsed the position taken by the Pope but also held that Catholic couples whose consciences compelled them to practice contraception could take communion without first confessing it as a sin. From this reaction, it would appear that in the United States, the church is no longer likely to oppose public or private programs of birth control.

Government birth control programs

Along with the shift in public opinion on birth control has gone a shift in public policy. Family planning activities have been initiated by federal, state, and local governments. Under the federal programs of maternity and infant care and aid to families with dependent children, the Department of Health, Education, and Welfare makes grants to state health and welfare agencies for the support of family planning services. In 1967, Congress made the provision of such services a prerequisite for these grants, requiring, in the case of AFDC, that they be offered without regard to age or marital status. The Department also makes grants for family planning under its programs of maternal and child health and medical care for the indigent. It conducts research on the biology of reproduction and, through the Food and Drug Administration, tests the safety of contraceptive drugs. It makes grants to the states for research and training and supports the development of sex education and counseling in the schools. While varied, the Department's program is small in scale. In 1967, only eight professionals among its 108,000 employees were engaged in this work. Its expendi-

---

[31] *New York Times,* October 8, 1968.

tures on the work amounted to only $9,000,000. Its efforts have been described as "leaderless and leisurely."[32]

Another federal agency, the Office of Economic Opportunity, set up in 1964, makes grants to finance antipoverty programs originated by local community action agencies. The activities of these agencies are to be discussed in Chapter 20. Among them, in particular cases, may be the provision of family planning services. At the outset, the OEO approached this part of the local programs with caution. It not only forbade the local agencies to require participation in the program or to confine it to members of particular racial or religious groups but also laid down a number of other rules: the family planning clinics were forbidden to promote particular contraceptive techniques, to provide information which was inconsistent with a patient's religious beliefs, to spend money on surgery, or to supply contraceptives to unmarried women or to married women who were separated from their husbands. Congress repealed the last of these conditions, allowing the others to stand. In 1967, it designated family planning as a program to be given national emphasis. But the program has been even smaller than that administered by HEW. Among more than 1,000 community action agencies, only 156 had family planning projects in 1968. OEO had only one specialist in the field. Its expenditure on family planning was around $9,000,000.

There were a number of developments in the states. In 1965, the Supreme Court of the United States held the Connecticut statute that made it a criminal offense for a married couple to use contraceptives to be invalid "as invading their rights of privacy."[33] In 1966, the legislature of Massachusetts repealed the law that made it a crime for a physician to furnish a married couple with contraceptive information or materials. By 1967, laws enabling the inauguration of public family planning services had been enacted by many of the states. In general, these laws provided that such services were to be administered as part of the states' maternal health programs; that they were to be provided only to families voluntarily seeking them and to families with low incomes; that they were to be rendered by qualified physicians and were to include a variety of contraceptive techniques. The number of states offering family planning services increased from 7 in 1960 to 37

[32] Elinor Langer, "Birth Control: U.S. Programs Off to a Slow Start," *Science*, May 12, 1967, pp. 765–67. See also Harkavy, *op. cit.*, pp. 11–19.
[33] *Griswold* v. *Connecticut*, 381 U.S. 479.

in 1967. In a few cases, these services were provided by the state itself. In Oklahoma, for instance, a law enacted in 1967 authorized the establishment of a state birth control center in each county to serve all citizens regardless of their income. Elsewhere the states gave financial support to clinics established by local governments. In California, under a law enacted in 1966, all local health departments are required to offer family planning services. In some cases, initiative has been taken by local governments. In Chicago, since 1964, the Board of Health has provided contraceptive services to all who request them, without regard to income and without charge. In other cities, the public hospitals have introduced or extended family planning. In New York, such services are supplied to all women who ask for them, whether they are married or not. In Philadelphia, they are provided at public expense to maternity patients in the public hospital and in a number of private hospitals. In some states, finally, the welfare authorities refer applicants for contraceptive information to private agencies. These agencies, with legal restraints on their activities removed, are operating on a growing scale.

All this shows progress. But the staff and funds so far provided fall far short of the need. In 1967, less than a third of local health departments and less than a fifth of hospitals with large maternity services provided any kind of contraceptive help for people who were medically indigent. The number of women requiring subsidized family planning is estimated at more than five million. In 1967, the number receiving it was only 700,000. As yet only 14 percent of those with low incomes have access to these services; 86 percent do not. In rural areas, only 6 percent have access; 94 percent do not.[34]

Birth control to prevent poverty

In a poor country such as India, already overpopulated and handicapped in its development effort by rapid population growth, birth control must have as its primary purpose restriction of the numbers of the population as a whole. In an affluent country like the United States, no such limitation is needed. Here, the importance of limiting numbers is confined to the lower income groups.

[34] Frederick S. Jaffe, "Family Planning and Public Policy" in Harkavy, *op. cit.*, Attachment B, p. 6; Sheppard, *op. cit.*, p. 732; and President's National Commission on Rural Poverty, *op. cit.*, pp. 81–83.

Amelioration of poverty is one of the purposes of family planning, but it is not the only one. Advisors on planned parenthood not only help some couples who do not want children to keep from having them but also advise others, who want children but have not had them, on practices that favor their birth. They are concerned not only with the number of children in a family but also with their timing, recommending that birth of the first child be delayed until the parents are prepared for it, both economically and psychologically, and that the birth of later children be so spaced as to safeguard the mother's health. Family planning attempts to improve marital relationships, releasing tensions that make for strife. It seeks to make sure that every child shall be a wanted child, assured of affection and given a proper start in life. Its objectives, thus, are broader than the prevention of poverty, with which we are here concerned.

The purpose of government birth control programs has been mistakenly denounced as racist. It is observed that clinics are established in the ghettoes, where the births to be prevented are births to mothers who are black. And this, it is charged, gives evidence of intended genocide. But acceptance of family planning services is not compulsory but voluntary. Exposure to contraceptive information could be coerced, to be sure, by making it prerequisite to the receipt of other forms of aid, but this is explicitly forbidden by law. And there is no way in which the *practice* of contraception can be coerced. The purpose of a public birth control program is to afford the poor, whatever their race, the same freedom of choice, the same ability to control their own destiny, that is already possessed by the well-to-do. Its purpose, in this sphere, is to provide equality of opportunity.

Benefits and costs of birth control

Birth control is among the antipoverty measures that yield the largest and most certain returns, the ones that produce the greatest ratio of benefits to costs. Among the benefits are avoidance of the cost of rearing an unwanted child. Arthur A. Campbell estimates this cost in the lower income groups at $470 a year or $7,986 to the 18th year. Discounting this figure at 4 percent per year, he arrives at a benefit of $5,617. He estimates the cost of preventing childbirth, on the other hand, at $20 to $25 per patient per year or $300 for every birth avoided. He thus arrives at a ratio of benefits to cost of $5,617 to $300 or 18.7 to 1.

Another benefit is found in the possibility that women who avoided unwanted pregnancies would accept gainful employment. Campbell estimates that the earnings of those who did so would amount to $2,178 per birth avoided. When this is added to the previous saving of $5,617, it gives a total benefit of $7,795 compared to a cost of $300, or a cost-benefit ratio of 26 to 1.[35]

The community would enjoy still other benefits. In 1964, there were 9.3 million children in families where there were four or more. If births beyond the third child could have been cut in half, it would have reduced the number of children in poverty by 4.6 million. If family size among the poor could have been reduced to that obtaining among the nonpoor, it would have cut the number by 6.5 million. Such a change in the volume of child poverty would have reduced the cost of public programs for health, education, housing, welfare, and the control of delinquency. It is estimated that such costs could be cut by $250,000,000 a year by a birth control program reaching 500,000 women at a cost of $20 each or a total cost of $10,000,000 per year.[36] In the public sector as in the private sector, the ratio of benefit to cost is as much as 25 to 1.

Characteristics of an effective program

An effective birth control program would undertake to make contraceptive information and materials as readily available to the poor and the near-poor as they are to the well-to-do. To this end, it would provide family planning services throughout the country in clinics operated by public welfare agencies, health departments, and hospitals and by private agencies subsidized by government. It would set its clinics up at convenient locations and keep them open at convenient hours. It would staff them with trained professionals. It would refer welfare clients to them for contraceptive information and materials. It would undertake to reach newlyweds to advise on family planning before the conception of their first child. In maternity hospitals, it would give advice on child spacing during the period of confinement for delivery and postpartum care. It would offer wide choice among the possible methods of control. It would provide these services without charge, supplying contraceptive materials to the poor at public

[35] Campbell, *op. cit.*, pp. 21–24.
[36] Sheppard, *op. cit.*, pp. 729–31.

expense. It would serve the unmarried as well as the married, reducing the extent of illegitimacy. The program would not only provide these services but it would advertise their availability and promote their use. It would launch an educational drive, giving instruction on the values and possibilities of family planning in the schools and in classes for adults.

The cost of an adequate program of birth control for the United States is estimated at $100,000,000 to $150,000,000 a year. Compared with the cost of other antipoverty measures, it would be small indeed.

"The war on poverty"

The war on poverty, as it came to be known, was not declared in response to pressure from the poor. It began rather as a response by President Kennedy to conditions he had seen in West Virginia when campaigning for the presidential nomination in 1960 and to journalistic exposures and economic studies of poverty throughout the United States that were brought to his attention by members of his secretariat and his Council of Economic Advisers. The war started with the passage of the Area Redevelopment Act in 1961 and the Manpower Development and Training Act in 1962, and work was under way on the formulation of a broader effort when the President was assassinated in 1963.The emerging program was to be based on the experience of private agencies and federal and local governments in providing opportunities for training and employment for the poor and in encouraging the betterment of poor communities. President Johnson adopted this program and made it his own. Embodied, in final form, in the Economic Opportunity Act, it was made a leading measure of his "Great Society." Presented in an atmosphere of political consensus, the Act was passed, with substantial majorities in both houses of Congress in 1964.

The Economic Opportunity Act

The policy of the Economic Opportunity Act was clear. It did not undertake to ameliorate poverty by raising public assistance payments or by creating government jobs. It sought rather to increase the employability of the unemployed. It placed its emphasis, in particular, on youth, providing added support for education, vocational training, and work experience. It also undertook to promote the improvement of community services for the poor. In all of this, it placed its reliance on the development of self-help and individual responsibility, and on group cooperation for the common good.

Administrative problems

When the war on poverty was being planned, it was decided not to entrust its administration to any of the existing agencies but to establish an independent body for the purpose. The Office of Economic Opportunity was accordingly set up in the Executive Office of the President. Among the programs covered by the law, however, there were some that duplicated those already being carried on. A struggle ensued within the bureaucracy to determine what programs were to be administered by what agencies. The upshot was a series of compromises that allocated certain programs to the Department of Labor and to the Department of Health, Education, and Welfare, leaving others to the OEO. The Office was also charged with responsibility for coordinating the government's antipoverty effort as a whole, an effort comprising more than a hundred different programs and the expenditure of $25 billion a year, in which the OEO itself played but a minor role. The Office, however, was given no real authority; its coordinating function was purely nominal.

The OEO might have contented itself with acting as a disburser of funds, leaving administration of the programs it financed to other agencies. It did not choose this course. Instead, it delegated some programs to other federal offices, administered others through contracts with private agencies, and administered still others itself. Administratively, the Office was thus a hybrid.

Throughout its life, the OEO has been a scene of great confusion. New and untried programs have been mounted at breakneck speed. Staff positions have gone unfilled. There has been delay in releasing funds. Congressional action has been uncertain. The agency's life has been extended for a year at a time. No one has known how long it would survive or what the size of its budget would be. Appropriations have been delayed. Payrolls have not been met. There has been a high turnover of administrative personnel. But, somehow or other, the work has been done.

Economic opportunity programs

In the fiscal year 1968, the Office of Economic Opportunity had a budget of $1.75 billions. It spent half of this on Community Action Programs, to be described in the next section; the other half, on programs that were nationwide in scope. These programs were varied in content; some were old, some new. Most important were the programs for training and employing young men and women, carried on at a cost of nearly $550 million: the Neighborhood Youth Corps, described in Chapter 17; and the Job Corps, described in Chapter 18. There were also work experience and training programs for adults— for the unemployed parents of dependent children and for others in poverty who had been chronically unemployed—expenditures for this purpose running to $215 million. There was assistance for other adult groups: advice and loans to help them in setting up small businesses, loans to small farmers, and aid for migrant workers, the sums spent for these purposes being relatively small. And finally, there was VISTA— Volunteers in Service to America—a domestic equivalent of the Peace Corps. Under this program, nearly 5,000 volunteers were each spending a year or more working in depressed areas, on Indian reservations, and in the slums, in schools, hospitals, and community centers, organizing day-care services, teaching retarded children, directing recreational programs, and performing many other helpful tasks. Expenditure on this program, too, was small, amounting to only $30 million a year.[1]

Some of these programs were administered by other agencies: the National Youth Corps by the Department of Labor, work experience and training by HEW, business loans by the Small Business Administration, and farm loans by the Farmers Home Administration. Other programs were administered by OEO: the Job Corps through contracts with universities and corporate enterprises; VISTA and the

[1] For a description of OEO programs, see Office of Economic Opportunity, *The Quiet Revolution* (Washington, D.C.: U.S. Government Printing Office, 1967).

Community Action Program, its largest undertaking, by the Office itself.

Community action

Community action is the one OEO program that is really unique. In the past, aid for the poor has been planned by private social workers and public welfare officials and administered by social agencies and local political machines. It has been handed down from above, with little or no participation on the part of its recipients. Such aid has also been fragmented, each program dealing with a particular problem, none with the needs of the poor as a whole. Community action, on the other hand, puts its emphasis on local initiative in the development of antipoverty programs and local participation in their administration and calls for a comprehensive attack on the problems of the poor. It invites the poor themselves to take part in the formulation and the execution of these programs, finding in their participation not only assurance that the aid provided will be better adapted to their needs but also hope that the participants will grow in self-reliance and responsibility, in dignity and pride. It seeks to elicit total community involvement, mobilizing all available resources, both public and private, in the attack on poverty.

A community action program may be started by any group of citizens: by social workers, by civil rights workers, by clergymen, or by other leaders of the poor. These people may meet on their own initiative or at the suggestion of the OEO, survey the needs of the community, formulate a program to meet them, and set up a private nonprofit organization to carry on the work. Or an agency of local government may develop such a program and enlist private support. In either case, the organization assuming responsibility applies to OEO for funds. If the Office approves the application, it designates the organization as a Community Action Agency. Until mid-1967, the Office provided nine tenths of the money spent by these bodies; since then it has provided four fifths.

Community action programs

There are over a thousand community action agencies in the United States, their programs a mixture of activities that varies from place to place. A number of the agencies have set up health centers, providing comprehensive medical service for the poor. A fourth of them provide legal services, advising the poor on such matters as juvenile offenses, divorce, and welfare claims and representing them in nonsupport cases and landlord-tenant disputes.[2] Some agencies maintain credit unions and offer instruction on purchasing and home management. Some give day care to the children of working mothers. Some provide homemakers and health aides for the aged. Some have recreational programs. Some promote housing improvement and community beautification. In more than 700 places, the community action agencies have set up neighborhood service centers. Here, all CAA activities are brought together along with other government services for the poor: employment counseling and job training, and family counseling and welfare work. Such services are thus brought within easy reach; information is provided and applicants referred to the programs that meet their needs.

In its first years when the local agencies were slow in getting programs started, the OEO initiated programs of its own and persuaded the agencies to adopt them. Of these, the most important was Head Start, a program preparing disadvantaged preschool children for school. Some 500,000 children, aged three through five, were cared for in 2,000 places during the summers; around 200,000 in 650 places during the school year. These youngsters were handled in small classes, given nutritional, health, and social services, trained in the use of language, and given other educational experiences. The results were both encouraging and discouraging. The children's intelligence quotients were raised by as much as 10 points. Their motivation, attitudes, and social behavior were improved. Where they went on to superior schools, they continued to gain. But where they went to inferior schools, the advantage of their head start was lost. The OEO therefore started 30 pilot programs in 1967–68 to follow through with compensatory education for Head Start groups. The Head Start program itself had reached 30 percent of the nation's disadvantaged three- and four-year-olds by 1968 at a cost of $220 per child during the summer and $1,050 per child during the school year. Its budget in fiscal 1968 was $283 million.

Another program initiated by the OEO was Upward Bound, mentioned in Chapter 10, designed to help underachieving high school

[2] On the CAA legal aid projects, see Herbert Mitgang, "The Storefront Lawyer Helps the Poor," *New York Times Magazine*, November 10, 1968, pp. 34 ff.

students in preparing for college. There were nearly 300 Upward Bound projects in 1968, aiding 26,000 students at a cost of $1,200 per student.[3]

Representation of the poor

Community action programs, said the Economic Opportunity Act, were to be "developed, conducted, and administered with the maximum feasible participation of residents of the areas and members of the groups served." This phrase was based on the experience of a committee appointed by President Kennedy to deal with the problem of juvenile delinquency and was written into the Act by administration draftsmen who had served with that committee. The phrase attracted little attention. Its possible significance was not appreciated by the administration. It was not questioned in either house of Congress.

The meaning of "participation" was not clear. But when the law was passed, OEO called for "involvement of the poor themselves . . . in planning, policy making, and operation of the program" and defined participation as "membership on the governing body or on a policy advisory committee" of a community action agency. Thereafter, the Office made it a rule of thumb that one third of the members of a governing board should be representatives of the poor. This rule was made a statutory requirement when Congress amended the law in 1966.

It was not clear whether representatives of the poor had to be people who themselves were poor and whether they were to be appointed or elected. The Office was not insistent on this matter, in some cases holding that the poor were adequately represented by appointees who themselves were well-to-do. But a common pattern came to be that of election of representatives from among the poor. The results were disappointing. In Philadelphia in 1966, only 2.7 percent of those eligible to vote did so; in Boston, only 2.4 percent: in Los Angeles, where a vigorous campaign was waged to bring out the voters, only 0.7 percent. In 14 elections held in New York city during

[3] On community action programs, see: U.S. Senate, Committee on Labor and Public Welfare, Subcommittee on Employment, Manpower, and Poverty, *Examination of the War on Poverty*, Staff and Consultants Reports, Vol. 3 (Washington, D.C.: U.S. Government Printing Office, 1967), pp. 739–70, 795–855; and National Advisory Council on Economic Opportunity, *Focus on Community Action* (Washington, D.C.: U.S. Government Printing Office, 1968), chaps. ii, iii.

1967, the average turnout was 3.5 percent; in the rest of the nation, the average that year was less than 2 percent.

Representatives of the poor on the governing boards might influence the community action programs by informing the other members concerning the needs of their communities and persuading them to vote for projects their constituents desired. But they could not exercise real power. They were always to be in a minority. They were unlikely to be a match for the sophisticated and powerful people who made up the majority. If not subservient to business or political interests, they might come to be dominated by the welfare bureaucracy. Those who retained the loyalty of their constituents might find themselves without influence on the board. Those who came to be influential might lose their popular support. Whatever the outcome, "maximum feasible participation" was not supposed to spell control.

Politics of community action

The community action program evoked widespread political opposition. In the past, delivery of welfare services had been a source of strength for local political machines. Now the community action agencies appeared as a rival source of power. They had money to spend, contracts to let, jobs to fill. And OEO dealt with them directly, bypassing the mayors and the machines. A struggle ensued in city after city to determine who should control the expenditure of antipoverty funds. In many cases, the mayors won out. Here, the community action agencies became subsidiaries or allies of local governments. Elsewhere they maintained their independence.

Where independent, the agencies were constant irritants. According to the National Advisory Council on Economic Opportunity, they played the gadfly role, reminding local governments of the need—

to mobilize and focus existing resources on programs designed to break the cycle of poverty in new and more effective ways. Sometimes they have succeeded by exerting internal pressures on governments. Sometimes they have challenged political units. And occasionally they have fought governments bitterly.[4]

In a few cases, action organized among the poor led to open conflict. Militant groups put pressure on landlords, merchants, and city officials,

---

[4] National Advisory Council on Economic Opportunity, *op. cit.,* p. 29.

calling rent strikes, imposing consumer boycotts, and staging sit-ins for jobs and larger welfare checks. And some of this activity was encouraged by persons identified in one way or another with OEO. Community action thus appeared to carry a threat to established interests. Local officials demanded that it be curbed.

Congress responded. In 1966, it amended the Economic Opportunity Act to specify projects on which community action money must be spent. The allocations thus required, together with those made for projects initiated by the OEO itself, preempted more than three fifths of this money, leaving the disposition of less than two fifths to be determined by the local agencies. The amendment thus impaired the program's basic commitment to local initiative. In 1967, Congress acted again, amending the law to require that bodies to be recognized as community action agencies after mid-1968 be state governments or their subdivisions or agencies designated by them. At that time, four fifths of the CAAs were nongovernmental groups. When the state and local governments made their choices, they took over only a tenth of these agencies, allowing nine tenths to survive. But under the law they retained the power to revoke these designations whenever they chose. The threat that community action seems to pose to local political interests was thus allayed.[5]

Appraisals and prospects

Critics complain that the war on poverty was misrepresented. Its character and scale were different than was claimed. Put before the people as a program composed of novel elements carefully integrated in a comprehensive plan, it was really a combination of familiar measures, some of them copied from the past, some already under way, hastily brought together by effecting compromises within the federal bureaucracy. Presented as an all-out attack on poverty, it was really small in scale. The numbers aided were small; the program was said to reach no more than 6 percent of the poor. The appropriation made was small, amounting to only $40 per person under the poverty line. The war on poverty, in the words of the National Advisory Council, was "little more than a large-scale research and demonstration program."[6]

[5] See John C. Donovan, *The Politics of Poverty* (New York: Pegasus, 1967), chap. iii, iv; and Ben B. Seligman, *Permanent Poverty* (Chicago, Ill.: Quadrangle Books, 1968), chap. x.

[6] National Advisory Council on Economic Opportunity, *op. cit.*, p. 37.

The promises made on its behalf went far beyond the performance the nation was willing to deliver. The expectations raised were not to be fulfilled.

This may be true. But granted the limits within which it has had to operate, the OEO must be credited with significant accomplishments. Its educational and employment programs—Head Start, Upward Bound, the Job Corps, and the National Youth Corps—have improved the opportunities of many thousands among the children of the poor. Its community action programs have been imaginative and constructive. They have eased the lives of many thousands dwelling in the slums, providing them with public services they had not had before, affording them a medium through which long-standing grievances can be redressed, giving them a measure of control over the conditions that surround them, a growing confidence in their role as citizens. These gains are difficult if not impossible to measure, but they are no less real. And, in achieving them, the government has obtained experience on which to build.

As this is written, the future of OEO is uncertain. Its results have not been spectacular; it has not prevented riots in the slums. The Office has attempted to pacify gangs of youthful offenders and has been charged, in consequence, with supporting criminal activities. It has sought to direct protest into peaceful channels and has been charged with sponsoring radical agitation. There have been scandals in some of its projects; cases of misappropriation of community action funds. The Office is unpopular with politicians in the South where the poor whose interests it serves are largely black. It is regarded with scant affection by politicians in the North. With first priority given by the government to fighting a war abroad, the war on poverty at home has taken second place. The hope that it inspired at the beginning has disappeared. The enthusiasm it aroused has been dispelled.

Unless extended by Congress, the life of OEO will end on June 30, 1969. The Job Corps is likely to be abolished and Head Start transferred to HEW. The fate of the agency's other programs is unknown.

PART V

The prospects

The strategy and the
feasibility of welfare

Public policy in the United States has moved consistently toward the goals of social welfare: toward security against life's hazards; toward equality of opportunity; toward the abolition of poverty. The nation's progress toward these goals has been substantial. For many years, it has come to the aid of those who were in need, providing assistance in cash, in kind, and in the form of social services. Since the thirties, it has insured nearly all of its citizens against dependent old age, survivorship, and disability; most of them against industrial accident and unemployment; and the aged against the cost of medical care. Since the fifties, it has outlawed discrimination in education and employment, in housing and in access to public accommodations, in elections and in treatment by the courts. It has taken affirmative action through training and employment to open the way to opportunity. During the sixties, it has recognized poverty as a national problem, attacking it through area development, urban renewal, and community action and through labor market services and manpower development. The nation's welfare programs have steadily grown in variety and in scope. In the fiscal year 1929–30, public expenditures on these programs amounted to 3.9 percent of the gross national product; in 1966–67, they amounted to 13.1 percent.

Income transfers to the poor have grown in scale. Income transfers are payments that are made not for services rendered by the recipients but to carry out the giver's purposes. They collect money from one group and distribute it to another in cash, in goods, or in services. The total of such transfers in the United States in 1964 is estimated at $97 billion. Of this, $16 billion took the form of private charity and employees' fringe benefits; $81 billion was effected through governments in the form of educational, health, and welfare services, social insurance benefits, public assistance payments, and various subsidies. Not all of these transfers go to the poor. Indeed, three fifths of the money and the services distributed go to the nonpoor and only two fifths to the poor. But the payments to the poor are still significant. In 1964, the poor received $38 billion in transfers and paid $8 billion in taxes, realizing a net gain of $30 billion. The transfers operated to move 4.5 million families across the poverty line. Before the transfers, 28 percent of the people were in poverty; after the transfers, only 18 percent. Before the transfers, the poor had 5 percent of personal income; after the transfers, the same people had 11 percent. The burden of poverty was substantially reduced.[1]

Progress toward the goals of welfare has been great. But certain questions remain. Is the strategy employed in promoting welfare as effective as it could be? Would other methods produce the same or better results at lower costs? Is further progress toward welfare feasible? Do we really know how to assure security, to provide equality of opportunity, to abolish poverty? If so, can we afford to pay as much as these reforms would cost? And if so, will we have the will to do so? It is to these questions that we now turn.

The strategy of welfare

The welfare programs in the United States are a hodgepodge of measures that were initiated at different times, with different objectives, at different levels of government. They are administered by a variety of federal, state, and local agencies. They are overlapping—often inconsistent and conflicting. There is no clear definition of purpose, no central direction in the welfare effort as a whole. But these are characteristics of governmental action that are not peculiar to the welfare field.

[1] Robert J. Lampman, "How Much Does the American System of Transfers Benefit the Poor?" in Leonard H. Goodman, (ed.), *Economic Progress and Social Welfare* (New York: Columbia University Press, 1966), pp. 125–57.

The methods employed in promoting welfare differ in their effects. Some may do more harm than good. Others are harmless but ineffective. Still others are effective but carry a high cost. Some welfare measures are mere palliatives for the evils they attack; others get at the causes of these evils and prevent their recurrence. Here, we summarize our appraisals of the programs adopted and the proposals made for enhancing social welfare.

How attack insecurity?

As it stands today, the structure of social security has its strengths and weaknesses. The systems of state insurance against industrial accident and occupational disease could be improved by extending their coverage to the uncovered fifth of the labor force, by raising the maximum limits that prevent full payment of their promised benefits, by making sure that negotiated settlements do not deprive the beneficiary of payments that are due him, by controlling the quality of the medical services that are provided, and by placing greater emphasis on vocational rehabilitation. But these are matters of legislative and administrative detail. In principle, the systems are sound.

The state unemployment insurance systems, like the industrial disability systems, could be improved by extending their coverage to the remaining quarter of the labor force and by raising the limits that prevent full payment of their benefits. But even if this were done, defects in principle would remain. Provision of insurance through 50 separate systems results in waste of resources and inequality of protection, with the reserves of some states standing idle while those of others approach exhaustion. Adjustment of employers' taxes in accordance with their employment experience does little or nothing to prevent unemployment but reduces reserve funds and makes it less certain that benefits will actually be paid. The risk of unemployment would be better met if insurance were provided through a single federal system and financed by a tax imposed on all employers at a common rate.

Protection against dependent old age, survivorship, and permanent total disability is afforded by a dual system, with social insurance providing the basic protection and public assistance serving as a supplement in cases where insurance benefits are lacking or low. Within its present framework, the insurance system could be improved by tying the level of benefits to an index of the cost of living, by raising the minimum benefits, and by changing the structure of benefits to pay relatively less to spouses and dependents and relatively more to single persons, widows, and larger families. But there are defects that are inherent in the nature of the system as it was first set up. Benefits and taxes were both related to earnings, and it thus appeared that benefits were purchased by contributions. This served at the time to make the system politically acceptable. And it established the claim to benefits as a right. But it had two unfortunate effects. It committed the government to the imposition of regressive taxes on wages and payrolls. It held down the benefits payable to the poor because their earnings had been low while distributing substantial benefits to persons above the poverty line whose earnings had been comparatively high. These effects could be avoided by setting up a different sort of dual system, one in which the lower benefits, adequate to meet the needs of the poor, would be financed from general revenues, and the higher benefits, related to earnings, would be financed by contributions. But this would require the substitution of a radically different system for the present one. Reform within the present framework would be more easily obtained.

The cost of medical care is met in part through a complicated combination of programs. For the aged who are covered by OASDI there is compulsory insurance, financed by wage and payroll taxes, to meet hospital costs, and there is voluntary insurance, financed by contributions from individuals and from the government, to meet other medical costs. For the aged who are not so covered, for dependent children, and for others who can prove their need, medical services financed from general revenues are provided as part of the public assistance programs. For those who are neither aged nor in poverty, protection against the costs of sickness is left to private initiative. Part of these people have no protection. For all of them, the protection purchased is less than adequate. This, as it has recently evolved, is the American system of health insurance. It should be possible, through a single national system of medical care, to get comprehensive coverage, with adequate benefits, at a lower cost.

How attack inequality of opportunity?

The methods employed in attacking racial discrimination are well designed for the purpose they serve. In a democracy, each man must stand alike before the law. Each must be accorded the same right to vote, to run for and to hold office, to be tried by a jury of his peers. Where laws prevent such equality, they must be repealed. Where administrative action prevents it, such action must be penalized. It is obvious, too, that each man should be granted the same access to public accommodations; and the same right to rent or buy a home. Where discrimination, whether public or private, denies these rights, it should be struck down. This is the course that has been followed in recent years by the Congress and the courts.

All men should have equal opportunity for employment. To insure this equality, government should avoid discrimination as an employer. It should forbid discrimination by its contractors. It should outlaw discrimination by all employers and all unions. These things have now been done. The fair employment practices laws put their initial emphasis on persuasion and negotiation. In the face of long-standing prejudice, this approach was doubtless wise. But for the laws to be effective, persuasion and negotiation must be reenforced by administrative and judicial orders and by the imposition of penalties. Such powers are granted by the laws.

Most important to equality of opportunity is equal access to education. Such access is denied by racial segregation. *De jure* segregation in the schools must therefore be forbidden. *De facto* segregation, too, should be ended. There are various means by which this can be done. In many places, one or another of them has been employed. In some communities, the balance of races is such that integration can be achieved. Elsewhere, imbalance may render it impossible. Here, the education offered to disadvantaged children should be strengthened. Efforts to compensate for their handicaps should be redoubled. Vocational training and employment counseling should be improved. Affirmative action should also be taken on other fronts. The federal government should extend financial aid to weak school districts. It should offer employment, loans, and grants to enable members of minority groups to carry their education as far as their capacities permit. These are the means of enlarging opportunity that are now being employed.

How attack poverty?

There have been three main approaches to the abolition of poverty: First, the needs of the poor have been met by giving them assistance in cash or in the form of goods and services. Second, the poor have been enabled to support themselves by affording them opportunities for employment. Third, employment has been facilitated by improving the operation of the labor market and by equipping workers with needed skills. Each of these approaches has advantages and limitations.

Charitable assistance, in cash or in kind, is the only method that can be employed in attacking the poverty of families that have no member in the labor force: the aged, the handicapped, and the single woman with small children in her care. Four fifths of the aid provided to the poor is in cash. This money can be spent as the recipient may please. His responsibility in spending is assumed. In some cases, the assumption is justified. In others, money provided to meet a family's basic needs may be diverted to other purposes. Less than a fifth of the aid is provided in kind. Such aid supplies specific goods and services. It takes whatever form the government may choose: surplus foods, for instance, or public housing. Some needs can be met only in this way: protection for neglected, abused, and abandoned children cannot be purchased in the marketplace. Government is the sole purveyor, too, of services that are collective in character: of public health, and of parks, museums, and libraries. Still other services are best provided in this way: this is true of public education and may be true of medical care. There are few who would question that aid must be extended both in cash and in kind. Opinions differ only as to emphasis between the two. Judgment as to their respective merits depends upon analyses made case by case. However provided, public assistance imposes heavy administrative burdens and carries substantial financial costs. But these are burdens and costs that society cannot avoid.

Provision of employment is superior in many respects to provision of aid in cash or in kind. It is less costly. It adds to the output of goods and services. It provides work experience and maintains labor skills. It yields a larger income and a higher standard of living. It produces self-reliance and contributes to self-respect. But each of the means by which government has undertaken or is asked to undertake to provide employment has its limitations: First, government has employed labor in the construction of public works. But, in doing so, it has created jobs only for labor in the construction industries. Second, government has promoted the economic development of depressed areas. But here its aid has gone to local authorities and private enterprises and may or may not trickle down to put the poor to work. Third, during the depression of the thirties, government made employment an alternative to other forms of aid. But it encountered difficulties in creating jobs that would not only be useful but would not compete with private enterprise, and in setting wages at levels that would not only be fair to labor but would preserve an incentive to return to private employment. Fourth, government has sometimes made acceptance of employment a prerequisite to the receipt of other aid. But this requirement has not in itself created jobs at which the poor could work. Fifth, it is now proposed that government provide jobs to all who seek them, serving as an employer of last resort. But this would require it to employ the least productive members of the labor force and to put them in many cases to tasks they were not equipped to do. Sixth, and most important, government maintains aggregate demand and stimulates economic growth by pursuing expansionist monetary and fiscal policies. Here, it makes its major contribution to employment. But, in doing so, it runs the risk of inflation. And it does nothing for the poor whose unemployment is a consequence not of inadequate demand but of structural change, for the people whose communities have been stranded, whose training and experience have been rendered obsolete. In all six cases, the attack on poverty is limited to families with members in the labor force who are equipped with needed skills. If families lacking such members are to be aided, it must be done in other ways.

A third approach to the abolition of poverty lies through improvement of the operation of the labor market and an increase in the mobility of labor. The operation of the labor market can be improved by modernizing and strengthening the public employment service, by offering job guidance, and by barring discrimination in employment. These are measures to which little or no objection can be raised. The mobility of labor can be increased by augmenting the skills of workers and enhancing their employability through manpower development; by reforming vocational training; by offering training to adults; and by providing more extensive and intensive personal counseling. In some cases, a job is all that is needed to lift a worker out of poverty. In others, there are handicaps to overcome. Here, employment opportunity alone is not enough. Manpower development goes much farther. Its goal is personal rehabilitation, enhancement of productivity, development of self-reliance, and attainment of self-support. But manpower programs, too, have limitations. Ultimately, they depend for their success on the availability of work. And they can help only those families who have members in the labor force.

There is no panacea for poverty. It would be possible, of course, to do away with poverty by transferring enough income from the nonpoor to the poor to lift them above the poverty line. But this would do no more than maintain the poor as permanent dependents. It would not attack the causes of poverty or prevent its occurrence. It would not provide the poor with capacities or opportunities for self-support. Nor would job creation, labor market improvements, or job training alone suffice to abolish poverty. None of these programs, as we have seen, would help poor families who have no member in the labor force. And job creation would be of no help to those who lack the skills that are in demand.

The poverty of different groups has different causes and must be attacked in different ways. The poverty of families that lack a bread-winner can be alleviated only by providing aid in cash or kind. The poverty of those with workers who are unemployed can be attacked through job creation, labor market improvement, and job training. The poverty of those with workers who are fully employed but earning less than a subsistence income can be attacked (through a negative income tax) by providing income supplements to meet their present needs, by raising their productivity, and by increasing their mobility. The ability of all low-income families to make ends meet can be enhanced by reducing the numbers of their dependents through birth control. All of these approaches must be followed simultaneously, with particular programs designed to meet the needs of particular groups. And this is what government has done.

Benefit-cost analysis

To attain efficiency in expenditures on governmental programs, resources should be devoted to those undertakings that will yield the largest benefits for the smallest costs. To this end, the benefits to be realized and the costs to be incurred are measured. Where the ratio of benefits to costs is favorable, a program may be undertaken. Where the ratio is unfavorable, it will not. Since resources are limited, programs may be ranked in the order of their benefit-cost ratios and priorities established accordingly.

Benefit-cost analysis was first introduced in the case of river valley development, where it has been used since the thirties to determine eligibility for investment but not to establish priorities. It is required by law only in this case. It has been undertaken by a few other agencies in appraising particular programs: manpower training, vocational rehabilitation, family planning, and the control of disease. It is not generally employed.

This type of analysis has its limitations. It is difficult to obtain agreement on the way in which benefits should be defined, since value judgments are involved. In the case of medical care, for instance, are benefits to be defined as reductions in morbidity or extensions in the life span? If the former, the ratio of benefits to costs will be higher if people die early, since older people are ill more often and demand more care. If the latter, the ratio will be higher if medicine succeeds in prolonging life, even though the incidence of illness may increase. So, too, with education. Its benefits for the individual include the higher wage he earns in a better job. Its benefits for the community include the larger output that results. But the benefits for the individual also include a better understanding of his environment and fuller enjoyment of his leisure. And benefits for the community include a greater capacity for self-government and conservation of the cultural heritage. Among these, which are to be taken as the goals?

It is difficult, too, to measure benefits once they are defined. In the case of medical care, gains in employment and output can be measured in dollars and cents; relief of pain and anxiety cannot. And whatever the definition of benefits, the part medicine has played in producing them is difficult to isolate. With education, likewise, earnings and output can be measured in money; intangible benefits, even though more important, cannot. The costs, moreover, must be incurred immediately while the benefits, however measured, may not be realized for many years.

Measurement of benefits is obstructed, too, by lack of information. In general, administrators of welfare programs do not know what they have accomplished. Health officials cannot prove that they have in fact made people healthier; doctors cannot prove that those who get regular medical attention are healthier than those who do not. Educators who offer literacy courses to adults do not know how many of their pupils have actually learned to read and write. Social workers cannot demonstrate that case-work methods have really been successful in effecting personal rehabilitation. In the absence of knowledge, investment in welfare programs is an act of faith.

The benefits obtained in different fields (health, education, welfare) may be weighed on different scales. But if this is done, they cannot be compared. The benefits of health programs may be measured in illnesses averted, the benefits of educational programs in achievement test scores, the benefits of welfare programs in reduced dependency. But the resulting figures cannot be used in establishing priorities. It should be noted, too, that the benefits of different programs go to different people. It is impossible to compare the satisfactions enjoyed by one recipient with those enjoyed by another. It is impossible, for instance, to compare the benefits realized through child care with those realized through aid to the aged or the benefits of expenditures, such as those on higher education, that go largely to persons in the upper income groups with the benefits of expenditures, such as those on rent supplements, that go to the poor. Here, again, value judgments must be made.

Even where benefits can be measured on a common scale, it does not follow that priorities should always be established in the same order as the ratios of benefits to costs. In vocational rehabilitation, the ratio is as high as 12 to 1. In programs for the training of the hardcore unemployed, it is much lower. But it does not follow that funds should be transferred from the second to the first. The attack on hardcore unemployment has broad social and political objectives that do not find expression in the measurement of benefits. Benefit-cost analysis, in short, has its uses as a tool. But its infirmities are such that it cannot be accepted as an inviolable rule.

Cost-effectiveness analysis

Another type of efficiency analysis, known as cost effectiveness, has come to be used in planning-programming-budgeting systems (PPBS). This type of analysis can be used in cases where benefits cannot be measured in money. Here, objectives are agreed upon, the costs of different methods of attaining them are measured, and the methods that promise the lowest costs are given priority. Cost effectiveness analysis is of no help in making choices among expenditures on health, on education, and on welfare, where the objectives cannot be compared. But it is helpful in making choices within these fields. It can show the comparative costs of averting illness under various programs of disease control, the costs of increasing earnings through different programs of vocational training, the costs of meeting the needs of the poor by providing assistance in cash and in kind.

This technique has been employed since 1961 in evaluating defense programs and budgeting defense expenditures. In 1965, President Johnson directed each department of the federal government to set up a PPBS unit to define its goals and to determine the cheapest methods of fulfilling them. In response to this directive, the Department of Health, Education, and Welfare undertook to ascertain the comparative costs of different methods of controlling disease, improving child health, and increasing workers' productivity and earnings. In the first of these studies, taking as its measure the cost of saving a life, it established as an order of priorities expenditures on (1) prevention of motor vehicle accidents, (2) early detection and control of cancer, (3) treatment of syphilis, and (4) treatment of tuberculosis. In the case of traffic accidents, it found that a death could be averted by spending $88,000 on improving driving skills, $45,000 on providing emergency medical service, $13,800 on tightening driver licensing, $3,000 on requiring motorcycle helmets, or $87 on requiring seat belts. The practical utility of such analysis is obvious. The results of the Department's other studies, unfortunately, were not so clear.[2]

PPBS is still in a primitive state, but in the field of social welfare, as elsewhere, its potential contribution to efficiency in budgeting is great. There are vast areas of ignorance concerning the comparative effectiveness and costs of welfare programs. No one knows how to spend the increased money available for elementary and secondary education so that it will have the greatest impact on pupil performance: whether to give priority, for instance, to programs for preschool children or to those for youths in high school; to programs increasing the ratio of teachers to pupils or to those affording cultural enrichment. There are no estimates by which to compare the costs of helping the unemployed by providing assistance and by providing jobs. The comparative costs of increasing employment through job creation and through improvements in labor market operations are still to be weighed. These and other problems of efficiency in expenditures on welfare are susceptible to the cost-effectiveness approach. As necessary information is accumulated through research and as experience is gained

[2] Elizabeth B. Drew, "HEW Grapples with PPBS," *The Public Interest*, Summer 1967, pp. 9–29.

in the analytical technique, PPBS should make it possible to establish priorities on a far more certain base.

Priorities in the attack on poverty

Antipoverty programs may be classified according to their effects as (1) those that may operate to worsen poverty, (2) those that alleviate poverty but do not prevent it, and (3) those that strike at the causes of poverty. Among the measures that operate to worsen poverty are minimum wage laws, slum clearance, rules that impair incentives (reduction of welfare payments and eviction from public housing as earnings rise), and action preventing birth control. Among the palliatives are public assistance, food distribution, rent subsidies, welfare services, and proposed income supplements. In the third group there are measures that are intended to strike at the causes of poverty but whose efficacy is open to question: area development, for instance, and the proposal that government be made an employer of last resort. In this group, too, are measures whose effects are more promising. Here we may list the maintenance of demand and the acceleration of economic growth, improvement of labor market operations and promotion of labor mobility, manpower development, and birth control. Measures that operate to worsen poverty should obviously be avoided. Measures that do no more than alleviate poverty must be continued as long as the poor remain. But the measures that public policy should emphasize are those that give a reasonable promise of removing the causes of poverty, reducing its magnitude, and preventing its further growth.

Given the present paucity of information and the primitive state of analysis in the field, choices among the programs attacking the causes of poverty must rest, not upon hard evidence, but upon informed judgment. On this basis, however, it may safely be concluded that the antipoverty effort should emphasize: (1) the maintenance of aggregate demand, (2) improvements in the operation of the labor market, (3) manpower development, and (4) birth control.

The feasibility of welfare

Is further progress toward the goals of welfare possible? Do we know how to go about it to assure security, to provide equality of opportunity, to abolish poverty? The answer in each case is yes. We do know how to meet the hazards of old age and survivorship, of sickness, disability, and unemployment. We do know how to eliminate racial discrimination and how to give all of our people an equal chance. As for the abolition of poverty, our answer depends upon the definition of the term. If we take it to mean that every person is to be made capable of self-support and public assistance rendered unnecessary, the goal is unattainable. There will always be needy families who have no breadwinners, people stranded by change who lack the flexibility to move to new locations or to acquire new skills, persons with crippled personalities who cannot be made employable, people whose productivity is too low to justify the payment of a living wage. These people will have to be supported in whole or in part by the state. But if by the abolition of poverty we mean that every human being in the United States is to be provided with living quarters that are safe, sound, sanitary, ventilated, and uncrowded; with clothing that will keep him warm, dry, clean, and self-respecting; with food that will supply him with the calories and nutrients that are required for health and growth; with medical care from the cradle to the grave; with education to the full extent of his ability—if this is the goal, we do know how to approach it. We can do so in some cases by providing employment; in others, by extending charitable aid. The question is not whether we know how to approach the goals of welfare but whether we can afford to pay as much as the attainment of these goals would cost and, even more important, whether we shall have the will to do so.

The cost of welfare

It is estimated that federal, state, and local governments in the United States spent just over $100 billion on welfare programs in the fiscal year 1967. This amounted to 13.1 percent of the gross national product and 42.5 percent of all government expenditures. Of the total, $46 billion was spent by state and local governments and $54 billion by the federal government.[3] The $100 billion does not include expenditures on city planning, urban renewal, recreation, or law enforcement but it does include other outlays whose benefits are not confined to the poor: all money spent on public health and public education, all social

[3] Ida C. Merriam, "Social Welfare Expenditures 1929–67," *Social Security Bulletin,* December, 1967, pp. 3–14.

insurance benefits and payments to veterans. The share of these expenditures that helps the nonpoor amounts to $53 billion. The share that aids the poor alone thus stands at $47 billion. This is the amount that was spent on public assistance, public housing, and other welfare programs, on the share of outlays on education and health that benefit the poor, and on the social insurance and veterans' payments that go to the poor. It stands at 6.5 percent of the gross national product and at 21 percent of government expenditures. Of the total, more than $17 billion was spent by state and local governments and nearly $30 billion by the federal government.

How much more would it cost to attain the goals of welfare? Suppose we sought to eradicate poverty by making income transfers. The poverty income gap is the amount by which the incomes of the poor fall short of their needs as defined by the government's poverty line. In 1968, it stood at $11 billion. This was only 1.4 percent of the G.N.P., 2.2 percent of personal income, and 4.5 percent of public expenditures. But the gap could not be closed by transferring $11 billion from the nonpoor to the poor. If this were attempted, people below the poverty line would discover that the payments made to bring them up to the line would be reduced by any amount they earned. In other words, their earnings could be subject to a tax of 100 percent. They would therefore find it advantageous to give up work and live on the dole. Some of those with incomes just above the poverty line might do the same. The poverty income gap would grow accordingly. The cost of closing it would be closer to $20 billion than to $11 billion. And this would do nothing to remove the causes of poverty.

Poverty and insecurity are less likely to be attacked through a simple system of income transfers than through an expansion of other welfare programs. Suppose that this is done. (1) Social insurance benefits are increased: industrial accident and unemployment benefits are raised by half; old-age, survivorship, and disability benefits by a third, with minimum payments raised to $75 a month—the cost of these changes coming to $9.35 billion. (2) A system of income supplements is introduced, with a minimum allowance of $1,600 for a family of four, payments continued up to a break-even point of $6,000, and earnings subject to a tax of 33⅓ percent, exceeding the present cost of public assistance payments by $6 billion. (3) Further assistance amounting to $2.5 billion is provided to those who can prove they are still in need. (4) Expenditures on welfare services are raised by half, at a cost of $2.5 billion. (5) Expenditures on food distribution are doubled, at a cost of $1.25 billion. (6) Expenditures on community action programs are also doubled, costing another $1 billion. (7) The sums spent on federal aid to schools in poverty areas are doubled, increasing these outlays by $3.5 billion. (8) Spending on manpower development is tripled at an added cost of $750 million. (9) Spending on urban renewal and housing is quadrupled, costing another $3 billion. (10) The sum of $150 million is spent on birth control. The annual cost of such an expansion in welfare programs would add up to $30 billion. It would increase present federal, state, and local expenditures on such programs by 30 percent.

Can we afford social welfare?

Can the United States afford to spend another $30 billion a year on social welfare? The answer depends upon the size of the gross national product, the share of the product that governments can take in taxes, and the competing uses to which tax revenues may be put. Governments might undertake to finance the added outlay by increasing tax rates. Or they might seek to finance it by diverting expenditures from other purposes.

There can be no question that the annual product of the American economy is large enough to permit the assurance of social security and the eradication of poverty. Standing at more than $3,900 in 1967, the G.N.P. per capita was half again as great as that in Sweden or Switzerland and twice as great as that in Great Britain or in any other country of Western Europe. Standing at $2,735 per capita, disposable personal income was large enough to provide $11,000 for each family of four, or more than three times the figure then set by the government's poverty line.

There is no question that taxes could be increased. Governments in the United States take a smaller share of the national product in taxes than do those of Great Britain, Western Germany, France, or Sweden. Another $30 billion added to the tax bill would raise it by 15 percent. Nearly 30 percent of the national product would then be taken in taxes. Such a share would still be lower than the 32 percent taken in Western Germany. But tax increases, whatever their purpose, are unpopular. It would not be easy to get them passed.

There is little question that if the nation wished to do so, the larger expenditure on welfare programs could be financed by diverting the money from other purposes. The federal government has been spending $75 billion a year on national defense. This outlay could doubtless be reduced to $60 billion and $15 billion saved without endangering the nation's security. Indeed, if the arms race could be checked, the nation would be more rather than less secure. The government is also spending more than $4 billion a year on a system of interstate highways, close to a billion on rivers and harbors, and more than $6 billion on an effort to put a man on the moon. If these expenditures were cut by two fifths, another $5 billion could be saved. The government, finally, is paying out more than $4 billion a year in subsidies to commercial farmers and around $6 billion in subsidies to other industries. If these were discontinued, the $10 billion saved would provide the rest of the $30 billion required to enlarge the welfare program. These shifts, however, are unlikely. The beneficiaries of existing expenditures are well entrenched.

The $30 billion that has been suggested for an expansion of welfare programs is the same amount that the government was spending each year in the late sixties to carry on the war in Vietnam. There was no complaint at the time that the country could not afford so large an expenditure. Nor did the outlay require anyone—other than the youths who were drafted—to make a perceptible sacrifice. It would seem that an economy that could so easily absorb the cost of a $30 billion war would be equally able to absorb the cost of a $30 billion increase in welfare programs. In fact, it was argued that sums of the size once spent on the war should be devoted to such programs when hostilities came to an end. The defense authorities replied, however, that this would be impossible, since the savings effected would be needed to construct new defense facilities, build new weapons systems, and replenish military stockpiles. The claims of welfare would have to be denied.

An expanded welfare program can be financed, however, without raising taxes and without diverting money from other purposes. It can be financed out of the annual growth in national output and the resulting growth of tax yields at existing rates. The average annual growth of the G.N.P. during the sixties has amounted to $45 billion. If the growth rate is continued into the seventies, this figure will rise as annual increments are compounded on a rising base. As a result, federal tax revenues will grow at the rate of $15 to $16 billion a year. Even when allowance is made for the higher costs resulting from continued inflation, the government will have surplus revenues mounting to tens of billions, that can be devoted to new programs. There will be enough money to rebuild the cities and enough to finance a generous system of income supplements.

Economically, the United States has it within its power to eradicate poverty, to assure full security for every citizen, to give all of its people an equal chance. If poverty, insecurity, and inequality of opportunity persist, it will not be because we lack the means to end them but because we lack the will to do so.

Prospects for social security

The prospects for continued progress toward social security, save in the case of unemployment, are bright. Employers whose tax rates are kept low by merit rating will oppose reform of the state unemployment insurance laws. But old-age, survivorship, and disability benefits under the Social Security Act are likely to be raised. Such action is both popular and easy. It is popular because the beneficiaries include not only people who are poor but many who are well-to-do. It is easy because the reserve fund from which benefits are paid grows steadily as payrolls grow. Benefits to railway workers, with their powerful unions, will also rise, and benefits to civil servants are likely to keep pace. Payments to veterans, too, will grow as Congress responds to pressures exerted by the American Legion and the Veterans of Foreign Wars.

Prospects for equality of opportunity

The strategy that will be most effective in attacking inequality of opportunity depends upon circumstances that vary from case to case. In situations where prejudice is deeply embedded, where discrimination is widespread, where the minority has few allies within the dominant group, and where the discriminator's cooperation is needed to effect a change—in such situations, modification is best to be obtained through compromise. But where prejudice is weaker and discrimination less pervasive, where the minority has strong allies, and where reforms can be effectively enforced, discrimination can be openly attacked. In this case, as in others, it is unnecessary to delay progress until all those who oppose it have been converted. But it is futile to enact reforms that have no real foundation in popular support.[4]

At present, the outlook for continued progress toward equality of opportunity is clouded. Riots in the city ghettoes, resort to violence and threats of violence, disorderly demonstrations and extravagant demands have frightened whites who once would have tolerated the Negro's progress, even some who were sympathetic to his cause. Sentiment has swung from accommodation to repression. The recommendations contained in the thoughtful report of the National Advisory Commission on Civil Disorders urging an all-out attack on the causes of disaffection have been ignored. The popular demand is for prevention of "crime in the streets," meaning disorder by Negroes, and for the maintenance of "law and order," meaning the use of force to keep Negroes under control. The country is faced with the unhappy prospect of prolonged race war. In such an atmosphere, legislation providing funds to improve conditions in the ghettoes is unlikely to be passed. And enforcement of laws requiring desegregation in education and nondiscrimination in employment and in housing is likely to be lax.

In time, one hopes this situation will take a turn for the better, as Negroes continue to press for reforms and as white people find that repression alone will not solve the problems presented by differences in race. Surely, the goal of equality of opportunity is not to be abandoned because there are prejudiced people in the white community who object. Nor is progress toward the goal to be halted because there are Negroes who reject it, demanding a separate identity, a separate culture, even a separate state. Equality of opportunity is demanded by democracy. It will not come quickly. But in the fullness of time, it is to be attained.

Prospects for the abolition of poverty

Progress toward social welfare is not steady but comes in spurts. Evils are exposed, reforms demanded, new laws enacted, and new programs launched. Then attention turns to other matters: to international conflict or to pressing domestic problems. Welfare programs

[4] George E. Simpson and J. Milton Yinger, *Racial and Cultural Minorities* (3d ed.; New York: Harper & Row, 1965), chaps. xxii, xxiii.

that were set up with high hopes and carried forward with deep devotion are now denied the support they need. Some programs encounter difficulties that were unforeseen: some end in failure. The hopes are disappointed; the devotion gives way to disillusionment. The zeal that once inspired the welfare effort is dispelled. But the gains achieved through past reforms are not lost. Welfare programs are continued on a higher level than before. With the next spurt of reform, they will ascend from this plateau.

At present, acceleration of progress toward the abolition of poverty seems unlikely. Dissension has largely dissipated earlier sympathy for the poor. The problem of poverty has come to be envisioned as a problem of race. Aid to the poor is thought to be aid to Negroes, who are only a third of the poor. The white reaction to the black rebellion denies support to measures that would be helpful to all the poor. Proposals to strengthen existing programs or to adopt new programs attacking poverty will have hard going in the years immediately ahead. Where problems are so pressing that they cannot be ignored, as is the case with deterioration of the cities and dependency in the slums, new initiatives may be taken. But this will be the exception rather than the rule.

But now, as always, the gains of the past will be retained. Monetary and fiscal policy will be directed toward the maintenance of demand, the acceleration of growth, and the provision of employment. No administration, however conservative, will stubbornly adhere to the dogma of an annually balanced budget while business declines, bankruptcies mount, and unemployment grows. Improvements in the operation of the labor market will be retained. Federal aid to schools in poverty areas will be continued. Medicare will not be repealed. Acceptance of birth control as an antipoverty measure will never be reversed.

Sooner or later, there will be another era of reform. The spectacle of poverty in the midst of affluence will move the conscience of America in the future as it has in the past. Ambitious new programs will be adopted; programs that seem as difficult today as social security seemed a third of a century ago. It is altogether possible that within the lives of men now living, poverty will be banished from the United States.

Bibliography

Bibliography

Chapter 1.   Inequality in income and wealth

Kravis, Irving B. *The Structure of Income.* Philadelphia, Pa.: University of Pennsylvania Press, 1962.

Kuznets, Simon. "Quantitative Aspects of the Economic Growth of Nations," *Economic Development and Cultural Change,* January, 1963, Part II.

Lampman, Robert J. *The Share of Top Wealth Holders in National Wealth.* Princeton, N.J.: Princeton University Press, 1962.

Miller, Herman P. *Income Distribution in the United States.* Washington, D.C.: U.S. Government Printing Office, 1966.

————. *Rich Man, Poor Man.* New York: Thomas Y. Crowell Co., 1964.

Morgan, James N.; David, Martin H.; Cohen, Wilbur J.; and Brazer, Harvey E. *Income and Welfare in the United States,* chap. xx. New York: McGraw-Hill Book Co., Inc., 1962.

Chapter 2.   Poverty

Citizens' Board of Inquiry. *Hunger, U.S.A.* Washington, D.C.: New Community Press, 1968.

Committee on Education and Labor, House of Representatives. *Poverty in the United States.* Washington, D.C.: U.S. Government Printing Office, 1964.

Council of Economic Advisers. *Annual Report, 1964,* chap. ii.

Davis, Allison. *Social Class Influences upon Learning.* Cambridge, Mass.: Harvard University Press, 1950.

Ornati, Oscar. *Poverty Amid Affluence*. New York: Twentieth Century Fund, 1966.

Orshansky, Mollie. "Counting the Poor," Joint Economic Committee, *Old Age Income Assurance*, Part II, pp. 178–231. Washington, D.C.: U.S. Government Printing Office, 1967.

———. "The Shape of Poverty in 1966," *Social Security Bulletin*, March, 1968, pp. 3–32.

President's National Advisory Commission on Rural Poverty. *The People Left Behind*. Washington, D.C.: U.S. Government Printing Office, 1967.

Riessman, Frank. *The Culturally Deprived Child*. New York: Harper & Row, 1962.

Sexton, Patricia C. *Education and Income*. New York: Viking Press, 1961.

Wilner, Daniel, *et al. Housing Environment and Family Life*. Baltimore, Md.: Johns Hopkins Press, 1962.

Chapter 3.   Insecurity

Brinker, Paul A. *Economic Insecurity and Social Security*, chaps. ii, vii, ix, xii. New York: Appleton-Century-Crofts Co., Inc., 1968.

Haber, William, and Murray, Merrill G. *Unemployment Insurance in the American Economy*, chap. i. Homewood, Ill.: Richard D. Irwin, Inc., 1966.

Pechman, Joseph A.; Aaron, Henry; and Taussig, Michael K. *Social Security: Perspectives for Reform*, chaps. ii, iv. Washington, D.C.: Brookings Institution, 1968.

Turnbull, John G. *The Changing Faces of Economic Security*. Minneapolis, Minn.: University of Minnesota Press, 1966.

———. Williams, Arthur, Jr.; and Cheit, Earl F. *Economic and Social Security*, chaps. ii, vi, ix, xi. 3d ed. New York: Ronald Press Co., 1967.

Chapter 4.   Inequality of opportunity

Conant, James B. *Slums and Suburbs*. New York: McGraw-Hill Book Co., Inc., 1961.

Commission on Race and Housing. *Where Shall We Live?* Berkeley: University of California Press, 1958.

Daedalus, Fall, 1965. "The Negro American."

Department of Health, Education, and Welfare. *Equality of Educational Opportunity*. Washington, D.C.: U.S. Government Printing Office, 1966.

Department of Labor, Bureau of Labor Statistics. Bulletin No. 1511. *The Negroes in the United States: Their Economic and Social Situation*. Washington, D.C.: U.S. Government Printing Office, 1966.

———. Report No. 332. *Social and Economic Conditions of Negroes in the United States*. Washington, D.C.: U.S. Government Printing Office, 1967.

———. Office of Policy Planning and Research, *The Negro Family*, 1965.

Grier, George and Eunice. *Equality and Beyond*. Chicago, Ill.: Quadrangle Books, 1966.

Johnson, Charles S. *Patterns of Negro Segregation.* New York: Harper & Bros., 1943.

Krosney, Herbert. *Beyond Welfare: Poverty in the Supercity.* Holt, Rinehart & Winston, 1966.

Marshall, Ray. *The Negro Worker,* chaps. ii–vi. New York: Random House, Inc., 1967.

Merton, Robert K., and Nisbet, Robert A. (eds.). *Contemporary Social Problems,* chap. ix, Arnold M. Rose, "Race and Ethnic Relations." 2d ed. New York: Harcourt, Brace & World, Inc., 1966.

Norgren, Paul H., and Hill, Samuel E. *Toward Fair Employment,* Part I. New York: Columbia University Press, 1964.

Ross, Arthur M., and Hill, Herbert (eds.). *Employment, Race, and Poverty,* Parts I, II, IV. New York: Harcourt, Brace & World, Inc., 1967.

Sheppard, Harold L., and Striner, Herbert E. *Civil Rights, Employment, and the Social Status of American Negroes.* Kalamazoo, Mich.: W. E. Upjohn Institute, 1966.

Silberman, Charles E. *Crisis in Black and White.* New York: Random House, Inc., 1964.

Simpson, George E., and Yinger, J. Milton. *Racial and Cultural Minorities,* chaps. xii–xv. 3d ed. New York: Harper & Row, 1965.

Chapter 5. *Private provision for security*

Brinker, Paul A. *Economic Insecurity and Social Security,* chaps. vi, xvi. New York: Appleton-Century-Crofts Co., Inc., 1968.

De Grazia, Alfred, and Gurr, Ted. *American Welfare,* chaps. i–xi. New York: New York University Press, 1961.

Kolodrubetz, Walter W. "Growth in Employee Benefit Plans," *Social Security Bulletin,* April, 1967, pp. 10–27.

McGill, Dan M. *Fundamentals of Private Pensions.* Homewood, Ill.: Richard D. Irwin, Inc., 1964.

———. *Life Insurance.* Rev. ed. Homewood, Ill.: Richard D. Irwin, Inc., 1967.

Reed, Louis S. "Private Health Insurance in the United States: An Overview," *Social Security Bulletin,* December, 1965, pp. 3 ff.

———. "Private Health Insurance: Coverage and Financial Experience, 1965," *Social Security Bulletin,* November, 1966, pp. 3 ff.

Somers, Herman M. and Anne R. *Doctors, Patients, and Health Insurance,* Part V. Washington, D.C.: Brookings Institution, 1961.

Turnbull, John G.; Williams, Arthur, Jr.; and Cheit, Earl F. *Economic and Social Security,* chaps. v, viii, xii. 3d ed. New York: Ronald Press Co., 1967.

Chapter 6. *Social security*

Burns, Eveline M. *Social Security and Public Policy.* New York: McGraw-Hill Book Co., Inc., 1956.

Carlson, Valdemar. *Economic Security in the United States,* chaps. iii, vii. New York: McGraw-Hill Book Co., Inc., 1962.

Myers, Robert J. *Social Insurance and Allied Government Programs.* chap. ii. Homewood, Ill.: Richard D. Irwin, Inc., 1965.

Turnbull, John G.; Williams, Arthur, Jr.; and Cheit, Earl F. *Economic and Social Security,* chaps. iii, xiii.–3d ed. New York: Ronald Press Co., 1967.

Chapter 7.   Occupational injury and unemployment

Brinker, Paul A. *Economic Insecurity and Social Security,* chaps. viii, xiv, xv. New York: Appleton-Century-Crofts Co., Inc., 1968.

Cheit, Earl F. *Injury and Recovery in the Course of Employment.* New York: John Wiley & Sons, Inc., 1961.

Haber, William, and Murray, Merrill G. *Unemployment Insurance in the American Economy,* chap. i. Homewood, Ill.: Richard D. Irwin, Inc., 1966.

Levitan, Sar A., *et al.* (eds.). *Towards Freedom from Want,* pp. 88–104, Milton J. Nadworny, "Unemployment Insurance and Income Maintenance." Madison, Wis.: Industrial Relations Research Assn., 1968.

Myers, Robert J. *Social Insurance and Allied Government Programs,* chaps. xii, xiii. Homewood, Ill.: Richard D. Irwin, Inc., 1962.

Somers, Herman M. and Anne R. *Workmen's Compensation.* New York: John Wiley & Sons, Inc., 1961.

Turnbull, John G.; Williams, Arthur, Jr.; and Cheit, Earl F. *Economic and Social Security,* chaps. vii, x. 3d ed. New York: Ronald Press Co., 1967.

Chapter 8.   Old age, survivorship, and disability

Brinker, Paul A. *Economic Insecurity and Social Security,* chaps. iii, iv. New York: Appleton-Century-Crofts Co., Inc., 1968.

Burns, Eveline M. *Social Security and Public Policy.* New York: McGraw-Hill Book Co., Inc., 1956.

Joint Economic Committee. *Old Age Assurance,* Part II. Washington, D.C.: U. S. Government Printing Office, 1967.

Myers, Robert J. *Social Insurance and Allied Government Programs,* chaps. iii–x. Homewood, Ill.: Richard D. Irwin, Inc., 1962.

Pechman, Joseph A.; Aaron, Henry; and Taussig, Michael K. *Social Security: Perspectives for Reform,* chaps. iii–ix. Washington, D.C.: Brookings Institution, 1968.

Turnbull, John G.; Williams, Arthur, Jr.; and Cheit, Earl F. *Economic and Social Security,* chap. v. 3d ed. New York: Ronald Press Co., 1967.

Chapter 9.   Medical care

Brinker, Paul A. *Economic Insecurity and Social Security,* chaps. x, xi. New York: Appleton-Century-Crofts Co., Inc., 1968.

Fein, Rashi. *The Doctor Shortage.* Washington, D.C.: Brookings Institution, 1965.

Feingold, Eugene. *Medicare.* San Francisco, Calif.: Chandler Publishing Co., 1966.

Harris, Reed. "Medicare," *The New Yorker.* July 2, 1966, pp. 29 ff; July 9, 1966, pp. 30 ff; July 16, 1966, pp. 35 ff; July 23, 1966, pp. 35 ff;

Harris, Seymour E. *The Economics of American Medicine.* New York: Macmillan Co., 1964.

Klarman, Herbert E. *The Economics of Health.* New York: Columbia University Press, 1965.

Somers, Herman M. and Anne R. *Doctors, Patients, and Health Insurance.* Washington, D.C.: Brookings Institution, 1961.

———. *Medicare and the Hospitals.* Washington, D.C.: Brookings Institution, 1967.

Chapter 10.   Educational opportunity

Bloom, Benjamin S.; Davis, Allison; and Hess, Robert. *Compensatory Education for Cultural Deprivation.* New York: Holt, Rinehart, & Winston, Inc., 1965.

Commission on Civil Rights, *Racial Isolation in the Public Schools.* Washington, D.C.: U. S. Government Printing Office, 1967.

Department of Health, Education, and Welfare. *Equality of Educational Opportunity.* Washington, D.C.: U.S. Government Printing Office, 1966.

Gordon, Edmund W., and Wilkerson, Doxey A. *Compensatory Education for the Disadvantaged.* New York: College Entrance Examination Board, 1966.

Harris, Seymour E. *More Resources for Education.* New York: Harper & Bros., 1960.

———. *Higher Education in the United States: Economic Problems.* Cambridge, Mass.: Harvard University Press, 1960.

Keezer, Dexter M. *Financing Higher Education.* New York: McGraw-Hill Book Co., Inc., 1959.

Meranto, Philip. *The Politics of Federal Aid to Education in 1965.* Syracuse, N.Y.: Syracuse University Press, 1967.

Passow, A. Harry (ed.). *Education in Depressed Areas.* New York: Teachers College, Columbia University, 1963.

Rivlin, Alice M. *The Role of the Federal Government in Financing Education.* Washington, D.C.: Brookings Institution, 1961.

Simpson, George E., and Yinger, J. Milton. *Racial and Cultural Minorities,* chaps. xix, xx. 3d ed. New York: Harper & Row, 1965.

Chapter 11.   Employment opportunity

Bullock, Paul. *Equal Opportunity in Employment.* Los Angeles, Calif. Institute of Industrial Relations, University of California, 1966.

Marshall, Ray. *The Negro Worker,* chap. vii. New York: Random House, Inc., 1967.

Norgren, Paul H., and Hill, Samuel E. *Toward Fair Employment,* Part I. New York: Columbia University Press, 1964.

Ross, Arthur M., and Hill, Herbert (eds.). *Employment, Race, and Poverty*, chaps. xiii, xviii, xix. New York: Harcourt, Brace & World, Inc., 1967.

Simpson, George E., and Yinger, J. Milton. *Racial and Cultural Minorities*, chaps. xii, xiii. 3d ed. New York: Harper & Row, 1965.

Sovern, Michael I. *Legal Restraints on Racial Discrimination in Employment*. New York: Twentieth Century Fund, 1966.

Chapter 12.   *Political and social opportunity*

Annals of the American Academy of Political and Social Science, January, 1965, *The Negro Protest.*

Commission on Civil Rights. *Political Participation*. Washington, D.C.: U.S. Government Printing Office, 1968.

Daedalus, Fall, 1965, *The Negro American.*

Grier, George and Eunice. *Equality and Beyond*, chaps. iv, v, vi. Chicago, Ill.: Quadrangle Books, 1966.

National Advisory Commission on Civil Disorders, Report. New York: E. P. Dutton & Co., 1968.

Simpson, George E., and Yinger, J. Milton. *Racial and Cultural Minorities*, chap. xv. 3d ed. New York: Harper & Row, 1965.

Chapter 13.   *Minimum wages*

Bloom, Gordon F., and Northrup, Herbert R. *Economics of Labor Relations*, chap. xviii. Homewood, Ill.: Richard D. Irwin, Inc., 1961.

Brinker, Paul A. *Economic Insecurity and Social Security*, chap. xxiii. New York: Appleton-Century-Crofts Co., Inc., 1968.

Cullen, Donald E. *Minimum Wage Laws*. Ithaca, N.Y.: New York State School of Industrial and Labor Relations, Cornell University, 1961.

Levitan, Sar A., *et al.* (eds.). *Towards Freedom from Want*, pp. 189–218, Jacob J. Kaufman and Terry G. Foran, "The Minimum Wage and Poverty." Madison, Wis.: Industrial Relations Research Assn., 1968.

Turnbull, John G.; Williams, Arthur, Jr.; and Cheit, Earl F. *Economic and Social Security*, chaps. xv, xvi, xvii. 3d ed. New York: Ronald Press Co., 1967.

Chapter 14.   *Public assistance*

Advisory Council on Public Welfare. *Having the Power, We Have the Duty*. Washington, D.C.: U.S. Government Printing Office, 1966.

Bell, Winifred. *Aid to Dependent Children*. New York: Columbia University Press, 1965.

Elman, Richard M. *The Poorhouse State*. New York: Pantheon Books, 1966.

Krosney, Herbert. *Beyond Welfare*. New York: Holt, Rinehart & Winston, 1966.

Leyendecker, Hilary M. *Problems and Policies in Public Welfare Administration*. New York: Harper & Bros., 1955.

MacIntyre, Duncan M. *Public Assistance: Too Much or Too Little?* Ithaca, N.Y.: New York State School of Labor and Industrial Relations, 1964.

May, Edgar. *Wasted Americans.* New York: Harper & Row, 1964.

Schorr, Alvin L. *Poor Kids.* New York: Basic Books, 1966.

Steiner, Gilbert Y. *Social Insecurity: The Politics of Welfare.* Chicago, Ill.: Rand McNally Co., 1966.

Wickenden, Elizabeth, and Bell, Winifred. *Public Assistance: Time for a Change.* New York: New York School of Social Work, 1961.

Chapter 15.   Income supplements

Burns, Eveline M. (ed.). *Children's Allowances and the Economic Welfare of Children.* New York: Citizens' Committee for Children of New York, Inc., 1968.

Green, Christopher. *Negative Income Taxes and the Poverty Problem.* Washington, D.C.: Brookings Institution, 1967.

Hildebrand, George H. *Poverty, Income Maintenance and the Negative Income Tax:* Ithaca, N.Y.: New York State School of Industrial and Labor Relations, 1967.

Krosney, Herbert. *Beyond Welfare,* chap. ix. New York: Holt, Rinehart & Winston, 1966.

Schorr, Alvin L. *Poor Kids,* chaps. v, vii, ix. New York: Harper & Row, 1964.

Theobald, Robert. *Free Men and Free Markets.* New York: Clarkson N. Potter, Inc., 1963.

———— (ed.). *The Guaranteed Income.* Garden City, N.Y.: Doubleday & Co., 1965.

Tobin, James. "The Case for an Income Guarantee," *Public Interest,* Summer, 1966, pp. 31–41.

————; Pechman, Joseph A.; and Meiszkowski, Peter M. "Is a Negative Income Tax Practical?" *Yale Law Journal,* Vol. 77 (1967), pp. 1–27.

Vadakin, James C. *Children, Poverty, and Family Allowances.* New York: Basic Books, Inc., 1968.

Chapter 16.   Housing

Anderson, Martin. *The Federal Bulldozer.* Cambridge, Mass.: Massachusetts Institute of Technology Press, 1964.

Bellush, Jewel, and Hausknecht, Murray (eds.). *Urban Renewal: People, Politics, and Planning.* Garden City, N.Y.: Doubleday & Co., 1967.

Fisher, Robert M. *Twenty Years of Public Housing.* New York: Harper & Bros., 1959.

Greer, Scott. *Urban Renewal and American Cities.* Indianapolis: Bobbs-Merrill Co., 1965.

Jacobs, Jane. *The Death and Life of Great American Cities.* New York: Random House, 1961.

Meyerson, Martin; Terrett, Barbara; and Wheaton, William L. C. *Housing, People, and Cities.* New York: McGraw-Hill Book Co., Inc., 1962.

Schorr, Alvin L. *Slums and Social Insecurity*. Washington, D.C.: Social Security Administration, Research Report No. 1, undated.

Wendt, Paul F. *Housing Policy*. Berkeley, Calif.: University of California Press, 1962.

Wheaton, William L. C.; Milgram, Grace; and Meyerson, Margy E. *Urban Housing*. New York: The Free Press, 1966.

Wilson, James Q. (ed.). *Urban Renewal: The Record and the Controversy*. Cambridge, Mass.: Massachusetts Institute of Technology Press, 1966.

Chapter 17.   Job creation and area development

Becker, Joseph M. (ed.). *In Aid of the Unemployed*, chap. viii, William H. Miernyk, "Area Development"; chap. ix., R. A. Freeman, "Public Works and Work Relief." Baltimore, Md.: Johns Hopkins University Press, 1965.

Fishman, Leo (ed.). *Poverty Amid Affluence*, chap. ix. Harry G. Johnson, "Unemployment and Poverty." New Haven, Conn.: Yale University Press, 1966.

Gordon, Margaret S. (ed.). *Poverty in America*, chap. xiii, Herman P. Minsky "The Role of Employment Policy"; chap. xxvi, Sar A. Levitan, "Area Development: A Tool to Combat Poverty?"; chap. xxvii, Varden Fuller, "Rural Poverty and Rural Areas Development." San Francisco, Calif.: Chandler Publishing Co., 1965.

Pearl, Arthur, and Riessman, Frank. *New Careers for the Poor*. Glencoe, Ill.: Free Press, 1966.

Princeton Manpower Symposium. *Unemployment in a Prosperous Economy*, pp. 67–81, Arthur M. Okun, "The Role of Aggregate Demand in Alleviating Unemployment." Princeton, N.J.: Princeton University, 1965.

Levitan, Sar A. *Federal Aid to Depressed Areas*. Baltimore, Md.: Johns Hopkins University Press, 1964.

——— (ed.). *Towards Freedom from Want*, pp. 135–61, Garth L. Mangum, "Government as an Employer of Last Resort." Madison, Wis.: Industrial Relations Research Assn., 1968.

President's Regional Commission, *Appalachia*. Washington, D.C.: U.S. Government Printing Office, 1964.

Chapter 18.   Labor markets and manpower development

Bakke, E. Wight. *A Positive Labor Market Policy*. Columbus, Ohio: Charles E. Merrill Books, Inc., 1963.

Becker, Joseph M. (ed.). *In Aid of the Unemployed*, chap. xi, Gerald G. Somers, "Training the Unemployed." Baltimore, Md.: Johns Hopkins University Press, 1965.

Cassell, Frank H. *The Public Employment Service*. Ann Arbor, Mich.: Academic Publications, 1968.

Committee on Labor and Public Welfare, U.S. Senate. *Examination of the*

War on Poverty, Staff and Consultants Reports. Vol. II, pp. 235–58, Garth L. Mangum, "Manpower Programs in the Anti-Poverty Effort."

Department of Labor, Bureau of Employment Security. "Public Employment Service in the Nation's Job Market, 1933–1963," *Employment Service Review,* June, 1963.

———, Employment Service Task Force Report. *Employment Service Review,* February, 1966.

Gordon, Margaret S. (ed.). *Poverty in America,* chap. xiv, Frederick Harbison, "Labor Market Strategies in the War on Poverty." San Francisco, Calif.: Chandler Publishing Co., 1965.

Lester, Richard A. *Manpower Planning in a Free Society.* Princeton, N.J.: Princeton University Press, 1966.

Levitan, Sar A. *Antipoverty Work and Training Efforts,* Institute of Labor and Industrial Relations, University of Michigan, Ann Arbor, Mich., and Wayne State University, Detroit, Mich., 1967.

Mangum, Garth L. *Contributions and Costs of Manpower Development and Training,* Institute of Labor and Industrial Relations, University of Michigan, Ann Arbor, Mich., and Wayne State University, Detroit, Mich., 1967.

———. *Reorienting Vocational Education,* Institute of Labor and Industrial Relations, University of Michigan, Ann Arbor, Mich., and Wayne State University, Detroit, Mich., 1968.

———, and Glenn, Lowell M. *Vocational Rehabilitation and Federal Manpower Policy,* Institute of Labor and Industrial Relations, University of Michigan, Ann Arbor, Mich., and Wayne State University, Detroit, Mich., 1967.

Nemore, Arnold L., and Mangum, Garth L. *Reorienting the Federal-State Employment Service,* Institute of Labor and Industrial Relations, University of Michigan, Ann Arbor, Mich., and Wayne State University, Detroit, Mich., 1968.

Princeton Manpower Symposium. *Unemployment in a Prosperous Economy,* pp. 126–41, Curtis C. Aller, "The Role of Government-Sponsored Training and Retraining Programs; pp. 153–66, Alice M. Rivlin, "Critical Issues in the Development of Vocational Education." Princeton, N.J.: Princeton University, 1965.

Ross, Arthur M. (ed.). *Employment Policy and the Labor Market,* chap. ix, Gerald G. Somers, "Retraining: An Evaluation of Gains and Costs." Berkeley, Calif.: University of California Press, 1965.

Weeks, Christopher. *Job Corps.* Boston, Mass.: Little, Brown & Co., 1967.

Wolfbein, Seymour L. *Employment, Unemployment, and Public Policy,* Part III. New York: Random House, 1965.

Chapter 19. Birth control

Committee on Labor and Public Welfare, U.S. Senate. *Examination of the War on Poverty, Staff and Consultants Reports,* Vol. 3, pp. 717–35, Harold Sheppard, "Effects of Family Planning on Poverty in the United States." Washington, D.C.: U.S. Government Printing Office, 1967.

Gordon, Margaret S. (ed.). *Poverty in America*, chap. xxi, Kingsley Davis, "Demographic Aspects of Poverty." San Francisco, Calif.: Chandler Publishing Co., 1965.

Harkavy, Oscar; Jaffe, Frederick S.; and Wishik, Samuel M. *Implementing DHEW Policy on Family Planning and Population*. Washington, D.C.: Department of Health, Education, and Welfare, 1967.

Jaffe, Frederick S. "Family Planning and Poverty," *Journal of Marriage and the Family*, November, 1964, pp. 467–70.

Kiser, Clyde V. *Group Differences in Urban Fertility*. Baltimore, Md.: Williams & Wilkins Co., 1942.

National Bureau of Economic Research. *Demographic and Economic Change*, pp. 77–113, Clyde V. Kiser, "Differential Fertility in the United States." New York: N.B.E.R., 1960.

Osborn, Frederick. "Qualitative Aspects of Population Control," *Law and Contemporary Problems*, Summer, 1960, pp. 406–25.

President's National Advisory Committee on Rural Poverty. *The People Left Behind*, chap. vii. Washington, D.C.: U.S. Government Printing Office, 1967.

Rainwater, Lee. *And the Poor Get Children*. Chicago, Ill.: Quadrangle Books, 1960.

Sulloway, A. H. "Legal and Political Aspects of Population Control in the United States," *Law and Contemporary Problems*, Summer, 1960, pp. 593–613.

Whelpton, Pascal K.; Campbell, Arthur A.; and Patterson, John E. *Fertility and Family Planning in the United States*, chaps. iii, ix. Princeton, N.J.: Princeton University Press, 1966.

Chapter 20.   *"The war on poverty"*

Committee on Labor and Welfare, U.S. Senate. *Examination of the War on Poverty*, Staff and Consultants Reports, Vol. 3, pp. 795–856. Washington, D.C.: U.S. Government Printing Office, 1967.

Donovan, John C. *The Politics of Poverty*. New York: Western Publishing Co., Inc., 1967.

Krosney, Herbert. *Beyond Welfare*, chaps. i–iii. New York: Holt, Rinehart & Winston, 1966.

Law and Contemporary Problems, Winter, 1966, "Antipoverty Programs."

Levitan, Sar A. *The Design of Federal Antipoverty Strategy*. Ann Arbor, Mich., Institute of Labor and Industrial Relations, University of Michigan, 1967.

National Advisory Council on Economic Opportunity. *Focus on Community Action*. Washington, D.C.: U.S. Government Printing Office, 1968.

Office of Economic Opportunity. *The Quiet Revolution*. Washington, D.C.: U.S. Government Printing Office, 1967.

Seligman, Ben B. *Permanent Poverty*, chaps. ix–xi. Chicago, Ill.: Quadrangle Books, 1968.

———— (ed.). *Poverty as a Public Issue*, pp. 231–71, Elinor Graham, "The Politics of Poverty" and "Poverty and the Legislative Process"; pp. 272–320, S. M. Miller and Martin Rein, "The War on Poverty: Perspectives and Prospects." New York: The Free Press, 1965.

The War on Poverty. 88th Congress, 2d Session, Senate Document 86.

Indexes

Index of names

Index of subjects

399

*This book has been set in 10 point Janson,
leaded 3 points and 9 point Janson, leaded 2
points. Part numbers are in 18 point Helvetica
Medium. Part titles and chapter numbers and
titles are in 14 point Helvetica Medium. The
size of the type page is 26 by 44 picas.*